The Employment Act and the Council of Economic Advisers

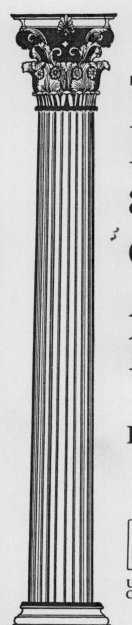

The Employment Act and the Council of Economic Advisers, 1946–1976

By HUGH S. NORTON

UNIVERSITY OF SOUTH CAROLINA PRESS
COLUMBIA, SOUTH CAROLINA

Library of Congress Cataloging in Publication Data

Norton, Hugh Stanton, 1921–
    The Employment act and the Council of Economic
Advisers, 1946–1976.

    Bibliography: p.
    Includes index.
    1.   United States. Council of Economic Advisers.
2.   United States—Economic policy—1945–1960.
3.   United States—Economic policy—1961–   I. Title.
HC106.5.N657   353.008   77-8664
ISBN 0-87249-296-6

Contents

v

Tables

Acknowledgments

The author is indebted to a large number of people with whom interviews and personal correspondence was conducted over the years from 1966 to 1971, during which research and manuscript drafting was in progress.

I am especially grateful to the late Gerhard Colm, to Grover W. Ensley, Gabriel Hauge, Theodore J. Kreps, Leon H. Keyserling, the late Edwin G. Nourse, Arthur Okun, John W. Stark, and Charles B. Warden—also to David E. Bell, Marriner S. Eccles, Mordecai Ezekiel, Alvin Hansen, Seymour E. Harris, Neil H. Jacoby, James W. Knowles, Isador Lubin, Walter S. Salant, Paul A. Samuelson, the late George Soule, and Henry C. Wallich. Interpretation of events and policies, evaluation of personalities, and errors of fact are, of course, the sole responsibility of the author.

Much credit goes to my colleagues in the Department of Economics at the University of South Carolina, especially Professor A. G. Smith, Jr., and James L. Cochrane, who read portions of the manuscript and with great patience lived through lengthy discussions and seemingly endless revisions and recasting of chapters. I am likewise indebted to my typist, Mrs. Flora Kees, for her efforts, and to my daughter Pamela, who helped with the bibliography. As always, I am indebted to my wife and family for their understanding.

The Employment Act and the Council of Economic Advisers

Introduction

In 1976, the Employment Act marked its thirtieth year, hardly mature by the standards of legislative acts. Yet, if most Americans feel secure today from the type of utter economic collapse that nearly capsized the nation in 1929–30, it is in large part due both to the institutions established by the act and to the concepts of which it is a symbol.

Of course, no single act created the awe-inspiring trillion-dollar economy that is the hallmark of modern America. For some, no doubt, a general sense of the enormous productive capacity of the nation is enough to assure them that, though hard times come, they also go, never staying long enough to become really serious. Other people go a little further and suppose that the nation is still protected from economic disaster by the reforms and safeguards that were built into the structure of government and the economic system by President Roosevelt and his New Deal.

There is just a tad of truth in both ideas but no more. For the Great Depression of the 1930s was ended, strangely enough, by Adolph Hitler; it was preparation for war that brought full employment, increasing national income. And it was the Employment Act of 1946 that created the climate of the economy we have lived in ever since, a system in which enough informed pragmatic economic advice is available to the President and Congress to enable them to avoid the worse extremes of unemployment and inflation and to attempt more control of the economy when this seems necessary in emergencies.

The Employment Act of 1946 was, like most successful legislation, the product of long thought and considerable compromise. Introduced by Senator James E. Murray of Montana and signed into law by President Truman, the act directed the Federal Government to use

all practicable means consistent with its needs and obligations and other essential considerations of national policy, with the assistance and cooperation of industry, labor, and state and local governments, to coordinate and utilize all its plans, functions, and

3

resources for the purpose of creating and maintaining, in a manner calculated to foster and promote free competitive enterprise and the general welfare, conditions under which there will be afforded useful employment opportunities, including self-employment, for those able, willing, and seeking to work, and to promote maximum employment, production, and purchasing power.[1]

The founders of the Republic and most of their late-nineteenth-century counterparts would have been startled by the suggestion that it was necessary to make provisions for economic specialists in the process of government, for political economy was in their time an adjunct of philosophy and agriculture, subjects in which almost all those involved in the early government of this nation considered themselves tolerably proficient. As men of their kind were gradually eased out of power in the first half of the nineteenth century, as the economic affairs of the nation became increasingly complex, and as economics became a distinct intellectual discipline, so began the separation between politicians and economists that was long a characteristic of American government. Indeed, from about 1830 to about 1930, politicians and intellectuals in the United States generally had little to say to each other, a condition which probably was detrimental to both the intellectual and socio-political life of the nation.

However, during the administration of Franklin Delano Roosevelt (and also, to a surprising degree, that of Herbert Hoover), the intellectual began to be accepted once again on the fringes of government. By "intellectual" I mean, for the moment, the man who, lacking any evident talent for winning elections, nevertheless has specific proficiencies of informed intelligence that can contribute to the process of making policy. The gradual restoration of the intellectual to his place in the inner counsels of government has been one of the notable features of American government for forty years now and has, of course, by no means been confined to economists.

This book confines itself to the role of economic advice exemplified by the Employment Act and to the development of those institutions through which professional economic advice has been implemented, the Council of Economic Advisers and the Joint Economic Committee.

The story is one of the gradual recognition of the need for informed economic advice in Washington, the installation of advice-giving mechanisms, and the consequences of the availability of such advice. It is the story of the Employment Act of 1946 and its implementation during its first three decades.

Our task is to observe the manner in which Presidents who served after 1920 dealt with the economic crises they faced and to determine the changes in approach brought by the Employment Act.

Our study will focus essentially on the Council, since it is part of the executive branch, but we cannot, of course, ignore its congressional counterpart, the Joint Economic Committee. The Joint Committee has by and large played less of an advisory role than the Council, but its function, though less direct, is integral to the act.

Ten presidents have been involved. Two—Harding and Coolidge—are essentially an interlude, a stage wait. Roosevelt with his New Deal laid the groundwork of economic control. Truman, the first president to utilize the Council, represents the transition period. Eisenhower, Kennedy, Johnson, Nixon, and Ford all faced major economic problems during which the Council and the Joint Economic Committee came of age. However, to understand the impact of the new era, we must appreciate the old, namely the pre-act years of laissez-faire.

Note

Introduction

[1] Public Law 304, 79th Congress (1946).

Part I

PRESIDENTIAL ECONOMIC LEADERSHIP IN CRISIS, 1920–45

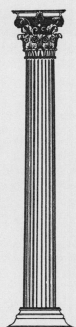

Chapter 1

Economics
and the Presidency

*"I sit here all day trying to persuade
people to do things they ought to have
sense enough to do without my
persuading them . . . that's all the powers
of the President amount to."*
— Harry S. Truman

As the election of 1976 approached, President
Gerald Ford made great efforts to improve the economic policies of his
administration. He had been much criticized, as had been Herbert
Hoover in 1932. Four decades earlier, Franklin Roosevelt drew both
high praise and bitter condemnation for his economic policies.

Economic catchphrases such as the "full dinner pail," the "New
Deal," the "New Frontier," the "Great Society," and the "New
Federalism" have served to identify whole galaxies of economic
policies from McKinley to Nixon. From Wilson's "New Freedom" to
Kennedy's "New Economics," in the public mind the President has
been in the center of economic policies, trials, tribulations, good times
and bad, thus to be condemned or praised as the course of the economy
rose in prosperity or declined into depression.

The American Presidency, the most powerful elective office in the
free world, includes among other elements awesome economic responsibilities, most of which have become attached to the office since 1921.
In 1920 the pressures on the office were lighter than they are at present
(although no one thought so then), but the powers were also much less
formidable. No serious body of citizens would have supported the idea

9

that the President had either the right or the responsibility to intervene in any meaningful fashion in economic affairs.

One must, of course, distinguish between formal and informal, or "political," responsibilities. The constitutional economic powers assigned the President are not extensive, but his informal or "political" responsibility is almost limitless. In the public mind, the President is guardian of the economy. He must "get the economy going again," or get the "system up on its feet."

As Clinton Rossiter expresses it:

There are limits, both strategic and physical, to what can be done in the White House, but certainly the alert President stands always ready to invite the managers of a sick industry or the leading citizens of a city plagued by chronic unemployment to come together and take counsel under his leadership. Of course, it is not his counsel but a well-placed government contract or a hike in the tariff or a dramatic recommendation to Congress for which they have come. Fortunately for the President, his position as overseer of the entire economy is obvious to even the most embittered spokesman for special interests. . . .

The very notion of the President as Manager of Prosperity strikes many people as an economic and political heresy, especially those who still swear allegiance to the tattered doctrine of the self-healing economy. Most of us, however, accept the idea of a federal government openly engaged in preventing runaway booms and plunging bust.[1]

By present standards, the economic powers of the Presidency at the turn of the century were severely limited. Most of the areas of economic power open to the modern Presidency remained largely unexplored. Monetary and fiscal policy in the modern sense were unknown. No federal responsibility for labor relations was contemplated by even the most liberal segments of the population. In 1902, despite the fact that a national emergency was clearly developing, Theodore Roosevelt was widely criticized for injecting himself into the coal strike. This view was by no means confined to management, but was held as well by a large segment of both middle-class people and workers, who were generally of the opinion that labor matters were no concern of the President. Of course, no concept of the aggregate economy existed, and such legislation as the Employment Act of 1946 would have been both inconceivable and inoperable. Of those parts of government to which some real economic significance was attached—namely, the Treasury, the tariff, and the tax program—only the Treasury was within the President's immediate jurisdiction. The tariff, an important matter at the time, was carefully kept in congressional hands. War, a phenomenon that usually acts to enhance executive power, had not occurred, except on a minor scale, since the Civil War. The long economic downturn during the 1870s had clearly demonstrated the inability of the President (as well as the rest of the federal establishment) to deal effectively with economic matters, but "hard times" and unemployment were expected to occur from time to time and no one seriously expected the President to handle them effectively (although, to be sure, people reserved the right to criticize him for economic troubles). However, if he served as scapegoat, he also got full credit for prosperity. Cleveland was to suffer through depression, while McKinley basked in the sunshine of the business upturn at the end of the century, taking credit for the "full dinner pail."

In the first decades of the new century, the parameters of presidential economic power were gradually extended, sometimes by strong Presidents who were anxious to expand the authority of the office, but more often by the exigencies of affairs. Theodore Roosevelt, always the activist, enlarged his economic powers extensively by assuming considerably more power than he actually had and by using the Presidency as a "bully pulpit" in the full sense. Taft, in contrast, was reluctant to face the conflicts inherent in such a course of action.

Neither Taft nor Harding was an aggressive President. They, as well as Coolidge, shrank from combat with the Congress. Wilson and Franklin D. Roosevelt, on the other hand, both by nature and by force of circumstances were inclined to enlarge the area of economic authority open to them. So in a sense was Hoover. It seems clear in every case that the power of the Presidency in economic and other matters was sought out and exploited by the President or arose out of unique circumstances. In few cases, and these only temporary, did the power pass without a struggle.

One might argue that the circumstances are stronger than the man. Thus, what Coolidge might have done if faced with a major crisis no one can say; what Truman would have done in the uneventful Coolidge era remains in the realm of speculation.

In judging the President's performance, Rossiter notes:

> In what sort of times did he live? A man cannot possibly be judged a great President unless he holds office in great times. . . .
> If the times were great, how bravely and imaginatively did he bear the burden of extraordinary responsibility? A successful President must do a great deal more than stand quiet watch over

11

the lottery of history: he must be a forceful leader—of Congress, the administration, and the American people; he must make the hard decisions that have to be made, and make most of them correctly; he must work hard at being President and see that these decisions are carried out.[2]

Much controversy exists as to just what influence the President alone can bring to bear on economic policy. Not only must he share power with others, he must also deal with the fact that much federal policy in the economic area is continuous and carries over from one administration to another. Policies that were once highly controversial and partisan tend to become embodied in the socioeconomic structure and to become bipartisan. One who realistically aspires to such high office will have long since shed his rough edges and extreme ideas in economics as well as other fields. Long before he reaches the White House, he will have learned the art of compromise, the need to conform his views, and the fact that solutions are seldom simple, clear-cut, wholly formed, or universally popular. The President must take the aggregate viewpoint; he must have in mind the entire economy. He begins as a candidate to face pressures that will influence his approach to economic issues. His appointment of key Cabinet officers and senior administrators will be closely observed and subject to comment in the press, forcing him to strive for balance in economic philosophy as well as in other viewpoints. Task forces established to explore significant issues will report on complex economic issues of the day, suggesting seemingly logical and reasonable courses of action that had somehow eluded the previous administration.

On assuming office, however, he soon finds that because of institutional rigidities, the number of ongoing programs, and other factors, his new men and new programs may have little impact on actual policy. Aside from such Cabinet posts as Treasury, Commerce, Agriculture, and Transportation, all oriented around economics, there are numerous policy-making boards, agencies, regulatory bodies, and similar groups to which the President appoints members and designates chairmen, or that he otherwise oversees, and that he and his supporters hope will reflect his economic views in a positive and forceful fashion.

Several Cabinet posts are concerned almost entirely with economic matters. Others, such as Labor and Health, Education and Welfare, have considerable economic impact. The President appoints the Cabinet members who head these departments and, in theory at least, attempts to mold their policies into a shape acceptable to himself and his party. His jurisdiction also extends to the overall supervision of the numerous regulatory commissions, although the "independent" status of the regulatory commissions gives them a substantial degree of detachment from the executive will. Some of these bodies have responsibility limited to one industry, while others have policy ramifications for many areas of the economy. In some instances the President has a large role in determining policy, whereas in others, such as the independent regulatory agencies, his role is more detached in both law and custom. That is, the regulatory agencies are so established as to be "independent," with members drawn from both parties and serving overlapping terms designed to minimize Presidential influence. Even when appointments can be made freely, the policy influence actually exerted by these appointees is questionable. The executive departments are cumbersome, with many long-term commitments and with permanent personnel in policy-making positions. That is, both personnel and programs are apt to be inflexible. The Civil Service system protects from removal a large number of federal officials who, in fact if not by title, occupy policy-making positions.[3]

In 1969–70, for example, Nixon found that the upper ranks of the Department of Health, Education and Welfare were not highly sensitive to his will. Further, even if the President were free to remove people in such cases, time and energy would be a major inhibiting factor. In a large agency, such as the Department of Agriculture, there are hundreds of employees in a position to exercise considerable policy influence by virtue of their expertise and long association with the technical problems and programs involved. These "old guardsmen" know the complexities of the policy issues confronting their departments; they have been around a long time and likely will be in office long after the current President has left his. They know the problems of implementation and how difficult it is to bring about a meaningful change in direction. It is said that there are three parties in Washington: Republicans, Democrats, and Bureaucrats.

Thus, while Nixon would not have appointed the liberal Senator William Proxmire as Secretary of the Treasury, it might be argued that it would have made little ultimate difference if he had. No secretary of a major department could go far in an unconventional direction without being pulled into line by day-to-day responsibilities such as Treasury Department functions or the ongoing force of vast technical programs such as those in Agriculture.[4]

Even a casual glance makes it clear that with such a wide variety of areas and the relatively short time that the President can spend on each area, they must receive a rather superficial analysis insofar as he person-

13

ally is concerned. Within the limits of his schedule, the President may pursue these matters largely as his interests dictate and as, in his judgment, may be necessary. Indeed, all evidence indicates that the President is forced to let routine matters run their course until some serious problem arises.[5]

This is hardly surprising in view of the pressing duties of his office and does not mean, to be sure, that a strong President will abandon the routine workings of various executive departments. It means only that he will have to delegate more, fight harder, and follow up more closely in order to prod the "huge federal beast" an inch or two in what he feels is the right direction. To be sure, these problems are not peculiar to government. Large organizations, such as universities and corporations, have the same difficulty and present the chief executive officer with the same frustrations.

It is said that President Kennedy spent much time personally and through the White House staff overseeing the State Department without making much headway (he called it a "bowl of Jello"). How much time was left to do the same thing in other areas can be left to the imagination. He had, for example, an interest in conservation, but conservation, then a quiet issue, got little of his time.

Most of the economic power exercised by the President is indirect, arising from his ability to use the White House as a platform and his access to the news media to dramatize an issue. A surprising amount of his formal power is negative—removal from office or use of the veto, neither of which is highly effective in formulating programs.

The President's economic responsibilities fall generally into seven broad areas:

1. Antitrust and the regulated industries;
2. Stabilization of the economy;
3. Encouragement of economic growth and development;
4. International economic matters (tariff, etc.);
5. Monetary matters, including banking;
6. Socioeconomic reform; and
7. Care of specific areas of the economy, such as labor and agriculture.

Clearly, no President can be expert in all of these fields, and the President is the head of a large and diverse group of agencies with numerous and often conflicting interests. Truman, pointing to his desk, used to say, "The buck stops here!" Perhaps more accurately he might have said, "All the bucks stop here!"

The major theme is clear: the President and his Cabinet are likely to be bound by policies, programs, problems, concepts, myths, and people inherited from past administrations. Consequently, the opportunities to carry out a major economic policy innovation are remote. Too much has come before and too much will come after.

Franklin Roosevelt, who probably had as much power and cooperation as any man ever to occupy the White House, expressed the matter thus:

> The Treasury is so large and far-flung and ingrained in its practices that I find it is almost impossible to get the action and results I want—even with Henry [Morgenthau] there. But the Treasury is not to be compared with the State Department. You should go through the experience of trying to get any changes in the thinking, policy, and action of the career diplomats and then you'd know what a real problem was. But the Treasury and the State Department put together are nothing compared with the Na-a-vy. The admirals are really something to cope with—and I should know. To change anything in the Na-a-vy is like punching a feather bed. You punch it with your right and punch it with your left until you are finally exhausted, and then you find the damn bed just as it was before you started punching.[6]

The President can suggest, cajole, plead, threaten, and use such direct power as he has over Congress, but he may get nowhere unless the political situation is favorable. Even the strongest President under the most favorable conditions can exercise only limited power. Yet, in the public mind, the President must adjust the domestic economy to the international situation while preserving national stability. He must keep wages high and prices low. He must preserve prosperity without inflation. He must reconcile free trade for rice farmers with high tariffs for textile firms. He must support the demands of labor and listen to the pleas of management.

Historically, this Augean task had to be done almost single-handedly. In 1920 the Presidency had almost no resources comparable to its present specialized staff, and technical matters requiring professional expertise were dealt with on a catch-as-catch-can basis. The doctrine of the self-healing economy was supreme in the land, and no President would have been able with impunity to claim power to intervene except in the most drastic emergency. In effect, except for platitudinous statements, the economy was none of the President's business. Theodore

15

Roosevelt sat by while J. P. Morgan dealt with the Panic of 1907, not only because he had no power or direct responsibility, but also because he had few advisers who would have been capable of telling him what to do and little machinery to effect such policies as might have been decided upon. Yet, even if there had been a host of capable advisers, what data would they have been able to use? The Employment Act of 1946, had it been passed in 1906 or in 1926, would have been a meaningless gesture. Where were the professional economists who now breathe life into the Employment Act and who stand ready to aid the President? They were in academic life; and most, like their fellow citizens, were convinced that laissez-faire was the order of the day. The few who had penetrated government circles were engaged for the most part in data gathering or in technical tasks involving application of microeconomics.

World War I, to be sure, forced the President to mobilize economic resources, and the glimmerings of macroeconomics began to emerge in shadow form. However, the swing back to laissez-faire was both rapid and decisive, and by the time Harding entered the White House, Presidential leadership in economic affairs had receded to its pre-1912 level.

Neither Harding nor Coolidge resisted this "return to normalcy," and few segments of the population found fault with their views. The businessman, the broker, and the advertising man saw their stars rising. By the late 1920s poverty was seemingly all but expunged from the land. True, farmers were not on the prosperity bandwagon, but, then, farmers had always been poor and, in any event, their sons were rapidly moving to the cities to sell stocks and bonds. Herbert Hoover, one of the finest examples to the enlightened businessman extant, was in office. Though no passive Coolidge and fully aware of the growing need for occasional intervention, his economic role was clearly to preside over and consolidate the gains resulting from the booming economy. Woodrow Wilson had long since retired to his quiet house on S Street, to die in 1924—a figure from the past. Yet, had Wilson, however dimly and fleetingly, glimpsed the future? Had the "scholar in politics," before his immersion in international affairs, really begun the era of economic involvement? Was the decade of the 1920s merely an interlude? Clearly it was. Even in the framework of the half century, the decade is out of the pattern. It is, of course, true that the Great Depression of the 1930s was the dramatic incident that marked the turn to a more controlled economy, but this was merely an incident. The tide had already turned. The war and the Harding-Coolidge years had interrupted this trend, but it was too strong to turn back. By the end of the Hoover era, economics and the Presidency had become inextricably intertwined.

16

Economics in the Oval Office

With all his responsibility, both formal and political, what are the President's resources with regard to information and advice? The President has many channels of economic information. In earlier years, the role of economic adviser was played by businessmen and financiers. Specific business problems and aggregative economic issues were not generally distinguishable, and even now most people do not draw a distinction between business problems and economic problems, taking the latter to mean problems of the aggregate economy as opposed to those of specific industries.

Before 1930 the distinction was even more blurred, and Presidents, like others, thought of them as interchangeable. Business problems required businessmen's solutions; problems of finance required the aid of bankers and financiers rather than that of economists, who, if considered at all, were thought of as academic people. Perhaps the President would have been more likely to consider economists useful for commenting on what now would be regarded largely as social problems.

Naturally, advice is often found close to home, and a major advisory role has been played over the years by confidential assistants, who, though not professionally qualified, had both the ear and the confidence of the President. These informal advisers, often able men who had close contact with the President, exerted substantial influence. This was especially true in the years before the more elaborate staff system was created and during which the presidential assistant played a broad "handyman" role. In *The Invisible Presidency* Louis Koenig has noted many examples. William Loeb, Jr., who served with great ability as Theodore Roosevelt's confidential secretary, was often able to influence the course of economic events:

> In his attitude on the policy issues of the day, Loeb was a replica of T. R., a foe of privilege, friend of the underdog, a good Square Dealer. He accepted the several planks of economic regulation and social improvement of the Square Deal with equal and sometimes greater enthusiasm than T. R. himself. . . .
>
> Loeb never sat down and outpoured advice to his chief. One couldn't do that with T. R. Instead, Loeb dropped comments and threw out opinions, often in a casual way, at any point in the many times he saw the President each day. The utterances made might jolt T. R. partly or completely from his determined course. The secretary's most opportune interludes for this kind of assertion came when he was taking dictation, but filled with

17

pauses when, at the spur of a Loeb comment or jab, a phase of policy might be discussed. Even as T. R. was dictating, Loeb would interject remarks.[7]

Roosevelt also absorbed information from businessmen and tapped the universities:

Of the businessmen intimates, perhaps the one of longest standing was George W. Perkins, partner of J. P. Morgan and architect of the labyrinthian corporate structure establishing United States Steel. Perkins' "straightforwardness and intelligence will commend to you whatever he has to say," wrote Speaker Tom Reed in introducing the business magnate to Roosevelt. Indeed they did, for T. R. persistently consulted Perkins in matters of business regulation.[8]

Franklin Roosevelt carried the use of advisers much further than Presidents who served up until his era.

Even after the formal machinery of advice giving was established in 1946 by the passage of the Employment Act, informal advice continued to be important. Koenig has written of Sherman Adams, Eisenhower's assistant:

Adams oversaw the mammoth preparation made in the Executive Branch each year for the impending session of Congress. His efforts were focused upon three great presidential documents conveyed to Congress in January: the Budget, the State of the Union Message and the Economic Report. To the departments these documents were crucial, for much of the program planning and policy innovation at the department level takes legislative form—appropriations, appointments, new statutory authority, and the like. . . .[9]

As much as any man, Sherman Adams held the administration to a predominantly liberal course, and away from the reefs of a politically unrealistic conservatism, toward which it naturally tended.[10]

Even at best, the informal sources of advice to the President are of limited usefulness. No informal adviser is likely to have continuing responsibility, nor is he always well informed on the problem as it relates to other issues. Until at least 1933 sound, unbiased economic advice upon which the President might rely was woefully inadequate. For many reasons, the professional economist was largely ignored, chiefly because the philosophy of the profession was for many years not oriented toward advice giving.[11]

Until 1920 the White House staff was not only small but essentially clerical and secretarial, and the present aggregation of highly trained professionals was unknown. No specialists in labor, foreign affairs, minority groups, and other technical matters were available. Hoover increased the staff considerably, Roosevelt more so, and in recent years the corps of White House assistants has become elaborately structured and highly influential.[12]

In Roosevelt's early days, the President was authorized only four staff positions above the level of clerical or secretarial. By tradition, such jobs carried little prestige and modest salary. Roosevelt's solution before 1939 was to place advisers in line jobs in the various executive agencies, where, though they were technically on the payroll of the department, they were at his disposal—a practice that often gave rise to confusion. By the 1939 reorganization of the executive office (brought about by the Brownlow Committee), however, the office was expanded, and this trend has continued.

By the 1970s the Executive Office of the President had a staff of some fifteen hundred to carry out six major purposes, which Rossiter lists as follows:

1. To insure that the chief executive is adequately and currently informed.
2. To assist him in foreseeing problems and planning future programs.
3. To ensure that matters for his decision reach his desk promptly, in condition to be settled intelligently and without delay; and to protect him against hasty and ill-considered judgments.
4. To exclude every matter that can be settled elsewhere in the system.
5. To protect his time.
6. To secure means of ensuring compliance by subordinates with established policy and executive direction.[13]

All of the top staff people are, of course, the President's own personal choices and owe him loyalty, but the "Presidency" is itself highly institutionalized, and only a handful of the staff have any regular day-to-day contact with him. One understandably has difficulty in distinguishing between the "President," the "White House," the "President's Office," the "Presidency," etc., in attempting to determine who did what when.

Size and quality of staff have varied over the years, but in general the present White House professional assistants number from ten to twelve men who function in broad areas but who are qualified by training and experience to specialize in such matters as labor relations, farm problems, and international economics. These people act as advisers, as administrative aides, as liaison with the Congress and executive departments, and in general make themselves useful to the President as dictated by his particular working style.

The upshot of this is the President is advised, assisted, backstopped, and otherwise aided in his policy-making role by a host of people, often unknown and unseen. How then does one know what policies and thoughts are the President's and which are those of one of his faceless helpers? Clearly, one does not entirely know. Which ideas were Eisenhower's or Sherman Adams', Kennedy's or McGeorge Bundy's, Johnson's or Bill Moyer's, Nixon's or H. R. Haldeman's? To some degree a study of the President's background, speeches, and the history of his administration gives some indication, but attribution is difficult. In the New Deal (a very unstructured administration), ideas percolated up from all areas, such as the Agricultural Adjustment Administration, and from outside advisers. In contrast, Eisenhower's famous staff system would have been difficult to penetrate.[14]

Acceptance of the Advisory Function

By the end of the Roosevelt years and the Second World War, the President's need for professional economic advice was generally accepted, but with certain very important limitations. The complexity of the economy and the high degree of government participation in the war years had brought about substantial change in public thinking and had convinced many skeptics that some professional advice was essential. Economists had demonstrated a degree of expertise during the war years that was to stand them in good stead.

There were, however, many reservations. Those who still opposed the New Deal and all its works (and there were many, especially in business) tended to equate planning, economists, advisers, "brain trusters," and other aspects of the Roosevelt years with "socialism," if not "worse."[15]

Despite this residue of distrust, there was general acceptance of the need for some organization that had the ability to coordinate and analyze the work under way at various levels of government. At the time the second Roosevelt Administration ended, the resources for economic advice were fairly well organized in the Federal Reserve System, and the departments of Commerce, State, Agriculture, and Labor. Elsewhere, they were less impressive or entirely absent. Although economists were increasingly active in the departments and independent agencies, few were close to the President or to the Cabinet officers.

The Presidency is by its nature a pragmatic office. (H. L. Mencken said of Coolidge: "There were no professors sweating fourth dimensional economics.") No President is likely to have had any substantial acquaintance with academic people, and until the 1930s the economist was seldom encountered outside the academic institution.[16] Of pre-Employment Act Presidents—Harding, Coolidge, Hoover, and Roosevelt—Roosevelt alone sought out economists as advisers, but he was by no means always satisfied with the results and never really understood modern economics. Only in a few of the executive departments and, to a degree, in the regulatory agencies did the economist carve out a real niche for himself before the Employment Act was passed.

Until the years following the Second World War, the economist had demonstrated little expertise to attract the high-level government official. Theoretical academic economics, most often micro-oriented, was of little use to a man faced with the problems confronting Hoover or Roosevelt.

The economist who would be successful in the role of Presidential adviser must combine an unusual mixture of qualities. He must be not only professionally competent in a difficult field; he must have great maturity and judgment. He must be willing to subordinate his ego to the President and to accept the fact that the President may for good (though perhaps unstated) reason ignore his reasoning and advice. Economists often enjoy the methodology of the problem as much as the solution and are unhappy when the advisee seeks only the answer, ignoring the careful step-by-step analysis that led up to it.

Until recent years the activities of the professional economists were not likely to draw them into public life. Few were interested in practical affairs, and fewer still had any concept of the aggregate economy. Those economists who did enter the public policy area often confined themselves to special segments of the economy, such as agriculture, railroads, and tariffs. They were apt to be interested in broad socioeconomic matters on the one hand or narrow statistical problems on the other.

With the passage of the Employment Act of 1946, the Council of Economic Advisers became the formal channel for providing the President with economic advice. Of course, he is not limited to that source. The President's time and energy are two of the most valuable items in Washington. The various accounts written about the Council of Economic Advisers make it clear that the Council chairman and members have had occasional difficulty in bringing matters directly before the President himself.[17]

Obviously, the further removed the economist is from the President, both in organizational and physical location, the less likely will he have frequent access. Professor Roy Blough, an early member of the Council has noted that if the economists were not part of the President's team they could hardly expect to get much of his time or have much influence on policy. On this basis, "the influence of the Council might be somewhat above that of a group of University professors with research and publishing facilities but probably not much above it."[18]

Under the act of 1946, the President has a clear obligation to entertain proposals and advice from the Council (although he can do so in a minimal fashion), but his relationship with other economists, both within and outside the government, is entirely what he may choose to make it. None of the five Presidents who has served since the Council was established has ignored it, and, in fact, its influence steadily increased, at least until 1971.

The passage of the Employment Act of 1946 made it the specific responsibility of the President to undertake the constant quest for economic stability. In numerous sections of the act the President is specifically designated as the responsible officer who must "foster and promote free competitive enterprise" and "promote maximum employment." Section 2 states:

> The Congress hereby declares that it is the continuing policy and responsibility of the Federal Government to use all practicable means consistent with its needs and obligations and other essential consideration of national policy, with the assistance and cooperation of industry, agriculture, labor and State and local governments to coordinate and utilize all its plans, functions, and resources for the purpose of creating and maintaining, in a manner calculated to foster and promote free competitive enterprise and the general welfare, conditions under which there will be afforded useful employment opportunities, including self-employment, for those able, willing, and seeking to work, and to promote maximum employment, production, and purchasing power.

Our task is to observe the manner in which Presidents who have served after 1920 have dealt with the economic crises they have faced and to determine the changes in approach brought by the Employment Act.

Notes

Chapter 1

[1] Clinton Rossiter, *The American Presidency* (New York: Harcourt, Brace & World, 1956), pp. 22, 23.

[2] Ibid., p. 112.

[3] In *The Ordeal of Power* (New York: Dell, 1962), Emmet John Hughes tells how Secretary Humphrey arrived in Washington with the idea that the budget could be cut and taxes reduced with enough will to do so. He found out differently.

[4] There doubtless would be general agreement that agricultural policy looked very much the same under Secretary Orville Freeman in 1967 as it did under Secretary Ezra T. Benson in 1954, or under Secretary Henry A. Wallace in 1934. No secretary, no matter how bold, could solve the agricultural problems without a much freer hand than he is likely to get from the Congress. Nor is it even likely that a man with wildly unconventional ideas would get the necessary cooperation from the "old heads" in the department who have seen numerous secretaries and Presidents come and go without having had much long-run impact.

[5] See Hugh S. Norton, *National Transportation Policy: Formation and Implementation* (Berkeley: McCutchan, 1967).

[6] Marriner S. Eccles, *Beckoning Frontiers* (New York: Knopf, 1951), p. 336. Truman makes the same point. See *Harry S. Truman, Memoirs, 1945, Year of Decisions* (New York: Doubleday, 1955), Mentor Ed., 1965, p. 105. Eccles' book makes interesting reading in the economics of the federal process, tracing the rise of an obscure Utah banker into the higher levels of New Deal policies.

[7] Louis W. Koenig. *The Invisible Presidency* (New York: Holt, Rinehart and Winston, 1960), p. 149.

[8] Ibid., p. 181.

[9] Ibid., p. 383.

[10] Ibid., p. 401.

[11] See Hugh S. Norton, *The Role of the Economist in Government Policy Making* (Berkeley: McCutchan, 1969).

[12] See for example, Patrick Anderson, *The President's Men* (New York: Doubleday, 1968).

[13] Rossiter, op. cit., p. 100.

[14] Indeed, some authors have indicated that some good Eisenhower ideas were killed off by the staff. Obviously, the staff system can protect the President, but it can also isolate him. Both FDR and JFK were inclined to seek outside the formal structure. Truman and Eisenhower were more organization bound; Nixon reached a new high in isolation and paid a high price for it.

[15] In the late war years, for example, the National Resources Planning Board fell into such political ill grace that Nourse refused to accept its former quarters for fear of association, even though the newly formed Council of Economic Advisers was desperate for space. See Edwin G. Nourse, *Economics in the Public Service* (New York: Harcourt, Brace & World, 1953).

[16] See Charles L. Schultz, *The Politics and Economics of Public Spending* (Washington: Brookings, 1968).

[17] See: Edwin G. Nourse, op. cit.; Edward S. Flash, *Economic Advice and Presidential Leadership* (New York: Columbia University Press, 1965); Seymour E. Harris, *Economics of the Kennedy Years* (New York: Harper & Row, 1965). See also, Arthur M. Schlesinger, Jr., *A Thousand Days* (Boston: Houghton Mifflin, 1964).

[18] Roy Blough, "Political and Administrative Requisites for Achieving Economic Stability," *American Economic Review* (Proceedings, May 1950), p. 176.

Chapter 2

The Years
of Laissez-Faire

*They burn the grain in the furnace while
men go hungry. They pile the cloth on the
looms while men go ragged. We walk
naked in our plenty.*
—Stephen Vincent Benet

The "incredible era," as Samuel Hopkins Adams
has characterized it, really began with the Wilson administration, World
War I, and the reaction that followed soon after the Armistice.

Though Wilson had been a Progressive and a reformer, his program of
domestic economic reform was limited, not only because of the press of
international affairs, but also in concept, as Arthur Link has noted:

> In the autumn of 1914 Wilson, moreover, thought his program
> to effect a fundamental reorganization of American economic
> life was complete and that the progressive movement had
> fulfilled its mission. "We have only to look back ten years or so
> to realize the deep perplexities and dangerous ill-humors out of
> which we have at last issued, as if from a bewildering fog, a
> noxious miasma," he wrote in a public letter to McAdoo in No-
> vember, 1914, announcing the consummation of the New Free-
> dom program. "Ten or twelve years ago the country was torn
> and excited by an agitation which shook the very foundations of
> her political life, brought her business ideals into question, con-
> demned her social standards, denied the honesty of her man of
> affairs, the integrity of her economic processes, the morality and

good faith of many of the things which her law sustained." And
so things stood until the Democrats came to power and the New
Freedom legislation righted fundamental wrongs. The nightmare
of the past years was over now, and the future would be a time
of cooperation, of new understanding, of common purpose, "a
time of healing because a time of just dealing."

Advanced progressives were puzzled by Wilson's remarkable
letter. Did the President mean what he had said? Was the progressive movement over? If so, then where could the social justice element go?[1]

Herbert Croly, a leading liberal, Wilson's biographer, and editor of
The New Republic, felt that Wilson was the victim of self-deception and
that his program of economic reform was superficial. Professor Link
comments:

Croly's analysis of the superficial character of Wilson's progressivism was essentially correct. There is little evidence that
Wilson had any deep comprehension of the far-reaching social
and economic tensions of the time. As Croly said, Wilson was
intelligent and sincere. But that did not make him a prophet or a
pioneer, or even a progressive of the advanced persuasion. He
had not taken office to carry out a program of federal social reform. He had promised to lower the tariff, reorganize the currency and banking system, and strengthen the antitrust laws, in
order to free the nation's energies and unleash the competitive
urges of the people. He had done these things, and with a
minimum of concession to advanced progressive concepts. He
had, moreover, turned over control of the public agencies established by the new legislation—the Federal Reserve Board and
the Federal Trade Commission—to cautious men. To try to por-
tray such a man as an ardent social reformer is to defy the plain
record.[2]

Clearly, the liberal Democrats had expected a more comprehensive
agenda of economic reform. Wilson's character, economic beliefs, and
the press of external events were to dictate otherwise. What had begun
as a gradual drift away from the program of economic reform was, of
course, much stimulated by war. The first casualty was the New Freedom, and a return to the New Nationalism, in the style of Theodore
Roosevelt, became apparent. Arthur M. Schlesinger, Jr., comments:

War completed Wilson's conversion. The requirements of
mobilization made him, in the end, the best New Nationalist of them

25

all. To meet the needs of war, central direction of the economy proved necessary; and the war itself, by creating clear and definite priorities, supplied the criteria that made the rational organization of industry possible. For a moment Washington became the unchallenged economic capital of the nation. . . . The national government had never gone so far in the operation and conduct of business.[3]

Despite liberal disappointment, Wilson's record of reform had not been unimpressive. Wilson's original philosophy had been favorable to a program of at least modest regulation. He clearly recognized the major economic change that had taken place since 1900, namely, the rise of concentrated corporate economic power; and he was convinced that a return to the pre-1900 economy was impossible. The obvious solution was, in his mind, a strong program of federal regulation designed to restore, or at least to preserve, competition.

The first areas to receive attention were the tariff and the nation's banking system. With substantial Democratic majorities in the Congress and a strong positive program, Wilson's first term was highly productive; however, the agenda proved to be limited in scope.

Reformers and liberals were pleased with the revision in the tariff but restrained in their praise for the Federal Reserve System, which they regarded as being too much under the control of the bankers. Likewise, their view of the Wilson antitrust program was less than enthusiastic. By 1916 Wilson's New Freedom program had become almost indistinguishable from Roosevelt's New Nationalism. As the election approached, however, the President was reminded that his victory in 1912 had rested largely on the fact that the Republican vote had been split between Roosevelt and Taft and that more attention must be paid to the liberal Democrats if he hoped to win again.

In January he appointed the liberal Louis D. Brandeis as Associate Justice of the Supreme Court and took a more advanced position on such issues as federal credits to agriculture. Child labor legislation, a favorite goal of the reformers, was passed in 1916; however, as Wilson had predicted, it was not upheld by the Supreme Court. Wilson's 1916 victory over Charles Evans Hughes seems to have been based only in part on the record of Progressivism and due principally to the fact that Wilson had kept the nation from war, a condition soon to change. War and its aftermath completely dominated his second term, and his administration ended in personal tragedy and national disillusionment.

The bitter postwar conflict over the League of Nations and Wilson's physical and mental collapse completely eliminated Presidential interest in domestic issues and made his renomination in 1920 impossible. After

26

forty-four ballots, the nomination went to James M. Cox of Ohio, with Franklin D. Roosevelt of New York as his running mate.

The election of a Republican President in 1920 had been regarded as a foregone conclusion, and, through a series of circumstances, the nomination fell to Senator Warren G. Harding of Ohio. The Republican candidates, Harding and Coolidge, won in a landslide (16.1 million to 9.1 million popular votes), and the new era began.

The State of the Economy, 1920

The United States in 1920 had changed greatly from the United States of 1915. America had become a major international industrial and financial power, and the industrial structure had been vastly expanded. Industries such as automobiles and aircraft, which in prewar days had been barely out of the developmental stage, were on the threshold of a period of incredible growth. Exports had skyrocketed, and by 1920 their value was more than $8.25 billion, a threefold increase over those of 1913. Domestic industry was emerging from the restrictions of wartime controls and was contemplating the prospects of new economic freedom. The federal budget for 1922–23 was a somewhat alarming peacetime $83.5 billion.

Though there was a short but sharp slump in 1919, recovery was rapid. Whetted by wartime bond issues, investors were increasingly interested in stocks and bonds. The modern concept of the corporation, only dimly seen in 1913, was becoming an increasingly influential reality in the economy.

Intercity transportation was still dominated by the railroads, just then being returned to their owners after wartime ownership and operation by the government. Labor and other groups had made strong moves toward continuing federal ownership, but the program had little popular support. The airplane and the radio were still of little economic significance, though they clearly had a great commercial future. Their development was much aided by the forward-looking Secretary of Commerce, Herbert C. Hoover. The war had greatly stimulated mobility among the population and contributed to the growth of urban areas and the decline of the rural population.

Though unionism had grown rapidly during the war (reaching a membership of some five million in 1920), its ranks were still filled largely with the skilled tradesmen. The postwar "Red scare," the open-shop drive in mass production industries, and the reconversion to peacetime industry combined to undermine further union growth. Aside from such closely knit groups as the railroad brotherhoods, the printing trades, and the

27

construction workers, unionism was weak and divided, with no encouragement from Washington.[4]

While the farmer had enjoyed prosperous times during the war years, rising land prices and declining demand for farm products were forcing him back into his prewar position. By July 1920 agricultural prices had fallen ten points below those for June and fell fifteen points more by August. Wheat, which had sold for upwards of $2.00 per bushel during the war, had fallen to 67 cents by the fall of 1920. Foreclosures mounted as the boom turned into the most serious agricultural depression in the nation's history.[5] Farmers were beginning to organize in an effort to fight for farm legislation, but they still did not have a really effective lobby in Washington.

By late 1920 business and industry were having their own troubles. The advance in rediscount rates begun by the Federal Reserve Board in late 1919 had continued into 1920 and this, coupled with the sharp decline in demand for farm equipment and industrial and durable consumer goods, dealt business a severe blow. Also by 1920 the heavy foreign lending that had been an important outlet for capital came to a temporary end. Before the year was over some 4.7 million men were unemployed. Thus the consequences of the postwar adjustment had begun to catch up with the economy.[6] More, of course, was involved than the war. It had served as a catalyst for social and economic change; beyond the war, the nation was adjusting to economic maturity.

Harding and Coolidge

Into this critical and fluid situation came Warren G. Harding. He was fond of comparing himself to his fellow Ohioan, William McKinley.[7] Harding was a newspaper publisher and a long-time politician, a man of personal charm and goodwill who had risen far beyond his limited ability. His formal education was modest. His business background was confined to the operation of the *Marion* (Ohio) *Star*. Though Harding has been looked upon as the weakest of modern Presidents, he was, in fact, a man of his times.

Drawn to politics early in his career, Harding had served in the Ohio state senate and as lieutenant governor, but lost as candidate for governor in 1910. In 1914 he was elected to the United States Senate.[8] His record as a Senator was completely undistinguished save for his standpat conservative Republicanism. William G. McAdoo said that Harding's style of oratory "left the impression of an army of pompous phrases moving over the landscape in search of an idea." Alice Roosevelt Longworth, who had a long association with him, said he was

28

not a bad man, "just a slob." Perhaps, but he was typical of his time and class.

When the new President entered the White House in March 1921, only minor problems were apparent. Prosperity was seemingly widespread, and Harding proposed to return the nation to "normalcy," away from the discord of reform and international problems that had dominated the past several years. The "sound business" outlook of the Cabinet was personified by Andrew Mellon in the Treasury and Herbert Hoover as Secretary of Commerce. Harding's economic orientation is easy to describe since it did not differ essentially from the outlook of the small-town merchant of his era—a philosophy composed of generalizations and platitudes relative to free enterprise, sound money, and other elements of conventional economic wisdom.

A kindly and limited man who avoided complexities, he looked upon himself as a harmonizer whose skill lay in bringing diverse views together. The tariff, problems of unemployment, monetary policy, and other esoteric economic issues were not within his sphere of interest. He admitted that, though books explaining such matters were available, he could not find them nor would he be able to understand them. As a small-town newspaper publisher, and an insular and mediocre Senator, he had no opportunity to become acquainted with such matters and he failed to realize that a harmonizer on his new level must be able to judge issues as well as men. It was his and the nation's tragedy that, in the end, he was a good judge of neither.

Andrew Mellon, Secretary of the Treasury, set the conservative tone of the administration. The secretary believed that high taxes on large incomes would discourage venture capital and thus retard economic development, and he set himself to work toward the goal of eliminating such discouraging factors.[9] One of the wealthiest men in the nation, he was taciturn and withdrawn, the complete opposite of the warm and friendly Harding. At his urging, Harding signed the Revenue Act of 1921, which eliminated the wartime excess profits tax and reduced the maximum surtax to 50 percent. The overall act was less favorable to business than Mellon had desired, but he was faced with serious opposition from the farm bloc Senators, who were determined that favors to business be balanced by favors to agriculture.

This frigid Pittsburgh banker and strong conservative was to dominate the fiscal policies of the Harding-Coolidge-Hoover era. (It has been said that three Presidents served under Mellon.)

Harding has been a much neglected figure. The biography by Francis Russell draws a more sympathetic portrait than that of most historians.[10]

In Marion, at the turn of the century, Harding built the *Star* into a profitable and influential regional newspaper. He was in many ways the prototype of the small-town booster, more successful than he had ever thought he would be, "bootstrapping" himself upward to the ranks of leading citizens—a "Babbit" come to life and soon to become a "Dodsworth." Some have attributed the success of the *Star* to his wife, but it seems clear that, although she made a contribution, the upward course of the enterprise had already been established when she came into the organization.

Harding was no more or less sophisticated in his economic thinking than the average small-town businessman of his age. He had watched Marion grow from a hamlet to a prosperous, small industrial city. Progress was evident on every side; his business, as well as that of his friends, was growing and profits rising. In this atmosphere, he and most of his fellow townsmen had risen from humble beginnings to financial and political success. The midwestern community with which Harding was so familiar was a microcosm of the American contemporary economy. Hard times might come but, in general, the course was upward. It was Harding's custom to purchase a few shares of stock in newly established businesses in the area, generally paying for them with advertising. Some of these enterprises failed, but most flourished. Eastern sophisticates were appalled by Harding's "traveling salesman" glad-handing, his smoking car jokes, and his general "oh-you-kid" approach, but his folksy ways had wide appeal to small-town America. In office, though, he found the job formidable and often told his assistant, Judson Welliver, that many issues (e.g., taxes) were beyond him.[11] Though overwhelmed by his problems, both official and personal, Harding had no choice but to follow his inclinations and those of his business-based advisers.

A conservative cast began to be noticeable almost immediately in the appointment of officials, especially those on the increasingly important regulatory commissions. The first appointment to the Interstate Commerce Commission went, much to the liberal Senator Robert La Follette's dismay, to Representative John J. Esch of Wisconsin. Esch, who had been co-author of the Esch-Cummins Act of 1920, replaced the Wilson-appointed Robert W. Wooley, whose attitude the railroads had found most uncooperative. This incident was minor compared to the outrage of the liberals when, in 1925, Coolidge appointed Thomas F. Woodlock of the *Wall Street Journal* to the ICC. Appointments to the Federal Reserve Board and the Federal Trade Commission served equally to convince the liberals that the conservative business community was in a powerful position. Mellon, as ex-officio FRB member, was reinforced in his fiscal view by D. R. Crissinger of Marion, whom Harding appointed Comptroller of the Currency.[12] One major contribution with great future significance, however, did emerge from the Harding years, namely, the federal budgetary process. Harding and General C. G. Dawes made a major breakthrough in policy control.

Harding's first appointment to the Federal Trade Commission (of which Wilson had expected great things) went to V. W. Van Fleet, an Indiana politician who had been assistant to Attorney General Harry M. Dougherty. The second appointment went to an Iowa farmer, one C. W. Hunt. Later, Coolidge made the direction even more obvious by appointing William E. Humphrey, a Congressman and long-time champion of big business.[13]

A major effort of Harding's administration was directed toward freeing the government of any taint of interference with business.

> The determination of the Republican administration to free itself as completely as possible from the slightest taint of competition with business was further strikingly manifest in its attitude toward the Muscle Shoals development. . . .
> One of the earliest actions taken by the Harding administration in April, 1921, was to terminate all work on the Wilson Dam, a decision, incidentally, that by destroying the existing organization for its construction, made the later resumption of building unnecessarily expensive.[14]

When Harding died in 1923 and was succeeded by Coolidge, the general outlines of his program remained unchanged. Coolidge had graduated from Amherst in 1895, been admitted to the bar, and practiced law in Northampton, Massachusetts. He had risen through the ranks of state politics to the governorship and became Harding's running mate in 1920 after a dramatic confrontation with the striking police force in Boston, which projected him into national fame more through press coverage than actual participation. Coolidge had risen in politics largely by not rocking the boat, a practice he continued with success into the Presidency.

Despite the Harding scandals and his own pedestrian performance, Coolidge had little trouble being reelected in 1924, and the course of business moved steadily upward. One troublesome spot, a portent of the future but not yet fully apparent, was the state of international trade. Protectionism was on the rise throughout the world, and protectionist sentiments in the United States found a ready acceptance by the business-oriented administration. The effects were unfortunate:

31

. . . the United States under Harding and Coolidge made an
exceptionally difficult situation far worse. If the United States
was to function as a creditor nation, it had to import more than
it exported. But the country moved in precisely the opposite
direction. By an emergency tariff in 1921 and the Fordney-
McCumber Tariff Act of 1922, the United States drowned any
hope that it would be more receptive to European goods. The
Fordney-McCumber Tariff restored the high prewar rates of
Payne-Aldrich and added a few new tolls of its own. (Harding
dumbfounded one reporter by explaining, "We should adopt a
protective tariff of such a character as will help the struggling
industries of Europe to get on their feet.") By including farm
products in the new tariff rates—from reindeer meat to
acorns—high-tariff advocated quieted traditional farm opposition
to protection.[15]

Harding's death brought little change except that personal honesty
was restored. Coolidge did not depart from the conventional economic
wisdom of the times. Schlesinger sums up the Coolidge economic philosophy in a revealing passage:

As he worshipped business, so he detested government. "If
the Federal Government should go out of existence, the common run of people would not detect the difference in the affairs
of their daily life for a considerable length of time." The Federal
Government justified itself only as it served business. "The law
that builds up the people is the law that builds up the industry."
And the chief way by which the Federal Government could
serve business was to diminish itself. "The Government can do
more to remedy the economic ills of the people by a system of
rigid economy in public expenditure than can be accomplished
through any other action." Economy was his self-confessed
obsession; it was "idealism in its most practical form"; it was
the "full test of our national character."[16]

Wall Street viewed Coolidge with apprehension since there was some
fear that his New England caution and conservatism would dampen its
freewheeling activities, but this fear proved groundless.[17] Though himself of modest means, and in many ways the very prototype of the thrifty
rural Yankee, he venerated the world of Wall Street.

In some ways, it can be said that Coolidge was the last of the
nineteenth-century Presidents, able to operate in a highly personal fashion with a small staff. His routine in the White House was more like that
of a mayor of a New England town, leisurely and unhurried without

pressure. He spent less time in his office than other modern Presidents. Coolidge enjoyed contact with the world figures who passed through the White House, but he valued most the opportunity to rub elbows with those in the highest ranks of finance and business. It is easy to be critical of the Harding-Coolidge years and to point out that the reluctance of these two Presidents to involve themselves led shortly to the collapse of credit and financial disaster. However, this is done only with the benefit of hindsight. Both Harding and Coolidge were fully convinced of the virtues of laissez-faire philosophy and, indeed, until the latter part of the Coolidge years, it is easy to understand and justify their inactivity.

The rather limited Wilsonian program of reform, with its narrow intellectual base, had never been really popular, nor was it demonstrably a success in the restoration of competition and the other goals that its proponents has set for it. As Coolidge and Mellon set about reversing these trends, there was little outcry of alarm from the nation as a whole.

Business activity scaled new heights as the midpoint of the 1920s was reached, with the rapidly growing automobile and electrical industries leading the progress parade. Sound, dependable men of large affairs were in key economic policy positions. Both Wall Street and Main Street were optimistic, so why should Pennsylvania Avenue dampen spirits? To be sure, the postwar depression in 1921–22 had been sharp, but except for farmers, it was short and it was expected. Consequently, in early 1923, when recovery began, the course of events seemed to be normal.

Hoover noticed that Coolidge had observed, "If one saw ten troubles coming down the road, nine would run into the ditch and only one would have to be dealt with." Hoover added, however, that when one did arrive, Coolidge was completely unprepared to deal with it.[18]

Coolidge was never really happy with Hoover in the Cabinet. Hoover impressed the President with his obvious ability, but he was far too aggressive for the President's taste—a young man in a hurry as far as Coolidge was concerned. Conversely, Hoover had a low opinion of the President's administrative talents.

The Coolidge luncheon guests (and likely economic advisers) included such men as J. P. Morgan, Jr., Clarence W. Barron of *Barrons*, and W. H. Grimes, editor of the *Wall Street Journal*—able men, but hardly unbiased on the subject of stock market credit or on the matter of governmental powers over business.[19] When the problems of the money market became too troublesome, Coolidge apparently took refuge in domestic affairs and in White House logistics.[20]

Industrial output rose, productivity increased substantially, and the

33

early signs of excessive speculation (e.g., the Florida land boom) began to surface as the 1920s wore on.[21] There were other disquieting factors to be seen by the farsighted: Agriculture refused to recover to its wartime levels, labor unrest was evident, coal and textiles were not prosperous; but, in general, as 1924 began there seemed to be adequate grounds for belief that the U.S. economy was on a rapidly rising plane and poverty was on the way out.[22]

With this growing business activity and the sympathetic views toward business prevailing in Washington, it is not surprising that those in the Federal establishment adopted the attitude that their greatest contribution would be to encourage industrial expansion and that a policy of noninterference would be the most productive course. The prewar era of Progressive-reform thinking had collapsed, and the next four years would find business attitudes more influential both in government and society in general than in any other period. Except for the state of the stock market, which was a constant topic of conversation, there was little economic discourse. Much more enticing were Prohibition, golf, sensational murders, Al Capone, and other topics of the day.

Businesses were venerated as never before. Industrial and financial leaders were in great demand as commencement speakers, and their words were carefully recorded. Even established religion was subjected to the test of sound business:

Religion was valued not as a path to personal salvation or a key to the riddles of the universe but because it paid off in dollars and cents. The Dean of the University of Chicago Divinity School told a reporter that a man could make more money if he prayed about his business. Reading the Bible, explained another writer, meant money in your pocket. Insurance men were advised that Exodus offered good tips on risk and liability, while a Chicago bond salesman confided that he had boosted his income by drawing arguments from Ezekiel.[23]

Bullish views were reinforced on every side by the evidence of mounting production of autos, output of steel, construction of new houses and factories. Technology was making substantial progress. Automobiles and electrical goods were not only expanding in output, improvements in design and quality were equally impressive.

"Scientific" management was much discussed; mass production was the key to prosperity. Henry Ford, the wizard of mass output, was a folk hero of immense stature. New and better methods were devised to make investment more efficient and productive. The investment trust was rapidly gaining favor, especially among those who were inexperienced in market operations. The trust seemed to be the answer to everything. It combined all the best securities, and, since all were rising, it required little or no attention from the small and unsophisticated investor.

Economics professors, long ignored as counselors when "practical advice" was needed, were anxiously sought and showed little hesitation about marketing their limited forecasting skills. Everyone was seeking "inside" information:

> To have a private economist was one possibility, and as the months passed a considerable competition developed for those men of adequate reputation and susceptibility. It was a golden age for professors. The American Founders Group, an awe-inspiring family of investment trusts, had as a director Professor Edwin W. Kemerer, the famous Princeton money expert. The staff economist was Dr. Rufus Tucker, also a well-known figure. (That economists were not yet functioning with perfect foresight is perhaps suggested by the subsequent history of the enterprise. United Founders, the largest company in the group, suffered a net contraction in its assets of $301,385,504 by the end of 1935, and its stock dropped from a high of over $75 per share in 1929 to a little under 75 cents.)
> Still another great combine was advised by Dr. David Friday, who had come to Wall Street from the University of Michigan. Friday's reputation for both insight and foresight was breathtaking. A Michigan trust had three college professors—Irving Fisher of Yale, Joseph S. Davis of Stanford, and Edmund E. Day, then of Michigan—to advise on its policies. The company stressed not only the diversity of its portfolio but also of its counsel. It was fully protected from any parochial Yale, Stanford, or Michigan view of the market.[24]

Unfortunately, for both their professional reputation and their clients' cash position, their degree of success was modest. As the market fell, these academic experts became even more active than they had been in sunnier days. Professor Joseph S. Lawrence of Princeton reached new heights in defending the level of brokers' loans when this matter began to be questioned. In the late summer of 1929 "the consensus of judgment of the millions whose valuations function on that admirable market, the stock exchange, is that stocks are not at present, over-valued . . . where is that group of men with the all-embracing wisdom which will entice them to veto the judgment of this intelligent multitude?"[25] Where indeed? Table 1 indicates the extent of economic activity that had been achieved by early 1929.

Table 1. **ECONOMIC GROWTH, 1919–29**

Year	Industrial Production	Cost-of-Living Index 1929=100	National Income (billions of $)	Real Income Per Capita, 1929 Prices
1919	—	101.6	64.2	543
1920	—	116.9	74.2	548
1921	58	104.2	59.4	522
1922	73	97.7	60.7	553
1923	88	99.5	71.6	634
1924	82	99.8	72.1	633
1925	90	102.4	76.0	644
1926	96	103.2	81.6	678
1927	95	101.2	80.1	674
1928	99	100.1	81.7	676
1929	110	100.0	87.2	716

Source: U.S. Department of Commerce

Gathering Clouds

By the latter part of the Coolidge Administration, the rise in the stock market was causing considerable unrest in prudent circles, and it was decided to bring this matter to the President's attention. The market had become almost an obsession. Businessmen, industrial workers, barbers, and maids studied the market, swapped tips, spoke knowledgeably of Dow-Jones, and watched their paper profits grow.

Professor W. Z. Ripley of Harvard, an authority on railroads and regulation, had written an article detailing what he thought were the dangers of this situation; and Judson Welliver, the presidential assistant, asked him to come to the White House and discuss the matter. Coolidge appeared to be concerned as Ripley painted an alarming picture. However, when the President discovered that the federal government had no specific authority (the stock exchange was under New York State law), he happily abandoned the whole matter, even though Welliver made a strong case for at least a presidential statement, which might have had a beneficial effect on the situation.[26]

The market continued on its course of "Coolidge prosperity." The degree to which Hoover as Secretary of Commerce might have used his influence to curb the situation is a matter of conjecture. Although there is little evidence that Coolidge sought out the counsel of economists, there was also a dearth of sound economic commentary in any form during this period. With few exceptions, academic economists were secure in their

36

ivory towers or were happily extolling the virtues of the expanding market. With superb luck, or perhaps masterful timing, Coolidge made his famous statement about choosing not to run in 1928. The field was thus left open to his rising Secretary of Commerce, who defeated Alfred E. Smith, the Democratic candidate. Hoover, as a recently converted Republican, was regarded with suspicion by the "old guard," and his appointment by Harding had been regarded with disfavor; yet by 1928 he was unbeatable.

Herbert C. Hoover won by some seven million votes. While the religious issue (Smith was a Roman Catholic) was the dramatic element in the election, the fact that few economic problems were apparent diluted Smith's appeal as a general reformer and friend of the "little man." One can only speculate as to the effect severe "pocketbook" issues might have had on the "Catholic problem," but, at any rate, the Republicans had taken title to the idea of prosperity, and there seemed no reason to change. There were no "little men" left. Everyone was going to be rich, and Smith's platform had only modest appeal.

The Engineer and the Price System

The Hoover Administration began under perhaps the most favorable circumstances that one can imagine. The flaws in the Coolidge prosperity had not been generally discovered; international tensions were, on the surface at least, at a low ebb; and the President appeared to be the best prepared in many years. The new President was a mining engineer by training, having been graduated from Stanford University in the first graduating class of that institution.[27]

Hoover's background in economic and business matters was far more complete than that of any recent President. He had had an outstandingly successful career as a mining engineer and, in later years, as developer, manager and investor in mining and related operations throughout the world. He had spent many years abroad, had lived for a long time in London, and had vast experience in international finance. No other American President had the foreign experience that Hoover had accumulated. He had retired at a comparatively early age to enter public life and had achieved considerable fame during World War I as a capable administrator of the war relief food program in Belgium. By 1920 he had become a formidable figure in Republican circles. As Secretary of Commerce in Harding's Cabinet, he was undoubtedly the most successful secretary before or since. The Department of Commerce had been one of the most carefree departments in that rather somnolent era.[28]

Hoover transformed it into one of the most respected. The department under his administration became an active and viable institution, with a substantial effort directed toward encouraging such rising activities as air transportation and radio communication. Hoover became one of the powers in the Cabinet, most unusual for the Secretary of Commerce. After his impressive electorial victory in 1928, Hoover entered the White House on March 4, 1929, the very epitome of the successful businessman-engineer devoted to public service. He was honest, conservative, wealthy by his own effort, an orphan who, by following the Horatio Alger tradition, rose to riches. His public image was that of a successful administrator of humanitarian projects. Every sign pointed to four more years of prosperity, honestly and efficiently administered.

Part of Hoover's appeal was that he was not viewed as a professional politician. He had never held elective office. He was efficient, a skilled and experienced man of large affairs who seemed to meld the national veneration for business with an equal regard for high-level, selfless public service. He had no need for more money, and his personal life was above reproach.

Many liberals who had supported Wilson, and to whom Harding and Coolidge were anathema, looked kindly on Hoover. In addition to his "Bull Moose" background (he had supported Theodore Roosevelt in 1912), his obvious ability and honesty impressed them.[29] The liberal popular economists, W. T. Foster and Waddill Catchings, wrote in his praise, "For the first time in our history, we have a President who, by technical training, engineering achievement, Cabinet experience, and grasp of economic fundamentals, is qualified for business leadership. 'I have no fears for the future of our country,' said Herbert Hoover in his inaugural address in March, 1929. 'It is bright with hope.'"[30]

To the economist the Hoover Administration is indeed a paradox. One looks in vain for an admission that the President would have made any policy changes in the light of subsequent events, or upon two decades of reflection. There is no concession that some policies were incorrect or short-sighted or that substantially different measures would have improved the chance of economic recovery. One is forced to conclude that Hoover, though a successful businessman, personally honest, and a thoroughly experienced and capable administrator, was, as President, faced with economic problems beyond his comprehension and that some three decades later he still did not understand them.

From what had appeared to be a high plateau of prosperity, the nation plunged into an apparently bottomless pit of depression. Despite his impressive background, like most Presidents before him Hoover had no overall economic policy, and he proceeded to formulate a procedure largely as he went along.

Several items of personal economic philosophy seem to emerge from the memoirs:

1. Hoover had a strong veneration for the "American dream," as typified by his own career. Raised "on the frontier" in Oregon and California in the 1870s and 1880s, he had lifted himself by his bootstraps. He was and remained opposed to any federally supported assistance to individuals suffering from economic misfortunes.

2. He had considerable faith in his own judgment and ability. (Had he not been a fantastic success in a highly speculative field, where he had been called upon daily to solve complex problems and where he had built a worldwide reputation?) His command of facts and figures was impressive throughout his life.

3. He was extremely conservative, a characteristic notable in personal dress and conduct as well as economic outlook. He called the McNary-Haugen proposal to support farm prices fascist in nature.

4. He was suspicious of the motives of others (e.g., Rexford Tugwell, Roosevelt's adviser) and he could not see why he should be subjected to abuse for following the "right" course. He complained about being called heartless because of his views on relief, pointing out his efforts to feed the victims of war.

5. He was very reluctant to admit that any of his policies should be changed. More than twenty years later (1952), the memoirs are without a shadow of admission that policy errors might have been committed.

6. When he was convinced he was right (e.g., on relief or his refusal to leave the gold standard), no one was able to sway him.

7. The President was systematic and precise, not given to action based on guesswork or hunch. During his administration, he appointed numerous committees, commissions, and study groups to supply him with facts.

8. He was a superb administrator and had almost total recall, often engaging in long summations of complex issues without notes or information from aides.

Much of his basic economic philosophy is clearly stated in his inaugural address. In this, his first official declaration of social and economic

39

policies at the opening of his administration, Hoover said among other things:

> The election has again confirmed the determination of the American people that regulation of private enterprise and not government ownership or operation is the course rightly to be pursued in our relation to business. In recent years we have established a differentiation in the whole method of business regulation between the industries which produce and distribute commodities on the one hand, and public utilities on the other. In the former, our laws insist upon effective competition; in the latter, because we substantially confer a monopoly by limiting competition, we must regulate their services and rates. Rigid enforcement of the laws applicable to both groups is the very base of equal opportunity and freedom. Such regulations should be extended by the Federal Government within the limitations of the Constitution and only when the individual states are without the power to protect their citizens through their own authority. . . . The larger purpose of our economic thought should be to establish more firmly stability and security of business and thereby remove poverty still further from our borders.[31]

Much has been written as to the responsibility of the Hoover versus Coolidge administrations as to what might have been said or done in regard to the stock market speculative boom which was then in progress. As we have seen, and as Hoover was well aware, Coolidge chose to remain detached from the situation, rationalizing his view by pointing out that direct responsibility rested with the Federal Reserve System or the State of New York. Coolidge has been almost universally damned by historians for his lack of constructive action.

Coolidge was a passive President in the extreme. Hoover, to the contrary, was an activist. (Coolidge complained that Hoover when in the Cabinet had often tendered unasked-for advice.) Though Hoover had responsibility only for Commerce, during his tenure as secretary he had not hesitated to involve himself in the affairs of other departments, especially Agriculture—he was often called Secretary of Commerce and undersecretary of everything else! Can one think that Hoover was able to ignore the financial situation then in the process of development? Is it not likely that he advised the President on these matters and also likely that Coolidge ignored his advice? It is known that Hoover was disturbed and, given his personality, his failure to speak out is not plausible, especially since, as H. G. Warren notes, when Hoover accepted the Commerce post, he was assured that he would have a voice in major economic policies, and all Cabinet members were so informed.[32]

40

Hoover did make cautionary statements in 1927, calling attention to the "fever of speculation," but they did little good.[33] Some controversy exists as to what might have been accomplished by White House statements, but John Kenneth Galbraith, in his lively account of events preceding the Crash, points out that moral suasion *was* effective on the rare occasions when it was used.[34]

Hoover is generally thought of as being very much the prototype of the laissez-faire Republican economic thinker. This of course is far from being completely true. Hoover was comparatively liberal, thought of himself as being progressive, and was, in fact, quite willing to intervene up to a point. He wrote to his friend and adviser Arch W. Shaw in 1933, complaining that his New Deal image was not accurate:

> I notice that the Brain Trust and their superiors are now announcing to the world that the social thesis of laissez-faire died on March 4. I wish they would add a professor of history to the Brain Trust. The 18th Century thesis of laissez-faire passed in the United States half a century ago. The visible proof of it was the enactment of the Sherman Act for the regulation of all business, the transportation and public utility regulation, the Federal Reserve System, the Eighteenth Amendment, the establishment of the Farm Loan Bank, the Home Loan Banks, the Reconstruction Finance Corporation. All are but part of the items marking the total abandonment of that social thesis. However, there are many other subjects upon which I could comment which are not news to you.[35]

On numerous occasions, he denied the conservative opinion that depression was self-curing and had to be endured until it was ended. After the 1929 crash, he said on one occasion:

> Mr. Mellon had only one formula: "Liquidate stocks, liquidate the farmers, liquidate real estate." . . . Secretary Mellon was not hardhearted. In fact he was generous and sympathetic with all suffering. He felt there would be less suffering if his course were pursued. . . . But other members of the Administration, also having economic responsibilities—Undersecretary of the Treasury Mills, Governor Young of the Reserve Board, Secretary of Commerce Lamont, and Secretary of Agriculture Hyde—believed with me that we should use the powers of government to cushion the situation.[36]

Other contemporary observers, such as the "Bull Moose" Republicans, considered him enlightened. Reporters and writers of the era looked upon him as a highly progressive and interventionist President.

41

Unfortunately, whatever his liberal inclinations, by the time Hoover took over, matters had reached a serious stage. The stock market, for example, had become a national mania far beyond recall by mild presidential statements. Frederick Lewis Allen has described the situation:

> The rich man's chauffeur drove with his ears laid back to catch the news of an impending move in Bethlehem Steel; he held fifty shares himself on a twenty-point margin. The window-cleaner at the broker's office paused to watch the ticker, for he was thinking of converting his laboriously accumulated savings into a few shares of Simmons. Edwin Lefevre (an articulate reporter on the market at this time who could claim considerable personal experience) told of a broker's valet who made nearly a quarter of a million in the market, of a trained nurse who cleaned up thirty thousand following the tips given her by grateful patients; and of a Wyoming cattleman, thirty miles from the nearest railroad, who bought or sold a thousand shares a day.[37]

What any President might have done with the tools available in a situation of such proportions is open to question.

In September 1929 the great boom era began to end. Thursday, October 24, was the most dramatic day in the history of the stock exchange. Galbraith has given us a vivid account:

> It was eight and a half minutes past seven that night before the ticker finished recording the day's misfortunes. In the board rooms speculators who had been sold out since morning sat silently watching the tape. The habit of months or years, however idle it had become, could not be abandoned at once. Then, as the final trades were registered, sorrowfully or grimly, according to their nature, they made their way out into the gathering night.
>
> In Wall Street itself lights blazed from every office as clerks struggled to come abreast of the day's business. Messengers and board room boys, caught up in the excitement and untroubled by losses, went skylarking through the streets until the police arrived to quell them. Representatives of thirty-five of the largest wire houses assembled at the offices of Hornblower and Weeks and told the Press on departing that the market was "fundamentally sound" and "technically in better condition than it has been in months." It was the unanimous view of those present that the worst had passed. The host firm dispatched a market letter which stated that "fundamentals remain unimpaired." *Senator Carter Glass said the trouble was due*

largely to Charles E. Mitchell. Senator Wilson of Indiana attributed the crash to Democratic resistance to a higher tariff.[38]

The postmortem investigation began immediately, and there were numerous reassuring statements that, while things may have got somewhat out of hand in the market, there was no reason to believe that the overall economy was in any danger.

There is some evidence that Hoover himself viewed the market crash in October 1929 with detachment, seemingly of the opinion that it had implications only for the market itself and not for the whole economy. The often repeated statement that business (as distinct from the speculative aspects of the stock market) was fundamentally sound was apparently more than a mere catchphrase so far as the President was concerned. The complex relationship between the stock market, the call money market, the investment trusts, and the commercial banking system was not fully understood, nor was it widely seen that much of the demand for automobiles and other consumer products that had sustained the industrial expansion had for the moment been satisfied. The superficial quality of the Coolidge prosperity had been overlooked by almost everyone.

Hoover's contention that as Secretary of Commerce he had been concerned about the speculative aspects of the market is probably true, but when he became President he faced a new dilemma. Secretary of the Treasury Andrew Mellon, bankers such as Charles E. Mitchell, and professors such as Irving Fisher of Yale were most optimistic and made frequent laudatory public statements as to the condition of the market. To his credit, the President did not engage in such practices; however, neither did he make statements urging caution. One source notes:

> It would be a serious mistake, however, to interpret the Great Depression as a problem which concerned and challenged one institution exclusively—the Presidency. To do so is to put too heavy a burden—an unfair and unrealistic emphasis—upon the power of that institution's custodian—Herbert Hoover. The economic collapse was not solely the President's concern, nor did he struggle to overcome it in some sort of splendid isolation. The Great Depression, like all momentous national experiences, engaged many other of the nation's major institutions as well.[39]

The System Is Sound

Although the President in late October repeated his view that "the fundamental business of the country, that is, production and distribution of commodities, is on a sound basis," he again refused to make specific statements about the market.[40]

On October 29 Dr. Julius Klein, the Assistant Secretary of Commerce, Hoover's friend and personal economic adviser, repeated Hoover's statement on radio and emphasized the soundness of the "mass of economic activities." It is obvious that the President was attempting to separate the stock market crisis from the basic manufacturing and distribution activities of the economy. Unfortunately, by this time the activities were not to be divorced. To be sure, only a minority of the population was actively engaged in speculation, but the banking and finance system was deeply and irrevocably involved. Unfortunately also, the "basic" economic activities were *not* as sound as had been thought.

In attempting to formulate some policy to meet this crisis, the President was handicapped by several weaknesses. First and perhaps the most significant was the paucity of sound economic intelligence. Information for decision making was both scarce and unreliable. Second, there were a number of highly placed persons in the financial world who had a personal interest in keeping the boom going as long as possible, and, in some cases, these individuals were closely tied to official policy, for example, through the Federal Reserve System. Third, the President was faced with the threat that any positive action on his part (given the state of affairs that had developed) might be the spark setting off the whole explosive situation. The President would have run considerable risk in making alarming statements that would have been extremely likely to pull down the whole house of cards. Finally, Hoover was hardly in a position to condemn too loudly the inaction of the previous administration, which not only represented his own party but of which he had been a part.

Overriding all was the President's own character. He was a conservative not given to action without considerable investigation and reflection, and the pace of events made deliberation a luxury beyond his grasp. He clung with tenacity to his view of what government could and should do:

> The purpose of government is to encourage and assist in the creation and development of institutions controlled by our citizens and evolved by themselves from their own needs and their own experience and directed in a sense of trusteeship of public interest. . . .
>
> Without intrusion the government can sometimes give leadership and serve to bring together divergent elements and

44

secure cooperation in development of ideas, measures, and institutions. This is a reinforcement of our individualism.[41]

Unfortunately, individualism—whatever its merits—was of little assistance to those caught up in the crisis rapidly overtaking the whole economy.

The President's first move to combat the crisis was shockingly "Keynesian." He announced a cut of a full percentage point on both corporate and personal income taxes. He undertook to stem the tide of uncertainty by extensive conferences with business leaders, who were requested to refrain from wage cuts, layoffs, and other action that would spread the depression throughout the economy. Railroad presidents, labor leaders, industrialists and financial leaders were called to the White House in turn and given essentially the same message. These attempts to rally businessmen make more sense when one recalls the modest size of the federal establishment as it then existed. Hoover had little fiscal leverage in government per se. The press statement issued at the conclusion of the meeting with railroad leaders is fairly typical of the general reaction: "The railway presidents were unanimous in their determination to cooperate in the maintenance of employment and business progress. It was stated that the railways which they represented would proceed with full programs of construction and betterments without any reference to recent stock exchange fluctuations; that they would canvass the situation as to further possibilities of expansion."[42]

Meanwhile, the stock market continued its slide, though the President was still assured from all sides that conditions were basically "sound." Among those supporting this position were the indefatigable Professor Irving Fisher; Stuart Chase, a popular economic writer; Alfred P. Sloan, Jr., of General Motors; William Butterworth of the U. S. Chamber of Commerce, and William Green of the American Federation of Labor.

Although he had personal misgivings about stock values, the President did not wish to increase alarm by a public statement voicing his doubts. This technique is illustrated by his message to Congress in December 1929, stressing the role of speculation; he spoke of:

> . . . a wave of uncontrolled speculation in securities, resulting in . . . the inevitable crash . . . a reduction in consumption . . . number of persons thrown temporarily out of employment . . . agricultural products . . . affected in sympathy with the stock crash.

Fortunately, the Federal Reserve System had taken measures to strengthen the position against the day when speculation

45

would break. . . . There had been no inflation in the prices of commodities and no undue accumulation of goods . . . past storms of similar character had resulted in retrenchment of construction, reduction of wages, and laying off of workers. . . . I have . . . instituted systematic . . . cooperation with business . . . State and municipal authorities . . . that wages and therefore consuming power shall not be reduced and that a special effort shall be made to expand construction work . . . a very large degree of industrial unemployment and suffering . . . has been prevented. . . .[43]

The conferences continued. By the end of the year, the President had conferred with farm leaders, state officials, leaders in the building and construction industry, and those in public utilities. Not only the President, but others apparently hoped for substantial benefit from these meetings. A program was started to stimulate useful public works and construction of Hoover Dam, a huge project, was authorized.

Hoover's closest personal economic adviser was Julius Klein, a professional economist with a Harvard Ph.D. who had held numerous federal posts and who was Assistant Secretary of Commerce from 1929 to 1933. Another who had some influence was Walter W. Stewart, a monetary theorist, investment banker, college professor, and adviser to both Coolidge and Hoover. (Stewart spanned an era and joined the Council of Economic Advisers under Arthur F. Burns during the Eisenhower years.) He had served on the War Industries Board during World War I and in the early 1920s was the first director of the Division of Research and Statistics for the Federal Reserve Board. He had also been on the faculty of various universities. Klein gave "able and devoted support and advice" to Hoover during the Depression (along with Robert P. Lamont, Secretary of Commerce). Another active figure was E. Dana Durand, Director of the Division of Statistical Research in the Department of Commerce. Durand served as economic adviser to the secretary.[44]

Optimistic statements were not very effective, but it would have been difficult to think of anything else under the circumstances. Frank W. Taussig, the well-known Harvard professor, bravely and honestly admitted in a radio address that little was known.[45]

Taussig was all too right. Though World War I had stimulated some study of the aggregate economy, information was far from systematic or complete. Basic economic data such as that fed into the present Council of Economic Advisers were nonexistent.

Hoover, systematic and precise as always, had undertaken to gather economic data, at least in a small way, during his tenure as Secretary of Commerce, and his reliance on the advisory capabilities of professional economists seems to have been greater at this time than it was during the years of his Presidency. In mid-1921, for example, he assembled a conference on waste through unemployment. This study included an analysis of the influence of the business cycle as related to unemployment. The committee concerned with this problem was under the chairmanship of Owen D. Young, the industrialist, and carried out its work with the assistance of the well-known economist W. C. Mitchell, an authority on economic fluctuations; but, in general, few economists appeared.[46]

A major immediate problem was to obtain an accurate count of the unemployed, which proved to be no easy task. A committee under Colonel Arthur Woods, made up of distinguished members, made little headway. Albert Romasco notes:

> But for the Woods Committee, vital facts were indifferently treated or unknown.
> Despite its elaborate connections, the President's committee attempted to make no surveys of national unemployment. They knew very little of what was happening in the rural sections of the country. Nor did they attempt to estimate the number of unemployed. When governors asked for the committee's plan, they were told that the committee had none, and the governors received instead a pamphlet on what others were doing. "The aim," Woods repeated to a congressional committee, "has been so to organize the country, so to help the country to organize itself, that it could meet whatever conditions might arrive."[47]

Unemployment rose rapidly as the fall in purchasing power began to cause inventory increases, in turn cutting into the industrial output. No really accurate unemployment data were available. Unions, public officials, and others made estimates, but these were most often inaccurate and most likely understated. Table 2 indicates the scope of the problem.

Table 2. **ESTIMATED* UNEMPLOYMENT, 1929–32**
(Estimated Labor Force: 40 Million)

Year	Persons
1929	5 million
1930	7 million
1931	9 million
1932	11 million

*Estimated from various sources.

As the Depression deepened, the chances of the unemployed obtaining suitable jobs, or indeed any jobs, became more remote. Men and boys (women and girls) drifted about the country searching for work, and camps of the unemployed sprang up near cities and at railroad junction points, dubbed in bitter jest "Hoovervilles."

Early in his administration, the President suggested to the Congress a program for revision in some portions of the banking laws and that consideration should be given to the impact of new developments such as chain banking. He suggested also the formation of a commission to study the problems of failures and losses, especially in rural banks. By 1932 the problem had become more serious, and the evil influence of speculation had become evident to the President:

> In soil poisoned by speculation grew those ugly weeds of waste, of exploitation, of abuse, of financial power.
> This depression has exposed many weaknesses in our economic system. There have been exploitation and abuse of financial power. We will fearlessly and unremittingly reform such abuses. I have recommended to the Congress the reform of our banking laws. Unfortunately, this legislation has not yet been enacted. The American people must have protection from insecure banking through a stronger system. They must be relieved from conditions which permit the credit machinery of the country to be made available without adequate check for wholesale speculation in securities with ruinous consequences to millions of our citizens and to national economy.[48]

In the fall of 1932, the President again noted the weakness which had been exposed by the Depression, stressed the importance of sound banking practices, and complained that suggested reforms had been rejected by the Democratic House of Representatives. Several days later, speaking in Cleveland, the President alluded to his proposal for a system of Home Loan Banks and again noted that the House had refused to act in sufficient time to prevent serious loss.

The early Hoover programs had two major objectives: (1) to restore confidence; and (2) to stimulate construction and industrial expansion. There was no overall plan for economic reform. In his view, none was necessary since the system was sound. That is, no long-run reforms were needed; and since speed was essential, only emergency treatment was to be considered. The President was, of course, aware of minor flaws, but his basic thesis—that the Depression was the fruit of speculation and foreign troubles—ruled out the need for basic alterations. What was called for, in his view, was a program for resuming the former level of activity. The National Business Survey Conference (largely built around the U. S. Chamber of Commerce) tried to promote a renewal of spending, just as the conferences with industrial leaders attempted to restore confidence and stimulate business construction. Neither was successful, and both demonstrate Hoover's preference for voluntary private enterprise over governmental policy.

Throughout the Depression the President expressed his devotion to the gold standard and his horror of the nation's being forced off gold. Late in 1932 he reviewed the economic situation and stressed the positive measures that had been taken:

> Being forced off the gold standard in the United States meant utter chaos. Never was our nation in greater peril, not alone in banks and financial systems, money and currency, but that forebode dangers, moral and social chaos, with years of conflict and derangement.
>
> In the midst of this hurricane the Republican Administration kept a cool head and rejected every counsel of weakness and cowardice. Some of the reactionary economists urged that we should allow the liquidation to take its course until we had found bottom. Some people talked of vast issues of paper money. Some talked of suspending payments of government issues. Some talked of setting up a council of national defense. Some talked foolishly of dictatorship—any of which would have produced panic itself. . . . The third peril, which we escaped by the most drastic action, was that of being forced off the gold standard. . . .[49]

The hoarding problem (not only gold, but currency) continued to plague the monetary system, and Hoover called attention to this situation on several occasions. The drain on gold continued to be a serious problem as international difficulties mounted, though it was to some degree eased by the passage of the Glass-Steagall Act of 1932, which liberalized acceptance of commercial paper by banks, thus freeing substantial quantities of gold. Maintenance of a gold standard seems to have become almost a mania with the President. He referred to it again and again. Though the pre-1914 international gold standard was a shambles, Hoover seems to have been completely convinced that its formal abandonment would be a fatal blow for the economy.[50]

The Relief Problem

Although the President had vetoed a bill by Senator Robert Wagner of New York to establish a subsidy system to encourage

49

states to establish employment agencies, he encouraged a study of European systems by the National Bureau of Economic Research. No study was made, however, since it was decided to wait until a British study on the subject was completed. No other such legislative proposals were introduced.

Many items of social reform, like the Garfield Commission on Conservation, were set aside due to "the congestion of Congress over recovery questions."[51] Foremost among these problems was that of relief. Here one finds the most paradoxical and tragic situation in the administration. As the Depression deepened, the President found it more and more difficult and unpopular to maintain that relief was a local matter.

The administration had generally taken the line that public relief was a city, or at most a state, responsibility. Unfortunately, these governmental units had very limited resources and, though they were supplemented by private charity, their funds were soon exhausted. Relief became a maze of inadequate and disjointed programs:

> . . . City after city has been compelled to abandon a part of its dependent population. "We are merely trying to prevent hunger and exposure," reported a St. Paul welfare head last May. And the same sentence would be echoed by workers in other cities with such additions as were reported at the same time from Pittsburgh where a cut of 50 per cent was regarded as "inevitable", from Dallas where Mexicans and Negroes were not given relief, from Alabama where discontinuance of relief in mining and agricultural sections was foreseen, from New Orleans where no new applicants were being received and 2,500 families in need of relief were receiving none, from Omaha where two-thirds of the cases receiving relief were to be discontinued, from Colorado where the counties had suspended relief for lack of funds . . . from Scranton . . . from Cleveland . . . from Syracuse. . . . But the individual localities present their own picture.[52]

As matters deteriorated further, the line became increasingly hard to hold, and Hoover realized it. He suffered greatly from bitter attacks by the opposition and was at a loss to understand why he, who had made a reputation as a great humanitarian, should be subject to abuse on this score. Apparently, the President could understand and sympathize with those who had suffered from war, flood, or other natural disasters; however, he seems to have failed completely to understand the problems of those who had suffered an economic blow by forces beyond their control. No one seriously taxed the administration with causing the Depression, and few seriously expected Hoover to produce an overnight solution, but the situation became more and more acute and bitterness mounted. Hoover was known to be a humane man. He was a superior administrator. Why, then, did he fail to act in the realm of individual relief? Perhaps, as some have suggested, he was increasingly reluctant to allow new ideas to be tried. He was by nature systematic and doctrinaire, and he attempted to draw a line between what should be permitted and not be permitted as interfering with the normal working of the system. "As his term wore on, the ideological obsession grew. He had himself done unprecedented things to show the potentialities of national action; but anyone who went a step beyond transgressed the invisible line and menaced the American way of life. His was the tragedy of a man of high ideals whose intelligence froze into inflexibility and whose dedication was smitten by self-righteousness."[53]

The President's strong view on this matter was reinforced by the need, as he saw it, to reduce federal expenditures and balance the budget. Consequently, there would have been little room for welfare programs, even if they had been looked upon as desirable.

Despite his generally cool view toward reform matters, the President was characteristically among the first to make systematic studies of social problems in an effort to obtain facts rather than to undertake hit-or-miss programs. Early in the administration, he appointed a committee to study broad social trends and charged it with the task of surveying the major social and economic changes that had taken place since the early years of the century. This committee was composed of leading sociologists and economists, and its work complemented that of another study committee on economic change.

The President made extensions in the coverage of the Civil Service, and he had a deep interest in the welfare of children. Although numerous conferences were held and studies were made regarding child welfare, and the economic status of blacks and other minority groups, legislative results were slim; these issues were buried in the debris of the collapsed economy.

Although he failed miserably on the relief front, thus damaging his political future beyond repair,[54] Hoover made some progress in improving financial affairs. Indeed, it was this effort to bring aid to banks and railroads, while failing to aid the people in a direct fashion, that provided Democratic critics with so much ammunition. Positive action taken included the strengthening of the Federal Land Bank System and the creation of the Reconstruction Finance Corporation as a means of supplementing credit available to farmers, business, and industrial corporations. The President made proposals early in January 1932 for further strengthening of the banking end credit systems, but most of these were lost in Congress. The RFC was a major anti-Depression accomplishment. Under the chairmanship of the able banker, Eugene Meyer, it acted as a last resort source of funds for banks and industrial corporations.

The collapse of the Insull utilities empire and the disclosure of fraud and mismanagement of other financial activities were severe blows to confidence in businessmen, the loss of which offset much legislation.[55]

A major mistake was the passage of the Hawley-Smoot Tariff Act, which further damaged the already precarious structure of international trade. In this case, as in others, Hoover, who had made much of seeking advice, ignored the advice that was available. The international situation was complicated by the war debts matter and by Hoover's growing tendency to point to Europe as the source of the Depression. As time passed, the President became more inclined to dwell on international causes of the Depression. Perhaps, to a degree, this had the effect of absolving domestic policies of responsibility, but it had no value in a positive sense.

European difficulties could be found there and isolated from the domestic scene.

> What the President had previously seen as the major causes prolonging the depression—world overproduction, the price collapse, political unrest—he now saw as part of a huger pattern of events which tied in with the European financial crisis. And none of them, in Hoover's estimation, was the basic cause of the depression. They were all simply effects that stemmed from one common source: World War I. Now that the root cause was exposed, Hoover quickly adjusted his interpretation of the depression.[56]

This view led, of course, to a desire to isolate the nation from European economic affairs.

Almost as paradoxical as the relief issue was the tax increase later in 1931. It is difficult to explain on administrative, fiscal, or political grounds. On numerous occasions (e.g., in the budget message of 1930), Hoover had indicated that he had an elastic and realistic concept of the balanced budget and that he was willing to accept a reasonable approach to "cyclical balance," as opposed to rigid annual balancing. He had, for example, pointed out that the budgetary surplus of past years might counterbalance the impending deficit, especially in a period of depression. To be sure, Britain's flight from gold brought problems in the form of gold outflow and rising interest rates. Yet Treasury operations showed no sign of lack of confidence in the framework of federal finance. One can only conclude that the administration's doctrinaire commitment to the balanced budget was commanding. The Congress, delighted to tag Hoover with an election-year tax increase, wrangled over its form and made comments about "a rich man's tax" but passed it nonetheless.

Whatever the President thought, domestic matters were not to be ignored. Troubles, both long- and short-range, beset the administration. In 1930 Senator Robert V. Wagner of New York introduced a proposal to provide for economic stabilization through planning, but the systematic President endorsed only the portion that related to improved statistical services, realizing that such information was not available.

Many who had contact with Hoover were impressed by his ability to analyze issues. Raymond Moley, when he accompanied FDR to the conference on war debts and the international crisis during the period of transition to the new administration, noted that Hoover spoke for an hour or more, marshalling facts and explaining in great detail without notes or reference to others. Warren notes that his information on social issues would have done credit to an expert, but when it came to positive action he remained unmoved in his views that federal policy had no positive role to play.

The transition to the new administration was especially painful. Both domestic and international financial crises were daily occurrences, and FDR refused to be bound by Hoover's policies. Europeans, of course, were anxiously awaiting the views of the new administration, and matters drifted dangerously.[57]

Despite Hoover's hard work and systematic approach, Depression problems continued to mount, and their solution escaped the President. As panic increased, each segment of the economy tried to save itself, and it is doubtful if any practical policies could have been devised at the time. The Democratic Congress, seeing sure victory ahead, did little to assure the success of the administration's program.

Hoover seems to have suffered from a peculiar defect. His record as Secretary of Commerce and his writings would indicate that he was in advance of his party in most areas of economic policy. Yet his measures for solution of the Depression were flawed in that they depended for execution upon the actions of others; that is, Hoover made exhortations to businessmen and state and local officials to take action beyond their capability. Again, this seems to stem from his unwillingness to engage in policies that would unbalance the budget. After a burst of activity, he retreated hurriedly to an unshakable insistence on a balanced budget, and the passage of time only strengthened his resolve.

With all the technological progress and the many socioeconomic changes that had taken place since 1920, the federal economic machinery designed to deal with them had been ignored. It was as though many years had gone by without fires and a city had decided that fires would no longer occur and had allowed its fire equipment to rust and fall into disrepair—indeed, not only to become obsolete but to be scrapped—while at the same time building larger and more complex buildings far from fireproof. Thus the President found himself largely helpless to know not only what had gone wrong and how far, but also what to do about it.

Wilson had watched some of these long-range developments in the early years of the century and had begun to formulate a positive program. for the integration of business and the public interest. International difficulties forced a realignment of priorities, and his program was never completed. Harding and Coolidge were fortunate. They rode the crest of economic prosperity—Coolidge, especially—to the last possible minute. Hoover, with superb qualifications, was to reap the wild wind of almost a decade of war and excessive speculation.

Each man had strengths, weaknesses, and traits of character that led him to react in a given fashion to the problems of the day; yet, they were largely at the mercy of events. No strength of character or administrative ability, both of which Hoover had in abundance, or economic erudition, of which he had as much as his contemporaries, would have enabled him to prevent the economic collapse. Hoover faced problems beyond his or his advisers' skill to interpret.

Despite heroic efforts, the situation deteriorated rapidly. The hardline stand on relief was a major political and pesonal blow for the President. As he worked harder, he became less tolerant of advisers who advanced new and unorthodox views. By the time of the 1932 election, the administration was at a low point. Yet, its positive accomplishments cannot be overlooked. The Debt Moratorium was clearly helpful in improving the international picture. The RFC, the Federal Land Bank, and the Home Loan Bank Board were helpful in restoring domestic liquidity and, indeed, were expanded by the incoming administration. The Glass-Steagall Act, releasing pent-up gold reserves, was also useful. Yet the President was reluctant to adopt a positive program of government policy. Positive programs were expensive, and Hoover viewed them with alarm. Nor could he escape the view that the major problem was financial and of wartime European origin.

54

Having begun a positive program in the first two years of his administration, the President turned away from its implementation and narrowed the scope of his policies to those concerned almost entirely with credit. Other issues, such as wages or housing construction, were, toward the end, hardly given consideration. Only for the implementation of these narrow policies was Hoover willing to cross the line from voluntarism to active federal policy, but by then it was too late.

For decades the doctrine of the self-healing economy had been accepted as gospel. Now, this idea was challenged on every hand. Even the most conservative businessman was seeking aid. Desperate measures seemed to be called for.

Professional economists had been of no consequence. They had not been called upon, and, given their philosophy, one is not surprised. Their day was at hand, but it would be a long time dawning.

End of an Era

To a considerable degree, the close of the Hoover Administration also marked the end of an era. Children then in kindergarten would complete college before the Republicans won the White House again. The extent of federal responsibility for economic policy would be greatly expanded as war followed depression through the next decade. Both the formal and informal responsibilities of the President would be vastly expanded, as would his resources to meet them.

The election of 1932, like that of 1920, was almost a foregone conclusion. Hoover defended his record without apology, but Roosevelt was elected by a substantial majority. Hoover carried 5 states with 59 electoral votes, and Roosevelt garnered the remaining 472 with 57 percent of the popular vote.

It had been thought that the more radical parties would capitalize on the uncertainty and dissatisfaction that existed, but, in the end, they made a dismal showing, with the Socialist and Communist parties together capturing slightly less than a million votes out of almost forty million cast. Farmers and war veterans, who had been restless in the closing days of the Hoover Administration, were quiet, waiting to see what course the new President would take.

Notes

Chapter 2

[1] Arthur S. Link, *Woodrow Wilson and the Progressive Era, 1910–1917* (New York: Harper & Row, 1954), p. 79.

[2] Ibid., p. 80.

[3] Arthur M. Schlesinger, Jr., *The Age of Roosevelt: Vol. I, Crisis of the Old Order* (Boston: Houghton Mifflin, 1957), p. 37.

[4] See John R. Commons and Associates, *History of Labor in the United States, 1896–1932* (New York: Macmillan, 1935).

[5] Theodore Saloutos and John D. Hicks, *Agricultural Discontent in the United States, 1900–1939* (Madison: University of Wisconsin Press, 1951).

[6] The major economic characteristics of the era are well covered by George Soule, *Prosperity Decade* (New York: Rinehart, 1947).

[7] John D. Hicks, *Republican Ascendancy, 1921–1933* (New York: Harper & Row, 1960), p. 25ff.

[8] See Joe Mitchell Chapple, *Life and Times of Warren G. Harding* (Boston: Houghton Mifflin, 1924).

[9] William S. Myers and Walter H. Newton, *The Hoover Administration: A Documented Narrative* (New York: Scribner's, 1936).

[10] *The Shadow of Blooming Grove* (New York: McGraw-Hill, 1968). Serious interest in Harding has been subordinated to the attention paid to his association with Nan Britton and the financial scandals that marked his administration.

[11] See Samuel Hopkins Adams, *Incredible Era: The Life and Times of Warren G. Harding* (Boston: Houghton Mifflin, 1930), pp. 32ff.

[12] Adams says that Crissinger's only apparent qualification was that he and Harding had stolen watermelons together as boys! Ibid.

[13] F. D. Roosevelt made an unsuccessful attempt to remove Humphrey in a landmark case testing the President's power to remove members of the independent regulatory commissions. However, Humphrey died before the litigation was complete: *Humphrey's Executor Vs. United States*, 295 U.S. 602, 625 (1935).

[14] Hicks, op. cit., p. 62.

[15] William E. Leuchtenburg, *The Perils of Prosperity, 1914–1932* (Chicago: University of Chicago Press, 1958).

[16] Schlesinger, *Crisis of the Old Order*, p. 57.

[17] Coolidge, like Harding, was personally honest, but, unlike Harding, he was able to keep his friends honest also. Whereas Harding was open and friendly, Coolidge was withdrawn and taciturn in the extreme. He saw no reason to involve himself in matters not required by law.

[18] Herbert Hoover, *The Memoirs of Herbert Hoover* (New York: Macmillan, 1952), Vol. I, pp. 55–56. See also, John K. Galbraith, "The Care and Prevention of Disaster," *The Liberal Hour* (Boston: Houghton Mifflin, 1960), p. 100ff.

[19] Irving Stone said that Coolidge had moved the White House across Pennsylvania Avenue to the U.S. Chamber of Commerce building.

[20] William Allen White, *Puritan in Babylon: The Story of Calvin Coolidge* (New York: Macmillan, 1938), pp. 35ff. Coolidge was much interested in how much food was served, how much it cost, how many dresses his wife owned, and other matters of a seemingly trivial nature to a President.

[21] These developments are discussed in popular style in George Soule, *Prosperity Decade* (New York: Rinehart, 1947), and John Kenneth Galbraith, *The Great Crash, 1929* (Boston: Houghton Mifflin, 1954).

[22] In the April 1 issue of *Graphic*, the Harvard economist, Sumner H. Schlichter, noted these structural changes with alarm, although most observers were quite content.

[23] William E. Leuchtenburg, op. cit., p. 189.

[24] Galbraith, *Great Crash*, op. cit., p. 60.

[25] Joseph Stagg Lawrence, *Wall Street and Washington* (Princeton: Princeton University Press, 1929), p. 179. See also Francis W. Hirst, *Wall Street & Lombard Street* (New York: Macmillan, 1931).

[26] See Broadus Mitchell, *Depression Decade* (New York: Holt, Rinehart and Winston, 1961), Chapter 1.

[27] Hoover was a fabulous success; he notes that his professional income probably exceeded that of any engineer in the nation. He had great appeal as a representative of the new political generation, scientifically trained in a hardheaded field. One can contrast his image with that of Wilson who was often regarded as the professor type, not highly regarded during the business decade. William Howard Taft spoke of Wilson as "the schoolmaster" in his private correspondence.

[28] Several of Hoover's fellow secretaries were amazed that he intended to spend the full day at the office, an unheard of thing in those days. *Herbert Hoover, Memoirs,* op. cit.

[29] His recent arrival on the scene and his support of Theodore Roosevelt in 1913 was less impressive to the "old guard" of the GOP. Nonetheless, like Eisenhower in 1952, he looked to them like a winner.

[30] W. T. Foster and Waddill Catchings, "Mr. Hoover's Road to Prosperity," *Review of Reviews*, January, 1930.

[31] *State Papers.* Vol. I, p. 34.

[32] H. G. Warren, *Herbert Hoover and the Great Depression* (New York: Oxford University Press, 1959).

[33] See Edward R. Ellis, *Nation in Torment* (New York: Coward-McCann, 1970), p. 28.

[34] John Kenneth Galbraith, *Great Crash*, op. cit., pp. 39–40.

[35] Arch W. Shaw File, Hoover Institution on War and Peace, Stanford University. Quoted with the approval of the Herbert Hoover Foundation.

[36] Herbert Hoover, *Memoirs*, op. cit., pp. 30–31.

[37] Frederick Lewis Allen, *Only Yesterday* (New York: Harper & Row, 1957), p. 315.

[38] Galbraith, *Great Crash*, op. cit., pp. 109–10.

[39] Albert U. Romasco, *The Poverty of Abundance: Hoover, the Nation and the Depression* (New York: Oxford University Press, 1965), p. 8.

[40] Galbraith, *Great Crash*, op. cit., p. 111.

[41] *State Papers.* Vol. 1, p. 572.

[42] William S. Myers and Walter H. Newton, *Hoover Administration*, op. cit.

[43] Ibid., p. 33.

[44] Ibid., p. 240.

[45] See Alvin Hansen, *The American Economy* (New York: McGraw-Hill, 1957). Hansen calls this an admission of bankruptcy.

[46] An interesting sidelight: Rexford Tugwell as representative of FDR lunched with Hoover in late February 1933; Hoover wrote to a friend that Tugwell "breathes with infamous politics devoid of every atom of patriotism." Myers and Newton, op. cit., p. 356.

[47] Romasco, op. cit., p. 148.

[48] *State Papers.* Vol. II, p. 257.

[49] Ibid., p. 262.

[50] Roosevelt, of course, had no attachment to gold and precipitated his own "gold crisis" by going off gold. See Dean G. Acheson, *Morning and Noon* (Boston: Houghton Mifflin, 1965), especially p. 166ff. When FDR went off gold, his conservative budget director, Lewis W. Douglas, resigned, saying, "Well, here is the end of Western Civilization!"

[51] Myers and Newton, op. cit., p. 481.

[52] "No One Has Starved," *Fortune*, Copyright© Time, Inc., October 1932, pp. 21–24.

[53] Schlesinger, *Crisis of the Old Order*, op. cit., p. 247.

[54] Technical matters such as banking and reform in securities trading were little under-

stood, but inaction in the relief area was understood by all.

[55] Large loans were made to administration stalwarts, to Hoover's embarrassment. On grounds that disclosure would cause bank runs and panic, RFC at first kept these loans secret. After several were made to administration figures, Democrats forced the RFC to disclose them.

[56] Romasco, op. cit., p. 185.

[57] These agonizing days are traced in Herbert Feis, *1933: Characters in Crisis* (Boston: Little Brown, 1966). See also, Laurin W. Henry, *Presidential Transitions* (Washington: Brookings, 1960), Part 4. This source is excellent, covering transition problems from Wilson to Eisenhower.

Chapter 3

Roosevelt and the Economics of Necessity

This great Nation will endure as it has endured, will revive and will prosper.
. . . Let me assert my firm belief that the only thing we have to fear is fear itself—nameless, unreasoning, unjustified terror which paralyzes needed efforts to convert retreat into advance.
— Franklin D. Roosevelt

Franklin Roosevelt faced greater economic responsibility and greater economic opportunities than any President had or, in some ways, is likely to face again. The election of 1932 was decided almost entirely on economic issues, and Hoover's failure to solve the Depression problem was a political disaster from which the Republican party did not recover for two decades. Strangely enough, Roosevelt by training and experience was far less qualified to exert leadership in economic matters than his immediate predecessor.[1]

Following his graduation from Harvard College in 1904, Roosevelt had remained to study economics, political science, and history before entering the law school at Columbia University in the fall of that year.[2] The fact that he served as editor of the *Crimson* (the main purpose of his stay) and the variety of subjects he studied make it obvious that he was not a serious student of economics or international finance.[3] Franklin Roosevelt, as a young man of wealth and distinguished family, had no personal knowledge of the money-making process which had shaped Hoover's young life—indeed, it would be difficult to imagine two youths with more divergent backgrounds. By family training and background, Roosevelt felt strongly the obligation of the wealthy to serve those less

59

well off, a feeling transmitted from both sides of the family. Although he practiced law in a half-hearted fashion in the early years of the century, his move into political life was almost immediate, and personal economic considerations were of little importance.[4]

Roosevelt dabbled a bit in business in the mid- and late-1920s, serving as New York representative of the Fidelity and Deposit Company of Baltimore. Both FDR and Mrs. Roosevelt had independent means, but, with a large and free-spending family, cash needs were high. Despite his occasional commercial ventures, however, Roosevelt obviously was never interested in business, nor was he interested in the law except as a vehicle into public life.

FDR was almost continuously in public life from 1910 until his death. He served as a member of the New York state legislature, Assistant Secretary of the Navy, and governor of New York. While out of office, he was engaged in extensive political activity and was an active supporter of Woodrow Wilson. By 1921, when he was struck by polio, FDR had served in the Wilson Cabinet and had been the Democratic candidate for Vice-President in 1920. Though his career appeared to be over, served by his family and his ever-faithful aide Louis Howe, he recovered in part, resumed his political life, and was elected governor of New York in 1928.

Roosevelt was never a scholar or a deep thinker in the Wilsonian tradition. He was a pragmatic man of great charm and had the ability to attract able people to his side and, in general, to hold their loyalty. As governor, he had shown an interest in low-cost electric power and conservation. He had been responsive to the relief problem in the state, but had formulated no overall philosophy.

Perhaps one of the few basic socioeconomic creeds that Roosevelt held throughout his life was his view that natural resources were much like an estate, i.e., one had the obligation to preserve them and improve them for the benefit of future generations. Any economic policy relating to resource preservation had his support. He also felt that an imbalance existed between rural and urban life, and, like Henry Ford, he was an advocate of village industry.

The highlights of FDR's personal economic philosophy can be discovered from numerous sources. Daniel Fusfeld, who has made a careful analysis of his economic education, notes that Roosevelt's economic training at Harvard was oriented toward regulation as the means of solving the economic problems of the day.

Roosevelt emerged from college when the Progressive movement was in its early stages. The theme of that movement was political and economic reform in the interest of the common man and it emphasized that concentration of economic power was the major reason for the failure of American democracy to realize fully its potentialities. Roosevelt's schooling in progressivism made these two points major elements of his economic-political philosophy. In his early political career FDR was in the progressive tradition, fighting bossism and big business, supporting welfare legislation, advocating conservation and other liberal causes. He was influenced by the example of his "Uncle Ted" Roosevelt; he supported the progressivism of Woodrow Wilson.[5]

He was influenced as well by W. Z. Ripley, O. M. W. Sprague, and the economic historian Frederick Jackson Turner. These men were apt to emphasize the value of regulation in controlling big business. Much stress was put on the growing maturity of the American economy and the disappearance of the frontier. In short, the program of study (whatever FDR took from it) was centered on the economic reform movement then in ferment. Roosevelt had his first experience in the real economic world when he became Assistant Secretary of the Navy. He had charge of both labor relations in Navy yards and the procuring of steel and soon became well acquainted with practical problems of monopoly. This experience was to stand him in good stead. Fusfeld notes that his economic sophistication was greater after this period.[6]

FDR had, up to this time, no occasion to put his ideas into actual practice nor to define the limits of his philosophy. His Navy years came just prior to the polio attack. During this period of forced inactivity, he had time to formulate and further refine his ideas. Roosevelt's philosophy was most cohesive in matters of long-range reform, especially those involving social welfare and use of resources. He was too conservative to think in terms of basic change, but thought in terms of improvement of the system then in existence.

Roosevelt was no economist, and he understood little of what would be considered essential knowledge to a professional. (Moley noted at the peak of the New Deal that neither he nor FDR would have been able to pass an examination in elementary economics.) He was, in the final analysis, a conservative and, as such, was always able, no matter how far away from basic thinking his advisers carried him, to return unerringly to home base—namely, to the conventional economic wisdom of the typical upper-class, educated American of the period. He had an immense political understanding of practical economic problems. His willingness to entertain new ideas was sometimes a trial to his orthodox

61

advisers, but his lack of economic sophistication always brought him back to rely on those whom he trusted. His flexibility was his great asset, offsetting lack of preparation. Despite his sincere interest in social legislation, his dedication to economic matters remained marginal and his ideas primitive. It seems clear beyond doubt that in the Presidency FDR made up his economic policy as he went along and at no time had a systematic and consistent policy. He departed from his predecessors chiefly in that he made a greater effort to utilize the resources of economic analysis and advice available to him.

It is difficult, four decades later, to realize the fear and uncertainty over economic issues that prevailed in the period between the end of the Hoover Administration and the beginning of the Roosevelt era. Professor Shannon has expressed this in graphic terms:

> . . . Saturday March 4, 1933. The nation's banks, the very heart of American capitalism, had closed their doors, and business generally was at a standstill. The first "bank holiday" had begun just before the election when the governor of Nevada closed the banks of that state for twelve days to prevent the failure of a banking chain. The first major state to close its banks was Michigan, whose governor issued a bank holiday proclamation on February 10. In order to prevent further runs and failures, the governors of Indiana, Maryland, Arkansas, and Ohio took similar action before the end of the month. In the first three days of March, seventeen other states closed their banks. . . .
> The new governor of New York, Herbert M. Lehman, himself a banker, reluctantly took the step in the early morning hours of March 4 as did twenty-four other governors.[7]

A moving speech by Roosevelt (as a candidate) illustrates both his thinking and the crisis atmosphere of the period, as well as his acceptance of the "mature economy" thesis:

> A glance at the situation today only too clearly indicates that equality of opportunity as we have known it no longer exists. Our industrial plant is built; the problem just now is whether under existing conditions it is not over-built. Our last frontier has long since been reached, and there is practically no more free land. More than half of our people do not live on the farms or on lands and cannot derive a living by cultivating their own property. There is no safety valve in the form of a Western prairie to which those thrown out of work by the Eastern economic machines can go for a new start. . . .[8]

Elected solely on economic issues and realizing that recovery from the Depression was the major task at hand, FDR had a plethora of advice and counsel. As the Hoover Administration neared its end, businessmen, economists, and journalists had begun to raise fundamental questions about the workings of the economic system, and economic discourse became widespread. Fresh ideas, both usable and useless, came from all quarters as the campaign proceeded.

Among the more articulate critics were Hugh S. Johnson, a retired Army General and amateur economist; Paul H. Douglas, a labor economist from the University of Chicago, later U.S. Senator from Illinois; George Soule and Stuart Chase, both economic journalists; Charles Beard, the noted economic historian whose "five-year plan for America" had attracted much attention; and J. M. Clark, the Columbia economist whose forte was an economic plan later useful in CEA legislation.[9]

Many of those who rallied to the early New Deal flag were veterans of the "Bull Moose" campaign and of Wilson's New Freedom. In numerous cases, they had supported Hoover and were now on the rebound from that shattered romance. Homeless since 1920, they were eager for a voice in the affairs of the new administration. In general, their economic ideas were Wilsonian.

As a candidate for the nomination, Roosevelt was forced to steer a course between two divergent economic groups: the powerful old-line Democratic powers, such as William G. McAdoo, Alfred E. Smith, Bernard Baruch, and John J. Raskob, all of whom were anxious for him to remain conservative; and liberals, such as Douglas, Soule, and Senator Burton K. Wheeler. A few extremists, such as Senator Huey P. Long of Louisiana, were far to the left, representing the more unorthodox economic views and criticizing FDR for being too conservative.

Then as now, the Democratic party was a big tent sheltering many diverse social and economic philosophies. Raskob, who was the representative of large industry (Du Pont); McAdoo, Wilson's son-in-law and Secretary of the Treasury in his administration; and Baruch and Smith were all powerful and conservative. Smith, who after he had left office as governor of New York became increasingly conservative, drifted steadily to the right as the New Deal progressed and became a leading FDR critic. Wheeler was a "La Follette Democrat," a reformer, and a liberal. Long, with his strong base in Louisiana, was the most practical politician of the far-out idealists, many of whom advocated some basic alteration—if not, indeed, the abandonment—of the capitalistic system.

The "Brains Trust"

Faced with these conflicting views and the necessity of coming forth with some specific ideas regarding the Depression, FDR utilized the so-called "brains trust."[10] Just whose idea the use of a "brains trust" was is not clear. Some credit goes to James A. Farley, but Judge Samuel I. Rosenman claims primary responsibility in his book, *Working with Roosevelt.*[11] The name, however, has been attributed to both Louis Howe and Walter Kiernan, a *New York Times* reporter.

Prior to the nomination, Rosenman had a discussion with the Governor relative to producing some new ideas on current problems and suggested the use of academic talent as a source of information.

"Usually in a situation like this," I went on, "a candidate gathers around him a group composed of some successful industrialists, some big financiers, and some national political leaders. I think we ought to stay clear of all these. They all seem to have failed to produce anything constructive to solve the mess we're in today. Now my idea is this: Why not go to the universities of the country? You have been having some good experiences with college professors. I think they wouldn't be afraid to strike out on new paths just because the paths are new. They would get away from all the old fuzzy thinking on many subjects, and that seems to me to be the most important thing."

"What would you have them do—exactly?" he asked cautiously. This was something new, and he was deeply interested. But he wanted to get nominated and elected—that was the important thing—and he was not sure whether this kind of a group would help or hinder. "I don't know exactly; we'll have to kind of feel our way as we go along. My thought is that if we can get a small group together willing to give us some time, they can prepare memoranda for you about such things as the relief of agriculture, tariffs, railroads, government debts, private credit, money, gold standard—all of the things you will have to take a definite stand on. You'll want to talk with them yourself and maybe out of the talk some concrete ideas will come."

After a pause and several puffs on his cigarette, his eyes on the ceiling, he said, "O.K., go ahead."

Following this discussion, Rosenman contacted Raymond Moley, whom he knew at Columbia University. Moley suggested R. G. Tugwell, an economist; Adolf A. Berle, a lawyer; and others as sources of advice. Tugwell generally specialized in agriculture and Berle in banking and corporate problems. These men were invited to Albany and engaged in conversation by the Governor, and, later, they met as a group in

64

Warm Springs, Georgia, with the candidate. A subsidiary goal of this effort was to sidetrack to FDR some of the reputation for advance thinking that Eleanor Roosevelt had gained and that his advisers thought put him in the background.

Whatever Roosevelt may have felt, his need to call on economic talent was inescapable.

> The overriding fact facing Roosevelt as he neared the Presidency was that the American economy had collapsed. The national income was less than half of what it had been four years earlier. Almost thirteen million Americans—nearly one-fourth of the labor force—could not find work. Mass starvation was at hand; perhaps revolution. The American system had broken down, and it was Roosevelt's job to make it work again. . . . They [Brains Trust] had an economic philosophy they believed would bring national recovery and which seemed to Roosevelt to make much sense.[12]

These academic thinkers filled a unique role in FDR's organization. A politician himself, Roosevelt was surrounded by those who had much the same talents. Louis Howe, for example, who had been and remained a close personal political adviser and alter ego, as well as Farley and other close associates of the candidate, was unable to play a role of the type needed. Howe and Farley were superb political tacticians; Basil ("Doc") O'Connor, FDR's one-time law partner, was a close personal friend and general adviser; but aid of a different sort was required. Technicians and idea men such as those in the present Council of Economic Advisers or those who are gathered into the campaign by a modern presidential candidate or President-elect were now needed. No present-day candidate would dream of entering the race on a serious basis or preparing to take office without position papers on various topics. Both prior to the nomination and in the interregnum after an election, his advisers remain active, drawing up programs and proposals designed to solve "the economic problem." Some forty years ago, however, this was not so common, and the "brains trust" was looked upon as a great innovation.

Moley (who died in 1975 at eighty-eight) became a very powerful figure in the "first New Deal" though his fall was almost as rapid as his rise in 1932. He was a forty-six-year-old Columbia University professor of government and public administration—not of economics. A lawyer, he had become a specialist in criminal law and public administration, which led to his Columbia appointment. Louis Howe had encountered him when Moley served as a member of the New York State Commission on the Administration of Justice. Moley impressed not only Howe, but Judge Rosenman as well. Tugwell has written of the tutorial efforts:

> I was not discussing this theory with a beginner. Roosevelt had studied economics and public law at Harvard, but that had been in 1902–1904, some thirty years earlier, and the economics of 1902 was as obsolete as the farms and factories of 1902. He was, however, like most people: what he had learned as a student had stayed with him. I concluded that he did not recall anything specific, but his attitudes were those he had worked out at that time. I guessed that even if he was as extraordinarily well informed as he seemed, it was hardly possible that his Harvard teachers could have prepared him for the crisis he was now having to meet. The whole system was in chaos, every part of it warring with every other part, and no means existed for relating each to the other, even in the way of conciliation, to say nothing of regulation. What would he do, I found myself asking, when and if he realized this?[13]

Tugwell became the "whipping boy" of the administration; he was young, handsome, brilliant, and often arrogant, a combination of qualities not likely to be endearing to the conservative businessman or congressional committee. The press and the Congress looked upon him as the theoretical professor who offered uncalled-for and wrong-headed advice and was in possession of far too much power and influence. Castigated as "Rex the Red," a "Communist," "a socialist," with his writings taken out of context, Tugwell was the target for those who disapproved of the "brains trust" and the whole administration.[14] He was often sent behind the scenes on overseas trips (at election time) and finally was appointed as governor of Puerto Rico. Later, he returned to academic life and to his career as a writer.[15]

For Moley these were busy days. Anderson says:

> But for Moley, in the crucial months between Roosevelt's election and his inauguration, these problems were far in the future. During the campaign he had emerged as the acknowledged leader of the Brain Trust, and in the pre-inaugural period he was (as *Newsweek* called him) the "one-man reception committee through whom ideas had to go to reach Roosevelt." Congressional leaders flocked to his rooms in the Carlton Hotel with ideas for the New Deal's legislative program. A joke circulated in which one of Roosevelt's oldest friends pleaded: "Franklin, can you do me just one favor? Can you get me an appointment with Moley?"[16]

The four-month period between the election and the inauguration was distressing. FDR was understandably reluctant to make any arrangements with Hoover that would tie his hands later. Hoover was equally anxious to avoid undue delay and to provide continuity. Neither man was comfortable with the situation, and, indeed, it was this sort of problem that resulted in the move, made some years later, to update the inauguration from March 4 to January 20.

After the election, these advisers were given various tasks in the administration, which Rosenman regarded as a mistake. When FDR asked what should be done with them, "I said that it would be particularly unfortunate if the members of the Brain Trust were to be given administrative jobs in Washington to which each would have to devote his major time and attention. No matter how large the particular job might be, it would be only a small part of the overall picture with which the President would have to deal, and these men could be more helpful in advice and discussion within that larger framework."[17]

Several of the "brains trust" group were placed in the Agricultural Adjustment Administration, which was a training ground of both economic and legal talent in the early New Deal days. Secretary Henry Wallace assigned to these men tasks that went beyond the technical and far exceeded the traditional confines of the department. Although Professor Allan Gruchy attributes much influence as policy makers to this group, it seems more likely that their influence was as "social architects" rather than economists in the technical sense.[18] Certainly, their activities ranged far beyond the collection and interpretation of economic data, and there is little evidence that FDR relied on them for economic advice in the modern sense.[19]

During Roosevelt's second term, and definitely by 1939, his close relationship with the "brains trust" came to an end. In fact, some like Moley became anti-Roosevelt, and all lost influence. Although some economists continued to be influential in various departments, their direct contact with the President was considerably less and by the beginning of World War II seems to have ceased entirely. The group was never well defined in the public mind. In his book on the work of the "brains trust" referred to earlier, Tugwell names in addition to himself, Moley, Berle, and, as associates, Robert K. Straus, Hugh Johnson, and Charles W. Taussig. He names Rosenman and O'Connor as founders.

In the formative years of the first New Deal, however, economic discourse was lively in all quarters, as businessmen, labor leaders, and economists under the lash of depression began to articulate their ideas. The economics of the New Deal began to take shape. Strangely enough,

67

those who had been critical of the prevailing system were no more prepared to cope with its downfall than those who had been its most ardent champions.[20]

It is an indication of the standing of professional economists and the pressing need of a solution to the economic problem that those who championed unorthodox solutions had a much larger audience than had been their lot for many years. No account of New Deal thinking would be complete without some mention of these lay "economists" who advanced solutions of an unconventional nature.[21] Symptomatic of the era is the fact that many of these prophets commanded more following than the professionals (which is not difficult to understand; very likely, the failure of the professional was a major factor that contributed to the influence of the noneconomist). They included Senator Huey Long, with his vague but attractive plans to share the wealth; the Catholic priest, Father Charles Coughlin, with poorly conceived monetary theories; Dr. Francis Townsend, a retired physician and founder of the pension plan bearing his name; and Howard Scott, who presented specific and comprehensive alternate economic plans. Scott, an engineer by training, was the founder of the system of "technocracy," an economic plan that attracted substantial numbers of adherents in the Depression years (its spiritual father was the economist Thorstein Veblen).[22] An offshoot group of technocrats held that the currency in circulation should be based on the output of electric power. For a while the technocrats were housed in Columbia's engineering school, but this became embarrassing as time passed, and they were eased out. The "far-outs" included the radical left of the Communists and the moderate left—to which Floyd Olson of Minnesota and Upton Sinclair and his End Poverty in California (EPIC) program belonged—as well as the extreme rightists who dreamed of fascism, such as Seward Collins, Lawrence Dennis, William Dudley Pelley, and others who advanced a variety of programs designed to modify or, in some cases, to replace the capitalist system.

These movements attracted a number of followers, and, while the real political significance was probably small, the administration was forced to follow a policy of accommodation for a time, at least insofar as Long and Coughlin were concerned. There also seems to be some evidence that Roosevelt acted to incorporate some of the views of these groups (especially Long's) in his program in order, at least in part, to undermine their standing. James A. Farley reportedly said after Long was killed that, had he lived, he would have received 2.5 million votes as a third-party candidate.[23]

It is difficult to estimate the degree of influence these unorthodox "economists" wielded. In most cases it is clear that their influence was substantially less than the publicity they garnered would indicate. They were colorful figures, but every indication is that their following was limited largely to the "born losers" of society who saw no hope of climbing the economic ladder by traditional means and who, in the stress of the period, were willing to embrace any philosophy that appeared to answer their problems. As even a modest economic recovery began, however, interest in unorthodox solutions faded and for all practical purposes disappeared completely as World War II began.

The Government Accepts Responsibility

Though no economist and a confirmed believer in orthodoxy, Roosevelt was willing to experiment within limits, and he did not shirk from the use of federal power to achieve economic ends. Less systematic than Hoover, he was also less rigid in his thinking and, perhaps being for the most part an economic illiterate, he was more able to accept advice. He therefore surrounded himself with diverse (perhaps too diverse) sources of advice. Whereas Hoover felt strongly that the government should adhere closely to its traditional functions, FDR was willing to admit that changing conditions demanded new and perhaps unorthodox solutions.

FDR was at this time cool to public works, especially the "massive" type being discussed. He shared Hoover's view that the unrealistic amounts of 2 to 5 billion dollars being bandied about were impossible with such a slender base as then existed. Also — and he was knowledge-able about these matters — he was dubious that such an amount would produce *useful* projects. That is, he doubted that there were 4 or 5 billion dollars worth of useful projects available. Like Hoover also, he felt that the time required to plan and complete such a huge program would be too great. If recovery should arrive, the government would be stuck with an array of semicompleted and costly projects. He, of course, hoped that recovery would take place long before many long-range projects would be complete. In a burst of economy he halted work on the Commerce Department building (a huge project at the time), until—perhaps recall-ing Lincoln's view of the uncompleted Capitol dome in the Civil War—he pushed it to completion as an aid to public morale. (Lincoln was castigated for using resources to complete the dome in wartime, but he decided that people would be more optimistic if they thought things were moving ahead.)

Finally, Roosevelt had no concept of the "multiplier"; that is, that

69

government expenditures would be magnified as they flowed through the economy, an idea now commonplace in fiscal policy. He envisioned benefits only to those directly employed. Hugh Johnson gives the impression in his writings that he had some such idea, but at this time, at least, FDR was unconvinced of the long-range merit of such a program.

The first New Deal in its simplest form was an experiment in industry-government cooperation. In general, the Coolidge-Harding view had been that the proper role of government was to leave business enterprise as much alone as possible. The old-line Wilsonian Progressives had, in contrast, proposed a program of regulation, Hoover occupied middle ground; more progressive than Coolidge or Harding, he was in some ways Wilsonian and more doctrinaire than Roosevelt. The first New Dealers (although they differed among themselves) sought a third alternative—planning and cooperation between business and government. This was largely Tugwell's concept, as expressed in *The Industrial Discipline and the Governmental Arts,* which was being published at that time.

Roosevelt generally accepted this view, until he became convinced that business would not cooperate. In the early New Deal, business, especially big business, was cooperative, but by 1935 it was much more critical and independent. A superb politician, he realized that Hoover's major errors had been twofold, namely, his hard-line stand on the issue of individual relief and his reluctance to strike out in new directions, acknowledging that the central government had the major responsibility for safeguarding the citizens in time of economic crisis. This philosophy was especially noticeable in the so-called "First New Deal," with its emphasis on direct relief and social experimentation. The multiple actions taken by the Congress in the famous "100 days" stimulated public confidence, not so much because the people understood or approved of what was being done, but because something was under way.

If the characteristic figures of the First New Deal were Tugwell, Berle, and Johnson, those of the second were Felix Frankfurter, Marriner S. Eccles, William O. Douglas, Leon Henderson, and Lauchlin Currie. The lawyers were students of Brandeis, but the economists were students of John Maynard Keynes. Frankfurter was a Keynesian convert and a powerful influence in the direction of active fiscal policy. Leon Henderson, chief economist of the National Recovery Administration (NRA) (and later chief of the wartime Office of Price Administration), viewed the major economic problem as one of restoring price competition. Unlike Brandeis, who clung to the virtues of smallness to the end, Henderson faced the facts of large scale in the economy. He was aware

70

of the tendency toward economic concentration and price inflexibility, and he put no great faith in the antitrust laws as a means of restoring competition.

Roots of New Deal Economic Thought

The various facets of the New Deal represented a number of economic philosophies, though they were never welded into an overall theory and its parts were often in conflict. Justice Brandeis, who had been appointed to the court by Wilson, illustrates the conflicting views. The aging justice was intellectual godfather to many of the most influential figures of the administration. Brandeis had an abiding distrust of bigness and centralization no matter where encountered—in industry or in government.[24] He had long opposed concentration and bigness in industry and finance, and he spoke sharply of this tendency upon his joining with the rest of the court in the decision to overturn the National Recovery Act.[25]

Though Brandeis was highly respected, others in New Deal circles were convinced that bigness was a twentieth-century fact of economic life that could not be ignored, but needed to be controlled and directed. George N. Peek and Hugh S. Johnson had seen the effectiveness of the War Industries Board under stress, and the extent of centralized control of industry had been demonstrated for the record by the Pecora investigation (which had in 1933–34 documented concentrated banker control of industry) and, later, the Temporary National Economic Committee (TNEC) hearings. Berle and Gardiner Means had documented the rise of corporate power and influence in their famous work, *The Modern Corporation and Private Property* (1932). Brandeis' view seemed more appropriate to the pre-1914 era.

Younger economists, following the thought of Veblen, began to pay more attention to, and to accept as normal, the noncompetitive economic system. The institutional economists—Walton H. Hamilton, Rexford G. Tugwell, John R. Commons, and J. M. Clark, for example—began to interest themselves in what Hamilton termed in 1918 the "larger and more comprehensive control of economic activity and development."[26]

In 1924, the "younger generation" published *The Trend of Economics*, in which W. C. Mitchell, J. M. Clark, R. G. Tugwell, A. B. Wolfe, Morris A. Copeland, and Sumner H. Slichter made a plea for an economic science paying more heed to the theory of production and less to the mechanics of a competitive price system. These economists had a degree of influence, not so much on FDR personally (who continued to the last to play it by ear), but on the rising New Deal economic tacticians, such as Henderson and Leon Keyserling.

As these observers viewed the situation, the American economy was too large and complex to be responsive to forces that shaped it in the years before 1900. Mass production industries organized on a huge scale were a reality that could not be ignored. Given this fact, it was, in their eyes, necessary to diffuse economic power. The antitrust laws were one means, encouragement of unions was another, and a third was the decentralization of financial control. All of these methods were used at various times by the Roosevelt administration—sometimes effectively, but often in confusion and conflict.[27]

Thurmon Arnold and his associates in the Justice Department worked in the Antitrust Division. The Norris-LaGuardia and Wagner acts were extremely encouraging to the union movement, while the Securities and Exchange Act and other measures dealing with holding companies were designed to decentralize and limit financial control as well as to alleviate specific abuses that had been brought to light by the crash of 1929.

The antitrust policies were spearheaded by the vast fund of information gathered by the TNEC in the Senate. Arnold, who was brought from the Yale Law School to head the Antitrust Division, began nearly a hundred new antitrust actions. The TNEC was guided largely by Senator Joseph C. O'Mahoney of Wyoming (who would later be a power in the legislation leading to the Employment Act of 1946). Never before nor since has such a thorough investigation of industry structure been undertaken. Even now, some four decades later, the data collected in these hearings are valuable. Arnold was of the opinion that the previous applications of the Sherman Act had failed to take into account consumer interests and had, in fact, encouraged business consolidation.

Roosevelt doubtless absorbed some of these conflicting ideas but, as Schlesinger points out, fundamentally his ideas were not well thought out.

> Roosevelt, in the center, had few clear-cut ideas of his own with which to reduce the confusion. Such economic furniture as stocked his mind was most conventional: he had written in 1930 that competition could almost be called a law of nature and in 1931 that a government could not keep running year after year if it spends more than it receives in taxes. But the seminars of the spring of 1932 had challenged his classical clichés, instructed him in the importance of purchasing power and given him strong doubts concerning the self-recuperative powers of the system. . . .[28]

72

By 1935, the first "New Deal" had begun to come apart in terms of ideology, due largely to lack of coordination and overall unity of goals. Hugh Johnson, a master of invective, condemned the antitrust acts as being a relic from prehistoric times and, in an article in the *Saturday Evening Post*, blamed the failure of the New Deal on the "Harvard Crowd," Justice Frankfurter's "Happy Hot Dogs." Tugwell blamed Brandeis and the "Cult of Antibigness." Johnson, Donald Richberg and Berle had all left by 1935. Only Tugwell remained, and his influence had faded considerably.

The later New Dealers viewed themselves as more pragmatic than their earlier counterparts, and they looked upon the first New Deal as an experiment that, though laudatory in purpose, was doomed to failure from the outset. The concept of national planning was, in their eyes, impossible in practice, requiring superhuman ability. The burden of administration and the state of economic knowledge were too great in one case and too little advanced in the other to assure reasonable success. Even if these barriers had not existed, they would have rejected the central idea, since they felt that, in a partnership between business and government, business would dominate the agencies of control. Time has proved that there was much merit in this view.[29] The later New Dealers pointed to the rise of business influence in NRA and in the Agricultural Adjustment Administration (AAA) as proof of this point. Tugwell found this disturbing and surprising. The later New Dealers found it disturbing but they were not surprised. The economic historian Louis Hacker has characterized the New Deal as largely a political, rather than an economic, plan.[30]

Keynes and Fiscal Policy

Roosevelt, like Hoover, had been generally committed to the idea of a balanced budget and during the campaign had gone so far as to castigate Hoover for failing to balance the budget. Like his belief in conservation, this concept was part of FDR's heritage and was deeply rooted in his background. Nonetheless as time passed his attitude became more flexible. In actual fact, as Table 3 shows, the administrative budget was increasingly in deficit from 1931 on. Those who endorsed the unbalanced budget as a fiscal tool noted that the sharp recession in May 1937 followed on the heels of the reduction in deficit spending that had taken place in the 1936–37 fiscal year, and they linked the two events.

Table 3.   UNITED STATES ADMINISTRATIVE BUDGET
1929–40
(billions of dollars)

Fiscal Year	Net Receipts	Expenditures	Surplus or Deficit
1929	3,861	3,127	734
1930	4,058	3,320	738
1931	3,116	3,577	- 462
1932	1,924	4,659	-2,735
1933	1,997	4,598	-2,602
1934	3,015	6,645	-3,630
1935	3,706	6,497	-2,791
1936	3,997	8,422	-4,425
1937	4,956	7,733	-2,777
1938	5,588	6,765	-1,177
1939	4,979	8,841	-3,862
1940	5,137	9,055	-3,918

Source: *The Economic Report of the President* (Washington, D.C.: U.S. Government Printing Office, 1968), Table B-63, p. 284.

Marriner Eccles, by then chairman of the Federal Reserve Board, and other advisers were willing if not eager to accept deficit financing. Tugwell claims that the turning point had arrived and that FDR was convinced: "This was the first time—after four years—that he appears to have accepted, not only theoretically but as a matter of positive governmental virtue, the management of income and outgo as a regulator of the economy."[31]

Seymour Harris indicates that Roosevelt and Keynes found little common ground.[32] FDR referred Keynes' letter to Henry Morgenthau, Secretary of the Treasury, who took pleasure in ignoring the policy recommendations. However, Alvin Hansen, Keynes' leading American disciple, was a mover and shaker in New Deal circles, and the Keynesian thesis was a fundamental influence upon New Deal economics, although he felt that FDR was not in sympathy:

Keynes found others in Washington more receptive. Steered around by Tugwell, he met a number of the younger men and told them to spend—"A monthly deficit of only $200 million," he said, "would send the nation back to the bottom of the depression, but $300 million would hold it even and $400 million would bring recovery." A few days later he sent Roosevelt the draft of another *New York Times* article entitled "Agenda for the President." Here he continued his running review of the New Deal, saying he doubted whether NRA either helped or

74

hurt as much as one side or the other supposed and again defending the agricultural policies. As usual, the best hope remained an increase in public spending; $400 million, through the multiplier, would increase the national income at least three or four times this amount. . . . With this, Keynes, pausing only to make astute investments in the depressed stocks of public utilities, returned home. . . .

Certainly, except for Marriner Eccles, no leading person in Roosevelt's first Administration had much notion of the purposeful use of fiscal policy to bring about recovery; and Eccles' approach, with its rough-and-ready empiricism lacked the theoretical sophistication and depth of Keynesianism. Roosevelt's own heart belonged—and would belong for years—to fiscal orthodoxy.[33]

Keynesian policies as such were never meaningful in an operative sense. Though many economists in high places had become convinced that such policies had a contribution to make, the real test never came in a clear-cut fashion.

FDR and most of his advisors were reluctant to embrace Keynes since they were generally adherents of economic orthodoxy:

Franklin Roosevelt, together with a large segment of the liberal movement, distrusted the Keynes-type argument in the early New Deal days. At heart they hankered for a balanced budget. Yet the idea of large-scale federal spending on relief, with its implied contempt for rigid economics, its assignment of a key role to the national government, and its promise of quick alleviation of human distress, was a natural for the President and his following. Amid the roar of the Hundred Days, Congress passed a half-billion-dollar relief bill, and the President gave the administration of the money to a *de facto* Keynesian (Harry Hopkins) whose economics consisted largely of an urge "to feed the hungry, and Goddam fast."[34]

Eccles, the most active Keynesian in high position, advocated a balanced budget, not by the traditional way of trimming expenditures or increasing taxes, but by increasing the level of economic activity. Beardsley Ruml was rapidly developing Keynesian ideas, but he was not in so strategic a position as Eccles. Eccles estimated that the budget would reach balance when national income had achieved the level of $80 billion. From the University of Chicago, Professors Paul Douglas, Jacob Viner, H. C. Simons, and H. A. Millis made a strong plea for deliberate deficits. William O. Douglas, Chairman of the Securities and Exchange

Commission (later a Supreme Court Justice), was a Keynesian.

Though not fully accepted by those in the administration (who viewed federal expenditures as only a temporary pump-priming tactic) and denounced by most of the business community, fiscal policy was to become a major weapon of the later New Deal.

Early in the administration, though Roosevelt would spend to achieve a specific purpose, the resulting deficit was, in his eyes, an undesirable and embarrassing by-product without intrinsic merit, requiring elaborate justification. In the 1936 campaign, there was some tendency to justify the deficits by noting their stimulative effects, but the President did not even imply, much less say, that deficits should be continued until full employment was reached. He was inclined to stress "structural remedies" for unemployment, such as keeping youth in school, intensified retirement programs, and reduction of the workweek. Hopkins, though more willing to spend than FDR, felt that in the long run substantial unemployment would be likely, and he recommended continued public works and work-relief projects on a long-term basis. As Herbert Stein points out, the point was that both FDR and Hopkins envisioned recovery and a balanced budget coexisting with a fairly high rate of unemployment. In summary, Roosevelt was at this stage prepared to accept a deficit only on the basis of serious emergency, and he still welcomed the prospect of balance or surplus.

Of high officials, Marriner Eccles alone saw merit in the deficit as such, and pointed with alarm to the danger of decline if vigorous efforts were made to reduce expenditures. Morgenthau, strongly opposed to deficits, recorded his view of Eccles' proposal:

> Eccles' December memorandum on the budget advanced, in his own words and in his own spirit, the ideas which had been given their classic statement by John Maynard Keynes. An attempt to balance the budget, Eccles argued, would put the country into an economic tailspin. The popular analogy between the debt of an individual and the debt of a nation was utterly false. The crucial consideration was not the size of the deficit but the level of national income. It would be unsafe to slash federal expenditures until the expansion of private enterprise took up the whole slack of employment. Meanwhile deficit expenditures were a necessary, compensatory form of investment which gave life to an economy operating below capacity. Ultimately they would lead to restored business activity and increased national income. An attempt to balance the budget for the fiscal year 1938, Eccles maintained, would be dangerously premature, would lead to a new wave of deflation and reverse

76

the processes of recovery thus far set in motion. This would spell doom for the Democratic party, perhaps even pave the way for totalitarianism.[35]

However, in the event Eccles' arguments proved to be premature, the budget might be balanced with only moderate reduction in spending. Happily, FDR was apparently not in need of a justification, and Morgenthau appeared to have carried the day.

> The revised estimates of the Bureau of the Budget seemed to him (Budget Director David Bell) and to the Secretary (Morgenthau) to constitute an overwhelming rejoinder to Eccles. The new figures, they agreed, demonstrated that recovery was well along, that the annual deficit was shrinking, that a balanced budget was in sight. "Golly," Morgenthau said on December 29, "I think we all got every reason to face the new year with the greatest of complacence and comfort. . . ."
> Surprised by the improved figures, the President teased Bell, who, he said, had been holding out on him. . . . Without argument, he subscribed to the long-run fiscal program which Morgenthau and Bell advocated.[36]

This happy state of affairs was much disturbed by the downturn in the fall of 1937. Paradoxically, both FDR and the Republicans were in an embarrassing position. FDR was unable to explain why conditions had deteriorated, and the Republicans were unable to claim that a decline had taken place without admitting that some improvement had first been made over 1932! That is, the opposition was able to say little about "recession" without admitting that the administration had, in the interval since 1933, made some headway, since "recession" would have represented a great advance over "depression." Such were the semantics of the era.

Stein suggests that there were five possible courses of action that the administration might have taken. He outlines them as follows:

1. Press firmly on with government economy to give assurance of a balanced budget in fiscal 1939 and thus encourage private investment. This was the key idea of Henry Morgenthau and James Farley, in which they had the support of Morganthau's distinguished economist, Jacob Viner.
2. Remove the "anti-business" aspects of the New Deal, notably the undistributed profits tax, and thereby stimulate private investment. This naturally was the dream of the business community.

3. Restore the planning features of the NRA, insofar as could be done constitutionally, probably by voluntary cooperation by business, and thereby sustain wages and stimulate investment. This was an idea always attractive to the President, and it had some support in business circles.

4. Attack the "private concentration of economic power" by trust-busting regulation, on the hypothesis that monopolies caused the recession either by following their normal economic practices of raising prices and restraining production or by a politically-motivated act of sabotage. Assistant Attorney General Robert Jackson was a leading promoter of this idea, with support from Harold Ickes, Leon Henderson, Benjamin Cohen, and Thomas Corcoran.

5. Resume spending and give up, at least for the present, the idea of balancing the budget. Hopkins and Eccles were the chief proponents of this course, which had the support of numerous economists in the administration, Lauchlin Currie, Mordecai Ezekiel, and Leon Henderson being the most prominent.[37]

Gradually, and largely for pragmatic reasons, the relative position of spenders and budget balancers had begun to change from their pre-1937 status. For one thing, spending programs had increased and a substantial number of major programs were in force (spending was a bureaucratic status symbol). Also, the business community was slowly beginning to recognize that budget balancing was not necessarily the key to recovery, and they had heard the "spending-ourselves-into-bankruptcy" record played so long without visible results that it had little influence. When Morgenthau made a reference to balancing the budget in a 1937 speech to the Academy of Political Science, the audience broke into derisive laughter, as well they might.

In addition, spending programs had gained a large number of important clients both in the government and outside it. Among the general population, as with businessmen, long experience with an unbalanced budget and a large debt without catastrophe had reduced the number who put the goal of debt reduction high on their list of priorities. Even Jesse Jones, a Texas tycoon and the hard-headed RFC chief, was a convert.

The growth of the federal budget relative to private spending and investment had given federal spending programs substantial leverage, and there was growing appreciation of this fact both among economists and laymen. Economists within the administration were beginning to correlate their own thinking on these matters. Some of the earlier, more

78

unorthodox approaches to recovery (e.g., gold-buying) had passed out of the picture, leaving more time and energy for more sensible programs.

Keynesian, or at least Keynesesque, ideas had made headway, and administration advisers were beginning to educate the President, who, in time, was educating the public, to the possibilities of spending as a positive stabilizing device.

By mid-spring of 1938, the President had made his decision (much against Morgenthau's wishes), but even now he was careful to explain that no real departure from tradition was being made:

> In the first century of our republic we were short of capital, short of workers and short of industrial production; but we were rich in free land, free timber and free mineral wealth. The Federal Government rightly assumed the duty of promoting business and relieving depression by giving subsidies of land and other resources.
> Thus, from our earlier days we have had a tradition of substantial government help to our system of private enterprise. But today the government no longer has vast tracts of rich land to give away, and we have discovered that we must spend large sums to conserve our land from further erosion and our forests from further depletion. The situation is also very different from the old days, because now we have plenty of capital, banks and insurance companies loaded with idle money: plenty of industrial productive capacity and several millions of workers looking for jobs. It is following tradition as well as necessity if Government strives to put idle money and idle men to work, to increase our public wealth and to build up the health and strength of the people—and to help our system of private enterprise to function.[38]

One of the virtues of fiscal policy as viewed by the New Dealers was that its influence was widespread; it was a "general" weapon helping to reinforce such specific tactics as the farm program and NRA, about which New Dealers had begun to be defensive. It also had the virtue of avoiding constitutional pitfalls that had tripped up several specific programs such as the NRA. Spending was transformed from the unwanted stepchild to the favorite son.

Viewing the era overall, the Keynesian influence cannot be denied. Professor Harris noted in 1947 that, though FDR and Keynes never understood each other, the administration as a whole had a Keynesian flavor. "Certainly, the economic historian interpreting the middle years of the 20th Century will characterize the period as the struggle for, and over, full employment. He may well refer to the period as the Keynesian period in the same manner as we now refer to the Mercantilist, the Physiocratic, and the Classical periods.''[39]

Fiscal Policy and Ideology

Fiscal policy influenced the overall goals of the administration favorably. There were, in brief, seven major thrusts to the New Deal economic program, all intended to operate within the general capitalist framework:

1. The general stabilizaton of and increase in the price level, approached with varying degrees of success, by such programs as devaluation, gold and silver purchase, and the NRA.

2. The restoration of credit and credit expansion. This was to be done by the RFC program, open-market operations, and other monetary policies.

3. Restoration of purchasing power, to be achieved by reform measures, such as elimination of child labor, increase in the minimum wage, encouragement of collective bargaining, and others.

4. Reduction of individual and business debt. This involved such activities as the Reconstruction Finance Corporation, the Home Owners Loan Corporation, and other agencies.

5. Revival of international trade. This goal was to be reached by the reciprocal trade agreements, the Good Neighbor Policy, and other devices under the general sponsorship of Secretary of State Hull.

6. The provision of individual relief through such programs as the Civilian Conservation Corps and the Works Progress Administration.

7. General programs of long-range reform and social uplift of various types concerned with labor, housing, Social Security, and reform in the securities markets and banking.

Hopefully, all these programs would reinforce each other and would integrate with other facets of the New Deal agenda. Their implementation called for an immense array of legislation, not always able to pass muster before the Supreme Court, especially in the first New Deal. The programs also required a large (for the era) body of administrators, sometimes incapable of meeting their responsibilities.

The second New Deal was more sophisticated, both in its politics and its economics. The second group of officials was more hardheaded and chose goals of a more limited and specific nature. The fact that Roosevelt understood the *practical* application of these programs is amply demonstrated by his press conferences where he engaged in give-and-take argument. His talk on the NRA, after the Supreme Court decision ruling it unconstitutional, was a masterful analysis of the issues. Abstract economic theory still held little interest for him, but, as Schlesinger remarks,

Considering the state of economic theory in the 1930's, this was not necessarily a disabling prejudice. Roosevelt had, as J. K. Galbraith has suggested, what was more important than theory, a set of intelligent economic attitudes. He believed in government as an instrument for effecting economic change (though not as an instrument for doing everything). In 1934, he complained to the National Emergency Council, "There is the great feeling that it is up to the Government to take care of everybody. . . . They should be told all the different things the Government cannot do." He did not regard successful businessmen as infallible repositories of economic wisdom. He regarded the nation as an estate to be improved for those who would eventually inherit it. He was willing to try nearly anything. And he had a sense of the complex continuities of history—that special intimacy with the American past which, as Frances Perkins perceptively observed, signified a man who had talked with older people who remembered many things back to the War of the Revolution.[40]

Roosevelt refused to think in terms of comprehensive economic philosophies. For him, economic planning was not an end but a means to an end. He was flexible; he had no hesitation in admitting contradictions or making changes in course, if needed. He did not hesitate to pick and choose from various ideologies, abandoning what appeared not to work and innovating when necessary. At no time were New Deal economic goals approached on a systematic basis, and there were constant conflicts and cross-purposes at work. Richard Hofstadter notes:

At the core of the New Deal, then, was not a philosophy (FDR could identify himself philosophically only as a Christian and a Democrat), but an attitude, suitable for practical politicians, administrators, and technicians, but uncongenial to the moralism that the Progressives had for the most part shared with their opponents. At some distance from the center of the New Deal, but vital to its public support, were other types of feeling. In some quarters there was a revival of populistic sentiment and the old popular demonology, which FDR and men like Harold Ickes occasionally played up to, chiefly in campaign years, and which Harry Truman later reflected in his baiting of Wall Street. . . .

The New Deal, and the thinking it engendered, represented the triumph of economic emergency and human needs over inherited notions and inhibitions. It was conceived and executed above all in the spirit of what Roosevelt called "bold, persistent experimentation," and what those more critical of the whole enterprise considered crass opportunism. . . .

The high moral indignation of the critics of the New Deal sheds light on another facet of the period—the relative reversal of the ideological roles of conservatives and reformers.[41]

At least four economic ideological groups were at work within the administration:

1. The agrarian "easy-money" advocates, especially strong in the Congress. This group was favorable toward inflation and approved the legislation designed to raise the price level. They were generally isolationist and looked inward rather than toward Europe. The leaders of this group—Senator Elmer Thomas of Oklahoma, Wright Patman and John Garner of Texas, and others—were midwesterners and westerners for the most part, descendents of the Populist Movement and the "Silverites." Patman remained in Congress until his death in 1976, still a "Populist" and foe of the Fed.

2. A small and increasingly limited group, who traced their roots to Grover Cleveland, whose goals were economy in government and the balanced budget. These traditional Democrats lost ground, especially as an economic rationale for large-scale spending was developed late in the second term.

3. The "Brandeis party," which continued to press for a restoration of competition and a small-unit economic system.

4. The followers of Herbert Croly, who embraced any ideas which would lead to a more positive role for the government in business in the style of Woodrow Wilson.

Speaking in more precise economic terms, there were also widely divergent views among FDR's associates. Such advisors as Gardiner Means and Senator O'Mahoney were followers of Brandeis, advocating the virtues of small scale and warning of the dangers of large firms, fearful of price rigidity and concentrated power.

Morgenthau was a doctrinaire balancer of budgets who worried about inflation. Others like Currie were advocates of corporate spending and advocated the short-lived excess (or undistributed profits) tax. Moderate Keynesians led by Alvin Hansen pressed for pump priming and later for compensatory finance, while left-wing Keynesians such as Paul Sweezy who had lost faith in capitalism, argued for more extreme forms of federal intervention in the system.

These groups waxed and waned in the course of the administration, and New Deal policy was sufficiently broad to encompass some elements of all these programs. Whatever the solid results of all these policies were, the electorate in 1936 and 1940 seemed to approve them. In 1940 and 1944, other matters were to be considered, but the 1936 election was a popular test of New Deal policies.

Despite the victory over Alfred M. Landon, however, after 1936 criticism became more marked, especially from the right, but also from the center and the far left. Huey Long had been a trial to the administration early and late, and in 1935 he published his *My First Days in the White House*, which the administration did not find humorous. H. L. Mencken in *The American Mercury* kept up a drumfire of critical comments.[42] Both right and left, however, were more powerful in the press than they were in the polls.[43]

Achievements and Failures

Sometimes designed to reform and at other times directed toward recovery, programs came and went in rapid profusion. Nonetheless, when the economic aims of the administration fell short, FDR seized political initiative. Roosevelt seems often to have chosen a course deliberately opposite to that of Hoover, seemingly to demonstrate that a poor administrator might be a great President while a good administrator might be a poor President.

The economists who passed in and out of the Roosevelt White House were a varied lot, and the New Deal policies reflected, in some part, their diverse views. Only Lauchlin Currie, borrowed from the Board of Governors of the Federal Reserve System, was formally installed in the White House as a professional economist, although, like most of FDR's staff, he had no title.

Currie, who had worked closely with Eccles, was well thought of, and this appointment was highly regarded; however, he was to find out, as many of FDR's people did, that his jurisdiction was not clearly marked out:

The appointment of a professional economist, and particularly of Lauchlin Currie, an administrative assistant to the President, was also an event of significance as a precedent for things to come. The public thought of Roosevelt as always having many intellectuals and Brain Trusters around him and tended to identify all of them as "economists." In fact, of those close to Roosevelt, only one, Tugwell, was an economist, and he was quite outside of the main stream of economists' thinking. Currie was a professional economist and in touch with the leading currents of economic thought of the time. Moreover his main competence and interest was in overall financial policy—originally monetary policy but increasingly fiscal policy. That the President should see many economic problems for the first time through the eyes of Lauchlin Currie increased the likelihood that weight would be given to the use of the budget as the lever with which to manage the economy.

However, Currie's role in domestic financial affairs was actually quite limited. "I quickly found that the President did not feel any pressing need for an economic assistant and the job would be what I made of it on my own initiative." Roosevelt used to pass Currie's memoranda on to Morgenthau, which annoyed Currie. An accommodation was reached under which Currie would work with the Treasury on Treasury matters but would not make suggestions on them directly to the President.[44]

Isador Lubin, Robert Nathan, Leon Henderson, Beardsley Ruml, and other economists had access to the President, though they were assigned to various agencies or were outside the government entirely. Ruml, for example, was treasurer of R. H. Macy Company and a member of the board of the Federal Reserve Bank of New York.[45]

A major weakness in Roosevelt's economic policies was his reluctance to give the Treasury post to a strong and well-qualified person. The original secretary, William Woodin, was president of the American Car and Foundry Company; however, his health broke early in the administration, and he was forced to resign. FDR then appointed Henry Morgenthau, who, though very honest, upright, and loyal to Roosevelt, was totally unqualified for the post.[46]

Within the Treasury, power was held and policy formulated at various times by various people, including Undersecretary Dean G. Acheson (later Secretary of State) and Harry D.White.

In many ways, of course, the Roosevelt Administration never really came to grips with the Depression. Many of the long-range reforms—Social Security, minimum wages, regulation in the securities markets, and other matters—became permanently established and played some role in stabilization, especially with regard to reestablishing confidence. The various devices designed to inflate the price level were largely unsuccessful, some doing more harm than good.

The President never formulated a comprehensive and coordinated economic policy, but by 1939 European affairs had begun to increase demand for American industrial products to a point where recovery was assured. And, as the international scene darkened, FDR turned his attention more and more to world affairs and less to domestic economics. Employment and income rose rapidly as the economics of recovery became the economics of war. Dudley Dillard has written:

> In summary, it may be concluded that the New Deal achieved certain important goals but failed to achieve the main economic objectives of any sound economic system, namely, full and efficient utilization of the available resources. Put slightly differently, the New Deal, despite the long distance it brought the economy along the uphill road to recovery, left a huge gap between the actual and the potential level of living of its citizens. More than a decade after the stock market crashed in 1929, the Great Depression remained unliquidated. Moreover, there were few indications that it would be liquidated in the foreseeable future. People were eating regularly and the private enterprise system had been preserved, but the performance remained unsatisfactory. Only the threat of war, and later the actuality of war, lifted the American economy from its moribund state.[47]

Brave words and some bold deeds went a long way toward the restoration of confidence in the dismal winter of 1932. A long upswing began, lasting until 1937 (more than fifty months—one of the longest until that date). Yet in part, due to the depths to which the economy had declined, recovery was painfully slow and pitifully incomplete. By 1939, ten million men remained unemployed and the gross national product was only $90.5 billion (about one-tenth of the 1970 figure). Wartime federal expenditures were able to accomplish what had seemed to be impossible in peacetime, and the Depression gave way to prosperity that would last many years.

Roosevelt's strengths as an economic policy maker were (a) his willingness to innovate and his flexibility; (b) his ability to dramatize issues and rally public support; (c) his willingness to shift positions as it became necessary; (d) his willingness to consider the overall performance of capitalism and judge it on that basis and not as an article of faith; and (e) his willingness to seek professional counsel.

His weaknesses, however, were (a) his tendency to embrace unorthodox ideas in a rather indiscriminate fashion; (b) his tendency to retain weak and ineffective, though loyal, men in key positions; and (c) his well-known practice of encouraging overlap and duplication of effort among high-level policy aides,a policy leading to confusion.

Some of FDR's policies would likely have worked if more adequate data or more capable administrators had been available. Others would have been better left alone. One must again remember that necessity, if not desperation, was the spur. One of the New Deal goals was the salvation of the capitalist system, which indeed appeared at times to be in danger. This goal was accomplished. FDR had been trained in the tradition of the virtues of reform and regulation, and the most durable of the New Deal innovations were in those fields.

Roosevelt's strong personality and the drama of the New Deal have sometimes overshadowed the fact that the reform program had deep roots not related to the New Deal as such. Professor Dexter Perkins comments:

> It is possible to argue that the New Deal had its roots in so-cial circumstance and is more wisely regarded as the reaction of the Americans to the Great Depression rather than as the accomplishment—worthy or unworthy—of any individual. The point can be made clear by recalling the circumstances in which the principal legislative measures of the era were enacted. The agricultural reforms of the New Deal, for example, were related to, if not precisely similar to, the abortive measures proposed (and vetoed) in the administration of Calvin Coolidge. The N.I.R.A. [National Industrial Recovery Act] owed its adoption in part to the trade-association movement of the twenties. The devaluation of the dollar in 1934 is reminiscent of the inflation-ary proposals of 1896, only one in a long line of such measures and not the only one adopted. Use of the Tennessee Valley dams was discussed long before Roosevelt took office. The awakening of labor was in line with the tendencies in every other industrial nation and was, in fact, long overdue in com-parison with the experience of Europe. Progressive taxes on the well-to-do were accepted long before 1933. And so might one go on to argue that in dealing with all these measures it was the spirit of the time that dictated action, not simply the will or the intelligence of the Chief Executive. . . .[48]

One of Roosevelt's great ideas was his acceptance of the need for planning, an idea that seems to have been in his mind for a considerable period, though, of course, it was much elaborated and sometimes misapplied in practice by his New Deal associates. Beyond question, the administration represented a major turning point in economic philosophy. While it had its antecedents, not a few of which were contributed by the Hoover Administration, it represented in many ways true innovative thinking—with welfare programs, long-range reforms, and less successful attempts to meet the emergency—superimposed upon basic capitalism. Did the New Deal rescue capitalism, or was it merely a way station en route to socialism? Decades later, the question remains unanswered. The change of pace and rapid movement of events following the entry of the United States into World War II make it difficult to trace the thread of policy. Quite clearly, the Truman and Roosevelt eras, though they overlapped, were also quite distinct. Two major events tend to cloud the issue: First, the upheaval of war and the end of the Depression; and, second, the partial systematization of economic policy making that came with the passage of the Employment Act of 1946. One doubts that the Council would have functioned had Roosevelt continued in office. But Truman was not Roosevelt, and 1946 was not 1932.

Notes

Chapter 3

[1] Daniel R. Fusfeld, *The Economic Thought of Franklin D. Roosevelt and the Origins of the New Deal* (New York: Columbia University Press, 1965).

[2] Rexford G. Tugwell, *The Democratic Roosevelt* (Garden City: Doubleday, 1957).

[3] During the campaign FDR almost completely ignored foreign affairs. See Raymond Moley, *The First New Deal* (New York: Harcourt, Brace & World, 1966).

[4] Joseph Lash, *Eleanor and Franklin* (New York: Norton, 1971). During his term as governor, his mother, Sara Delano Roosevelt, supplemented his salary and met many other family needs.

[5] Fusfeld, op. cit., p. 252.

[6] Fusfeld, op. cit., p. 252. See also, Rexford G. Tugwell, *The Brains Trust* (New York: Viking, 1968).

[7] David A. Shannon, *Twentieth Century America* (Chicago: Rand McNally, 1963), p. 321.

[8] *State Papers*. Vol. I, p. 860.

[9] *Forum*, July, 1931. Among other things, this article mentions an "economic council" as a means of solving problems. Reproduced in *History of Employment and Manpower Policies in the U.S.*, Part V. Committee on Labor and Public Welfare, U.S. Senate, 88th Congress, 2d Session.

[10] The humorist, Will Rogers, noted that having tried everything else, the country was now willing to try brains.

[11] Samuel I. Rosenman, *Working With Roosevelt* (New York: Harper & Row, 1952), p. 56ff. See also, Tugwell, *Brains Trust*.

[12] Patrick Anderson, *The President's Men* (New York: Doubleday, 1969), p. 22.

[13] Rexford G. Tugwell, from *The Brains' Trust*, p. 36. Copyright© 1968 by Rexford G. Tugwell (Reprinted by permission of Viking Press, Inc.).

[14] *The Chicago Tribune* ran frequent cartoons of a long-haired, bespectacled professor in academic garb, offering silly advice to older and wiser men. Even Tugwell's college years' poems were unearthed!

[15] See Bernard Sternsher, *Rexford Tugwell and the New Deal* (New Brunswick: Rutgers University Press, 1964).

[16] Anderson, op. cit., p. 23.

[17] Rosenman, op. cit., pp. 87–88.

[18] Allan Gruchy, *Modern Economic Thought* (New York: Prentice-Hall, 1948), p. 1.

[19] The range of Moley's activities is indicated by his book, *After Seven Years* (New York: Harper & Brothers, 1939).

[20] See Arthur A. Ekirch, Jr., *Ideologies and Utopias, the Impact of the New Deal on American Thought* (Chicago: Quadrangle Books, 1969).

[21] Marriner Eccles in his book mentions the influence of these lay economists and points out that one of his attractions in the eyes of FDR was that he was a hardheaded banker-businessman who had met a payroll. Likewise, Raymond Moley notes in *After Seven Years* that in 1932 Washington had become a mecca for single taxers, socialists, and others who had unorthodox economic ideas. Eccles was a unique figure. A Utah banker with wide business interests, he was shaken by the Depression, not so much financially as intellectually. Though not widely read, he began to develop Keynesian ideas on an independent basis. He came to Tugwell's attention. Passed on to FDR, he was appointed to the Federal Reserve Board.

[22] Veblen, an unorthodox economist in the early years of the century, had emphasized the role of technicians in *The Engineers and the Price System* (1921).

[23] Arthur M. Schlesinger, Jr., *The Politics of Upheaval* (Boston: Houghton Mifflin, 1947) p. 80ff. See also, T. Harry Williams, *Huey Long* (New York: Knopf, 1969).

[24] See Alpheus T. Mason, *Brandeis: A Free Man's Life* (New York: Viking, 1946).

[25] Jonathan Daniels, *The Time Between the Wars* (Garden City: Doubleday, 1966), p. 269.

[26] Walton H. Hamilton, "The Place of Value Theory in Economics," *Journal of Political Science*, 26 (March 1918), pp. 345–407.

[27] By the mid-1950s economists had begun to be more doubtful of unions, since they too had begun to be powerful and monopolistic and were often in concert with industry.

[28] *Crisis of the Old Order*, p. 420. FDR was a master of fence straddling. He startled Moley early in the administration by asking for a speech endorsing (in one document) both free trade and protection!

[29] Many students of the present regulatory agency list industry domination as a major weakness of the process.

[30] Louis M. Hacker, *American Problems of Today* (New York: Crofts, 1938), p. 204.

[31] Rexford G. Tugwell, *The Democratic Roosevelt* (Garden City: Doubleday, 1957), p. 449.

[32] Seymour Harris, ed., *The New Economics*, Chapter II; Seymour Harris, "Keynes' Influence in Public Policy" (New York: Knopf, 1947), p. 16ff. Hoover also disliked Keynes, and called him "most conceited."

[33] Schlesinger, *Politics of Upheaval*, pp. 406, 408.

[34] Eric F. Goldman, *Rendezvous with Destiny* (New York: Knopf, 1953), pp. 330–31.

[35] John M. Blum, ed., from *The Morgenthau Diaries*, Vol. I, *Years of Crisis, 1928–1938* (Boston: Houghton Mifflin, 1958), p. 280.

[36] Ibid., p. 281.

[37] Herbert Stein, *The Fiscal Revolution in America* (Chicago: University of Chicago Press, 1969), p. 102. In his autobiography, former Supreme Court Justice William O. Douglas, who was SEC Chairman in 1937, notes that in June FDR asked him if the declining stock market was the result of a Wall Street conspiracy against the administration. Douglas expressed the opinion that the downturn was due to the spending cut and not to any Wall Street conspiracy. See, William O. Douglas, *Autobiography* (New York:

Random House, 1974) p. 284.

[38] Roosevelt, *Public Papers*, 1938, Vol. VI, p. 97.

[39] Seymour Harris, ed., *The New Economics:* "Keynes Influence on Theory and Public Policy" (New York: Knopf, 1947), p. 15.© Augustus M. Kelley, Inc.

[40] Schlesinger, *The Coming of the New Deal* (Boston: Houghton Mifflin, 1959), p. 650. FDR told Frances Perkins, "I saw your friend Keynes. He left a whole rigamarole of figures. He must be a mathematician instead of a political economist." Frances Perkins, *The Roosevelt I Knew* (New York: Viking, 1964), p. 119.

[41] Richard Hofstadter, *The Age of Reform: From Bryan to FDR* (New York: Knopf, 1955), pp. 323–24.

[42] See for example, H. L. Mencken, "Three Years of Dr. Roosevelt," *The American Mercury*, 37, 1936.

[43] See Benjamin Stolberg and Warren Jay Vinton, *The Economic Consequences of the New Deal* (New York: Harcourt, Brace & World, 1935).

[44] Herbert Stein, *The Fiscal Revolution in America* (Chicago: University of Chicago Press, 1969) p. 129. See also Alan Sweezy, et al., "The Keynesian Revolution and Its Pioneers," *Proceedings*, American Economic Association, May 1972. Vol. 62, No. 2, pp. 116ff.

[45] Currie later went to the Treasury, leaving federal service after World War II, Lubin became associated with the Twentieth Century Fund, and only Nathan, a Washington consultant, retained his close political ties.

[46] Morgenthau made many errors, but his final mistake was the so-called Morgenthau Plan propounded late in World War II. This plan called for the breaking up of German industry and the establishment of a number of small German agricultural states in the postwar settlement. In *The Founding Father: The Story of Joseph P. Kennedy and the Family He Raised to Power*, Richard J. Whalen notes that Kennedy, who had been a strong FDR backer and contributor, hoped for the Treasury post. Instead he was named the first chairman of the newly formed Securities and Exchange Commission, and later, Ambassador to Great Britain (New York: Signet, New American Library, 1964).

[47] Dudley Dillard, *Economic Development of the North Atlantic Community, Historical Introduction to Modern Economics* (Englewood Cliffs: Prentice-Hall, 1967), p. 609.

[48] Dexter Perkins, *The New Age of Franklin Roosevelt, 1932–1945* (Chicago: University of Chicago Press, 1957), pp. 72–73.

Chapter 4

Truman and
the New Approach

Democracy attacks the problem of
government the hard way—that is the
most fundamental way.
　　　　　　　　—Edwin G. Nourse

By Roosevelt's death in early 1945, the new era
was at hand. Naturally, interest in domestic economic policy had been
minimal during World War II, but now, as the new President took office,
victory in a short time was no longer in doubt, and thoughts might safely
be turned to the postwar era. There was, of course, immense interest in
the postwar world. One has the impression that, as the war drew to a
close, the economic future was viewed with a mixture of fear and
anxious optimism.

Popular commentators on the economy found a wide audience for
articles on the future of the economy and postwar expectations. In the
New Republic (August 1942), George Soule began a two-part article
entitled "Full Employment After the War." Professor Sumner Slichter,
writing in the *Harvard Business Review* in the autumn of 1942, noted that
the war had been instrumental in developing the greatest and most
skilled labor force and the most complete plant in history:

> The prospective increase in the Nation's plant fills many peo-
> ple with dread. They fear that we are likely to be poor because
> we are able to produce so much. Before Pearl Harbor a *Fortune*
> survey found that 69.9 percent of persons interviewed expect

90

things to be worse after the war than before. Early in June, 1942, the Gallup poll found a slight majority of people had given up the idea of a post-war depression. Businessmen were expecting prosperity by two to one. Farmers and lower income groups, however, were expecting depression. Is there any basis for this fear? If we really have the kind of economy in which a gain in productive capacity reduces living standards, it is high time that we changed it.

The National Resources Planning Board had begun as early as 1941 to discuss postwar plans for employment. The NRPB noted that, on the basis of wartime experience, it was entirely possible for the United States to attain a national income of $105 billion. In 1929, GNP had reached $104.4 billion, but had fallen to $56 billion in 1932. It had peaked at $211.4 in 1944, but, of course, no one expected such levels to last long once the war was over.

Wartime Changes in the Economy

The war years brought enormous change in the American economy, but it was difficult to determine how many of these changes were fundamental and to identify those that were merely incidental to the war and would disappear with war's end. Perhaps the most dramatic change was that related to employment. Even the staunchest defenders of the New Deal were forced to admit that it had largely failed in its efforts on this front. In 1940 unemployment had still been a serious problem, with some nine million either unemployed or employed at tasks below their skill. The war in Europe rapidly changed this situation, however, and by the time the United States became actively involved, in 1942, labor shortage had replaced the redundancy of the past decade.

By the peak period of 1944, with some thirteen million men and women in the armed forces, unemployment had declined to the lowest practicable levels. It was assumed, of course, that many of those in the wartime labor force would return to other roles; housewives and retired persons, for example, had entered war industries in large numbers. On the other hand, the returning servicemen would be seeking jobs. One of the major forces behind the Servicemans Readjustment Act of 1946 (the "G. I. Bill") was the need to ease the return of the troops and to feed them into the labor market with a minimum of strain. Plant and equipment additions had been significant both in number and in quality as new processes were adopted. Many industries were able to operate at full capacity for the first time in years. Railroads, for example, were able to

Table 4.   SOME SELECTED ECONOMIC INDICATORS, 1935–45

Year	Total Gross National Product[a] (billions of $)	Total Gross National Product[b] 1958 Prices (billions of $)	Implicit Price Deflators for GNP[c] (index numbers 1958=100)	Total National Income[d] (billions of $)	Per Capita Disposable Personal Income ($)[e]	
					Current Prices	1958 Prices
1935	72.2	169.5	42.6	57.2	459	1,035
1936	82.5	193.0	42.7	65.0	518	1,158
1937	90.4	203.2	44.5	73.6	552	1,187
1938	84.7	192.9	43.9	67.4	504	1,105
1939	90.5	209.4	43.2	72.6	537	1,190
1940	99.7	227.2	43.9	81.1	573	1,259
1941	124.5	263.7	47.2	104.2	695	1,427
1942	157.9	297.8	53.0	137.1	867	1,582
1943	191.6	337.1	56.8	170.3	976	1,629
1944	210.1	361.3	58.2	182.6	1,057	1,673
1945	211.9	355.2	59.7	181.5	1,074	1,642

Source: *Economic Report of the President*, transmitted to the Congress, February 1970.
[a]Extract from Table C-1, Gross National Product of Expenditure, p. 177. Source: Department of Commerce, Office of Business Economics.
[b]Extract from Table C-2, Gross National Product of Expenditure, Billions of Dollars, 1958 Prices, p. 178. Source: Department of Commerce, Office of Business Economics.
[c]Table C-3, p. 180, ibid.
[d]Extract from Table C-16, Total and Per Capita Disposable Personal Income and Personal Consumption Expenditures in Current and 1958 Prices, 1929–1969. Source: Department of Commerce (Office of Business and Economics and Bureau of Census).
[e]Extract from Table C-12, National Income by Types of Income, 1929–1969, p. 191. Source: Department of Commerce, Office of Business Economics.

Table 5. **EMPLOYMENT STATISTICS, 1935–45**

Year	Total Civilian Labor Force[a]. (thous. of persons 14 yrs. of age & over)	Total Employment Civilian Labor Force[b] (thous. of persons 14 yrs. of age & over)	Total Unemployment Civilian Labor Force[c] (thous. of persons 14 yrs. of age & over)	Unemployment as Percentage of Civilian Labor Force[d]
1935	52,870	42,260	10,610	20.1
1936	53,440	44,410	9,030	16.9
1937	54,000	46,300	7,700	14.3
1938	54,610	44,220	10,390	19.0
1939	55,230	45,750	9,480	17.2
1940	55,640	47,520	8,120	14.6
1941	55,910	50,350	5,560	9.9
1942	56,410	53,750	2,660	4.7
1943	55,540	54,470	1,070	1.9
1944	54,630	53,960	670	1.2
1945	54,860	52,820	1,040	1.9

Source: *Economic Report of the President*, transmitted to the Congress, February 1970.
a b c and d Extracted from Table C-22, Noninstitutional Population and the Labor Force, 1929–1969, p. 202. Source: Department of Labor, Bureau of Labor Statistics.

Table 6. PRODUCTION STATISTICS AND PRICE INDEXES

Year	Total Industrial Production [a] 1957–59=100	Total Manufacturing [b] 1957–59=100	Total New Construction [c] (value put in place, millions of $)	Consumer Price Index, [d] All Items 1957–59=100	Wholesale Price Index, All Commodities [e] 1957–69=100
1935	30.7	30.6	4,232	47.8	43.8
1936	36.3	36.4	6,497	48.3	44.2
1937	39.7	39.7	6,999	50.0	47.2
1938	31.4	30.5	6,980	49.1	43.0
1939	38.3	37.9	8,198	48.4	42.2
1940	43.9	43.8	8,682	48.8	43.0
1941	56.4	58.3	11,957	51.3	47.8
1942	69.3	73.1	14,075	56.8	54.0
1943	82.9	88.7	8,301	60.3	56.5
1944	81.7	86.3	5,259	61.3	56.9
1945	70.5	73.0	5,809	62.7	57.9

Source: *Economic Report of the President*, transmitted to the Congress, February 1970.
[a] Extract from Table C-35, Industrial Production Indexes, Major Industry Divisions, 1929–1969, p. 217. Source: Board of Governors of the Federal Reserve System.
[b] Ibid.
[c] Extract from Table C-40, New Constructive Activity, 1929–1969, p. 222. Source: Department of Commerce, Bureau of the Census.
[d] Extract from Table C-45, Consumer Price Indexes, by Major Groups, 1929–1969, For City Wage Earners and Clerical Workers, p. 229. Source: Department of Labor, Bureau of Labor Statistics.
[e] Extract from Table C-48, Wholesale Price Indexes, by Major Commodity Groups, 1929–1969, p. 232. Source: Department of Labor, Bureau of Labor Statistics.

Table 7. STATISTICS ON MONEY SUPPLY AND PROFITS

Year	Total Reserve Bank Credit Outstanding a (averages of daily figures, millions of dollars)	Total Federal Reserve Member Bank Reserve b (averages of daily figures, millions of dollars)	Total Corporation Profits c (billions of dollars)		Current Assets & Liabilities of United States Corporations d (billions of dollars)	
			Before Tax	After Tax	Assets e	Liabilities f
1935	2,494	5,716	3.6	2.6	—	—
1936	2,498	6,665	6.3	4.9	—	—
1937	2,628	6,879	6.8	5.3	—	—
1938	2,618	8,745	4.0	2.9	—	—
1939	2,612	11,473	7.0	5.6	54.5	30.0
1940	2,305	14,049	10.0	7.2	60.3	32.8
1941	2,404	12,812	17.7	10.1	72.9	40.7
1942	6,035	13,152	21.5	10.1	83.6	47.3
1943	11,914	12,749	25.1	11.1	93.8	51.6
1944	19,612	14,168	24.1	11.2	97.2	41.7
1945	24,744	16,027	19.7	9.0	97.4	45.8

Source: *Economic Report of the President*, transmitted to the Congress, February 1970.
aExtract from Table C-54, Federal Reserve Bank Credit and Member Bank Reserves, 1929–1969, p. 241. Source: Board of Governors of the Federal Reserve System.
bIbid.
cExtract from Table C-71, Profits Before and After Taxes, All Private Corporations, 1929–1969, p. 125. Source: Department of Commerce, Office of Business Economics.
dIbid.
eExtract from Table C-75, Current Assets and Liabilities of U.S. Corporations, 1939–1969, p. 265. Source: Securities and Exchange Commission.
fIbid.

increase output nearly twofold in the 1933–44 period with almost no increase in their physical plant. Many of these changes were not readily apparent. It was clear to all that a tremendous demand for autos, appliances, and housing had developed, but no one knew the dimensions of this demand or how long it might last. Both businessmen and workers found it difficult to shake off Depression thinking. This cautious consumer and business attitude, coupled with the program of price and wage controls, kept prices from rising unduly.

Many of the dramatic changes in the decade 1935–45 are shown in Tables 4, 5, 6, and 7. Underlying these figures lay the tremendous capacity of the economy to produce. With only a mild reduction in consumer goods (indeed, except for autos and certain other durable items, real standards of living actually rose), the system produced a vast volume of war material. Many thousands of men and women had learned new skills and had gained industrial experience.

Many changes (women in the labor force, new technology in aircraft, for example) would set patterns for the future. Other far-reaching socioeconomic forces—such as the growth of suburbs, continued movement off the farm, and northward movement of blacks—were obscured by the drama of the war, but nonetheless potent. It was then impossible to trace or measure the impact of these changes, and no one was able to forecast the future with confidence.

In planning for the future the ideas of John Maynard Keynes, which had enjoyed currency among government economists as well as academicians (in wartime many were in both groups), were central to postwar analysis. Alvin Hansen, a Harvard professor and leading American Keynesian, in 1943 prepared for the NRPB a lengthy statement entitled, *After the War, Full Employment*.

> When the war is over, the Government cannot just disband the Army, close down munition factories, stop building ships, and remove all economic controls. We want an orderly program of demobilization and reconstruction. The Government cannot escape responsibility. To fulfill its responsibility it needs the hearty cooperation of business, labor, farmers and the professions in the great task of developing a vigorous, expanding and prosperous society.

Keynesian economic thinking was in the forefront of postwar policy formulation and especially the legislation leading to the Employment Act. Stephen K. Bailey comments on Keynes' role:

> There are few who would question the contribution of John

Maynard Keynes to the theoretical underpinnings of the Full
Employment Bill. Care should be taken, however, in assigning
his proper historical role. Keynes was not the inspired prophet
of a new mystical theology. He was the great verbalizer and
rationalizer of a theoretical attitude which was being forced, by
the cold facts of the depression experience, upon a number of
European and American economists.

The Bill's terminal reliance upon a program of Federal investment and expenditure cannot be understood without an
appreciation of the theoretical contributions of the late Lord
Keynes and the movement of which he was a symbol.[1]

From a policy standpoint, linking Keynes to postwar policy plans had
both advantages and disadvantages. Keynesian policies, insofar as they
had been used to combat the Depression and as understood by businessmen or conservative economists, had not been universally popular.
American adherents of Keynes built up the so-called "maturity thesis."
Hansen, perhaps its leading exponent, had long held that investment
opportunities had diminished following the close of the frontier at the
end of the nineteenth century.[2] The idea was expanded by others.[3]

This thesis was by no means widely accepted, and the federal
economists and others to whom Bailey refers as the "intellectual mid-
dlemen" were careful to avoid overstressing the stagnationist theme. As
Bailey makes clear, the long-range analysis largely originated in the
fiscal division of the Bureau of the Budget:

The Budget Bureau, under the leadership of Harold Smith,
began as early as 1939 to think of the budgetary process in the
broader context of government fiscal policy and economic program formulation. In 1939, a Fiscal Division was established in
the Bureau to examine "questions of fiscal policy and [to give]
staff assistance in the formulation of the President's financial
program."

Under the intellectual guidance of J. Weldon Jones, Gerhard
Colm, Arthur Smithies, and Grover Ensley, the Fiscal Division
during the war years gradually evolved a conception of the "Nation's Budget" which found its way into the President's Budget
Message of January 3, 1945. The concept of the nation's budget
was a logical off-spring of Roosevelt's statement in January,
1941, that "the Budget of the United States presents our national program. It is a preview of our work plan, a forecast of
things to come. It charts the course of the nation." What had
been added by 1945 was an official recognition of the essentially
Keynesian proposition that the federal budget should be used to

contribute to the larger context of the total national economy. An analysis of the budget messages from 1940 to 1945 gives a clear indication that the annual budget was on its way to becoming an important instrument of national policy programming in the economic field.[4]

Despite all the foregoing evidence of interest in the Employment Act among economists and labor groups, there was little indication of much involvement on the part of the general public; nor was there much understanding of the implications of the act. There was, in fact, a great deal of suspicion of government control and an understandable desire to free the economy from wartime measures as rapidly as possible; out of this dichotomy came the act. In summarizing the forces which preceded the legislation, Bailey says:

> A major policy bill does not burst like a mature Athena from the head of Zeus. The Full Employment Bill had a gestation period of at least six months, and its ancestry dates back a long way. If we are searching for the moment when the idea of a separate Full Employment Bill came into existence, we should probably have to choose that instant of time in August, 1944, when the Patton amendment to the Kilgore bill was first brought to the attention of Senator James E. Murray of Montana. . . .
> In this general awareness by Senator Murray and his War Contracts Subcommittee staff that limited reconversion legislation was not enough that the Patton amendment had created a new frame of reference for thinking about postwar employment problems, the Full Employment Bill of 1945 had its real beginning.[5]

After a dramatic struggle, the Congress came to agreement and the era of informal Presidential economic advice came to an end (see Appendix E for some personalities involved in passage of the act). However, the new era did not mean that the function of economic advice and analysis had decisively emerged from the twilight zone it had so long occupied. Much doubt still remained as to whether the objectives of the act were feasible or, indeed, even desirable.

It was hoped that the uncoordinated federal economic policies would be brought under a more or less unified control and that a sense of direction would be provided. The Act made it a specified federal responsibility and policy to maintain a framework of full employment and to devote the resources of the federal establishment to economic stability, saying in Section 2:

The Congress hereby declares that it is the continuing policy and responsibility of the Federal Government to use all practicable means . . . to coordinate and utilize all its plans, functions, and resources for the purpose of creating and maintaining, in a manner calculated to foster and promote free competitive enterprise and the general welfare, conditions under which there will be afforded useful employment opportunities . . . and to promote maximum employment, production, and purchasing power.[6]

The function of the Council of Economic Advisers (CEA) created by the Act was to be the preparation of an economic report which would be transmitted, with or without comment by the President, to the Joint Economic Committee of Congress (originally called the Joint Committee on the Economic Report). The Joint Economic Committee would then hold hearings and make to the whole Congress such reports or recommendations as it saw fit. The CEA report, including that portion specifically written for the President, was to be made public, so that the recommendations, or at least those printed in the report, would be in the public domain, a major state paper. Discussion between the CEA and the President leading to the report, however, was private.

The machinery of the act was fairly simple. The Council members appointed by the President were to be aided by a small staff of professional and support personnel. The Council was to use statistical and data collection services provided by other federal agencies, and it was not contemplated that it would be a large agency.

The need for such services was painfully obvious. The Roosevelt years, then closing, had, as we have seen, witnessed an enormous increase in governmental policies in the field of economics. The administration had introduced a wide variety of complex and interrelated policies aimed at stabilization and recovery. Whatever their merit, no serious attempt had been made to view them in the aggregate. Each policy stood more or less on its own, sometimes complementing and sometimes clashing with other policies. No one in the administration had a clear view of the entire New Deal program, nor was anyone able to see all the relationships.

Successful economic planning on a large scale, incident to World War II, was another factor in the acceptance of the legislation. Many of those who were favorable toward the act pointed out that wartime planning and careful utilization of resources had been highly successful. Was it not possible to apply such techniques to the peacetime economy? Economists who had been the object of much abuse in the years of the

New Deal had been useful in wartime, and their ranks had been supplemented by the influx of younger men trained during the years of the "Keynesian Revolution."

Though still anathema to many, the leading edge of economic planning was becoming more respectable. Thus both the Congress and the administration, though they would have been reluctant to admit it, were being pushed inexorably toward more systematic economic policy—policy which required more elaborate machinery than was then available. Thus the twin events of depression and war had brought the idea of formal economic analysis into existence and acceptance. The former had made it necessary and the latter had made it respectable. This is not to say, of course, that the Congress suddenly embraced planning and planners as the new faith. Far from it. Yet a new era had clearly begun.

Transition and Truman

These legislative actions, of course, coincided with the entry of Harry S. Truman into the White House, and his administration was only in the formative stages with regard to domestic economic policy when the Employment Act was passed.

By Truman's time the White House had grown substantially from the informal days of Coolidge and even in comparison with those of the early Roosevelt period. It had become common to have science advisers, military advisers, and advisers on problems of minority groups and other issues—often on a full-time basis with formal titles and fairly well-defined responsibilities. Truman was a better and more systematic administrator than FDR, but he was, like Roosevelt, highly pragmatic. Unlike Roosevelt, Truman liked tidy lines of authority, and he did not put his aides at cross purposes and create overlapping authority if he was able to avoid it. He had less inclination toward advisers in general and little use for economists.

Although he had a large staff, he had no professional economists in residence as economic advisers. Dr. John R. Steelman, a labor economist, seems to have attended to economic matters, assisted by various people, none of whom were professional economists.[7]

Truman, who had never attended college, came to the Senate with a strong sense of his lack of background in national affairs. Sensitive of his lack of higher formal education, he announced his intention of attending Georgetown University Law School at night, but the pressures of his job, of course, quickly made this impossible. In Kansas City, he had pursued law and accounting on this basis but never graduated. A "quick study" and a voracious reader, the Senator soon developed a reputation as one who "did his homework." He worked with Senator Burton K. Wheeler on railroad and other transportation legislation and impressed not only Wheeler but the staff, who had been inclined to look down their noses at him as "the office boy" of Kansas City's political boss Pendergast.[8]

He began to widen his horizons and develop new intellectual interests. Jonathan Daniels recounts his meeting with Justice Brandeis:

"I'm not used to meeting people like that," he said. It was true. Most of his growth and studying had been free from great intellectual companionship, as his voracious reading as a small town boy had been largely self-directed. Before he went to Washington he had met practically no intellectuals or theoretical students. His companions were small town businessmen and politicians. He had no such feeling then, as Arthur Meier Schlesinger, Jr. expressed, after his election in 1948: "The conceptions of the intellectual are at last beginning to catch up with the instincts of the democratic politician." Truman was aware only of how much he had to learn.

After his first meeting with Brandeis, he went often to California Street—almost every other week—to the open houses which the Justice held for his selected friends.

"The old man would back me into a corner," Truman said in affectionate memory of Brandeis, "and pay no attention to anybody else while he talked transportation to me. He was very much against the control of financial credit—hipped on a few insurance companies controlling too much of the country's credit."

That apartment of Louis Brandeis at 2205 California Street was a new world to Truman. He met there people unlike those he had been accustomed to knowing in politics and the public service of Missouri. His old world remained; however, he had no wish to escape from the practical political world in which he had grown.[9]

When Truman came into office, he knew little of many events both foreign and domestic.[10] Within a week after the Japanese surrender, the President had submitted to the Congress a program which suggested a second run of the first New Deal, calling for extension of Social Security, increase in the minimum wage, a permanent Fair Employment Practices Commission, slum clearance, public housing, flood control, and reclamation plans, as well as a plan for full employment. Shortly thereafter, he asked for legislation to nationalize atomic energy, to provide the St.

101

Lawrence Seaway, national health insurance, and federal aid to education. It is easy to overlook the scope of these requests in the welter of international and domestic strife of the immediate postwar years.

The Employment Act

Let us retrace our steps to the period shortly after Truman assumed the Presidency and during which time the act was still under consideration in the Congress. Truman apparently did not have a clear idea of the purposes of the Employment Act. In his second press· conference after becoming President, he stated he was not familiar with it.[11] However, in this hectic period (May 1945), he was beset with more pressing problems than the "Full Employment Bill." He had been in office less than a month, the war was drawing to a close in Europe, and great decisions were being made on a global basis. Early in September, Truman sent to the Congress a statement covering twenty-one points of needed legislation, including the full employment legislation.[12]

The actual assistance the Truman Administration gave the act during its consideration by Congress was spotty, beginning with the unfortunate testimony of John Snyder (then Chief of the Office of War Mobilization and Reconversion, and later Secretary of the Treasury). Snyder was apparently unsympathetic toward the bill or, at best, was mildly interested. However, in October, Truman made a strong personal appeal on radio, taking the case of full employment directly to the people.[13] Bailey comments on responsibility for passage of the Employment Act:

> Certainly President Truman cannot be held responsible. It is true that he attempted to provide political leadership through his messages to Congress, his radio appeals to the public, the testimony of members of his Cabinet before the Senate and House Committees, his conversations with key Congressional leaders, and his appointment of a Cabinet committee under Fred Vinson to press for passage of a strong bill. It is true also that he signed the final compromise Act. But the forces which shaped and modified the legislation were far beyond his control, and it is almost certain that if he had vetoed the conference bill he would have got nothing in its place.[14]

In his memoirs, Truman takes a large share of credit for passage of the Employment Act, noting that it was included in his recommendations to the Congress shortly after the war ended.[15]

Whatever his views may have been, the President took the act seriously and was careful to appoint qualified members to the Council, the act making it mandatory that the appointees be professionally qualified. Although his appointments were commendable, it was unfortunate that so little rapport existed between the President and the CEA members. For example, although they were almost the same age, it is hard to imagine two people more different temperamentally than the cool, precise Dr. Edwin G. Nourse, who was chairman of the Council, and the outgoing, politically minded President.

The President quite obviously took the appointment task seriously and was careful to keep politics at a minimum. His choices were Edwin G. Nourse, John D. Clark, and Leon H. Keyserling. All three men were well trained, highly respected, and experienced in government affairs. Nourse and Clark were professional economists. Keyserling was a lawyer with substantial economic training and, as Wagner's assistant, had been a figure in the drafting and passage of the Wagner Act in 1937.[16]

Perhaps the first source of confusion was the overlap between the duties of the Council and those of the White House assistants who had taken care of such matters previously. Who would perform the role now? Would Dr. Steelman act as a bridge between the Council and the President, or would the CEA chairman perform this task? Just what role would the chairman play?

At that time, the White House work load was generally split in two parts. The "Steelman Side" was, for the most part, in charge of day-to-day matters, while the "Murphy Side," under Charles S. Murphy, was, in theory, concerned with long-range planning. Although Truman ran a tighter ship than FDR, there was, in fact, much crossing-over from one side to the other. The work of the Bureau of the Budget in attempting to coordinate economic policy has been mentioned. The fiscal division of the Bureau after 1935 performed many of the duties later performed by the Council. The late Gerhard Colm, who transferred to CEA (where he was, in effect, chief of staff), had been in the Bureau along with Arthur Smithies (later at Harvard) and Everett Hagen; all were pioneers in national income accounting. David E. Bell, who was then a junior staff member and who was later in high policy positions himself, has characterized the role of the organization as "remarkable."[17]

Long after the Council was well established, the Bureau of the Budget continued to be a highly influential group, and, in any event, its work on federal expenditures, fiscal policy, and other aspects of federal finance put it in a pivotal position. Further, the Bureau's directors had been for the most part broad-gauge types who took a serious view of their duties. It will be recalled that Charles G. Dawes under Harding had worked hard to establish the authority of the organization, and that tradition had continued.

The President had been a strong supporter of the New Deal and endorsed its domestic programs without reservation. Nonetheless, the Employment Act was a challenge to the traditional method of formulating economic policy and obtaining economic advice, going far beyond anything Roosevelt had done. Implementation of a new governmental concept is never a simple matter; and the President, understandably, was not anxious at this period to strike out in strange directions. He was still very much under the shadow of Roosevelt, and there were many serious doubts about the practical aspects of the new legislation. Not surprisingly, many viewed it as just another agency that would make some splash and then pass from the scene. And it is more than likely that, seeing the situation from the White House in 1946, the President took the view that CEA was less than crucial to the future of the Republic.

Not until July did Truman appoint the Council members.[18] The six-month delay was apparently not due to any specific displeasure on the President's part, but to general pressures of other affairs and the desire to move cautiously in starting off a completely new direction.

The press was fairly favorable. Some of the more conservative papers expressed the thought that the Council would be a "fifth wheel," but only a few on the far right and far left were hostile.

It was no doubt fortunate that the Council was small and held a "low profile." With the rapid scaling-down of the federal establishment in the postwar period, the creation of an agency that totaled no more than twenty people passed almost unnoticed, and, while some were apt to characterize the Council as useless, few were concerned about its cost or its size.

Nourse, the Pioneer

Nourse was at the time of his appointment sixty-three years old (he died April 10, 1974). A highly respected economist, he had been associated with the Brookings Institution for many years. He had received his Ph.D. in economics from the University of Chicago in 1915 and had spent some years in academic life in the early years of the century.

In his book, Nourse notes that the appointment came out of a clear sky, but in a memorandum prepared in August 1963 for deposit in the Truman Memorial Library he speculates at greater length on the reason for having been chosen:

How the Lightning Struck

I had not been sounded out by anybody, and the possibility of such an appointment had never entered my head—much less been activated by me (see *Economics in the Public Service*, pp. 103–8). But in retrospect I see two clues that may be of passing interest. President Truman and his White House staff intended that Council appointments should meet with approval both from the economics profession and from the business and labor world. At the same time, these appointments had to be confirmed by the Senate. This would involve Senator Murray, author of the "Full Employment" bill; Senator Taft, a staunch supporter of the revised measure when it came up for passage; and Senators O'Mahoney, Wagner, Capper, *et al.* Several well-known economists came under such active consideration that various newspapers and weeklies had predicted their appointment for the chairmanship. Two of the most prominent and most meritorious candidates were Winfield Riefler, top of staff for the Federal Reserve Board, and Professor George Taylor of the University of Pennsylvania, an outstanding labor specialist. [Author's note: By coincidence, Riefler's obituary appeared in the *New York Times* on the same day as that of Nourse.]

What influences or circumstances led to the by-passing of these or other names, I never heard or inquired. Subsequently, partisans of all four of the major interested groups—labor, management, agriculture, and the economics profession—expressed to me their satisfaction at my appointment, and several of them stated or intimated that they had had some part in bringing it to pass. Gradually, I synthesized in my own mind an explanation that embraced some four elements: (1) my long and active identification with agricultural problems and farm organizations; (2) later but extensive studies in industrial problems and policies and association with labor and business circles; (3) the reputation of the Brookings Institution for realistic and timely scholarship; and (4) some acquaintance with the Washington Establishment gained from 24 years of research work on national economic issues in their administrative setting. But the one individual whose voice probably was decisive in the matter was Senator James E. Murray.

As chairman of a Senate subcommittee "to investigate war contracts, the termination of war contracts, and related problems," Senator Murray conducted a series of public hearings that ranged quite widely into issues of price and wage policy as related to prospects for private employment after demobilization. In some way my books on *Industrial Price Policies and Economic Progress* and *Price Making in A Democracy* had come to his attention and had moved him to invite me to testify in the hearings of his committee. Afterwards he wrote me a cordial letter, which I accepted as merely in the pattern of Senatorial courtesy. But on July 31, 1946, one day after the announcement of my appointment, I received the following letter:

Dear Dr. Nourse:

As sponsor of the Employment Act of 1946, I should like to extend my congratulations on your appointment as Chairman of the Council of Economic Advisers.

It is with great pleasure that I recollect your splendid testimony on postwar problems before my Military Affairs Sub-committee back in the spring of 1944. In speeches and statements of my own I have often quoted extensively from your conclusions on the desirability of industry's adopting a policy of low prices and high production. In fact, before the Banking and Currency Committee met to consider your nomination, I showed your testimony to the Chairman of the Committee and pointed out that you had helped develop the philosophy which was finally embodied in the Employment Act of 1946.

As chairman of the Council of Economic Advisers, you now have a splendid opportunity to win wider acceptance for the principles you have set forth so lucidly in your writings. Please be assured of my wholehearted support of your efforts in this direction.

Looking forward to seeing you in the near future and discussing this entire problem with you, I beg to remain

Yours sincerely,

James E. Murray
Chairman
Committee on Education and Labor

This letter will no doubt be something of a surprise to those who have viewed Senator Murray in the light only of the Full Employment bill which he introduced in the Senate in 1945, with its dominant emphasis on Federal spending as the means of preventing an "unemployment gap." It is idle to speculate on how much of the text of the 1945 bill derived from the thinking of Murray himself and how much of it was supplied by a corps of draftsmen who found him a somewhat guileless "front." But the bill which he initially sponsored did posit "full employment in a free competitive economy through the concerted efforts of industry, agriculture, labor, state and local governments, and [lastly] the Federal Government." And in the letter quoted above one may well ponder the meaning of the remark that I

106

had helped develop *the philosophy which was finally embodied in the Employment Act of 1946.*

Keyserling, then thirty-eight years old, was a lawyer by profession, having graduated from Columbia University in 1931. He studied economics at Columbia on a part-time basis and joined Rexford Tugwell in Washington in the early 1930s, serving on the legal staff of the Agricultural Adjustment Administration. From then until 1946, he served as Senator Robert F. Wagner's assistant, in a number of federal agencies, as a staff member of the Senate Committee on Banking and Currency, and, finally, as general counsel of the National Housing Agency. It was generally known that he was the choice of Senator Wagner. In 1944 Keyserling had attracted much attention by winning second prize ($10,000) in the Pabst Postwar Planning Essay Contest with a paper that stressed growth as an important economic goal.[19] He had been associated with the inception of the original legislation.

Keyserling has been described by an associate as having the "heart of a missionary and the ego of a politician." His prize-winning essay, written immediately before the close of the war, reflected his observations of the difficulties of mobilization and the effect of specific production goals set by the President. In his essay, Keyserling had suggested the establishment of an economic committee.

> To start, Congress should establish an American Economic Committee, with 3 members from the Senate and 3 from the House of Representatives, appointed by their presiding officers, 3 members appointed by the President from his Cabinet, and 6 members appointed by the President to represent American enterprise, including 2 each from industry, agriculture and labor. The President would designate the Chairman. The Committee would have a small technical staff, supplemented by experts from Government agencies who would serve in rotation, staying for a time and then returning. Each Committee Member could be called before Congress for questioning and exposition.[20]

Although less well known, perhaps the most personally interesting of the trio was John D. Clark. A lawyer, he had in middle life resigned a vice-presidency of Standard Oil of Indiana to earn a Ph.D. in economics in 1931 from Johns Hopkins University. Later, he had become involved in Wyoming politics and was an associate of Senator O'Mahoney. At sixty-two, he left the post as dean of the College of Business at the University of Nebraska to accept an appointment on the Council. Liberals were pleased, conservatives were alarmed about Keyserling, while both groups were neutral on Nourse and Clark.

The immediate economic policies of the early Truman Administration centered about problems of reconversion and inflation, intensified by the underlying fear that mass unemployment would return to haunt the nation as it had prior to the war.

The economy, however, was more buoyant than had been thought. After falling slightly to $208 billion in 1946 the GNP began an upward climb to $345 billion in 1952. (Truman's "sailing orders" to the Council had been to maintain a GNP of $200 billion.)

Unemployment rose from its wartime (and all-time) low of 1.9 percent to 3.6 percent in 1944, but fell again as the Korean War began to be an influence. In broad outline, the anticipated economic problem of deflation became instead a problem of inflation.

A series of legislative acts to provide for transition and stabilization had been passed in the early days of the administration. These included the "G.I. Bill," legislation for the settlement or renegotiation of contracts, a federal aid to highways act, legislation for flood control, and other related matters.

Between May 1945 and mid-February 1946, 7.6 million men were released from the Armed Forces; some 3.7 million were laid off in aircraft and munitions-type industries. However, most were absorbed into the economy, and by February 1946 unemployment was only 2.7 million.

Following an interlude of strikes and confusion about price controls and with the passage of the Employment Act, the shape of administration policy began to emerge.

The formal termination of hostilities did not take place until December 31, 1946. With almost full employment and reconversion substantially completed, 1947 was, in the President's view, a year for federal fiscal restraint. The first *Economic Report* noted that a budget surplus was desirable in time of full employment, and the President called for a budget expenditure of $37.5 billion, with a projected income of $37.7 billion. No tax cut was called for, and, in fact, the President suggested an increase in excise taxes, which had been enacted as a wartime measure.

Controls over consumer credit had been established in 1941 and were administered throughout the war by the Federal Reserve Board. On December 1, 1946, all controls except those dealing with autos and a dozen other consumer durables were lifted. By 1947 all such controls had ended.

The President suggested a program to ease monetary pressure and help increase the flow of consumer goods. The Congress was asked to enact a wide range of control legislation, and when the second session of the 80th Congress began the President again addressed himself to the problem of inflation. However, as the election of 1948 approached, the Republicans and many Democrats showed no interest in "regimentation" of the economy. Installment controls and rent controls were extended, but the rest of the program was ignored.

Early in 1950, the President had again called for fiscal restraint, estimating the fiscal budget deficit at $5.5 billion; however, with the outbreak of the Korean War, the signals were reversed. In July the call was made for an additional $10.5 billion for defense, coupled with a tax increase of $5 billion, a move unanimously recommended by the Joint Economic Committee. In December, another $20 billion was requested and quickly appropriated. To a large extent, the balance of the Truman years were dominated by the economic effects of the Korean War.

Public opinion shifted toward a favorable view of economic controls as prices rose rapidly, and standby rationing procedures were adopted along with price controls in August, although the legislation was amended (amid great confusion) to the point where it was of little value. The Defense Production Act of 1950 was passed in September, authorizing the President to control priorities of goods and prices, operational authority being delegated to the National Production Authority in the Commerce Department. The Economic Stabilization Agency was established to encourage voluntary methods of control. In December, the Office of Defense Mobilization was established, with general authority over production, manpower, stabilization and transportation.

Faced with a 1952 budget of $71.6 billion and a prospective deficit of $16.5 billion, Truman requested an immediate $10 billion tax increase to balance the budget. However, due to rising income and a slowdown in defense outlays, the budget deficit was turned into a surplus of $3.5 billion and a tax rise of only 5.7 percent was enacted. In fact, the situation was better than the·noise and tumult of politics would have indicated:

> For all the controversy, inflation was checked in 1951. The surges of speculative buying that had sent prices soaring in 1950 ended in January, when wholesale prices began a slow but steady drop that extended into 1953. Although the consumer price index continued to rise, the rate of advance was slow. Price, wage, and credit controls, together with higher tax rates, helped to limit the inflationary impact of the rapid increase in federal expenditures. But it was the offsetting effect of a pronounced decline in civilian demand that removed much of the

pressure on prices in a period of full employment and rising personal income.[21]

On a longer-term basis the Administration recommended an assortment of bills, including among other things, a program to stimulate investment in housing for middle-income families, foreign aid, and increased authority over banking reserves on the part of the Federal Reserve Board.

The Council report included a scholarly dissertation on the function of the price system and concluded (just prior to Korea) that "the price level is now within a range where stability should be feasible at workable levels." Substantial space was devoted to the working fiscal policy as a tool of stability and growth.

The 1951 and 1952 reports were dominated entirely by the economic problems of war and stabilization incident to Korea.[22] A highlight of the 1953 report was a cogent statement on the purposes of the Employment Act and a review of the achievements of the legislation.

The Role of the Council

From the first, it was apparent that the exact role of the Council was not clear. The most serious uncertainty centered around the issue of *advice* as opposed to *advocacy*. That is, to what degree should the Council merely advise the President and to what degree should it justify and perhaps even *promote* the President's policies? The core of this problem was the fact that the report was to be made public. When programs and predictions are made public and widely distributed, the question arises as to how much these policy positions bind the administration in its future action. The council also faced the vexing question of what and how much information should be made public, and the members soon became divided on these issues. Nourse was of the opinion that they should stick closely to the task of giving *economic* advice. Clark, and especially Keyserling, felt strongly that their advice should cut across advisory lines and include *social and political* aspects.

President Truman, a highly pragmatic man, took little interest in the methodology of economics or in the internal problems of the Council. In general, he supported the Clark-Keyserling view. Keyserling maintained that Nourse was unable to adjust himself to the problems of the White House and could not understand that the President did not have time for "economic bull sessions," as was the custom at Brookings. By late 1948 matters had become such that the council was no longer able to speak with one voice.

Nourse became more and more frustrated with the situation and, shortly before he resigned, he said:

> The events of recent weeks have confirmed my belief that it is useless to try to go on in my post under present conditions. The physical and nervous strain is so great that at several times I have seen my breaking point just around the corner. Further, the President's handling of the Mid-year Report shows how little real opportunity there is for having our work adequately considered in actual policy making. Although the President said when we submitted our draft materials, "I want to study these very carefully and discuss them fully when I get back" [from a weekend cruise], he never consulted with us thereafter, nor did he sit in with the Cabinet-Council—it was a couple of Steelman's assistants who had the chance to talk to him.[23]

In another context he said:

> Some cynical people have alluded to the Council as "The Three Wise Men of Economics" standing at the President's elbow to give him smart answers to economic riddles or to tell him just what to do in every economic crisis or situation as it arises. Now I do not regard myself as 33⅓ percent of the Three Wise Men. I do not claim that the Council is composed of the three greatest economists in the United States or even that it includes any one of that sacred three. As I understand the matter, we have, by the vicissitudes of politics, been entrusted with the task of organizing an agency through which, over the years, the Chief Executive of the United States may see the economic situation and problems of the nation in their entirety and through professional eyes. It is the responsibility of this agency to process for his consideration the materials which should be of most use to his course of action with reference to the national economy. . . . I conceive this agency as the doorway through which the best thinking of systematic economics (not forgetting the lay brothers) may be brought into clear and effective focus at the point of executive decision as to national economic policy and action.[24]

Nourse's view was clearly that of one who thought of himself as an adviser to the President in a confidential role. He did not see himself as being an active participant in, or advocate of, the President's program, involved in day-to-day affairs, or in the promotion of the program. In his view, the Council was to operate in detached fashion, giving the President technical advice.

Keyserling and, to a lesser extent, Clark did not embrace Nourse's view and soon made it clear that they did not see anything improper in the Council's active participation in the President's program, nor was Keyserling, unlike Nourse, opposed to testifying before Congress. Keyserling stated his philosophy thus:

> It is clear that the members of the Council are employees of and advisers to the President, and that they are not employees of and advisers to the Congress in the same sense. But this does not mean, in my opinion, that the members of the Council cannot or should not testify before, cooperate and consult with, and in a sense give advice to committees of the Congress just as this is done by heads of other agencies in the Executive branch and even other agencies in the Executive Office of the President, such as the National Security Board, who are appointed by the President and confirmed by the Senate under statutes defining their functions and responsibilities, and who are employees of the advisers to the President in the sense that they work under his direction as members of his "official Family" and may, of course, be dismissed by him. . . .
> In addition, it has been the almost universal custom and entirely appropriate for such officials (Cabinet Secretaries) to appear before congressional committees and to make analyses and give advice in the fields in which they operate under statute, even when this has not been preceded by a Presidential message covering the specific matters before the committee. In appearing before committees on the Congress in this role, I cannot see where the Council of Economic Advisers is doing any different or appearing in any different light from what is done by heads of other agencies working in different fields. And I have never seen any valid reason why the members of the Council, in view of the statute under which they operate and the nature of their role, should follow a contrary course or differentiate between themselves and heads of the other agencies to whom I have referred above.[25]

One staff member who was close to the situation holds that Nourse was apt to object to liberal advice as "political," whereas he was, on the other hand, apt to regard conservative advice as entirely within the legitimate purview of his position. Keyserling complained with some justice that Nourse made speeches to "conservative" groups while objecting to Keyserling's similar activities before "liberal" groups. However, Keyserling has also maintained that the differences between Nourse and himself were not on the basis of economic theory and

112

methodology, but in terms of political organization and procedure. Keyserling has said that the differences should have been settled by the President instead of his telling Council members to work things out among themselves.[26] Nourse agrees, but holds that some basic economic differences were present.[27]

Truman wanted his staff to support his programs, especially in public, and it can be argued that it would be impossible for an adviser to disassociate himself from his chief. One can imagine the political capital that the opposition could make of an adviser who refused in public to endorse the President's program! This difference of opinion in the CEA was, of course, widely known and much discussed among economists.

Roy Blough, another CEA member, has considered the problem carefully:

> . . . What the individual in an inconsistent position like that facing the Council may do is to carry on as well as he can, thinking and speaking as independently as possible but being discreet and cautious, never abandoning his standards of integrity by saying what he does not believe to be true. Almost inevitably in the end, the inconsistency of the position will become too clear and he will be obliged either to withdraw from some aspect of his work or resign his position. I have no criticism of any economist who is not willing to put himself into such an inconsistent position, or who, being in it, prefers to retire. That is clearly the most comfortable choice and the most unequivocal position. But unless economists are willing to carry on in the Council under the conditions I have outlined, I doubt if we shall be able to achieve through the Council the various goals we would like to see achieved. Perhaps we should look on Council members as expendable, each carrying forward the work as far as he individually can and then retiring in favor of others who can carry it farther before they, too, drop by the wayside. I suggest that even the institution of the Council itself is expendable and that sooner or later it will be cut down politically to be replaced by some other organization carrying forward the same functions in somewhat different ways.[28]

The basic question is to what degree should the Council restrict itself to broad economic advice? Should the economist give advice that obviously conflicts with political reality? Or should he temper his recommendations in the forge of practicality? Should he present various policy choices and let the President or the Congress (by means of the Joint Economic Committee) decide what is practical? Clearly, what a President needs most from the Council is *professional economic advice,* not political counsel. But an economist who gives impracticable advice would certainly not succeed as an adviser. Thus, the economist who wants his counsel to prevail must be a *political* economist. As the Council was without precedents, each man who served was forced to formulate his own procedure for meeting these philosophical problems in such a way as to satisfy his personal code of ethics.[29]

This methodological issue was compounded by an organizational matter. Although Nourse was designated chairman, the precise role of the chairman was not clear. What was his authority over the other two members? Obviously, since they were presidential appointees, the chairman could not dismiss them. What did being chairman mean? In the regulatory commissions, for example, the chairman was sometimes elected, and, in some cases, the office rotated year by year. Generally, the chairman was the "executive officer," attending to housekeeping duties; but he had only one vote among his colleagues in making decisions. Nourse never got the President to decide this issue, nor, in fact, did he in all probability get the President even to think seriously about it.

After much delay and some apparent misunderstanding, the President accepted Nourse's resignation. He departed from the Council on November 1, 1949.[30]

Keyserling and Expansionism

The departure of Nourse completed the first phase of the active operation of the Council. The original team had worked together with reasonable harmony and performed extremely useful service for three eventful years, which, in view of the newness of the tasks, was remarkable. The resignation brought about a mild crisis in the affairs of the Council. Nourse's view of its proper conduct had substantial support in the Congress and among economists, especially those in academic life. At the annual meeting of the American Economic Association in December 1949, a session was devoted to an analysis of the administration of the act. The general tone of papers presented was critical of the Council for being too politically oriented. (Nourse says the idea that Truman got rid of him because of his economic views is "laughable; he never bothered about what my views were.")[31]

Nourse's departure focused new attention on an organizational question raised by the Hoover Commission in 1949, when it recommended that the Council be replaced by an office of economic adviser with a single head, thus clarifying the role of the chairman.[32] This problem was to arise later; however, the immediate problem was one of finding a new chairman.

114

Some controversy exists as to Keyserling's candidacy to succeed Nourse. As vice-chairman, Keyserling would be a natural candidate. Although Truman reportedly assured Keyserling that he would be appointed, six months elapsed before this was done. Keyserling was apparently sensitive to the fact that he did not have a Ph.D. in economics, having never written a dissertation. Like many government economists, Keyserling, though he had done graduate work in economics and had had many years of practical experience in Washington agencies, did not possess the badge of the academic economist. During the period of his acting chairmanship, Keyserling had often incurred the displeasure of the conservatives by actively attending Democratic Party functions and, in other words, being "political."

Nourse notes that a list of thirteen names of prominent economists had been compiled by Dr. Steelman, to which he (Nourse) added "three or four" as possible candidates. None of these to whom the post was offered accepted; some declined "pretty brusquely," according to Nourse.[33] Keyserling denies this.

There is no doubt that Keyserling was a bit sensitive about this relationship to the "professional" (mostly academic) economists. Keyserling wrote to the author in this regard:

> Perhaps an important factor in the attitude toward the Truman Council was the attitude of so many of the so-called professional economists toward me, and their state of shock when I was made Vice-Chairman of the original Council in 1946, and Chairman later on. Prior to 1933, I had majored in economics as an undergraduate at Columbia, returned there for two years of graduate economics study after graduating from law school, served in the Economics Department there, and participated in the writing of an economics text. From 1933 to 1946, I had been more creatively and actively engaged in the forging and administration of important national economic policies and programs than any other economist, in addition to speaking and writing very widely on these subjects. Despite all this, the general viewpoint among the so-called professional economists was that I was unqualified for CEA membership because I had not completed the essay requirements for a Ph.D.! If, instead of coming to Washington in 1933, I had completed these requirements, taught a course or two during these years, and written a few of the entirely useless (for practical purposes) types of econometric articles which usually appear in the *American Economic Review*, the so-called professionals would have deemed me entirely qualified.

115

I must state categorically, although I will not labor the point nor attempt to prove it, that the various stories, to the effect that I was made Chairman of the Council only after search for and offers to others, is another pure canard. President Truman promised me that he would appoint me Chairman almost as soon as the vacancy occurred, and he was not one to break his word. That some conservative members of the Cabinet were able to achieve some delay does not negate this. In any event, it would have been more fruitful if the discussion of who should have succeeded Dr. Nourse had been on the merits rather than the subject of the gossip and prejudice set forth above. On the merits, both of my work in other categories and my work as Vice-Chairman entitled me to be Chairman, and my record as Chairman vindicated the designation.[34]

Keyserling took over formally May 10, 1950, as chairman. Professor Roy Blough of the University of Chicago assumed duties as the third member.[35] As he took over the helm, Keyserling was able to look back with some satisfaction. While not a member of the White House inner circle, his relationship with the President was satisfactory. Within the CEA, his subordinates generally agreed with and supported his views. The spring of 1950 saw the economy in good balance. Inflation was no longer a problem. Aggregate demand remained strong and the postwar readjustment had been achieved without serious dislocations. Cold-war pressures had dictated an expansion of military spending. Thus began an active period. Keyserling, who had been a disciple of Rexford Tugwell in his student days, was a born expansionist. The new chairman at forty-two was twenty-one years younger than Nourse and a dedicated New Dealer, deeply involved in social problems.[36]

He immediately became operative on many fronts. Keyserling had numerous Washington contacts and he hastened to make use of them. Under Keyserling's aggressive leadership, the Council took a part in the argument over direct controls after the onset of the Korean War, and much of 1950 and 1951 was spent on this issue. The Council took an active part, along with the Office of Defense Management, in preparation for the Korean War and in the struggle toward stabilization of the economy under wartime conditions. All this activity was in addition to its regular workload.

The Council was much involved in the national debate over price and production controls. It was quick to move into the unoccupied territory of stabilization and remained there until the mobilization agencies were able to establish their own expertise. The stabilization agencies, functioning much like their World War II counterparts, were temporary agencies, headed by nonprofessionals performing duties that were largely entrusted to the Council by later Presidents.

One has the impression that so long as things moved smoothly Truman had little interest in what CEA did or did not do, vis-à-vis other agencies or within its own house. Generally, Keyserling had a free hand so far as the White House was concerned.

The Council played a part in the famous accord between the Treasury and the Federal Reserve Board, an issue which merits some attention. The financial burden of the Korean mobilization effort had reopened the long-smouldering dispute between the Treasury and the Federal Reserve Board. At issue, essentially, was whether the Federal Reserve Board would continue to support the government bond market at the expense of what it viewed as its freedom to pursue an active monetary policy. The Treasury, supported by Truman and the Council, took the view that the Board should do so.[37]

In mid-1950 the Board withdrew support from certain Treasury issues, which brought the conflict into the open. Truman was strongly supported by Secretary of the Treasury Snyder and by both Keyserling and Clark on the Council.

When, in late December 1950, the Federal Reserve Board announced that reserve requirements would be increased in January and February, the conflict between the Treasury and the Board became a major public issue. Treasury bills had increased from 1.09 percent in January to 1.38 percent by the end of the year (1950). Yield on nine- to twelve-month issues averaged 1.44 percent in the fourth quarter of 1950, as compared to 1.09 percent for the corresponding quarter of 1949, and open-market rates had likewise increased.[38]

At this point, the President met with the Open Market Committee, argued the administration viewpoint, and subsequently issued a press release indicating that the issue had been resolved to his satisfaction.[39] Unfortunately, the Board took a different view, and Marriner Eccles, the veteran member, released to the press his view of the meeting, which conflicted sharply with that of Mr. Truman, maintaining that no such commitment had been made.[40]

The Council was concerned about this issue, having mentioned some months earlier the need for eliminating uncertainty, saying, "The consequence of leaving the issues in suspense will be most dangerous."[41] It is an interesting exercise in bureaucratic byplay that Blough, as a newcomer to the Council (and one who had not associated himself with the Keyserling-Clark position) played an unofficial role in the settlement,

117

along with William McC. Martin, Assistant Secretary of the Treasury. Though he had served in Treasury, Blough was more acceptable to the Fed than either Keyserling or Clark, who had gone on record as being critical of the Board. Thus, although the Council had no direct role in the accord, it was able through force of personality to play an important part. Edward S. Flash notes that Keyserling was upset by the exclusion of the Council, since he regarded the dispute as a matter of economic policy upon which he should have been formally consulted.[42] This incident is typical of Keyserling's general approach, namely, that there were few, if any, economic policy incidents from which CEA should be excluded.

The Council and the Korean War

Keyserling's activist orientation was again evident in the mobilization decisions as the Korean War progressed, and the President established a number of World War II type agencies to deal with prices and production. Always the interventionist, he attempted to break into the policy-making process via the Office of Defense Mobilization. He also tried to have the Council designated as economic adviser to the Office of Defense Management as it had been to the National Security Resources Board before the Chinese intervention in Korea.[43] In addition, he attended staff meetings as Council representative and in other ways tried to project CEA into the situation.

In the Economic Report of January 1951 and in a special report to the President, Keyserling warned of inflationary pressure. However, as the military situation in Korea reached a stalemate and as domestic measures became effective, pressure on prices relaxed and it became administration policy to stretch out the mobilization program.

Keyserling objected to this tactic, since he felt that too much emphasis on the control of inflation would be used as a rationale to reduce spending and thus to limit growth. However, the President had multiple noneconomic factors to consider and, likewise, many advisers to listen to. A combination of calculated military risks and budgetary and debt considerations made it inevitable that the Council would lose influence. Under these circumstances and as the newly dominant agencies acquired their own economic staff resources, the Council lost touch with day-to-day mobilization affairs. As they acquired staff, ODM, Office of Price Stabilization (OPS), and the Economic Stabilization Agency became less dependent on the Council, with ODM taking over the area of

118

mobilization policy, which Keyserling had coveted. This was clearly the President's intention; in mobilization matters ODM had the President's ear.

Throughout his tenure, Keyserling had espoused the doctrine of expansionist economics, but this time his stock-in-trade was not very salable. As a basis for his "Fair Deal," Truman applauded this orientation but was unable to follow beyond a point, and the point was much closer than liberals had hoped. David Bell has noted that "The President let Nourse go and promoted Keyserling because Keyserling fitted better the economic tone the President wanted for his Administration. A five-percent annual increase in GMP would not have been a natural way for Mr. Truman to have described his objective, but what Keyserling was driving at appealed to his understanding, convictions, and hopes for the nation."[44] This was the general view, but when other factors became more important the Keyserling theme had to be played in a minor key.

The Council's performance during the mobilization period cannot be viewed as entirely satisfactory. Yet its failure was integral with that of the entire administration, which was, in turn, due to the fluidity of the situation and the diffusion of authority. On the eve of the war, the Council had enjoyed a large measure of prestige. It had, in the period of partial mobilization, shifted successfully from its role as setter of economic sights to an active posture central to the stabilization effort. During this period a "twilight zone" condition between "police action" and war existed in Korea. The mobilization agencies and the Economic Stabilization Agency had not yet got under way. As a small and flexible agency, CEA had, almost on a free-lance basis, rushed into the breech early in the war and exercised a positive role. Keyserling had warned that forward planning must be done; yet, when the Chinese intervention in Korea (November 26, 1950) plunged the Administration into confusion, CEA was part of the confusion.

The emphasis upon expansion was a major factor in extending the Council's influence into other agencies and facets of governmental policy. However, it seems clear that the rise (and subsequent fall) in the Council's fortunes under Keyserling was, in part, an accident of time. The theme of expansionist economics as played by the Keyserling trio was short lived. Truman was essentially a fiscal conservative and as an adjunct to the Fair Deal he accepted the CEA view of expansionist economics, but in the long run was unwilling to give it free rein, especially in the face of other complex domestic and international problems. Unlike the Roosevelt Administration, which before 1940 was concerned almost solely with economic matters, the Truman years were dominated

119

by international political issues. Domestic economic problems were chronic but not critical.

The stabilization issue was squarely faced by the administration. While the President was able with some justice to castigate the Republican 80th Congress for failing to enact meaningful controls, he, a supreme political realist, certainly never expected anything else. His characterization of the "do-nothing 80th Congress" and the "terrible Capehart Amendment" were good for political mileage but for little else.[45]

Facing problems of reconversion from a major war and within a short period remobilization for another war of uncertain dimensions and duration, the economic problems of the Truman years were immense and, under the circumstances, well handled.

It is not apparent that the Council made any great progress in coordinating economic policy, and, as in the Roosevelt era, policy seems to have been formulated on an ad hoc basis. The Fair Deal never approached the New Deal in scope of economic innovation.

Truman Economics

Truman was a man of mature years when he reached the Presidency. Like many of his generation, he bore the personal scars of the Depression. He entered the Senate in 1935 at the peak of New Deal influence. He had unbounded admiration for Roosevelt, Senator George Norris, Wagner, and the movers and shakers of the early New Deal period. His natural habitat was the Senate. Projected into a position of leadership at the most difficult time imaginable, he found the Employment Act awaiting implementation. Nourse was inclined to move cautiously and to adopt a view of scientific detachment that Truman found difficult to understand. Although he respected Nourse, he was clearly unable to endorse Nourse's view of the Council's role.

Keyserling was an aggressive chairman who headed an agency not yet five years old. Various accounts make it clear that his personality was not one that made him universally liked. He did not hesitate either to articulate his views (one source says that "Keyserling was apt to mount his verbal bicycle and pedal furiously!") or to push the Council into areas of influence.

Not surprisingly, because of his apparent inclination toward expansion and his undoubted attachment to the Fair Deal ideology, he became a figure of controversy, and so, of course, did the Council. Several powerful and conservative members of Congress had never accepted the Council, and they were happy to find a rallying point against it. Few doubted Keyserling's ability as an economist and none his skill as an advocate. His detractors, however, felt that he was expanding the Council into political and policy areas beyond its intended scope.

Keyserling argues very persuasively that, though he was closely connected with early New Deal matters (e.g., the Wagner Act), he was not slavishly devoted to New Deal doctrine per se, and, also, that much of the New Deal policy later looked down upon by economists had a great deal of merit:

> It is also true that I have never abandoned certain characteristics of the New Deal which I believe are enduring. These include the spirit of innovation; the concept that the core economic problem, both economically and socially, is the improved distribution of the national income (unfortunately neglected during more recent years by both economists and Government); the belief in the increased use of the national power in the modern industrial age. . . .
>
> I also continue to adhere to the view, more manifest during the New Deal than later, that people in high public posts should stand for what they believe in and make sacrifices for and then rationalize that position. I think the Heller Council went far too far in that direction, not to speak of later CEA's. I gave substantive demonstration of my adherence to this position when, as Vice-Chairman of the CEA, I urged stronger measures against the 1949 recession than the President was willing to advocate, and at one time I almost lost my job for doing this.[46]

Much credit is due to the senior CEA staff members, such as Colm, Walter Salant, and Benjamin Caplan. With good government contacts and sound professional reputations, they lent much prestige to the Council. Colm, a scholar with very extensive academic contacts, was especially important in the early days. The Keyserling staff was excellent and, by and large, they agreed with his views. As the Truman administration neared its end, the Council, even more than the rest of the dying administration, shared in its loss of influence.

It is instructive to compare the Nourse-Keyserling philosophies. Nourse rejected the view that the Council should play an active part in advocating the Truman program. To what degree this reluctance was based on adherence to a view of his role as adviser or, in part, on his general lack of strong interest in the ultimate aims of the Fair Deal is impossible to say. Keyserling viewed the chairmanship as a vehicle for promoting liberal policies. Perhaps he would have been equally at home or, likely more so, as a presidential assistant or as a U.S. Senator. Nourse, in contrast, was a professional economist and career scholar who did not view himself, as Keyserling seems to have, as part of the administration, taking part in or promoting policy. Perhaps it was inevitable that the Council should have become involved in policies of a broad nature. It may be that Keyserling's fault was that he went too far too fast, given the climate of the times. To what degree the attempt to reduce the CEA budget, which we shall consider shortly, was a result of factors far beyond Keyserling's control (and, given its source, such a prospect is likely) is a matter of dispute; however, Keyserling must bear some blame.[47]

The Truman period can be viewed with great interest since its six-year span represents the pioneer years of the Council and the formative period of formalized economic advice on the presidential level.

Mr. Truman, clearly, was never willing to use the Council beyond a limited degree. Nourse complained frequently that the President did not take sufficient notice of its advice or spend enough time on Council affairs.[48] Keyserling, although involved in many issues, was often upstaged by others, particularly after the Korean War became a major concern. It seems obvious that Truman was never really sold on the merits of the Keyserling expansionist economics and remained a traditionalist in economic matters. In the end, Keyserling disturbed the uneasy peace between the Council and the conservative element of the Congress by his insistence on the expansionist theme.

It seems likely, after more than two decades of observation of the Council under several chairmen, that both Nourse and Keyserling were, in a sense, victims of rigidity. Each took extreme positions, and neither would make basic alterations in his mode of operation. It must, of course, be kept in mind that no precedent existed. The incoming Republican chairman, Arthur F. Burns, was able to chart a course somewhere between their positions and emerge successfully.

A major element of successful advisership is clearly rapport between the adviser and advisee. All evidence suggests that Nourse was never able to achieve an easy relationship with Truman.[49] It is likely that Nourse was at a disadvantage as to age and the fact that he had a firm reputation built on a long career when he came to the Council. Most importantly, he began a new and demanding line of work, the outlines of which were ill defined. Nourse also suffered from the fact that not only Keyserling, but Clark, was often in basic disagreement as to procedure. Yet Nourse made a major and long-lasting contribution in establishing procedures and techniques.

Despite all the problems, one is reminded of the talking horse; it is not so much what it says but the fact that it can talk at all that is remarkable.

The Truman-Nourse-Keyserling Council survived, which was remarkable. The precedent for formal economic advice was established and survived a very eventful six years.

Let us pause briefly and recall what had taken place. By the end of the Truman years the Council had become an operating body. Nourse, the first Chairman, had taken a view detached from the political goals of the Administration. Keyserling, his successor, had operated the Council in an aggressive fashion. A combination of Keyserling's personality, the Korean War, distrust of the Council among conservatives, and other factors had brought it into controversy. These events took place as the Democratic era of two decades came to a close, and an apparently conservative Republican administration came into office. Thus, the future of the Council was in some doubt.

The central thrust of the Truman years was not domestic policy but foreign affairs. As the early months of the administration were dominated by the closing scenes of World War II, the last days were occupied with Korea.

Economic policy in 1945–46 was concerned with the problems of reconversion to peacetime and with the issue of stable prices. The early reports of the Council dealt largely with these immediately pressing issues. These issues were central to the goal of maintaining a $200 billion economy. The years 1948–49 were dominated by a desire to control inflation, and the reports dwelt on these matters at length.

By early 1950 the administration, under less immediate pressure, had become more willing or able to focus on long-range problems, and considerable space was devoted to what was referred to as "a unified national economic policy." As described in the 1950 report:

> There is no previous experience with an economy of the size
> that ours has now reached, from which there may be drawn any
> firm rule as to the proportion of the national income which may
> safely in the long run be channeled back into the economic
> stream through the Government. But the Council's whole ap-
> proach focuses upon the objective of economic expansion
> through the enlarging activity of consumers and of business, and
> this means that Federal expenditures should be held as low as
> the requirements of programs essential to national growth and
> welfare will permit.
>
> Because so large a proportion of present Government pro-
> grams is devoted to purposes which, while essential to national
> security and world political stability, make little direct contribu-
> tion to increased standards of living, we wish to emphasize the
> desirability of working toward lower levels of expenditures as

rapidly as international conditions permit. We also wish to emphasize the importance of constant vigilance against the dangers of waste and inefficiency everywhere and at all times. Measures of economy, however, must not be so distorted in application as to involve the sacrifice of essential objectives.[50]

With little opportunity to formulate a program, and with only modest personal background in economic affairs, Truman faced major economic problems, but they were often overshadowed by the immediacy of international matters.

Truman's great weakness in matters of economic policy was that he failed to generate new ideas. His program was a replay of the New Deal. Domestic economic problems, though troublesome, were not critical. Employment and income remained high.

Professor Calvin B. Hoover has written of the period:

> In summary, under the Truman Administration the New Deal economic legislation which had been initiated by President Roosevelt and which was partially in abeyance during World War II gave evidence of having become an integral part of the American economic system. The process of price and wage determination in industry had become one involving large corporations and large labor unions. It could no longer be considered substantially an approximation of the purely and perfectly competitive process assumed as characteristic of laissez-faire capitalism.
>
> It had been assumed that full employment would automatically exist in a purely and perfectly competitive laissez-faire economy, but under the changed character of the economy this no longer could be taken for granted.[51]

Unlike his predecessor, Truman did not use his advisers to innovate boldly. No period comparable to the "hundred days" occurred in the Truman years. Some of the New Deal figures were still present, but they were no longer active. No one trained in economics was in the Truman White House as adviser in such matters. Keyserling was a man of force and imagination, but his relationship with some elements of the Congress was strained, and he was often isolated in the Council. Some commendable policy programs, such as the Brannan Plan (on agricultural price supports), were lost in the Congress. No doubt, neither the Congress nor the people would have viewed a vast array of socioeconomic legislation with great favor.

The Truman Administration was the bridge between information advice from many varied and different sources and the structure of formal advice provided by the Employment Act of 1946. Though President Truman administered the act for more than six years, his mode of operation and his philosophy belong more to the pre-1946 period.

Can one really doubt that he looked upon CEA for the most part as an organ of the administration and its policies rather than as a viable source of information and advice? What would he have done if the Council had recommended policies completely different from those that he had in his own mind? Truman was a strong-minded man; as Nourse says, he used CEA as a "dignified front" for his policies. The President respected Dr. Nourse, but Nourse was not part of the "team," and the team played the game according to Truman rules. Keyserling was on the team (second string), but his wearing—indeed, flaunting—of the Fair Deal colors made him suspect to the opposition and the neutrals. Whatever Keyserling's merits, and they were many, it is also clear that many in the Congress and in the press did feel that he was "too political" to maintain his credibility as an adviser. In short, Truman viewed the Council much as Roosevelt would have done—nice to have around, lending a patina of disinterested "science," but of no real value in a political and operational sense.

This can be said without subtracting from Truman's stature. He was faced with a new agency with which no one was familiar. His time and interest were limited. Many of his comments, especially to Nourse, indicate that he had only the most casual interest in it. The substantial prestige held by the Council a quarter century later was not, of course, then in existence. Neither the Congress nor the executive branch was completely sold on its virtues. Thus, at this stage, economic policy making was still largely without central direction or coordination. The old-line system had changed very little from its prewar pattern.

Notes

Chapter 4

[1] Stephen Kemp Bailey, *Congress Makes a Law* (New York: Columbia University Press, 1950), p. 1. The ideas of Keynes are difficult to separate from those of other interested economists: "The point is that Roosevelt and his advisors were likely to have been influenced by pre-Keynesian economists and perhaps even by Keynes himself, although the latter is not as willingly conceded here as elsewhere." Reprinted by permission of J. Ronnie Davis, ©1971, *The New Economics and the Old Economists* (Ames, Iowa State University Press), pp. 152-53.

[2] See "Economic Progress and Declining Population Growth," *American Economic Review* (March 1939), Vol. 29.

[3] *An Economic Program for American Democracy* (New York: Vanguard 1933). Seven Harvard and Tuft's economists: Richard V. Gilbert, George H. Hildebrand, Jr., Arthur W.

Stuart, Maxine Y. Sweezy, Paul M. Sweezy, Lorie Tarshis, and John D. Wilson.

4 Bailey, op. cit., p. 25. See also, Grover Ensley, "A Budget for the Nation," *Social Research* (Sept., 1943), Vol. 10, No. 3, pp. 280ff.

5 Bailey, op. cit., p. 37.

6 Public Law, 304, 79th Congress (1946).

7 Steelman had obtained a Ph.D. in economics from the University of North Carolina and taught briefly at the Women's College of Alabama in the early 1930s. In 1934, he met Frances Perkins and accepted a job in the Labor Department. Remaining there until the late 1940s and after a short tenure as a consultant, he entered the White House to assist on labor matters of which the new Secretary of Labor Schwellenbach knew little. Steelman remained there until the end of the administration. Most accounts agree that he was extremely aware of his position and careful to eliminate serious competition. David Stowe, his assistant, was a former North Carolina school teacher. Truman's staff was a very mixed bag with some old Missouri pals, a few Roosevelt holdovers, and some top-drawer professionals. Clark Clifford probably emerged as the most skilled and successful. A good view of Truman's attitude with regard to economists and intellectuals in general appears in Paul H. Douglas' *In the Fullness of Time* (New York: Harcourt Brace Jovanovich, 1972), pp. 222ff.

8 See Jonathan Daniels, *Man of Independence* (Philadelphia: Lippincott, 1950). Pendergast had been instrumental in Truman's election, but no one ever questioned Truman's honesty, though many had doubts about Pendergast. Truman was a Senator's Senator. He shunned the limelight, spoke rarely, and worked hard on his committee assignments. These qualities plus his friendly personal manner made him an "insider" in a short time, and his work on the wartime investigating committee was later to make him a national figure.

9 Ibid., pp. 186–87.

10 Much has been made of the sudden death of FDR and the elevation of Truman, yet Truman had told several friends that FDR would not last too long and he dreaded being in the White House. Though shocked at Roosevelt's death, he was hardly as surprised as press accounts indicated.

11 Bailey, op. cit., p. 161.

12 *Congressional Record,* 79th Congress, 1st Session, December 14, 1945, p. 12267.

13 Bailey, op. cit., p. 235.

14 Ibid., p. 237.

15 Harry S Truman, *Year of Decisions,* p. 545.

16 Leon H. Keyserling, "The Wagner Act: Its Origin and Current Significance," *George Washington Law Review,* Vol. 29, (December 1960), p. 199ff.

17 Letter to the author from David E. Bell, November 25, 1969.

18 The full story of these early days is recounted in detail in Edwin G. Nourse, *Economics in the Public Service* (New York: Harcourt Brace, 1953).

19 A word about this Pabst essay contest is of interest since it relates to postwar planning. Of the 17 winners, 8 were government economists (in 1943). These were Herbert Stein, who served on CEA in the Nixon years (1st prize, $25,000); Leon H. Keyserling, Grover Ensley, Mordecai Ezekiel, Joseph M. Gillman, Leo Grebler, Everett M. Hagen, Albert G. Hart, and John H. G. Pierson. These essays, published by the Pabst Brewing Company, make very interesting reading. See also, "The Keynesians and Government Policy, 1933–1939," *American Economic Review, Proceedings,* May 1972, pp. 116ff.

20 *The Winning Plans in the Pabst Postwar Employment Awards* (Pabst Brewing Company, No Date), p. 11. This publication contains all the seventeen essays and brief biographical sketches of the winners.

21 *Federal Economic Policy* (Washington: Congressional Quarterly Service, 3rd Edition, 1968), p. 37.

22 In 1952 the midyear report was issued for the last time.

23 Nourse, op. cit., p. 280.

[24] Ibid., pp. 393–94.

[25] *Monetary Policy and the Management of the Public Debt.* Hearings before the Subcommittee on General Credit Control and Debt Management, 82nd Congress, 2d Session, March, 1952.

[26] Personal interview, 1968.

[27] Personal interview, 1968.

[28] Roy Blough, "Political and Administrative Requisites for Achieving Economic Stability," *American Economic Review,* Vol. 40, No. 2 (May 1950), pp. 177–78. See also, Roy Blough, *The Role of the Economist in Federal Policy Making* (Urbana: Institute of Government and Public Affairs, University of Illinois Bulletin No. 28, Vol. 51, 1953).

[29] Seymour Harris, "The Gap Between Economists and Politicians," *New York Times Magazine,* April 14, 1965.

[30] Nourse had submitted his first resignation on December 15, 1948, after the Truman victory of that year. No direct reply was made, and he resigned again on August 9, 1949. This letter brought some discussion as to a replacement, but no real action and a final resignation was submitted September 9, which became effective November 1, 1949. One cannot read Nourse's account of the incident without forming the opinion that Truman was guilty of failure to face the issue squarely, since in the end, the matter was dealt with by Steelman. Nourse, op. cit., p. 272ff.

[31] Letter to the author, December 23, 1969.

[32] Commission on Organization of the Executive Branch of Government (Hoover Commission), *General Management of the Executive Branch* (1949), p. 17.

[33] Nourse, op. cit., p. 286.

[34] Letter to the author, June 10, 1971.

[35] After much discussion, the author has concluded that Keyserling is correct in saying that no serious consideration was given to an outsider. No doubt Truman did feel constrained to consider opposing views and one cannot escape the feeling also that Truman really cared little about the matter. His relationship with CEA had been minimal. One can imagine that he might have told Steelman, "If Leon wants the job, go ahead."

[36] His post-council career has made this clear. After leaving the Council in 1952, Keyserling became a practicing lawyer and a consulting economist in Washington, and, later, founder and Chairman of the Conference on Economic Progress, remaining active as a commentator on CEA affairs. He has written countless monographs, published widely and testified frequently before the Congress.

[37] This issue is thoroughly discussed in the monumental study by the Joint Committee (then the Joint Committee on the Economic Report), *Monetary Policy and the Management of the Public Debt* (Washington: U.S. Government Printing Office, 1952).

[38] *Economic Report of the President,* January, 1951, p. 142.

[39] Truman, *Memoirs,* op. cit., p. 62. See also, Eccles, *Beckoning Frontiers,* Chapter 6.

[40] *Monetary Policy and the Management of the Public Debt.* U.S. Congress, Joint Committee on the Economic Report, 72d Congress, 2d Session, Doc. No. 123, Part 2, 816.

[41] Ibid.

[42] Flash, op. cit., p. 49.

[43] *Hearings* on the Independent Offices Appropriations Bill for Fiscal Year 1952, 72nd Congress, 1st Session, pp. 90–91, U.S. Congress, Senate Committee on Appropriations.

[44] Flash, op. cit., p. 96.

[45] The "Capehart Amendment" to the Defense Production Act of 1951 allowed manufacturers to include in their ceiling prices all cost increases since the start of the Korean War. This in the President's opinion was a major weakness. Senator Capehart was a conservative Indiana manufacturer of musical systems and radios. He and Truman had been (and continued to be) close friends.

[46] Letter to the author, June 10, 1971.

[47] Many of those interviewed by the author pointed out that both factors were at work, i.e., a residue of distrust of such agencies was present. Yet as one observer noted, the

Democrats were in control of Congress, and the Republicans who instigated the move were obviously able to obtain Democratic support for their views. Consequently, they tended to assign a sizable share of the blame to Keyserling.

[48] Nourse says, "The President continued to make protestations as to the value of the Agency. But it seemed to me that he valued it only as a dignified 'front' for his policies. As soon as we ventured to challenge any of them, he retreated behind his Presidential prerogative and 'put us in our place.' "

[49] Personal factors were no doubt of major importance; for example, many close observers have commented on the fact that Kennedy and Heller were able to achieve a close personal relationship, sharing many personal characteristics. Neither Keyserling nor, even more so, Nourse, was a type to fit closely into the group of Truman cronies of those years. See the statement "Professional Background of the First Chairman of the Council of Economic Advisers," which Nourse prepared for deposit in the Harry S. Truman Memorial Library, pp. 15ff, for some background of the appointment.

[50] *Economic Report of the President*, 1947.

[51] Calvin B. Hoover, *The Economy, Liberty and the State* (New York: Twentieth Century Fund, 1959), p. 244.

Part II

THE
COUNCIL
OF ECONOMIC
ADVISERS
1952–76

Chapter 5

Eisenhower and Modern Republicanism

Arthur, my boy, you'd have made a fine
chief of staff overseas during the war.
　　　　　—Dwight D. Eisenhower

Dwight D. Eisenhower assumed office in January 1953. He had spent his entire career as an officer in the United States Army except for a brief, and professionally meaningless, period as the president of Columbia University. It seems fair to say that his economic philosophy, if any, was largely a matter of conjecture. The Republican Party, taking office after an interlude of twenty years, was—on the surface at least—dedicated to a reversal of many New Deal-Fair Deal economic policies.

The Modern Republicans

The Republicans and their candidate in 1952 were in an ambivalent position. Long out of power, they had been critical of the economic policies of the Roosevelt-Truman years. The more extreme elements of the party were wont to refer to "creeping socialism" and to stress the more unorthodox and wasteful aspects of the New Deal-Fair Deal as being typical of Democratic rule. On the other hand, it was clear that a program vowing to eliminate Social Security, the Wagner Act, and other welfare or reform elements of the Roosevelt-

131

Truman era had limited appeal. Alfred M. Landon in 1936, Wendell Wilkie in 1940, and Thomas E. Dewey in 1944 and 1948 had all faced the problem of attacking the methods of the New Deal-Fair Deal without implying that the social reforms would be undone if they took office.[1] All these candidates were generally more liberal than the party's "old guard" and, as a consequence, had some difficulty in securing the nomination. Neither of the two candidates since 1936 had been completely able to bridge the gap between the old guard and the electorate. In 1952, Eisenhower was accepted reluctantly by the conservatives, whose hearts belonged to Robert A. Taft, Senator from Ohio and "Mr. Republican." In his economic policy, Taft was far from being an old guardsman, but he was a regular Republican and acceptable to the old-line party leaders. As a popular wartime commander, Eisenhower was a political windfall, but his views on economic and social questions were not known.[2]

The younger, "modern" Republicans (e.g., Henry Cabot Lodge, Jr.) were Eisenhower's first supporters. They recognized that the economic clock was not to be turned back and thus generally endorsed the social reforms of the Democratic years. Some even accepted such unorthodox ideas as an unbalanced budget, at which Republicans had raged for two decades though, as we shall see, this was to prove a two-edged sword.

Perhaps typical of Eisenhower's views at this stage was an incident reported by Arthur Krock. Eisenhower had met informally in 1947 with a group of influential Republicans, including Taft and Senator Vandenberg. The discussion turned to the problem of inflation.

> [Eisenhower] The only group in a position to make sacrifices, and make them quickly and effectively, is industry. Labor is "political, and so is politics, which I don't know anything about and don't want to." Congenital in these latter groups are delay, compromise, and inaction on a spiky issue like inflation. So why should not someone—for instance, Benjamin Fairless, President of the United States Steel Corporation, announce prices, taking the risk of forgoing profits, saying, "You will put us in the red if you want to, and you can ruin us"; and urge other industries to emulate? Then, said Eisenhower, a wonderful example would be set for labor, and politicians, and the general public that would strike effectively at the spiral of inflation.
>
> The Senators were not impressed. And except for Martin [Pennsylvania], they began to needle the General, sometimes humorously. . . .
>
> But Taft's needling was wholly serious. "Oh, it's not that

simple," he said; the farmers would not go along with the sacrifice idea, and inflation could not be effectively attacked without their cooperation. Bridges wisely commented that only by Presidential leadership could inflation be effectively restrained, and with this the Republican Senators agreed. The conversation also made it clear that the Pennsylvania businessmen and politicians present, except Governor Duff, were hostile to Eisenhower's basic suggestion and thoroughly approved the heckling to which he was being subjected.[3]

Eisenhower as a candidate benefited, no doubt, from his economic illiteracy and the fact that he had no record of having taken stands on this or that issue that could be used to embarrass him in the future. Relatively little was said about economic issues in the campaign (the emotional issues were Korea and the Nixon "fund"). Gabriel Hauge was recruited from the McGraw-Hill Publishing Company by Herbert Brownell to serve as economic speech writer. Hauge was a professional economist with a Harvard Ph.D. who understood modern economics and was able to put the Eisenhower view into writing.[4]

Though he had never been in business nor earned a living in the profit-making world, Eisenhower was apparently impressed by and enjoyed the company of successful businessmen. One might speculate that the career of a professional soldier, at least that of field commander, is one which would be least likely to demand the articulation of a comprehensive economic philosophy. While he was completely unacquainted with the practical side of business or economic issues, as a candidate of the Republican party, he was in general interested in a reversal of the interventionist economics of the Roosevelt-Truman era. It was expected generally that he would follow a conservative line. The fact that his ultimate record was reasonably liberal is a tribute to both the "modern" Republicans and to the professional skill of the Council of Economic Advisers. Many critics have faulted Eisenhower for being too detached and isolated by his staff. There were doubtless instances, especially in domestic affairs, where his detachment constituted a serious problem. Secretary of the Treasury George M. Humphrey as a prominent businessman had been tagged at an early date as the strong man of the Cabinet, and he had a grasp of financial affairs.[5] To some degree, his conservative strength was counterbalanced by Hauge in the White House and Arthur F. Burns in the Council, both highly capable men, more liberal than Humphrey. Despite his regard for Humphrey, his dependence upon the professionals, and his extensive social contacts with industry leaders, one gets the impression that Eisenhower generally had somewhat more progressive economic ideas than those that managed to filter out through the staff.[6] Perhaps one of the shortcomings of the staff system is that professionals tend to take over and amateur ideas have little currency. Eisenhower pretended no knowledge of economic matters and was often at his worst when commenting on them "off the cuff." He made the observation that the reason people voted for him was his knowledge of military affairs, which, in the cold-war era, the electorate viewed as essential to the office.

But the issue cuts deeper. The administration was not just the captive of the staff system; it was also the captive of the facts of economic life in the latter half of the twentieth century and of the two previous decades of policy making. Too many things had been done that were not to be undone; the impact on the economy of a quarter century of Depression and global war was not to be ignored. Secretary Benson, for example, made manful but fruitless attempts to recast the national agricultural policy, while Secretary of the Treasury Humphrey attempted, with little more success, to get the Treasury on a paying basis. As Budget Director Joseph M. Dodge had warned, budget cutting was not as easy as it looked from outside. The Eisenhower team went through a painful but educational experience. By various means, the Truman budget was cut by $8.5 billion. Eisenhower, the Republican leader and savior of the nation from "creeping socialism," was never able to completely carry out his avowed program because of the responsibilities faced by Eisenhower, President of the United States. He walked the endless tightrope between the extreme and the moderate, the right-wing old guard and the liberal-independent groups, constantly attempting to placate one at the expense of the other. Sherman Adams gives the following account of a revealing incident in *Firsthand Report.*

Taft's violent and most embarrassing attack on Eisenhower occurred when the President, with Secretary of the Treasury George M. Humphrey and Budget Director Joseph M. Dodge, met with the Republican leaders in Congress on April 30, 1953, to break the bad news that the new Administration would not be able to balance the first budget, as Taft and his cohorts had expected.

Taft heard the President out in grim silence and listened impatiently to further explanations from Dodge and Roger Kyes, who was then Deputy Secretary of Defense. Then Taft exploded, losing control of himself, pounding his fist on the Cabinet table and shouting at the stunned President, who was sitting opposite him.

"With a program like this, we'll never elect a Republican

134

Congress in 1954," he shouted. "You're taking us down the same road Truman traveled. It's a repudiation of everything we promised in the campaign!"[7]

Later, Taft passed the incident off, but it illustrates Eisenhower's task of trying to mesh traditional conservative demands with modern-day Presidential responsibilities. Taft was never really satisfied with this performance, but by this time his illness was well advanced, and he died several months later.

For the most part, so long as the administration worked through the Council of Economic Advisers and the immediate White House staff, its economic policies made practical sense, but occasionally it took on the patina of nineteenth-century conservatism.

Several interesting aspects of the Eisenhower approach to the Presidency deserve mention. The President was not a politician in the usual sense. He had never held public office, and he delegated "political" chores to others, mostly to Vice-President Richard Nixon and Sherman Adams. Like many who come late into politics, Eisenhower refused to recognize that almost every institution is "political" in a sense. No one, for example, had a better grasp of "army politics" than he. He was devoted to the staff system and viewed it as a means of allowing himself to concentrate on the "major issues." Domestic economic matters were generally among those delegated to Humphrey, to the Council, or to the White House "economic legman," Hauge.

The early days of the administration were watched with more than usual interest. If the administration were to follow the traditional Republican line, it might be expected that it would attempt to reduce federal spending, balance the budget (a goal close to the heart of the new Secretary of the Treasury), reduce the scope of federal planning, cut taxes, and, in other ways, reverse the "drift toward socialism," for which the Democrats had so long been taken to task. There was an understandable desire to "liberate" the economy and remove controls. This was done, but taxes were to prove another matter.

Trouble from the Hill

One of the first issues to face the new President was the future role of the Council of Economic Advisers. As we have seen, some elements in Congress, even those friendly to its creation, had begun to take a dim view of its mode of operation and philosophy in the last days of the Truman Administration. Some observers have indicated that it was mainly congressional antipathy to Keyserling's activist

135

policies that led to the crisis that we must now consider.

In some congressional quarters, opinion as to the value of the Council had been lukewarm at best. The more conservative elements, especially in the House, had been mildly critical from the first, and the professional economizers looked upon the Council as an organization of limited usefulness compared to its cost, even though the cost was modest (about $500,000 per year).

This incident, like that concerning Keyserling's appointment, is surrounded with controversy. Keyserling cites considerable evidence, both in personal correspondence and in public print, that he had good and often warm relationships with numerous key Senators and Congressmen. In a letter to the editor of the *Journal of Commerce* in 1968, he recounted the highlights of the move to cut CEA's budget:

> . . . Late one afternoon on the House floor, with most members absent and with no roll-call vote, there was an "economy" flurry, and a number of agencies were cut drastically, including not only the Council but also the Labor Department and a number of others. The MC who proposed the CEA cut was not even a member of the Joint Economic Committee which deals with CEA work.
>
> Although [others] argued, they were not successful in restoring their cuts in full. I was successful in having the Council cut restored in full and without difficulty. Those who helped me most on the Senate side were Senators Taft, Saltonstall, Ellender, and Maybank, all of whom were conservatives, two of whom were Republicans, and three of whom were on the Senate subcommittee dealing with this appropriation. The person who helped me most on the House side was Congressman Albert Thomas, chairman of the House Appropriations Subcommittee and a conservative Southern Democrat.
>
> The method chosen to help us was unusual and sprung from the fertile brain of Senator O'Mahoney. He suggested that, in view of the "Economy" drive, and the lack of success on the part of other agencies which had been cut, the Council should be permitted to spend the fiscal 1953 reduced appropriation in nine months rather than twelve. This was agreed to without any significant opposition anywhere. It had precisely the effect of permitting us to spend at the originally asked for rate and not to have to reduce our activities in any way as the amount allotted was authorized to be spent from July 1, 1952, to March 31, 1953. I did not regard this as a very good way to accomplish the result.

But it was clear that there would be a new President, a new

Administration, and a new council come January, 1953, and it would then be their responsibility to take care of themselves and they would have a period of three months grace in which to do so. If the Congress had had any disposition to move against me, they would not have taken action which deliberately helped me to continue full speed ahead and which would pose a problem only a couple of months after it was certain that I would no longer be in the job. That is not how the Congress vents its displeasure. I know of no other occasion when the Congress helped any other agency in this manner to avoid entirely the consequences of a cut engineered by a small minority under the conditions of confusion as I have described them above.[8]

To be sure, in the latter days of any outgoing administration, the Congress is apt to attempt to eliminate or reduce the scope of any programs of which it disapproves and which lack broad popular support. In this instance, the Council was included among various agencies in a move to reduce expenditures.

Fortunately, this attitude was not universal, and by legislative strategy those Senators who were favorable toward the Council managed to overcome a move to reduce its operating budget by 25 percent. This was done, as Keyserling notes, by applying the full sum to three quarters of the year, thus enabling the Council to operate at full capacity that long, but creating a serious problem for the incoming administration, the views of which were apparently unknown (no one in authority took pains to make them known directly; Hauge tried, but he was not a line official, merely an adviser).

The status of the Council was thus unclear when the new administration opened for business. At best, the Eisenhower Administration was not expected to be sympathetic to the general idea of the Council, and the economy-minded chairman of the House Appropriations Committee, Representative John Taber of New York (long a foe of the Employment Act), refused a request for $75,000 to provide funds to the end of the fiscal year. He was supported by John Phillips of California, who was determined that CEA must go. Apparently, Taber did feel that Eisenhower was either intending to end the Council or that he would be indifferent to the matter. How much blame must rest on Keyserling is difficult to say. No doubt, many conservative Congressmen and most of the incoming White House staff viewed him as the very prototype New Dealer.

On the other hand, the more influential Republicans in the Congress (e.g., Taft) thought highly of him. Keyserling argues that Burns greatly overplayed the incident in order to force reorganization of the CEA staff:

> This distortion of the record was utilized by Burns and his Administration in an attempt to discredit their predecessors, gild their own record, and indulge in some spoilsmanship. Instead of outside economists being taken in by this, they would have been better informed and fairer if they had really studied the situation, and given more credit for what I did to keep the Council vigorous, useful, and accepted during difficult pioneering years (in contrast with such other previous planning agencies as the National Resources Board, which was really abolished by the Congress). In short, Burns did not really "clean up" or "rescue" anything.[9]

"The Best Man in the Country"

Amidst this confusion, Dr. Arthur F. Burns arrived to serve as chairman of the Council. Eisenhower had told his staff to search for "the best man in the country on the ups and downs of business." It was Taber's idea that the Council should be replaced by a single economic adviser (with a small staff), and he stood ready to approve an appropriation of $50,000 for the operation of such an office. Taber was apparently under the impression that the President shared this view. However, at this point, Eisenhower and Adams made an appeal to the chairman of the Senate Appropriations Committee, Styles Bridges, to provide funds to carry the Council through the fourth quarter. The President told Bridges that he intended to rebuild the Council and improve its status. As a consequence, the Senate voted $60,000, but this was reduced to $50,000 in conference and given, not to the Council, but to the President for an adviser in line with the Taber idea.[10] Meanwhile, the President had announced the Burns appointment and noted that the "Fair Deal slate would be wiped clean."

In *Firsthand Report*, Adams has written a revealing account of Burns' arrival at the White House and the circumstances surrounding the Council as the new administration began:

> The unpalatable theories of Leon Keyserling were too fresh in their recollection to stimulate any enthusiasm for restaffing the agency. Indeed, some of them [i.e., White House staff members] would have been happy to have the Council abolished altogether. Having the President's office budget in mind, I was inclined at first toward cutting the Council down to one man,

138

whereupon I listened to a stern lecture from Gabriel Hauge on the reasons for continuing the C.E.A. and recommending Burns.

. . .

When I took my first look at Burns on the day he came to my office, I was to take him in to meet the President, I had a sinking sensation. If somebody had asked me to describe the mental image I had of the type of New Deal official we were in the process of moving out of Washington, this was it—a glassy stare through thick lenses, peering out from under a canopy of unruly hair parted in the middle, a large pipe with a curved stem: the very incarnation of all the externals that were such anathema to Republican businessmen and politicians. I wondered if we would both be thrown out of Eisenhower's office. But I swallowed hard and invited the professor to follow me in.

If Eisenhower had any misgivings, he kept them to himself. To me, Arthur Burns turned out to be a pleasant surprise. He and Eisenhower got along fine. They shared the same outlook and philosophy. Far from being the abstract and impractical professor, Burns had his feet planted solidly on the ground and had no difficulty in more than holding his own in arguments at the Cabinet table with such hardheaded protagonists as Humphrey and Dodge. As soon as the 1954 downturn began to appear, Eisenhower set aside ample time at Cabinet meetings so that Burns could discuss the economics of the situation. These periods lasted often as long as thirty minutes, and Eisenhower listened to him with fascination. The President was particularly impressed by the importance Burns placed on the time factor in his analysis of business conditions. Going back, as he often did, to his Army experiences, in one such exchange on the role of time in the economy, Eisenhower remarked that a commanding officer in combat could recover lost men and lost weapons, or a strategic position on high ground, but he could never recover lost time. One morning, after Burns finished a detailed outline of contributions that various government departments could make toward strengthening the economy, Eisenhower said to him admiringly, "Arthur, my boy, you would have made a fine chief of staff overseas during the war."[11]

Despite the fact that he had been confirmed as chairman of a group whose future was uncertain, Burns began to assemble a staff and formulate policies. Not surprisingly, the period of confusion during which the matter of the future status of the Council was being decided (and no funds were available) did not facilitate Burns' search for personnel. Burns and other top professionals went on the White House payroll on a

139

temporary basis, but about twenty of the staff were let go. When CEA was refunded, many new people were hired—a blow to the organization. Aside from this immediate difficulty, there was some feeling among economists that the general atmosphere of the Republican administration would not be amenable to economic policy making. Burns was naturally anxious to assemble a cadre of well-qualified economists who shared the general views of the administration.

The new chairman was forty-nine at the time of his appointment. He had been professor of economics at Columbia University and had long been associated with the National Bureau of Economic Research as a student and colleague of Wesley C. Mitchell, the authority on economic fluctuations. He had received the Ph.D. from Columbia University in 1934.

Burns was classed generally as an inductive economist; that is to say, he drew his conclusions from the observable facts of the economy, in contrast to reasoning deductively from theoretical models. Nourse and Keyserling were generally of the same type, while later CEA members, and especially the staff, were apt to be more inclined toward theory and deductive economics. Though not a Keynesian, Burns was willing to admit the usefulness of the Keynesian apparatus. Burns was a natural for Hauge to seek out and was at once attracted to the job. Soon he began to assemble his associates.

Neil Jacoby, then forty-four, came to the Council from the University of California at Los Angeles. He had obtained his Ph.D. from the University of Chicago in 1938. Jacoby is one of the few CEA members who has formally recounted that the element of politics, as well as professional standing, enters into appointment. Writing recently in *History of Political Economy*, Jacoby tells of the pre-appointment process:

> Members of the Council differ from many other Presidential advisers in that their appointments require senatorial confirmation. This means, in practice, that under long-standing rules of senatorial courtesy the nominee must be agreeable to the senior Senator of the nominee's state and to the leaders of his political party. I first cleared my nomination with the chairman of the Republican Committee for Los Angeles County, McIntyre Faries, a leading attorney who later became a judge of the U.S. District Court. Although I had never engaged in partisan activity, Faries was mainly concerned that my economic ideology would not conflict sharply with Republican views. Later, he informed me that I had the support of his committee, and this would be communicated to the senior Senator from California,

William F. Knowland. When I called upon Senator Knowland to seek his support, he readily agreed to sponsor my nomination. When I appeared before the appropriate committee of the Senate in February, 1954, the proceedings were as brief as they were cordial. There was no probing of my professional education, experience, or capacity. Evidently, my acceptability to the California Republican organization and to Senator Knowland was all that was needed by the U.S. Senate to prove my fitness to advise the President upon economic policy!

As an academic economist I was at the time annoyed at the requirement of obtaining partisan approval of my appointment. Subsequent reflection, however, led me to conclude that this can have positive values. The President of the United States is not only a head of state and the chief executive of the federal government; he is also the leader of a political party. If his advisers are to have his confidence, they must share a common ideological approach to the issues before the nation. Parties should have a part in the selection of presidential advisers, if they are to play a vital role.

Because President Eisenhower wished to have a personal acquaintanceship with his advisers prior to their appointment—an eminently sensible practice—the White House requested me to meet him in Denver, Colorado, during July, 1953, where he was taking a fishing vacation with friends. I remember sitting in a swinging settee on the front porch of the late-Victorian home of Mrs. Doud, the President's mother-in-law, discussing economic policy with the President. He was dressed informally, and was completely relaxed. As so many millions of people did, I liked and trusted him immediately for his openness and obvious integrity. He said, "Jacoby, my people have checked your professional competence; but if we are to work together, you should know more about my economic views." Thereupon, he launched into an hour's discourse on what seemed to be favorite themes. He concluded by saying that he expected his Council to tell him the truth about the economy at all times no matter how unpalatable or what the political consequences might be.[12]

In a subsequent book, he outlines the essential elements for success as an economic adviser:

Members of the Council are most likely to serve their chief effectively if they possess a "passion for anonymity." The Council is wise to avoid the spotlight, to do its work behind the scenes. Councillors should be reluctant to speak for quotation in the newspapers. They should be reticent about making public

141

address. They should avoid so far as possible, public testimony before Congressional committees. If the Council governs its behavior by these precepts, it will minimize the risk of being publicly at odds with the President or of being charged with "political" bias. Needless to say, the effort to live by these rules is difficult because of the great pressures in Washington to elicit news from Presidential advisers.

A member of the President's Council obviously is dutybound to respect the policies of the President. He must forgo the privilege of public criticism of the administration. When he disagrees with a policy, it is his duty to work within the government to change it.[13]

The Council's senior member, Walter W. Stewart, at sixty-eight had been an adviser to Hoover and had long government service. In his long career, he had been on the faculty of several universities, an investment banker, and a faculty member of the Center of Advanced Study. Though not a Ph.D., Stewart was described as a brilliant economic theorist and one of the world's leading authorities on gold and foreign exchange. He was CEA's elder statesman, with vast experience.

Burns' operating philosophy was noticeably different from that of Keyserling, and he indicated a desire to play a role more in the Nourse tradition. The issue of his relationship to the Congress arose at the time of his confirmation, when he told Senator John Sparkman, "My own personal inclination would be to stay out of the limelight, make my recommendations to the President, indicate to him . . . the basis of the recommendation, . . . and remain eternally quiet."

Burns, although he did not take a position as extreme as that assumed by Nourse, apparently agreed with him that his usefulness would be diminished if he responded to any and all questions from a political group. There were, in his view, several areas in which he could cooperate without impairing his advisory relationship to the President. Burns recognized that the Council members were more than advisers; they were also "administrators" of the Employment Act. Thus, it would be entirely proper for Council members to advise Congress in this regard. A second area in which Burns was willing to testify was with reference to a technical matter, such as derivation of data. Third, he was, of course, fully willing to testify on matters relating to the Council itself, such as defending its budget requests.

In the fourth area, testimony dealing with economic conditions and policy, Burns noted two major dangers:

First, in some cases the President had to adopt policies that he

142

didn't like and that I didn't like. He had to do it for reasons of overall political policy, but his heart was bleeding over it. What should I do before a committee of Congress in such a case? Should I criticize the President when I happen to know that he shares my views? Would that be fair? In any case, how could I criticize the President publicly and still remain a useful member of his administration? On the other hand, how could I say to a congressional committee that something is sound when I believed it otherwise?

The other major danger in testifying is that once an adviser takes a strong position in public, he is apt to become a prisoner of that position. I wanted to give the President the fullest benefit of my knowledge and thought. Hence, I wanted to be free to advise the President one way one day, and yet be able if necessary to go in the next day and say, "I've been thinking it over. What I told you yesterday was wrong. I overlooked some important points. What really ought to be done is thus and so."[15]

Despite these pitfalls, as time passed Burns frequently gave testimony on semipolicy matters, although he often requested permission to testify in executive session. In both Republican and Democratic Congresses, Burns was able to make this precedent effective, as Miss Silverman notes: "Burns established his policy. He would express his preference to the congressional committees dealing with economic issues. If the committee in question accepted his preference, that was all to the good. However, if the committee insisted on different terms, Burns would accept those terms."[16] She quotes Burns on the issue subsequent to his leaving the Council:

Keyserling took an extreme position and in the process ignored a vital distinction. Cabinet officers are directly responsible to Congress. Their responsibilities are largely defined by Congress. But the Council is not an administrative agency. It is advisory only—advisory to the President by law, and advisory to the Presidency by practice.

Nourse also took a rigid position. To the extent that the Council had duties defined by law it is responsible to the Congress and must answer to it—that is why I placed no conditions on my testifying on proposed changes of the Employment Act or on the statistical gathering functions of the government or on the defense of the Council's budget.

But I want to add this: if there had only been the type of Council that Keyserling envisioned, I never would have taken it for granted that the Council Chairman must, as a practical matter, support the President's views at public hearings, and I would not place myself in that position. But because there had been a Nourse I could conceive of there being a practical alternative and could try to find it. So Nourse did more than make my job easier by taking the position he did; because there had been a Nourse my job was possible.[17]

As a result of the congressional reappraisal of the Council at the beginning of the new administration and subsequent consultation with the Bureau of the Budget, a change in the organization of the Council was made. Reorganization Plan No. 9, which reads as follows, was adopted:

> The functions vested in the Council of Economic Advisers by section 4(b) of the Employment Act of 1946 (60 Stat. 24), and so much of the functions vested in the Council by section 4(c) of that Act as consists of reporting to the President with respect to any function of the Council under said section 4(c), are hereby transferred to the Chairman of the Council of Economic Advisers. The position of Vice Chairman of the Council of Economic Advisers, provided for in the last sentence of section 4(a) of the said Act, is hereby abolished.[18]

The essence of the plan was that the chairman was designated the operating head of the Council; he would be responsible for reporting to the President, as well as for such executive tasks as making staff appointments. Thus, hopefully, the stress that had resulted from the situation of equal power among the three members (with no real executive power vested in the chairman), which Nourse had found so difficult, might be eased. To what extent this reorganization plan was responsible for Burns' mode of operation and to what extent his own personal preference was influential is difficult to say. Some observers have commented on the fact that Burns was inclined to "play the game close to his chest" and to take little account of staff views. Although Burns was able to gain frequent access to the President and was successful in introducing him to the rudiments of economics, there is some doubt as to his real influence on policy issues vis-à-vis Secretary Humphrey. One close observer told the author, "While Burns was successful in the game of words and phrases, Humphrey played the power game." However, another participant pointed out that *any* Secretary of the Treasury is in a very powerful position by the very nature of his job. Secretary Humphrey was especially powerful, and the fact that Burns won a number of issues speaks very well for his position in the administration. Under

Burns' leadership, the Council, then only a child by agency standards, was holding its own in company with the strongest Cabinet post in the government, occupied by a man not only admired by the President, but also one who had accepted only with the understanding that he would have the last say on matters of federal finance.

Issues relating to money were often seized upon by the opposition to embarrass the administration, and the Eisenhower-Burns-Humphrey procedure was to put more weight on monetary policy than had been the case in the Truman years. The lack of congressional control early in the administration was a problem. John Taber (R., N.Y.), Robert Rich (R., Pa.) and other "professional economizers" ran wild and embarrassed the White House with calls for impossible budget cuts. Fiscal policy was assigned a somewhat more modest role, and it was hoped that direct controls might be abolished quickly and largely avoided in the future.

Congressional Democrats lost no time in noting that attempts to raise interest rates, the early move by Humphrey to lengthen maturity periods for the Treasury issues (to ease refunding), and other actions were beneficial to bankers. Throughout the administration, a running battle with Congressman Wright Patman, Senator Paul H. Douglas, and other Democrats took place over interest rate policy. Democrats generally charged the administration with being too "deflationary" in its policies, and labor groups joined gleefully with the opposition to castigate the administration for being the party of "big business."

Burns had been determined to preserve the reputation of the Council, and by and large he managed to do so despite the general conservative, "hard-headed" atmosphere of the administration. In contrast to both Keyserling before and Walter Heller after him, Burns had strong ideas about staff function: "I believed that the staff functioned primarily to advise me; it was not supposed to go about selling programs."[19] The staff members did not become involved in policy matters as a consequence, but were given assignments that were essentially requests for data or information, often stripped of all policy overtones insofar as possible.

Burns, however, did create an innovation in the operation of the Council which gave him good channels to other areas of the federal establishment, namely, the Advisory Board on Economic Growth and Stability (ABEGS). This group, under Burns' chairmanship, met with representatives from Agriculture, Commerce, Labor, the Federal Reserve, and the Bureau of the Budget, as well as the White House. It proved to be a valuable organization. Burns was new in Washington, as was Jacoby, and, while Stewart had a vast fund of experience on the

145

federal level, most of it was years in the past. Outside contacts made at first through ABEGS and then in other ways involved the staff in some degree of policy operations. Typical of the informal machinery was staff member David Lusher's "Tuesday group," a gathering of professional economists on the operating levels of the federal agencies involved in policy making. Burns used his former National Bureau of Economic Research connections to sponsor a conference on antirecession policy at Princeton University that resulted in a series of papers. Thus, despite a degree of centralization, the Council utilized the various channels of information open to it much in the same manner as had been done previously. Although Burns was the only member who spoke for CEA in public and testified before Congress, he was at pains not to endanger his advisory relation with the President, and he managed to operate in close harmony with Gabriel Hauge.

Hauge occupied a unique position vis-à-vis the Council. In the Truman years, no professional economist had been on the White House staff. Likewise, in the Kennedy years, as we shall see, Heller was anxious that no one in the White House should play the role of economic adviser. Hauge had combined a career in teaching, research, and government service. He left a position as assistant to the chairman of the McGraw-Hill Publishing Company to join the White House staff in 1952 (after serving on the campaign staff). Hauge attended the Monday morning conferences to brief the President, helping to increase his grasp of economic affairs. Although this seems at first to be an overlap with Burns' functions, several factors must be kept in mind.

First of all, Hauge constituted a link with the White House, although, clearly, he could have been a barrier if other circumstances or personalities had prevailed. Second, and perhaps of overriding importance, Hauge was able to field the wide range of economic problems that landed on the President's desk. Matters regarding such issues as farm policy, import quotas, and tariffs demanded top-level attention. Hauge was able to extinguish these "brush fires" without involving CEA time and effort. Also, since Eisenhower was completely without either economic or political experience, Hauge was able, along with Burns, to play an unusually important educational role. Eisenhower became a great admirer of Burns and, since Burns was the senior of the team and an economist of great reputation, probably gave his views more weight than those of Hauge. Although Hauge was highly capable, his daily contact with the President no doubt had some influence in reducing his prestige in Eisenhower's eyes. Likewise, Hauge was careful not to upstage Burns, for whom he had much regard.

146

In addition to ABEGS and other conduits of information, Burns made use of task forces that undertook to examine specific problem areas. As Burns became better oriented in Washington, ABEGS suffered some eclipse, but he retained his view of its usefulness and recommended that the institution be formalized in the guise of an economic policy board to relate to economic matters, in much the same manner as the National Security Council relates to matters of defense.

While Burns was working out his mode of operation and rebuilding the Council, he was occupied also with the economic problems that began to beset the administration. The Humphrey "stretch-out" of federal financing, along with tax extension difficulties with House Republicans, had created or intensified a decline.

By April 1953 a noticeable weakening was taking place in four of the National Bureau's eight leading economic indicator series. Other economists had warned of a decline shortly after the first of the year. Despite this, the administration, committed to a reversal of the "spending policies of the Democratic party," had begun to follow a restrictive budget policy in planning for fiscal 1954. Aside from this commitment to administration policy in general, CEA faced confusing signs. While some indicators were falling, GNP was on the increase and unemployment was at the very satisfactory level of 2.7 percent. Industrial output was steady. Moreover, the administration had already taken positive steps to stimulate business confidence (to some degree, of course, the very fact that a Republican was in the White House increased business confidence). Eisenhower had reduced the Truman budget of $72.9 billion (fiscal 1953) to $64.4 billion (fiscal 1954), while urging agencies to make further reductions in preparation for greater fiscal restraint in 1954 and 1955.

In May the Open Market Committee began a policy designed to ease pressure on bank reserves. Care was taken not to attribute this action to a potential recession, but to point to increased tension in the financial markets. In July reserve requirements were reduced. Through this period, Burns apparently played only a minor part. By August, however, warning signs had begun to multiply, and the Council, now fully in operation, began to take positive action. Burns requested the staff to prepare an analysis of possible anticyclical moves to be made if matters continued to deteriorate. The Council's major concern was the accumulation of business inventories, coupled with a decline in sales. ABEGS and other task-force groups were asked to undertake studies of measures to encourage stabilization and economic growth to be pursued in the event of a further slowdown in economic activity.[20] In late September 1953 the *New York Times* reported that the Council had indicated its concern to Secretary Humphrey, who expressed alarm. Humphrey sought advice from Burns, who, in turn, urged his staff to explore various measures upon which action might be taken quickly without congressional approval.

Both as part of the overall Eisenhower program and to stimulate the economy, numerous proposals were made the latter including tax reform and reduction and housing and welfare proposals, including improvements in unemployment insurance. The Council was involved to a degree in all of these matters, although its contribution was largely indirect, such as helping the housing agencies get more staff to expedite their affairs.

The general tone of the administration was to discount the use of federal encouragement to economic activity, characteristic of the Roosevelt-Truman years, while at the same time using these means to full advantage. As we shall see, the same technique was applied to budget balancing.

The Republicans Face Recession

A recession early in the first Republican administration since 1932 was a political disaster beyond contemplation, and, as the economy slowed, action was essential. Using sound strategy, the 1954 *Economic Report of the President* emphasized a positive tone of confidence and reassurance. The performance of the economy had never been brighter, according to the State of the Union Message and the *Economic Report* of that year:

> The upsurge of production and employment, which has been sustained with but brief interruptions in the United States for about a dozen years, continued in 1953. New records were established in industrial activity, employment, and the disbursement of incomes. Unemployment reached the lowest level of any peace-time year in recent decades. The average level of prices was remarkably steady. The fruits of expanding production and enterprise were shared widely. Perhaps never before in their history have the American people come closer to realizing the ideal of high and expanding employment without price inflation.[21]

Despite the optimistic tones of the *Economic Report,* there was considerable feeling in various quarters that the situation, especially with regard to unemployment, was more serious than the report indicated. By

148

early February the Council began to acquaint the administration with the dimensions of the problem.

The President was understandably anxious to avoid another debacle like that of 1929, and the issue dominated Cabinet discussion until June, when the danger appeared to be over. Donovan has recorded items from Cabinet meetings:

Cabinet, February 5, 1954

The President informed the Cabinet that he had asked Burns to coordinate reports from the various departments and agencies on their plans for public-works projects. It would be essential, he said, to have planning advanced sufficiently to insure that men would be put to work quickly.

Projects actually under way, he noted, gave the government flexibility in speeding them up or stretching them out, as conditions required. . . .

Humphrey then made his position known. He said that a broad public-works program would be desirable if operations then in progress should fail to turn the tide. He felt, however, that they might very well succeed. . . .

To cap the discussion Lodge praised the care that was being taken by the administration to master the economic setback. He said that this attitude refuted charges that Republicans were bound to the "trickle-down" theory of economics—the theory of helping the few at the top in expectation that the benefits will then seep down to the rest of the people.

[An interesting aspect of this discussion, as well as of similar discussions in the next few months, was the muting of emphasis on balancing the budget. . . .]

Cabinet, March 12, 1954

The President was in a deadly serious mood. The unemployment situation had worsened. In March the number of jobless reached the peak of 3,725,000 or 5.8 of the entire civilian labor force. The fact that unemployment was then at the crest, however, was not known on this date.

Cabinet, March 19, 1954

Burns reported that some favorable trends were appearing, but he urged that judgment be suspended for a while. The Council of Economic Advisers, he said, was moving ahead rapidly with projects that might be started if need should arise.

[Charles] Wilson [Secretary of Defense, formerly President of General Motors] noted the upturn in the automobile industry—

a factor that was to prove extremely important.

Burns then called attention to another encouraging and unusual situation: Plant expansion and building contracts had been continuing at a very high rate through nine months of general decline.

He attributed this to confidence in the administration's ability to maintain a stable economy. Pointing out that public confidence was a precarious thing, he said that he could only fear what the outcome might be if the administration should betray signs of timidity or impotence. . . .

Cabinet, April 30, 1954

Burns came armed with hopeful omens again. . . .

Cabinet, June 11, 1954

Burns made his presentation. He noted definite evidence that recovery was under way, but said the possibility remained that it would fizzle out. He recommended a number of measures, again stressing housing, building, interest rates and highway construction.

"Arthur, you'd have made a fine chief of staff during the war," the President told him. . . .

There was a note of elation in the Cabinet on July 23 when Burns announced that the midyear economic indicators showed definitely that the decline had come to an end. To have passed from the Korean War economy to a peace-time economy without a far more serious drop, he said, was a tremendous accomplishment.

With the Congressional elections approaching, the Cabinet cheerfully discussed various opportunities for making all this clear to the public, especially the now favorable comparison between 1954 and 1952, the last year of Democratic rule.[22]

During this critical period, the President and Burns were in frequent contact, and CEA had been designated as the command post for planning antirecession measures. Burns was one of the few who had regular private meetings with Eisenhower, and Adams reports that sometimes the President would sit and "listen to him with fascination."[23] Burns, however, did not play it alone:

During this entire period, Martin and Humphrey also maintained close communication through regular Monday lunches, other meetings, and frequent telephone calls. The Federal Reserve nonetheless remained somewhat aloof from the inner circles of government policy-making. It had only recently regained its independence and did not want to risk losing it again so soon.

Interestingly, Sherman Adams suggests that George Humphrey lost standing with the President on economic issues, and Martin gained, when Humphrey in 1953 "slowed down normal growth" by bringing out "an attractive issue of . . . bonds that mopped up enough money that would otherwise have gone into corporate stocks and mortgages to cause a mild panic." Adams continues: "Coming to the rescue, William McC. Martin, Chairman of the Federal Reserve Board, took steps to ease the situation, lower interest rates and loosen up the money supply."[24]

Likewise, Burns maintained constant contact with ABEGS, departmental and Cabinet officials, and other concerned parties. There was much talk about the "arsenal of weapons" to be used in economic stabilization. The *Economic Report* mentioned such tools as debt management policies, mortgage credit policies, agricultural support policies, tax policies, and public works.

Burns had a lively interest in public works, and he was especially attracted to highway improvements, to which he attributed extraordinary "multiplier effects." Burns believed highway improvement encouraged shopping centers, subdivisions, and other forms of economic activity beyond the immediate effects of construction. Undoubtedly, he had these ideas in mind when he supported the Federal Aid Highway Act of 1954, which began the present interstate system.

Burns, of course, recognized that, in the immediate crisis, public works would be of little use, since they take too much time to get under way and for benefits to materialize. Although it is common to speak of a "shelf of public works," from which projects can be pulled, dusted off, and put into effect, the actual process is quite different, due to the problem of timing. Professor Raymond J. Saulnier, who succeeded Burns as chairman, has noted that, in any event, increased federal spending is not likely to do much good unless there is at the same time an atmosphere that is conducive to private spending.[25]

A key issue with portents for the future was the tax-cut matter fought out between Humphrey and Burns. Although recovery was well along by the time it took place, it is illustrative of the personalities and inner workings of the administration. Jacoby has recounted:

The specific question which then divided the President's inner circle of advisers, particularly Secretary of the Treasury George Humphrey and the Council of Economic Advisers, was whether to reduce federal taxes and to allow certain expiring taxes to

151

terminate. The Council strongly favored tax reduction as a necessary step to strengthen consumer purchasing power and to stimulate private demand at a time when unemployment was 5.8 percent of the labor force and growing. Humphrey opposed tax reduction, because of his adherence to the ancient fallacy of "balancing the budget" annually under all circumstances.

Through the winter and spring of 1954 the issue between Humphrey and the Council became more clearly defined as the recession deepened. Burns and I made clear to the President our strong convictions about the need for tax reduction. We stated that we could not predict a timely economic recovery unless tax reduction took place. The President said, "Talk to George Humphrey." There followed a series of luncheon meetings with the Secretary of the Treasury, often extending well into the afternoon, where taxation issues were heatedly debated. . . .

Humphrey met his match in Arthur Burns. With his face wreathed in smoke from an omnipresent pipe and his shock of grey hair protruding over large, piercing eyes, Burns was a man of forceful presence, whose arguments were always logical and buttressed by weighty evidence.

Unable to persuade Humphrey of the need for tax reduction, Burns and I finally reported our failure to President Eisenhower and again urged his support in the strongest possible terms. The President then did sponsor the tax cuts. Humphrey was shattered; but he did not resign. Tax reductions totaling $7 billions a year took effect between April and June, 1954—the first time massive tax cuts were made at a time of Federal budgetary deficit to counter a recession. They had an important effect in strengthening the forces of the economic revival which began thereafter.[26]

In general, there was little reliance on a policy of increased federal spending. Instead, the administration preferred to put its faith in the antirecessionary effects of the stabilizers, including transfer payments of various types. The Federal Reserve's easy-money policy included reductions in reserve requirements, an increase in the money supply, and lower interest rates. It seems possible that the recession might have been prevented, or at least substantially mitigated, if the administration had taken more account of the deflationary effect of the cut in military spending following the Korean War.

The short recession was succeeded by a rapid recovery concentrated in the durable consumer and producer goods sectors of the economy, while agriculture and the soft-goods industries remained depressed. The economic expansion of 1955–57 was sectoral rather than general;

wholesale prices of durable consumer goods rose at an annual average rate of 5.5 percent in the three years 1955–57, while agricultural prices fell on the average of 1.7 percent in the same years. Wholesale prices of nondurables increased at a rate of 1.7 percent in the period, while the general wholesale price index increased 2.1 percent in the period 1955–57.

These divergent price trends reveal the spotty character of the economy. "Structural" or "sectoral" inflation was to be a continuous problem in the future.[27] Rising prices in machine tools, electrical gear, and related industries spilled over into the other sectors, causing an increase in the general price level.

The administration was aware of these facts, but policy in general was directed more toward overall, rather than selective, credit controls. That is, the policy was intended to control an overall "pull" on prices resulting from an excess of demand throughout the economy. No change was made in tax rates, and fiscal policy was aimed at securing a cash budget surplus through a reduction in federal expenditure, with the tax level unchanged. In large part, the burden of controlling inflation was placed on monetary and credit instruments. This policy was designed to create credit constraints by raising interest rates and by controlling bank reserves through open-market operations and by restraining the money supply.

The capital goods expansion, coupled with a decline in demand, gave rise to a capital goods recession in 1957–58.[28] Although industrial capacity rose from 1953 to 1957, the index of manufacturing remained almost stable, with idle capacity becoming a serious problem. The reaction of the business sector was to reduce its capital expenditures (via the multiplier effect), which brought a decline in national income, personal consumption spending, and expenditures for inventories. GNP fell from a rate of $410.1 billion in the second quarter of 1957 to $393.1 billion in the corresponding quarter of 1958.

Some discussion of further tax reduction took place, but the administration took no action other than a passive move to extend excise taxes for one more year. Again, faith was lodged in the automatic stabilizers, along with accelerated governmental expenditures, such as the highway program, and increases in transfer payments. These fiscal policies were backed up by the Federal Reserve with reductions in reserve requirements and open-market operations. However, recovery from this recession was never really vigorous, and the economy faltered again by the late 1960s.

While it was mild and short, the recession of 1957–58 brought to light a

153

number of disturbing trends that were to be troublesome to both the Eisenhower and Kennedy administrations. The first of these problems was the continued rise in prices, despite the substantial drop in demand. Whereas in the first two postwar recessions prices had remained fairly stable, both wholesale and retail prices rose in the latter period. In part, this phenomenon was explained by the long-term wage contracts undertaken in 1956 in durable goods industries and by the increase in the number of service workers relative to production workers.

A second and perhaps more disturbing fact was the stubborn refusal of unemployment to fall below 5 percent. Especially unsettling was the *structure* of unemployment. Even after the economy had recovered fully from the recession, unemployment was still highly concentrated among older workers, young workers, the unskilled, and minority groups.

The administration mounted an attack upon the unemployment problem by taking various steps, described by the Council in its report for 1960–61, in which unemployment was called "the most complex challenge to public and private policy." Thus began the well-known argument between those who adhered to the "structural" school, who argued that unemployment resulted from technological change and regional shift of industry, etc., and those who maintained that there was overall an insufficiency of aggregate demand. The Eisenhower Administration leaned toward the structural arguments and attacked the problem by technical assistance to depressed areas, programs of vocational training and retraining, and assistance to small businesses through the Small Business Administration. In its last report (forecasting for 1961), the Saulnier Council recommended legislation to enlarge existing programs designed to treat structural unemployment, but by the time the administration ended, little real progress had been made in this sector.

Stress and Strain

The ambivalence within the administration relative to economic policy is illustrated by the "budget crisis" of 1957–58. On January 15, the day on which the budget was submitted, Secretary Humphrey noted that there were, in his view, many places where the budget might be cut, and, inviting Congress to do so, added his famous statement to the press that unless future budgets were cut over time, "I predict we will have a depression that will curl your hair."

Humphrey's reaction to the resulting furor was almost as startling as his original statement.

"I may have gone overboard a bit this afternoon," Humphrey

reportedly remarked, shortly thereafter, to the bemused Budget Director, Percival Brundage. To much of Washington that would have seemed an extraordinary understatement. Never in the history of executive budgeting since 1921 had there been anything to match the spectacle of a first-rank Cabinet officer publicly assailing the presidential budget on the very day it was sent down. Budget Bureau officials were furious; some of the aides within the White House were appalled. "Modern" Republicans in the Cabinet and their departmental staffs—and many a sharp-minded Pentagon official—took umbrage, as well they might, for obviously they were in the line of Humphrey's fire. At the Capitol and in the press corps, and among spokesmen for the private groups most vitally concerned, reactions were as unsure as the situation was unusual.[29]

Not surprisingly, the opposition made much of this seeming contradiction. House Democrats (in House Resolution No. 19) asked Eisenhower what to cut. Although Capitol Hill Republicans tried to tag the move as a political gesture (which, of course, it was), it was embarrassing to the White House and confirmed the suspicion that there was a wide gulf between the economics of the Council and that of the conservative elements in the administration. The net result of the incident was a "paper" cut of $4.9 billion, most of which melted away as the year passed.

In large measure, Burns was successful in his professed desire to rely more heavily on monetary policy than previous administrations had done. He worked closely with the Federal Reserve and lost no opportunity to seek its cooperation.[30] The independence of the Federal Reserve makes it difficult to evaluate the precise role of the Council in the general easing of the situation, but it clearly deserves some credit. The Council did make effective efforts to ease credit in the field of housing that were of substantial benefit.

Though Burns' role of tutor was very important, perhaps his most significant contribution was his success, at least in appearance, in removing the Council from the area of partisanship into which it had fallen in the late Truman-Keyserling period. Further, he managed to accomplish this feat in an administration not overly sympathetic to the Council and its objectives. To what degree this was merely an illusion is debatable, but at least he created the image.

Overall, the Eisenhower Administration, although it came into office with an intent to balance the budget, ultimately adopted the idea that the budget need not be in balance each year.[31] In fact, the administration was able to secure a surplus in only three of its eight years in office. Likewise, despite the often expressed desire to curb the federal debt, it increased $20 billion in the period 1953–60.

Another troublesome problem which continued into the Kennedy years was the increasing drain on gold. Rising expenditures abroad (largely for economic aid and for military purposes) reduced gold reserves from $22.8 billion in 1957 to $17.8 billion in 1960. Despite various measures taken to stem this outflow, it continued on a large scale.

The Burns Council recognized the importance of the growth problem, but was reluctant to put the goal into quantitative terms. In 1955 the Council made a ten-year projection of GNP on the basis of an assumed growth rate of 3 percent, but published no national economic budget. By 1958, the Council had reached the conclusion that "although the rate of economic growth that is best suited to the nation's capacity and requirements cannot be stated precisely, the low current rate would clearly be unsatisfactory as a condition."[32] While the administration was unwilling to fix an "adequate" rate of growth, it did embark upon numerous programs designed to enhance the existing rate. These programs were in the area of natural resource development, research and development, aid to health and education, aid to small businesses, and regional assistance.

Eisenhower's last year in office did not see a resolution of the conflict between price increases and unemployment, and the continuation of a sluggish economy, combined with the drive for a surplus, was a factor against which Vice-President Nixon, the Republican candidate in 1960, had to defend himself. The net performance of the administration was frustrated by the classic dilemma that faces modern economics—the provision of an adequate supply of investment and consumer spending, allowing productivity of the economy to advance at a satisfactory rate, while at the same time controlling inflation. The realities of modern economic life weighed heavily on the administration:

Many businessmen were, of course, greatly disappointed that the New Deal and Fair Deal programs were so little changed by the Eisenhower Administration. Still, however much as American businessmen disliked "government in business," they nevertheless felt much more relaxed and confident now that interferences with and intervention in business were in the hands of a Republican administration. Their acceptance in large part of the "New Order" as "capitalism" naturally helped to obscure recognition both in the United States and abroad of the substantial transformation of American capitalism which had in fact occurred. Communist and socialist opponents of capitalism, both in the United States and in foreign countries, of course denied that any fundamental changes had occurred. They insisted that the contemporary American economic system was undoubtedly capitalism, although a late stage characterized by monopoly instead of by competition.[33]

The Burns Council was the instrument that in large part enabled the Republican party to skirt the crevasse of economic depression, while linking Eisenhower's generally conservative outlook and welfare liberalism to the stated purposes of the Employment Act. This was an accomplishment of which Burns might well be proud. He did much to polish the image of the Council as a meaningful institution.

His relationship to Humphrey was founded on the realistic thesis that Humphrey was in an operative position, a line officer, while Burns was an adviser, a staff man. Given these facts, Burns would have been both foolish and short-sighted had he attempted to undercut the powerful secretary.

Some staff criticism was directed toward Burns for his tendency to write large portions of the reports personally or to rewrite in detail. Though he continued this practice, he reportedly became responsive to staff views and is said to have toned down the opening parts of the 1954 report which staff members found too conservative and had characterized as looking "like material from the National Association of Manufacturers."

In the area of day-to-day operations, Burns was again a model of success. He met weekly with the President and Gabriel Hauge, thus briefing the President and the White House "resident economist" and improving the President's understanding of economic matters. Burns, and Burns alone, was Council spokesman before both the Congress and the press, and almost all White House-CEA relations were channeled through him. The close relationship with Hauge made this possible, and one has the impression that Hauge was an unsung hero of the administration who got far less credit than he deserved. One may speculate, for example, as to what the situation would have been if Nourse had been able to work through Hauge instead of Steelman.

Performance of the Administration

Though Eisenhower was never completely able to attain the goal of "security with solvency," nor to reconcile the more conservative elements of the Republican party to the economics of the

157

twentieth century, he did make considerable progress in adjusting the administration to the economic policy demands of the era. However, the administration was never free from partisan attacks on its policies, and it was almost continuously accused of favoring the financial community with its "hard-money" policy.

The President was himself willing to accept an expanded governmental role. In the budget message of January 1956, he noted that labor and management should join with government in guarding the integrity of the dollar. Critics of the administration contended that, for some reason, the President and the Council were excessively concerned with inflation. Likewise, the often reiterated concern with balancing the budget gave the administration both blame and credit it did not deserve. Liberals were critical for what they believed to be an excessive amount of attention directed toward this goal by both Eisenhower and Humphrey. However, as Stein notes, this was to a degree illusory:

A second source of misunderstanding of the Eisenhower fiscal policy was the identification of budget-balancing with old-fashioned or reactionary policy. Modern fiscal policy was derived mainly from the depression when deficits were appropriate. Willingness, and indeed eagerness, to accept deficits came to be the litmus-paper test of modernity. But there was nothing in the new ideas to suggest that balancing the budget or running a surplus was *never* the proper course. The essential point was that the desirability of balancing the budget was not given by some eternal principal but depended on economic conditions which would vary.

The Eisenhower administration's conspicuous attention to budget-balancing, sometimes interpreted as evidence that they had not learned the lessons of the previous two decades, was based upon a judgment about the economic condition of the country between 1953 and 1961. The administration believed that the underlying problem of those years, and most of the time the current and overt problem, was inflation. Given this diagnosis, a prescription of balanced budgets was consistent with, indeed required by, modern fiscal policy. The diagnosis was not unique with the administration, or even unusual at the time, and there was abundant evidence in the preceding years and in the current experience to support it. The diagnosis may have been wrong; it may have been pressed too far and too long. But this is a matter of judgment in the application of a flexible, functional policy; it raises no question about the acceptance of policy itself. When *its* diagnosis was temporarily different, the administration not only tolerated large deficits but took steps to expand them.[34]

In actual fact, Eisenhower performed the feat of *talking* a balanced budget, while, except on rare occasions, not delivering—a fact that aroused the envy of Kennedy in later years. Although Kennedy was to find the balanced budget to be a paper tiger when really tested, Eisenhower and his associates, as Republicans, can perhaps be excused for being somewhat more inclined to pay homage to the concept. Concern with a balanced budget, especially by Republican Presidents, seems to be akin to political opposition to liquor in the "Bible Belt." No one expects the promise to be kept, but it must be made.

The recession of 1957–58 brought on increasing economic debate between the administration, the Democrats, and the labor unions, which resulted in a series of antirecession proposals in the Congress. These were designed to accelerate military spending, bar reduction of agricultural price supports (or acreage allotments), and promote other devices designed to increase spending. Spending was to be accelerated by such actions as an emergency housing bill, an emergency highway bill, and an omnibus rivers and harbors bill. All these proposals were developed by the Democratic majority under the leadership of Senator Lyndon Johnson and sent to the White House before the Easter recess.

Although he did not respond to this challenge with any formal antirecession program, the President proposed two measures designed to have an immediate impact on spending; both were accepted by the Congress. These proposals were the authorization of accelerated spending of some $840 million by executive agencies and an advance of unemployment funds to those states in which funds had been exhausted.

By 1959 declining revenues had resulted in the largest peacetime deficit in history ($12.9 billion). The deficit in administration eyes clearly called for fiscal restraint, but what would happen to unemployment? Unemployment, which had leveled off at about 3 percent of the labor force after the 1947–48 recession and at some 4 percent after the 1953–54 dip, rose slowly thereafter and remained stubbornly at the 5 percent level. This dilemma brought on prolonged internal and external debate over economic policy, lasting until the end of the administration and influencing the election of 1960. Democrats in the Congress viewed the unemployment rate as symbolic of sluggish economic growth due, as Lyndon Johnson put it, to "the intolerable burden of laggard government."

Kennedy, as the 1960 Democratic candidate, was quick to capitalize on this situation and made much of the low level of growth with his pledge to "get the country moving again." In *Six Crises,* Nixon notes that the sluggish economy was a factor in the election, but the Vice-President found himself powerless to change the situation.

Nixon had been warned in February 1960 that the economy was, according to Burns' analysis, heading into a decline. Burns, who had left the Council at the end of 1956 and returned to the National Bureau of Economic Research, cautioned Nixon that his chances in the election would suffer if this proved to be true. Nixon heeded this advice and attempted through the Cabinet Committee on Price Stability, which he headed, to take fiscal action to stimulate the economy. However, the administration had a strong desire to accumulate a large surplus at its close, a goal from which neither Eisenhower nor others were to be diverted. Nixon attributed a large share of his defeat to this situation, and he was impressed with Burns' forecasting ability. Nixon has said:

> Unfortunately, Arthur Burns turned out to be a good prophet. The bottom of the 1960 dip did come in October and the economy started to move up again in November—after it was too late to affect the election returns. In October, usually a month of rising employment, the jobless rolls increased by 452,000. All the speeches, television broadcasts, and precinct work in the world could not counteract that one hard fact.[35]

In *The Fiscal Revolution in America,* Herbert Stein commented:

> Whether or not the 1958–1960 fiscal policy was a mistake economically, it was certainly a great irony politically. For one of the chief victims of President Eisenhower's determination to have a large budget surplus was probably Mr. Nixon and the Republican Party. Reflecting later on the 1960 Presidential campaign, Nixon said that two developments occurred before the conventions "which were to have far more effect on the election than all our carefully considered strategy decisions put together." One was the shooting down of the U-2 reconnaissance plane over the Soviet Union. The other was the failure of the administration to respond to Nixon's request, prompted by Burns' advice and forecast, for an expansive economic policy.[36]

George L. Bach, the long-time student of monetary policy (expressing a widely held viewpoint), said:

> In retrospect, the Eisenhower fiscal policy of 1958–60 was one of the major fiscal policy mistakes of the postwar period. The push was for a big surplus instead of the "timely flexibility" against economic slack that administrative officials emphasized

so frequently in their public pronouncements. With a recession in 1960, the administrative budget surplus was $1 billion, while the full-employment budget surplus soared to nearly $15 billion, as restrictive tax policy created a "fiscal drag" on economic growth. The monetary authorities at the Federal Reserve by and large shared the White House view. Money was tight in 1960, though the Federal Reserve acted to ease it somewhat after early 1960. Lack of communication and coordination cannot be blamed for the failures of monetary and fiscal policy during this period.[37]

Thus, in some ways, the end of the Eisenhower years was much like the beginning, with threats of economic downturn.

Several recent authors have given Eisenhower much more credit for political know-how than has been customary. Garry Wills, for example, notes that throughout his administration, especially in his relationship to Nixon, Eisenhower was a master politician who always managed to look good.[38] In contrast, Nixon always looked bad. Nixon and Adams carried the political ball while Eisenhower, the best "politician of them all," acted the role of statesman. Eisenhower had been an expert poker and bridge player in his Army years, and he had not lost his skills.

Like his chief, Burns had been a bit more fortunate and, perhaps, more astute than his successor, Raymond Saulnier; and he, like Eisenhower, kept his image bright and shining.

In summary, the economics of the Eisenhower Administration was marked by five major factors:

1. The administration, though anxious to alter the "drift toward socialism" and to operate on a balanced budget, was generally locked in by the realities of the economy at mid-century.
2. Eisenhower made little pretense of being an economic thinker and left the major task of policy formulation to his staff and to the Council.
3. The Council, which began the administration under a cloud, became, under Burns, a respected and viable agency.
4. Eisenhower was the first Republican President since Hoover; and, not surprisingly, the administration was sensitive on the issue of economic stability and was apt to overreact when the charge was made that it was under the domination of big business.
5. Eisenhower was not an imaginative policymaker, nor was the Council apt to embark on innovation.

161

Burns operated the Council in a manner that would have appealed to the first chairman, Nourse. That is, Burns conducted an advisory group in the best sense and successfully put its expertise to work as directed. It is noteworthy that, while the administration had its quota of inept performances (Secretary Oveta C. Hobby in Health, Education and Welfare; the U-2 Affair; and Senator Joseph McCarthy and the Army, for example), economic performance was generally good, and the CEA performance was all but flawless (it was Humphrey who was critical of the President's budget). To be sure, the Council had its share of luck. The economy continued to operate at a high level; and extraordinary fiscal demands, such as those that were to flaw the Johnson Administration, were largely absent.

Most observers, watching the early confusion that marked the relationship between the Council and the new administration—with the Council existing only in shadow form—would have predicted a pedestrian performance. Hauge, Burns, Saulnier, and the President himself deserve a substantial measure of credit that it was not.

Members of the Burns-Saulnier Council, although thoroughly professional, were somewhat more subdued than either their predecessors or those who were to take office in 1960. Their use of "modern economics" was often carried out quietly and, as in the case of budgetary deficits, not generally talked about outside the shop.

Burns was succeeded by Saulnier, who continued to the end of the administration. In all, eight men served during the Eisenhower years. In addition to the original group and Saulnier were Joseph S. Davis, Paul W. McCracken (who was to return in 1969), Karl Brandt, and Henry C. Wallich. All of these were academic economists, representing, in order, Stanford, Michigan, Stanford, and Yale. All returned to academic life at the close of their service.

By the end of the Eisenhower years, the Council had been in operation for fourteen years, six under Truman and eight under Eisenhower. Those eight years were very meaningful and saw the Council firmly installed as a fixture in the policy-making process. No doubt the Council benefited from the fact that Eisenhower made no pretense of economic understanding and had been trained to depend on a staff. However, we cannot overlook the fact that the traditional machinery for policy making was still functioning and that the Council had begun to play an integral part in the process. The dark days when the Council's fate hung by a slender thread were long in the past, and new influence was at hand. Moreover, the administration clearly recognized and accepted responsibility for the promotion of economic stability. Republicans, both liberal and conservative, had accepted, if not endorsed, modern economic policy.

Notes

Chapter 5

[1] Wilkie, president of Commonwealth and Southern, a utility holding company, who ran in 1940, probably represented the most innovative of the Republican candidates. He was not a favorite of the "old guard."

[2] For some time Democrats had hoped that Eisenhower would run on their ticket, since Eisenhower had never registered and no one was sure of his party leanings. No less a Democrat than Harry Truman had shared this view.

[3] Arthur Krock, from *Memoirs, Sixty Years on the Firing Line*, p. 283. Copyright© 1968 by Arthur Krock. Reprinted with permission of the publisher, Funk and Wagnalls, Inc.

[4] After White House service Hauge joined the Manufacturers Hanover Trust Company and later became its president.

[5] Humphrey was an industrialist (president of the M.A. Hanna Company) and a long-time GOP power. He was a pragmatic man who often seemed to take delight in displaying a tendency towards antiintellectualism.

[6] The famous Eisenhower "staff system" was in reality a mild extension of the White House establishment that had been growing up since Roosevelt's day, and had been greatly improved by Truman.

[7] Sherman Adams, *Firsthand Report* (New York: Harper & Row, 1961), p. 21.

[8] *Journal of Commerce*, December 31, 1968.

[9] Personal correspondence, June 10, 1971.

[10] The move to reduce the budget of the Council was made by Representative Rees (R) of Kansas. It was opposed by a group of Senators who devised the method of dealing with it: Maybank (S.C.), Ellender (La.), O'Mahoney (Wyo.), Saltonstall (Mass.), and Taft (Ohio). Saltonstall and Taft were Republicans; the others were Democrats. This "fumble" was a serious one for the morale of the civil servants who watched it closely, and the lack of coordination was no credit to the Administration. A good account appears in Laurin W. Henry, *Presidential Transitions* (Washington: The Brookings Institution, 1960), pp. 548ff.

[11] Adams, op. cit., pp. 155–56.

[12] Neil H. Jacoby, "The President, the Constitution and the Economist in Economic Stabilization," *History of Political Economy*, Vol. 3, No. 2 (Fall, 1971).

[13] Neil H. Jacoby, *Can Prosperity Be Sustained?* (New York: Holt, 1956), pp. 56–57.

[14] Nourse agrees with these points saying, "I only wish I had been smart enough to differentiate these cases as explicitly as Burns has done from the fourth issue, the one on which I took my stand. . . ." See C. Silverman, *The President's Council on Economic Advisers*, Inter-University Case Program, Case Study #48, (Indianapolis: Bobbs-Merrill, 1959) p. 16. Reprinted with the permission of the Inter-University Case Program.

[15] Ibid, p. 17.

[16] Ibid, p. 18.

[17] Ibid, p. 18.

[18] Plan to Reorganize the Executive Branch (Hoover Commission Report, 1949).

[19] Quoted in Flash, op. cit., p. 165.

[20] *Economic Report of the President*, January 1954, p. 123.

[21] Ibid., p. 76.

[22] Robert J. Donovan, *Eisenhower: The Inside Story*, pp. 214–22. Copyright© 1956 by New York Herald Tribune, Inc. Reprinted by permission of Harper & Row.

[23] Adams, op. cit., p. 156.

[24] G. L. Bach, *Making Monetary and Fiscal Policy* (Washington: Brookings, 1971), p. 92.

[25] Raymond J. Saulnier, *The Strategy of Economic Policy* (New York: Fordham University Press, 1963), p. 44.

[26] Jacoby, "The President, the Constitution and the Economist," pp. 407–8.

[27] See Joint Economic Committee, *Recent Inflation in the United States* (Washington: Government Printing Office, 1959) and "The Postwar Inflation," Chapter 5 in *Employment Growth and Price Levels*, 1960.

[28] See *Economic Report of the President*, 1959, "Economic Developments in 1958 and Outlook for 1959," Chapter 3, pp. 7–32.

[29] Richard E. Neustadt, *Presidential Power: The Policies of Leadership*. Copyright© 1960 by John Wiley & Sons, Inc. Reprinted with the permission of the publisher.

[30] On June 14, 1954, the *New York Times* reported that the Federal Reserve was resisting "feelers" for a reduction in rediscount rates put forth by the Administration. Yet only a week passed before the "independent" Federal Reserve reduced, not rediscount rates, but reserve requirements.

[31] The 1961 *Report* (p. 59) noted: "A tax system must, of course, provide the reserves needed to cover governmental expenditures over reasonable periods, though a balance is not required every year. A budgetary surplus in prosperous times helps to curb inflationary pressures, and a deficit during a period of recession may help to reverse the downturn."

[32] *Economic Report of the President*, 1958, p. 3.

[33] Calvin B. Hoover, op. cit., p. 252.

[34] Stein, op. cit., p. 283.

[35] Richard M. Nixon, *Six Crises* (New York: Doubleday, 1962), p. 311.

[36] Stein, op. cit., p. 370.

[37] Bach, op. cit., p. 102.

[38] See Garry Wills, *Nixon Agonistes* (Boston: Houghton Mifflin, 1970).

Chapter 6

Kennedy and the Age
of the Professional

*I gave them straight Keynes and
Heller, and they loved it.*
—John F. Kennedy

J ohn F. Kennedy brought to the Presidency a wide
variety of talents and a unique economic background. The first President
born in the twentieth century, Kennedy was not only the youngest man
to serve, but perhaps also the wealthiest and among the best educated in
a formal sense.

Kennedy had graduated from Harvard, briefly attended Stanford's
Graduate School of Business, and the London School of Economics,
acquiring at some point a taste for economic methodology and a talent
for expressing economic concepts unshared by other recent Presidents.
Following service as a Naval officer in World War II, Kennedy spent
some time in journalism and considered the idea of an academic career.
However, though he had done some fragmentary graduate work, his
A.B. from Harvard represented his only earned degree.

Still undecided as to a career, he entered the congressional race from
an east Boston district and, winning, found himself in Congress from a
"safe" district, though barely past his middle twenties. In 1953, he
abandoned his House seat and defeated Henry Cabot Lodge, Jr., in a
Senate race.[1]

Although articulate and well informed on issues, JFK was, in comparison to other Presidents, short on practical experience, having except for short periods been engaged in public service all of his adult life, and having been spared the necessity of seriously earning a living.

In *A Thousand Days*,[2] Schlesinger points out that Kennedy had received his highest grade (only "B") in his freshman year at Harvard in the introductory course in economics. The course made no deep impression on him. Indeed, he remembered his grade as "C," or so, at least, he liked to tell his economists in later years.

His stay at the London School of Economics was brief, and in *Economics of the Kennedy Years*, Seymour E. Harris (a long-time adviser) argues that the social views of Harold Laski had no influence on Kennedy's economic philosophy.[3] Nor, according to Theodore Sorensen, did JFK express much interest in finance or in the many family enterprises established by his father. As a Senator he attempted to keep his household finances in balance, but as a man of great wealth money had no real meaning to him.

In his early congressional days, JFK showed more tendency to reflect the outlook of Joseph P. Kennedy, but as he moved to broader areas of endeavor this tendency was less evident. He said later, "I had just come out of my father's house." In any event, by 1960 the father was aging and probably made little serious attempt to press his viewpoints on the maturing son. Sorensen makes the point that Kennedy, though largely unschooled in formal economics, had great native intelligence and an ability to gather and use to the best advantage a wide variety of advisers.

To this combination of influences, Kennedy added his own devouring curiosity about the way things worked. If at the start of his administration he was sometimes unsure of technical detail, he readily acquired an excellent command of economic analysis. In addition, he had shrewd economic intuitions, though perhaps more on national than on international problems. "He was the most perceptive of critics," Walter Heller later said— "he could pick out a sentence or a paragraph and see its weakness. Even though he might not have understood the analytic bases for its weakness, he had the feel for it, and this was uncanny." His approach to economic and social policy, in short, was that of an experimentalist and activist, restrained by politics and prudence but unfettered by doctrinal fetish or taboo.

As President, he meant to assure himself a wide range of intelligent advice. Having chosen Douglas Dillon as Secretary of the Treasury, he chose Walter Heller as Chairman of the Council of Economic Advisers. "I need you both," he told Heller, "for a proper balance in economic matters. . . ."

Dillon, if to the right of Heller, was by no means an economic conservative. He understood the value of academic advice, restored the economists to the Treasury Department, from which they had been driven out by George Humphrey, made Seymour Harris (on Kennedy's suggestion) his economic adviser, and encouraged Harris to set up a panel of outside consultants, whose meetings the Secretary regularly attended. Harris, who had a realistic grasp of the political problems of economic policy, became an effective bridge to the Council. Nevertheless, both Dillon's personal background and the institutional predilections of the Treasury inclined him to a particular solicitude for the business community. He was also an exceptionally skilled operator within the bureaucracy, ready to pull every stop and cut many corners to advance the Treasury view, always and justifiably confident that his charm could heal any feelings hurt in the process.

Heller, on the other hand, had the knack of composing breezy memoranda on economic problems—some hundreds in three years—and Kennedy read them faithfully. Both Heller and Dillon were urbane and articulate men; and much of the debate between them was conducted in the President's presence. . . .[4]

He also had an ability to learn and to judge people and was capable of listening to diverse viewpoints and coming to logical conclusions on empirical grounds. Sorensen also states that Kennedy's view on federal finance and budgeting were much more conservative than many of his supporters had believed (or perhaps hoped).[5]

Harris claims that, in terms of economics, Kennedy was the most sophisticated President who has served in recent years. By background and training, he was inherently conservative, although he became more Keynesian in his thinking as his administration progressed. Harris says: ". . . after the first eighteen months of the Kennedy Administration the President underwent a fundamental change. He had become convinced that deficits would stimulate the economy, that with large amounts of unemployment they would not bring on inflation, and that there were some objectives much more important than the balanced budget."[6]

He had, of course, been forced to think largely in terms of regional economic problems in his congressional years:

The special character of his New England problems led him in the Fifties to think less about fiscal and monetary problems and more about structural remedies—in other words, direct attempts to strengthen New England's position in the national economy.

His membership on the Labor and Education Committee encouraged the structural approach. (Though he sought appointment to the Joint Committee on the Economic Report, which dealt with fiscal and monetary issues, he did not make it until 1960.) In general, he looked for programs which he thought would at once benefit New England and the Nation, like redeveloping depressed areas (he served as floor manager of Paul Douglas's first area redevelopment bill in 1956) or raising the minimum wage (and thereby reducing the South's competitive advantage) or repealing the Taft-Hartley Act (and opening the way for the unionization of the South). On occasion, he would vote against what Massachusetts considered its local interest, as when he supported the St. Lawrence Seaway. On other occasions, he was ready to help New England at possible expense to the general welfare, as when he favored special protection for textiles or, for a while, opposed farm price supports on the ground that they worsened New England's terms of trade with the rest of the country.[7]

As a Congressman and Senator, Kennedy was (like his fellow Congressmen) inclined to take a highly pragmatic and localized approach to matters of economic policy; perhaps his lack of experience made him more inclined to do so than most. He generally supported those measures that he thought would be good for Massachusetts and opposed what he thought would be damaging. He sometimes voted against costly regional proposals in agriculture and reclamation, matters requiring some explanation when his ambitions for national office were paramount.[8]

In the Senate, however, though he still was a "Senator from New England," Kennedy took a somewhat expanded view. He began to gain some breadth of vision as he faced the challenge of the Senate with its more encompassing problems.

Many observers feel that a liberalizing influence was exercised by his contact with Theodore Sorensen, his senatorial assistant who accompanied him to the White House and became one of his biographers. Sorensen was a Nebraska liberal, a lawyer eleven years younger than the Senator, but who, unlike Kennedy, had already formed an economic philosophy. Over the years of their contact—in the Senate, in particular—Sorensen was successful in infusing Kennedy with liberal ideas, at the same time himself adopting the more pragmatic and less idealistic viewpoint of the Kennedys.[9] There is no doubt that Sorensen as a young Midwestern liberal (Senator George W. Norris, the great Nebraskan, was his hero) represented a species that was totally new to the wealthy and urbane Senator from the Northeast. Sorensen was able to educate Kennedy on such matters as rural electrification and reclamation, farm problems, and other matters largely alien to Massachusetts.

In 1956, when he narrowly lost the vice-presidential nomination to Senator Estes Kefauver, JFK set his sights on the White House, and the next four years saw an intensive effort to obtain the nomination in 1960. During these years he traveled throughout the nation, studied national economic problems intensively, and discussed them with Sorensen and others. To be sure, Sorensen was one of many factors, and his influence can easily be overrated.

Moving from House to Senate is, in any case, a broadening experience calling for a new outlook. Certainly, Kennedy was thinking further ahead than the Senate and thus desired to demonstrate economic understanding that transcended the borders of New England. Kennedy was never a power in the Senate "establishment." Yet he did his homework; in counsel with Professor Seymour Harris of Harvard, he became an expert on New England's postwar economic difficulties. As in the House, he continued to have some interest in labor matters, but his ideas on fiscal affairs were still unsophisticated, and from time to time he questioned the feasibility of spending in the face of an increasing national debt and voiced other economic ideas based in conventional wisdom. During this period he received instruction from both Harris and from Professor Paul Samuelson—MIT professor, Nobel Prize winner, and probably America's most distinguished economist—emerging in 1960 with a far more sophisticated grasp of economic affairs than had been true of the young Representative from Massachusetts.[10] As the campaign for nomination began, all resources were made ready. Theodore White noted:

> Ideas, next. From Harvard now the professors began to gather. Ever since 1952, individual professors of the Harvard faculty had been furnishing this most prominent of their living alumni with ideas, information, and analysis, to shape his national thinking. He had over the years drawn them one by one into his closeness, until Harvard's faculty seemed his intellectual harem. In January of 1960 he had assembled his Brain Trust at the Harvard Club, on Boston's Commonwealth Avenue, and at dinner had bluntly told them they were now mobilized (permitting the Stevensonians among them to take leave if they so wished). Now, in July, they were to act. Professor Archibald Cox of the Harvard Law School was to establish himself with a speechwriting detail in Washington; the professors were to think, winnow, analyze, and prepare data on the substance of

national policy, to channel from university to speech writer to Cox to Sorensen—and thus to the candidate.[11]

In 1960, he narrowly defeated the Republican candidate, Richard M. Nixon. Kennedy had taken full advantage of the downturn in economic activity at the end of the year, charging that the Eisenhower years had been marked by stagnation and decline. Kennedy was critical of the Eisenhower economic policy on four counts, holding that the Republicans had allowed a decline in growth to take place (not absolute, but relative), and a rise in unemployment (8 percent in 1961); had pursued an over-restrictive monetary policy; and had allowed the balance of payments to deteriorate. These views reflected those of his economic advisers, principally Samuelson, Galbraith, and Harris.

Both Kennedy and Nixon put considerable stress on economic growth and progress, and JFK's general economic theme was "to get the country moving again." The campaign was marked by a substantial barrage of statistics, references to growth rates, etc., that shed little light on the depth of the issues involved. During the campaign, Sorensen reports that Nixon referred to Kennedy as an "economic ignoramus," who did not understand high-school-level economics. Neither candidate showed much economic sophistication, and the campaign generated more heat than light. As Herbert Stein notes, JFK still had a long way to go in his economic education.

Stein argues that JFK, who gained a reputation as a sophisticated economist, gained it only after considerable "education."

Kennedy has been called the first modern economist in the American Presidency. This may have been true in 1963, but it was not true on Inauguration Day. At that time Kennedy's fiscal thinking was conventional. He believed in budget-balancing. While he was aware of circumstances in which the budget could not or should not be balanced, he preferred a balanced budget, being in this respect like most other people but unlike modern economists. But if he brought into the White House no very sophisticated or systematic ideas about compensatory fiscal policy, neither did he bring with him any deep intellectual or emotional commitment to the old ideas. This was partly a matter of his youth. He was not the first Keynesian President on Inauguration Day, but he was the first who was not a pre-Keynesian— the first who had passed the majority of his life in the post-Keynesian world where the old orthodoxy was giving way to the new. This characteristic he shared with his contemporaries. But he had in addition special characteristics which helped prepare him to accept the new economics he did not yet know. The son

170

of an extremely wealthy, urban, Catholic family, he was unlikely to confuse personal budget-balancing with financial acumen or financial acumen with moral virtue.[12]

Both as candidate and as President-elect, Kennedy made much use of task forces. The most significant economic task force in the early period was asked to address itself to the issues of recession and growth. This group was headed by Professor Samuelson, whom JFK tried to recruit as CEA chairman. The product of this group, a report entitled *Prospects and Policies for the 1961 American Economy,* set the tone for much of the early Kennedy economic policy.

In terms of the economic policy role of the President, Kennedy faced some unique problems: (1) the aggregate demand resulting from World War II and the Korean War had been largely satisfied, and economic growth would slow in any case; (2) his margin of victory over Nixon was so small that it hardly constituted a mandate for basic economic change; (3) the balance-of-payments problem made expansion policies difficult to pursue since it limited the effectiveness of fiscal policy; (4) the alliance between Republicans and conservative southern Democrats made for relatively little control over the Congress; (5) for largely personal reasons, his relationship with the Congress was not as sound as it might have been; and (6) he and the business community were mistrustful of one another, especially after the "steel price incident" in April 1962.

This incident deserves some attention, since it was to be of great future interest. The President had obtained agreement from the United Steel Workers for a new contract with a wage settlement that the Council believed would not disturb wage-price relationships. The wage-price guideposts, which were to become widely known in later years, were not then fully understood, although they were introduced in the *Economic Report* of January 1962. After the contract was signed, the major steel producers announced price increases that the Council believed to be inflationary and excessive. Kennedy lacked the emergency powers used a decade earlier by Truman in a similar situation, but, relying on public indignation, he denounced the steel companies and began a vigorous campaign to force a price reduction. His strategy involved several points: presenting evidence that the steel price increase was unnecessary for the welfare of the steel industry; attempting to encourage a split in the industry by encouraging the second-level major firms, such as Inland and Kaiser, to hold the price line; and emphasizing the adverse effects on the steel industry in the international market if prices were increased. Within seventy-two hours, the companies had reversed themselves.[13] There is some question as to the relative influences of the pressures involved. Grant McConnell suggests that the marketplace played a major part in the reevaluation, and no doubt this is true. However, the power of the Presidency (backed by the technical competence of the Council) was a major factor. Though he won, the incident stirred up considerable controversy and influenced the President's relationship with the business community for some time. Some harsh words were exchanged and the administration used some rough tactics that upset the press as well as the steel company officials. It also injected CEA into the operational side of the Presidency, where it was to remain for good or ill throughout the Kennedy and Johnson years.

Despite his later efforts to make a favorable impression on the business community, he was never really able to do so and, following the steel incident, his relations with the Business Advisory Council and its chairman, Roger Blough (president of U.S. Steel), were cool, although Heller and Blough worked cooperatively. In fact, this incident merely intensified ill feeling generated when JFK attempted to reduce the influence of the Business Advisory Council. BAC had been established as a communications device between government and industry. Over the years, it had become dominated by "big business," and Kennedy felt that it was being used to secure unfair advantage. The reaction was more adverse than had been expected, and the administration was forced to make a modest withdrawal in order to preserve such rapport with the business community as it had. In his book, *The Free Enterprisers,* Hobart Rowen quotes Lee Lovinger, assistant attorney general, as saying that the antitrust policy followed by the administration was limited to rather conventional matters in an effort to avoid further acrimony with businessmen.[14] The business community did not overlook the fact that JFK appointed a large number of academic people to high-level positions in which Eisenhower had generally placed businessmen and industrialists.

Rowen also argues that the Yale speech on "economic myths," widely admired by the academic community as a classic, fell flat with businessmen. Unlike Eisenhower and Johnson, Kennedy was more at home with artists and scholars than executives and, despite his efforts, he never managed to gain the full confidence of the business community. Like his father, he was always an "outsider." Joseph P. Kennedy had always been considered a "maverick" by the upper levels of business and doubtless JFK reaped some of this ill will.

172

Kennedy and His Economists

Kennedy was a natural to attract the able academic economist. In Roosevelt's day, though the need was great, there were few capable professionals who had experience in high-level affairs. In the Kennedy years, need and availability often coincided; economists of ability and experience were available, and the administration was anxious to use them. As he left the businessman cold, Kennedy seemed to have been made to order for the intellectual community. Both groups overstated his defects and virtues. It should not be thought, however, that the Kennedy Administration was a haven for the pure theoretician who had no pragmatic views.[15] Kennedy was first, last, and always a hardheaded politician, appreciating capable performance and intolerant of vague concepts, fuzzy thinking, or a general lack of competence.[16]

Many distinguished economists in addition to Samuelson, in and out of the administration, were known to have influence on the Kennedy philosophy. John Kenneth Galbraith and Carl Kaysen were frequently consultants. Seymour Harris, a Kennedy adviser of long service, organized a group of economists who met at irregular intervals with the Council, the officials of the Treasury (where, Harris told the author, "Humphrey had run all the economists out"), and the Bureau of the Budget. The President apparently enjoyed raising questions on policy matters and obtained varied viewpoints from any economist with whom he came into contact. Galbraith was anxious to exert a potent liberal influence. Before his departure to India as ambassador, the Harvard economist spent several weeks commuting between Washington and Cambridge and was involved in a number of economic issues and events that took place in the early days of the administration:

> On the issue of economic recession and a tax cut, I urged that needed public expenditures be pressed first as an anti-recession measure. Thereafter, if unemployment was still high, taxes could be reduced. I believe JFK agrees. He faces trouble with William McChesney Martin, Jr., Chairman of the Federal Reserve, and dislikes the prospect of a fight with him—which he thinks may be inevitable. Martin has been in office for a long time, and, in his chosen sphere, obviously regards himself as superior to the President.[17]

January 27—Washington

We had a long meeting at the White House to consider the State of the Union message—economic aspects. Dillon, Fowler, Leddy, from Treasury; Goldberg from Labor; Heller, Gordon,

173

Tobin from the Council of Economic Advisers; and several others. There was a further long discussion of repealing the 25 percent gold cover clause which Dillon supported but not with fervor. I opposed it with fervor. It would, as I have said, set off a hideous debate; everyone would be persuaded in the process that something horrible was happening to the dollar; the gold outflow would be worse than ever. Better wait. The need for action may not arise; if necessary, it can be done at the last minute; in any case, there are powers to suspend the clause requiring a minimum cover which could be used. In the end, I had the better of it; there is a great advantage in being certain.

This afternoon Walter Heller and I had a long talk with the President—an interruption in an even larger meeting on the economic message.[18]

January 31—Washington

This morning I had a long visit with Robert Roosa. I asked him why the banks and the Federal Reserve could never bring themselves to express any warmth and compassion for the unemployed and needed always to warn of the dangers of action. I had as text a draft on internal interest rate policy agreed upon by Federal Reserve and Treasury.[19]

From his post in New Delhi, Galbraith sent frequent comments on domestic economic matters and on his visits to Washington continued in his advisory role:

The bedroom meeting was on economics—Dillon, McChesney Martin, Heller, Gordon, and Roosa. This was interesting. The Federal Reserve, pressed by the higher interest rate lobby, has been actually raising interest rates of late although unemployment is still around seven percent. Dillon, who is an excellent operator, entered only a partial defense. But then Martin, who isn't so clever, went all out. "The Federal Reserve," he said, "could not keep interest rates artificially low." They had been doing their best; in the last few weeks, they have been buying government bonds to keep the money market easy. I asked if such purchases were not artificial and went on to ask that he define the difference between natural and artificial action on the part of the Federal Reserve. I did this with great mildness and many assurances of my desire to help Martin clarify his position. In response, only static came out. The President then made a magnificent statement saying he did not want the recovery choked off by premature increases in interest rates.[20]

Some writers have suggested that Kennedy would have done well to keep Galbraith in Washington, since he was so articulate. One suspects, however, that JFK had in mind the fact that Galbraith had a very liberal image, much too liberal for many (he had been president of the Americans for Democratic Action), and he would be less visible in India.

Despite his frequent use of, or at least conversation with, outside economists, Kennedy did not lose sight of CEA nor the other resources officially available to the President in his role as economic policy maker. The emphasis was on the "new economics." The members of the Council appointed by Kennedy—Heller, Tobin, and Gordon (later Gardner Ackley and John P. Lewis)—were all adherents, generally speaking, of the postwar Keynesian views of fiscal policy. Heller, Tobin, and Gordon were, like the President himself, born in the twentieth century and trained in the years of the "Keynesian Revolution."[21] Kennedy appointed Walter W. Heller of the University of Minnesota as the chairman. This appointment was announced at the same time as the Cabinet appointments.[22] This protocol, though minor, was a departure from past practices. One of the unfortunate aspects of the Council crisis at the beginning of the Eisenhower years was the delay in naming CEA members, which contributed to confusion as to the fate of the Council.

Harris claims that Heller was able to bring the President around to his view on modern economics, whereas Keyserling, Burns, and Saulnier in the Truman and Eisenhower years were dealing with Presidents who already shared their views. This claim is hard to support. Truman and Eisenhower were both "educated" and, to a degree, "liberalized" by the Council. Eisenhower, especially, came to depend on Burns and Hauge, despite an occasional backslide. Harris gives Heller primary credit for being Kennedy's teacher of modern economics; but he also has substantial praise for Secretary Dillon, who was a good balance for Heller. As an activist, Kennedy recognized the Council's policy-making potentiality:

> Kennedy's economists did not dictate either his ideas or his actions in the field of fiscal policy. Nevertheless, he was more influenced by professional economists than his predecessors had been. In part this was simply the continuation of a rising trend of influence which dated back to Roosevelt and his Brain Trust and ran through the Truman-Keyserling and Eisenhower-Burns relationship. But while the trend of economists' influence was rising anyway, it made a leap upward with the Kennedy Administration. Kennedy was especially prepared to accept new ideas. Moreover, he had, for a President, an unusual interest in abstract thinking; he read a great deal, enjoyed the company of intellectuals, and was for these reasons open to education by economists.

Council of Economic Advisers, a free hand to take more advanced positions than the Administration was ready to adopt. To be sure, there was a political dividend in this for Kennedy, in that it accorded the Administration a useful liberal facade. But Heller can also be a genuine frontrunner, as Dillon suggests, generating new ideas. The CEA's annual reports have contributed greatly to the public's economic education, especially the 1962 report which developed what might be called the "economic conscience" of the New Frontier. This may eventually be regarded as a unique state paper, because it urged the nation "to face the question of public versus private expenditures pragmatically, in terms of intrinsic merits and costs, not in terms of fixed preconceptions.[28]

Heller was much like Kennedy in personality, and many of the descriptive terms used to describe JFK—articulate, pragmatic, witty—apply equally to Heller. Heller's pragmatism enabled him to overbalance advisers who, though perhaps more liberal, lacked his sense of practical affairs.

The Great Debate over the New Economics

Perhaps no incident more clearly illustrates the growing role of CEA than the now famous debate over expansionist policy that went on in the Kennedy Administration in the early 1960s on the issue of economic growth and the continuing problem of unemployment. These issues, of course, were carried over from the Eisenhower years, and the debate was more or less continuous.

Among administration economists, two basic schools of thought contended. The first group, of which Heller was a member, was of the opinion that there was insufficient aggregate demand for goods and services. Citing the experience of the war years, these economists argued that the need was for public spending, public works, and other such activities designed to increase aggregate demand. In Keynesian terms, the nation's capacity to produce, or "aggregate supply," depends upon various factors, such as population, technology, participation of the labor force, and supply of natural resources. Clearly this capacity was great in the United States during the early 1960s. On the other hand, "aggregate demand" depends upon consumption, investment, and expenditures for net foreign imports. If the aggregate amount spent on these items is inadequate, there will be a gap between the potential capacity of the economy and the consumption. In some way this gap must be closed. If the private sector is unable to do so, then it must be closed by government expenditures.

The second school held that excess unemployment stemmed from structural deficiencies in the economy. That is, there were large numbers of people who, because of lack of training or obsolete skills, were unable to participate in the modern economy, whatever the demand. To these observers the obvious remedy was a policy of preparing the unemployed through programs of training, upgrading, and relocation.[29] Those who endorsed the structural view argued that increased spending would not only fail to solve the problem but would, in fact, further aggravate it by contributing to inflationary pressures, raising wages and prices, and further impairing those seeking jobs. To look at the matter in another way, they argued that federal expenditures of sufficient magnitude to draw these people into the labor force through increases in aggregate demand (as in war time) would be intolerable.

The Council, viewing the tax burden as a drag on the economy, was in favor of increasing demand through greater purchasing power by a tax reduction. Galbraith, however, opposed this route on the ground that it would merely increase spending for personal consumer goods, of which, he had argued in *The Affluent Society,* there was already a more than adequate supply. In Galbraith's view, the real need was for increased spending in the public sector, which had been far outstripped by private affluence (the doctrine of social imbalance). While there were many worthwhile programs to be considered, neither Congress nor the administration was anxious to embark on complex, time-consuming ventures. A quick and simple tax cut was in many ways desirable, but political problems complicated the picture. Bach has recounted some of the pressures and problems:

> The Kennedy Administration inherited a recession when it took office in January, 1961. . . . [its economists were committed to action]. . . .
>
> At the Treasury, Secretary Douglas Dillon, a respected financial authority and former high offical in the Eisenhower administration, had doubts; and these doubts were shared by Chairman William McChesney Martin, Jr., at the Federal Reserve. They knew the arguments for an active fiscal policy, but nonetheless remained concerned about the dangers of inflation, of a large unbalanced budget, and of a weakening U.S. balance-of-payments position. Dillon was soon joined by Robert V. Roosa from the Federal Reserve Bank of New York as Undersecretary of the Treasury; Roosa played a leading role in both international monetary arrangements and debt management. His views

179

were similar to those of Dillon, and the generally conservative trio of Dillon, Roosa, and Martin constituted a powerful force in the new administration.[30]

On the other hand, the Council put the matter into a cogent and powerful argument strongly in favor of a cut, stating, "Faster economic growth in the United States requires, above all, an expansion of demand, to take up existing slack and to match future increases in capacity. Unless demand is adequate to buy potential output, accelerating the growth of potential is neither an urgent problem nor a promising possibility."[31] To analyze the impact of government fiscal policy on the economy, the Council emphasized a new concept, the "full-employment surplus."

The Full-Employment Surplus and Other Concepts

The Heller Council, with its young and well-trained staff, articulated many concepts of macroeconomic analysis that have found their way into the elementary economics textbooks of recent years.

The tax cut proposals of 1964, for example, were based upon the fact that the modern economy, given the current tax structure, generates substantial revenue that varies automatically with increases and declines in personal and corporate income. In fact, due to the progressive nature of the income tax, the tax yield (or loss) is multiplied, and up or down movements are escalated accordingly. That is, as personal and corporate incomes rise, increasing amounts automatically accrue to the government as tax payment. As gross national product increases by, say, 4 percent, federal tax receipts (at a given rate of taxes) rise by $8 to $10 billion annually. Thus, in a given year, if the budget is in balance, it will show an $8 to $10 billion surplus in the following year, even if there is no increase in federal spending or tax rates. To avoid this automatic "drag," the advocate of modern fiscal policy argues that in prosperous times taxes should be cut or a "fiscal dividend" declared through an increase in federal spending programs; that is, the surplus should be expended and put back into consumption or investment spending by the private sector. It is argued that the key concept is not the surplus or deficit of the budget per se but the *full employment* surplus or deficit.

There were numerous occasions during the 1950s and early 1960s when, although a deficit existed, the economy was not expanding, since the deficit was due to low incomes and low levels of employment, which produced low tax receipts. In these years, the federal budget exercised a

180

drag on the economy in that tax receipts exceeded government spending well before full employment had been reached. The persistent deficits thus reflected mainly the involuntary results of a depressed economy that pulled tax receipts below government spending levels. In short, tax rates were *too high* even though a deficit existed. Under these circumstances, the budget was pulled back to a surplus condition long before full employment was reached. As Heller said, the "vaunted built-in flexibility is a mixed blessing" in that it causes improper signals to be flashed under the circumstances then existing.

In 1962, for example, the realized federal deficit was $4 billion, but the tax rates then in effect would have produced a surplus of $10 billion at full employment. A drag was thus imposed on the upswing long before the appropriate time, i.e., when full employment had been achieved.

The appropriate fiscal policy target of the mid-1960s for "full" or "high" employment under these assumptions would have been that level of GNP associated with a 4 percent rate of unemployment. The "full employment surplus," under these circumstances, would have been the excess of revenues over expenditures that would prevail at 4 percent unemployment. Heller calculates that the 1961 budget would have run a surplus of about $10 billion at full or high employment. Fiscal policy brought the surplus down from about $13 billion, but it was still too high to avoid a "drag."[32]

As Heller notes, modern policy making must have quantitative as well as qualitative targets, and these targets must be flexible:

> But even if the employment act had not required quantitative targets, activist policy does. Without them, how can the decision maker aim at finite economic objectives and make hard choices among alternatives, as he must? Presidents need to know—to the best of their economists' ability—how high they can push employment and output with reasonable price stability. If, for example, we had followed the advice of those who urged us to fix our job sights on a 5-percent rather than a 4-percent level of unemployment, it would have automatically lowered our GNP target by $20 billion.
>
> Standards of economic performance must be recast from time to time. Recasting them in more ambitious terms was an indispensable prelude to the shaping of economic policies for the 1960's which would be suitable to the tremendous output capabilities of the U.S. economy.[33]

Divergent views on the issues were articulated by the various advisers, and the President considered them carefully. But, as President, he was forced to temper professional advice with practical politics. Others outside the administration lent a hand; for example, Paul Samuelson met with the President at Hyannisport and made a plea for an early cut.[34] The President, however, was not fully convinced, as Schlesinger says:

> . . . in the President's mind what was theoretically desirable had to be tempered by what was politically feasible. His campaign had emphasized discipline and sacrifice; his victory had been slim; his Congress was conservative; and, at least in the mind of the business community, his party had a reputation for fiscal irresponsibility. As Kennedy told Heller in December, 1960, "I understand the case for a tax cut, but it doesn't fit very well with my call for sacrifice." Nor did it fit very well with the need, increased by the shaky balance-of-payments situation, to appear, though a Democrat, a defender of the dollar. . . .
>
> As Kennedy told Walter Lippmann and me at luncheon a few days later, most economists were evasive when he tried to pin them down as to what exactly government could do to stimulate growth, but [Robert] Nathan had been frank; and an additional $50 billion to the national debt would of course be very little compared to the extra growth and revenue which could thus be induced. Only the systematic creation of annual deficits, he said, was the one thing which the political situation, short of depression, precluded his doing. "I don't want to be tagged as a big spender early in this administration," he said on another occasion. "If I do, I won't get my programs through later on."[35]

This was, in the true sense, an exercise in the art of *political economy*. Many factors and personalities were to be taken into account. The late Harry F. Byrd, Sr., then senior Senator from Virginia and long-time chairman of the Senate Finance Committee, was unalterably opposed to a tax cut at this time. Even more important, Congressman Wilbur D. Mills, then the powerful chairman of the House Ways and Means Committee, was opposed to a cut, unless it incorporated a basic reform of the tax situation. While the Kennedy forces were not opposed to a reform, they felt that it would be a long-term proposition—much too long for any immediate economic gains. Flash notes:

> Kennedy was restrained by other noneconomic factors. Mills was strongly opposed to immediate reduction because of the lack of clear indications of recession and because such a step would deny an essential sweetener for the structural reforms in which he was primarily interested and which had yet to be presented to Congress. Further, Mills felt that imposition of the tax cut without accompanying reduction in expenditures would

increase the risk of inflation. Without Mills' support, no tax legislation was possible. The slow and tortuous progress of the 1962 revision dulled any remaining optimism that a bill could be passed quickly. Furthermore, to push the tax cut would jeopardize other priority legislation by risking a fight within Congress at a highly inappropriate time. Although Dillon favored cuts in the next year (the nature and extent of them yet to be determined), he was strongly opposed to any immediate cuts for reasons paralleling those of Mills. The likelihood both of a sizable deficit instead of a modest surplus for fiscal 1963 and a congressional refusal to enact a postal rate increase for additional revenue made the prospect of further deficits stemming from a tax reduction all the more unwelcome. (William McChesney) Martin's distaste for deficit financing and the power of the Federal Reserve to react to its use by raising interest rates were an additional restraint. A few enlightened sophisticates might not be worried about deficits, but the general public was, and in an election year this was an important consideration. Kennedy wished to meet the criteria of fiscal responsibility as applied by the general public and by the business community both at home and overseas.[36]

While this controversy was perhaps the most illustrative example of economic advice at work in the administration, other serious economic problems were troublesome.

Unemployment continued to be of concern, and the problem of gold outflow was far from solved. The argument over attacking unemployment or recession continued over most of the early months of the administration. As the Kennedy Council took over, unemployment had reached almost 7 percent. Within days after the Council was organized, a special message on a "Program for Economic Recovery and Growth" was in preparation. This message, coming on February 7, only four days after the State of the Union Message, was largely the work of the Council and provided an excellent opportunity for the CEA to demonstrate its ability to the President, as well as enabling its members to separate the strands of their own thoughts.

Within a brief period, the Council participated in messages on gold and the balance of payments, national resources, and the federal highway program, while at the same time laying down the outlines of its own testimony before the Joint Economic Committee on March 6 (i.e., its support of the President's emergency program).

Although the economic downturn with which the Council was also concerning itself was mild, countercyclical operations centered around

183

the diminishing rate of economic growth as seen in the increased frequency of recession and the ominous weakness of recovery after each downturn.

The basis of action on this front was a report (indeed, a classic of economic advisership), commissioned by Kennedy while President-elect, made by a task force committee under Paul Samuelson. Entitled *Prospects and Policies for the 1961 American Economy* and largely written by Samuelson, the report nonetheless reflects the views of other highly respected professionals. The tone of the report was generally expansionist, but, again, the President was reluctant to embark upon a major program of federal expenditures.

The Heller Approach

Having in mind the controversy between Nourse and the Joint Committee and Burns and Senator Douglas in regard to testifying before the Joint Committee, Heller took steps to avoid difficulty and, in fact, turn it to his advantage. In a presentation early in March, the chairman pledged cooperation with the Committee but included these significant words:

> We assume the Committee does not want the Council to indicate in what respects its advice has or has not been taken by the President, nor to what extent particular proposals, or omissions of proposals reflect the advice of the Council.
>
> Subject to the limits mentioned, members of the Council are glad to discuss . . . as professional economists, the economic situation . . . in achieving a better understanding of our economic problems and approaches to their solution.[37]

Heller clearly recognized that testimony, in addition to being a useful lubricant in congressional relations, also gave him an invaluable "launching pad for economic ideas." He recognized the educational value of the Council's role in putting forth and domesticating new economic concepts. For example, he brought his ideas on fiscal policy into sharp focus in his testimony on the role of stabilizers. Typical of his educational technique was his comment on the balanced economy:

> The success of fiscal and budget policies cannot be measured only by whether the budget is in the black or in the red. The true test is whether the economy is in balance. Only an economy which is realizing its potential can produce the goods and create the jobs the country needs. If at the end of this year the unemployment ratio is still near 7 percent, our fiscal policies

would have to be viewed with great concern, even if there is little or no deficit in the budget. On the other hand, if we have succeeded in reducing the unemployment ratio and expanding output significantly by the year's end, we will be on our way to the goals of a stronger economy and the restoration of budgetary strength.[38]

These were relatively bold forays into advanced economic policy; and, in stating them in public, Heller was pushing beyond the public thinking of the administration, although some of these ideas had been presented in a Joint Economic Committee study.[39] Heller recognized the value of the platform provided by the opportunity to testify, as would Ackley, his successor. Kennedy, of course, helped to set the tone in June 1962 in his famous Yale speech on economic policy.[40]

Kennedy always allowed Heller to introduce or comment upon matters that he himself was unable for political reasons to touch and often used Heller to take the "flack" from controversial issues, once telling him, "Walter, I want you to know I resent these attacks on you."

The Heller Council employed a mode of operation different from both the Burns and Nourse-Keyserling Councils and was highly informal in its internal organization. The young and generally inexperienced staff members were not entirely suitable for high-level representation, leaving the burden of this task upon the members of the Council, especially on Heller himself. Further, it had been agreed between the President and Heller at the time of his appointment that there would be no Kennedy counterpart of Gabriel Hauge, the White House resident economist and "legman" under Eisenhower. While this assured Heller that the Council would be the economic authority, it was to prove troublesome. A White House in-house economist is able to undertake many urgent semipolitical economic chores for the President. With no such talent available, Heller and the other CEA members were engaged in such "errands," which took time and effort from other long-range matters, and involved them in day-to-day crises.

The late Gerhard Colm commented on this matter during the Twentieth Anniversary Symposium, noting a weakness: "the Council [under Kennedy and Johnson] has had to act frequently as a fire brigade for the President, particularly for the implementation of the price-wage guidelines."[41] It may well be that the "fire brigade function" is the price paid for Council involvement; there is no doubt that the Heller Council was involved. Whatever the arrangement, however, economic talent in the White House was both available and used. For example, though he was not on the White House staff as an economist per se, Professor Carl

Kaysen, a noted economist, was influential and played a large role in the tax cut drama.

Unlike the procedure in the Burns Council, intra-Council discussion of issues, wide staff participation at all levels, and flexibility were encouraged; consultants and part-time experts were used extensively, especially at report-writing time. In general, the Heller Council staff was a three-level structure: the members and career staff; the academic economists who served for a year or more; and the consultants (often former Council or staff members) on call to deal with special problems.

In its external relations, the Council was somewhat more formal and maintained close contact throughout the government with other groups who shared its concerns. Kennedy's Secretaries of Labor Arthur Goldberg and Willard Wertz, for example, pressed hard for a solution to unemployment. Chairman Heller, Treasury Secretary Dillon, and Budget Director David Bell were closely allied in the "Troika," a group that often expanded to include Chairman William McC. Martin of the Federal Reserve. Apparently there was more personal rapport among this trio (or quartet) than had been the case among their counterparts in the Eisenhower years. Heller made early efforts to establish good congressional relations, and, similarly, he did not overlook the importance of nongovernmental groups. Contacts were maintained with the Brookings Institution, the Committee for Economic Development, the National Planning Association, and similar organizations.

To the economic scholar, the Kennedy period has great fascination. It is most likely that, in some part, this stems from the fact that the policy-making process has been so well documented. Heller, Harris, Schlesinger, Sorensen, and others who were close to the administration have left extensive records. The "Kennedy myth," stemming from his untimely death and the general charisma of the Kennedy clan, has caused an outpouring of literature, almost all of it highly laudatory. In fact, Kennedy made little real economic progress but, like most Kennedy performances, what was done often had a patina of glamour unmatched by other Presidents, and an almost day-to-day record of the administration exists. The economic education of the President can be closely followed. The reaction of the administration to various sources of economic advice can be discovered and, at least to a degree, evaluated.

President Kennedy entered office with no fixed economic philosophy and little experience other than as a legislator observing economic problems from a regional viewpoint. Over the three years of his Presidency, he absorbed a great deal of economic education both from the facts of economic life and from his advisers, formal and informal. Though his performance on the tax cut matter was excellent, the administration was far from solving its economic problems to the satisfaction of the nation or itself. The President continued to be troubled by the "sticky" unemployment situation and, despite his desire to reach the goal of a full-utilization economy, by a substantial gap between potential and actual output. The administration estimated that there was a gap of $40 billion between potential and actual GNP in 1961 ($518 billion, as compared to $558 billion).[42] Kennedy sought to close this gap and put the economy on the historic track of a real increase in GNP of 3.5 per year, but the closing of the "job gap" was never completely accomplished. Unused potential expanded as large numbers of new workers entered the labor market (the high birthrates of 1940–43 were making their impact), and unemployment remained around 5.5 percent. The Kennedy Council, concluding, as we have seen, that the main obstacle to expansion was the tax burden, declared in the 1963 report that "for all its advances, the Nation is still falling substantially short of its economic potential. . . . Private initiative and public policy must join hands to break the barriers built up by the years of slack since 1957 and bring the Nation into a new period of sustained full employment and rapid economic growth. . . . The main block to full employment is an unrealistically heavy burden of taxation. The time has come to remove it."[43]

In general, the Kennedy Administration continued the wage and price policies of the Eisenhower years. The unemployment problem was attacked on both cyclical and structural fronts. The tax proposals were designed in large part to solve this problem, and structural effects were to be treated by programs such as the Area Redevelopment Act and the Manpower Development and Training Act. Various facets of the poverty programs were also directed toward structural unemployment, but their overall effectiveness at best was limited.

Kennedy was unable to push through the Congress all the measures necessary to achieve adequate economic performance. In the first days of his administration, he had proposed an extensive program including increases in unemployment compensation and in Social Security, an increase in the minimum wage, and a massive program to aid depressed areas. Area redevelopment appeared at first to be a signal success, but congressional reluctance to finance it adequately limited its effectiveness.

The Kennedy Council was deeply interested in growth and devoted considerable space to the subject in the 1963 report. The administration reverted to the Truman practice of stating growth goals in quantitative terms, the 1962 report noting that, in view of the rapidly expanding labor force, a rate of 4.5 percent was well within the capability of the economy. The administration returned to this theme frequently, devoting much discussion to development of human resources.

Kennedy's strength as an economic policy maker can be attributed to several factors:

1. His interest in, and ability to absorb, economic information and his interest in methodology.
2. His wise choice of advisers—Heller and Dillon were capable and articulate and balanced each other well. Also, though he did not undercut the official advisers, he had no qualms about "bouncing their ideas off others" when the opportunity arose.
3. His skill as an advocate. His urbane and low-pressure presentation of new views eased the acceptance of such ideas throughout the nation. Kennedy enjoyed a very "good press" throughout his term.

The President's weaknesses as an economic policy maker were

1. His failure to obtain real support from the business community.
2. His failure to move legislation through the Congress.

That is to say, Kennedy's articulation of economic policy was better than his performance. Words and phrases came easier than acts and viable programs. He faced a Congress often hostile or indifferent to his program. He had to deal with the constant problem of dividing his time between multiple crises, foreign and domestic. Much of his economic program, including the tax cut, was still not passed on November 22, 1963.

Kennedy and the New Economics

The Kennedy program was, in large part, a reflection of the views of the CEA and other advisers. Never before had the Council achieved such influence as a policy-making body and vendor of new ideas. In an article in *Playboy* (Vol. 5, No. 6, June, 1968), John Kenneth Galbraith says that the most significant accomplishment of the Council was the conversion of the President to Keynesian economics.

One must, however, take care not to overemphasize the CEA role. Heller had great access to the President, probably more than any chairman before or since, and he won many battles but lost, in all probability,

188

a larger number. Dillon, Martin, and Roosa were all important policy makers, often on the opposite side of the fence from Heller.[44]

In some ways the skill and, to a degree, the luck of the Heller group made their tasks more difficult later on. Heller made things look easy. His self-confidence and his access to Kennedy tended to obscure the fact that congressional roadblocks stalled a substantial number of measures.

Heller sold the new economics to the President, but both the Congress and the business community were yet to be convinced. He made a hard sell—perhaps too hard. There is some evidence, however, that the effects of the tax cut were much oversold and that CEA generally underrated the impact of structural unemployment, in part because treatment of structural unemployment would have called for massive spending (which Kennedy wished to avoid) and in part because of methodology. In *New Frontiers*, Heller describes both the Council's reasoning and some of the problems encountered:

> Careful analyses of the statistical record within CEA convinced us that the structural-unemployment thesis was more fancy than fact, since the structural component of unemployment had not risen, that the 4-percent unemployment target was not only attainable but should be viewed as an interim target, later to be reset at a lower level.(after manpower programs had increased labor skills and mobility); and that we had a sound method of translating the employment goal into a GNP target and thus defining the gap between actual and potential GNP.
>
> The reactions to the 4-percent figure—both from those who thought it too high and from those who thought it too low—removed any illusions I might have had about political economy being able to abstract from values and emotions. On one side, we were condemned as heartless for setting a goal, even an interim goal, that would leave three million people unemployed. On the other, we were assailed as reckless for believing we could drive the economy that far without colliding with structural barriers and bringing on a rash of inflation. Employment developments in 1965–66 rendered a clear-cut verdict on the structural-unemployment thesis: the alleged hardcore of unemployment lies not at 5 or 6 percent, but even deeper than 4 percent—how deep still remains to be ascertained.[45]

Much has been made of and written about the relationship between Kennedy and his economists, constituting a mixed blessing for the economic historian or analyst. One can seldom determine how much routine policy was glamorized and made to seem more important by observers who were on the scene, or who were self-serving.

The hallmarks of the Kennedy economists were imagination and innovation. The debate over the tax cut was highly educational, and it is unlikely that such a question would have been so fully ventilated by any preceding administration. CEA shared in the general regard for the administration on the part of the press and the intellectual community. The appointment of the Council members at the same time as the appointment of key Cabinet officials and the personal rapport between JFK and Heller both played a part in solidifying the position of the Council in the establishment and in the public mind. Kennedy went far beyond any other President in demonstrating an understanding of economic issues in a political context.

Yet, for all its articulation, the solid accomplishments of the administration were not impressive. In contrast to the Eisenhower Administration, the atmosphere of expectations was overly favorable, whereas they had been overly dark in 1952. That is to say, whereas the Eisenhower-CEA performance had been better than expected, the Kennedy accomplishments were less than advertised. Many of the most serious issues regarding gold outflow and unemployment remained largely unsolved when Johnson took over the reins.

Improvements in technique and operation were impressive. The operations of and interactions between CEA, the Treasury, and the Board of Governors were nicely attuned, and JFK left a smoothly working group for the incoming Johnson Administration. What the Kennedy Administration might have been able to accomplish with more time is, of course, open to speculation. The tax cut carried to completion by Johnson was a prime creation of the Kennedy-Heller Council. Kennedy had inherited a solid institution as a legacy from Eisenhower and Burns. By his close working relationship formulated with Heller and with his interest in methodology, Kennedy improved the advisory function in form, if not in substance. In contrast to Truman, for example, he not only accepted the reality of the Employment Act de forma but also took a deep interest in the operations designed to implement it.

Recognition of the dynamic aspects of economic advice was a major virtue of the Heller Council. To be sure, Heller had many advantages in his advisory role. Unlike Nourse with Truman, he enjoyed a sound and easy personal relationship with the President. He fully understood the "outrider" value of the Council and used it often as an educational device; indeed, this was one of his strongest contributions. Interchange between the Council and the Joint Committee was marked not only by frequency but by high quality and sophistication during the period.

Yet one has the impression that, though the Council was well lubricated, polished, and running smoothly, its potential performance exceeded its actual performance. Perhaps this stems essentially from the fact that the premature end of the administration prevented the President from carrying out his full program. A thousand days is a brief time to formulate and complete a major course of national action.

In the epilogue of his biography of John F. Kennedy, Theodore Sorensen has written that it will not be easy for historians to compare him to other Presidents, "for he was unique in his imprint on the office." He was indeed, and his relationship to the Council was unique. He left the new President a superb policy instrument.

Notes

Chapter 6

[1] One of the reasons Lodge lost was that he had spent a great deal of time on the Eisenhower presidential effort and somewhat neglected affairs at home. Lodge was one of the "modern" Republicans who helped to shape the Eisenhower views. Most state political observers had thought him unbeatable and cautioned JFK not to leave his safe seat.

[2] Boston: Houghton Mifflin, 1964.

[3] Seymour E. Harris, *Economics of the Kennedy Years* (New York: Harper & Row, 1964), Chapter 2.

[4] Op. cit., pp. 623–24.

[5] Theodore C. Sorensen, *Kennedy* (New York: Harper & Row, 1965), p. 440.

[6] Harris, op. cit., p. 93.

[7] Schlesinger, *One Thousand Days* (Boston: Houghton Mifflin, 1964) p. 622.

[8] James McG. Burns, *John Kennedy: A Political Profile* (New York: Harcourt Brace & World, 1959). Every Senator who aspires to the White House is faced with the problem of explaining his regional outlook on economic issues which stood him in good stead in his senatorial days. LBJ had the same problem.

[9] See Patrick Anderson *The President's Men* (New York: Doubleday, 1968). Anderson observes that JFK as an independently wealthy man was able to become more idealistic as he grew older, whereas Sorensen, as with most men, was forced to grow more pragmatic as he grew older and faced growing personal economic responsibilities.

[10] Professor Canterbery says: ". . . most American Presidents went to the White House wholly ignorant in economic theory and left with no visible improvement." He holds that JFK was unique because (1) he was informed on economic matters as a candidate, (2) he had great intelligence and mental flexibility, and (3) at the end of the thousand days, he had learned more economics than many graduate students do in about the same time. E. Ray Canterbery, *Economics on a New Frontier* (Belmont: Wadsworth, 1968), p. 9.

[11] Theodore White, *The Making of the President* (New York: Atheneum, 1960), p. 297. Copyright© 1961 by Atheneum House, Inc. and copyright© 1965 by Theodore H. White, Reprinted by permission of the author and the publishers.

[12] Stein, op. cit., p. 375.

[13] Both this incident and the Truman steel incident are discussed in detail in Grant McConnell, *Steel and the Presidency* (New York: Norton, 1963).

[14] Hobart Rowen, *The Free Enterprisers, Kennedy, Johnson and the Business Establishment* (New York: Putnam's 1964).

[15] The volume of economic memoranda which was passed to Kennedy was immense.

Heller notes that more than 300 economic memos were passed to JFK in the thousand days of his presidency. Walter W. Heller, *New Dimensions of Political Economy* (Cambridge: Harvard University Press, 1966), p. 29.

[16] Most of his biographers, (Sorensen, Schlesinger, Lincoln) make this point clear.

[17] John Kenneth Galbraith, *Ambassador's Journal* (Boston: Houghton Mifflin, 1969), p. 7.

[18] Ibid., p. 18.

[19] Ibid., p. 21.

[20] Ibid., pp. 116, 117.

[21] Heller, Gordon, and Tobin were all in graduate school in the early or late 1940s, at the peak of academic Keynesianism.

[22] Heller was not well acquainted with JFK, having only met him during the campaign and then more or less off hand (through Hubert Humphrey). Heller, like most, was impressed by Kennedy's quick mind. *See* Harry Brandon, "Interview with Walter Heller," *The Sunday Times* (London), June 13, 1965.

[23] Stein, op. cit., p. 379.

[24] Ibid., p. 380.

[25] Heller, op. cit., p. 32.

[26] It was on the occasion of his appointment that JFK made his celebrated remark: Tobin had been reluctant to accept for several reasons, pointing out his orientation toward theory, saying to the President, "I am afraid that I am only an ivory tower economist." Kennedy replied, "That's the best kind; I am an ivory tower President."

[27] Heller, op. cit., p. 42.

[28] Rowen, op. cit., p. 181.

[29] These arguments are well summed up by Robert Theobald in his book, *Free Men and Free Markets* (Garden City: Doubleday, Anchor Ed., 1965). An excellent statement of both cases is the address by Gardner Ackley, Vandeveer Memorial Lecture, Southern Illinois University, October 26, 1966 (mimeographed).

[30] George L. Bach, *Making Monetary and Fiscal Policy* (Washington: Brookings, 1971), p. 112.

[31] *Economic Report of the President*, January, 1962, p. 108.

[32] Heller, op. cit., pp. 66ff.

[33] Ibid., p. 61.

[34] Ibid., p. 32.

[35] Schlesinger, *A Thousand Days*, pp. 628–29.

[36] Flash, op. cit., pp. 246–47.

[37] U.S. Congress, Joint Economic Committee, *Hearings on January 1961 Economic Report of the President, and Outlook*, 87th Congress, 1st Session, pp. 312–14.

[38] Ibid., p. 361.

[39] U.S. Congress, Joint Economic Committee, *Study of Employment, Growth and Price Levels* (1959).

[40] Heller, op. cit., p. 37. This speech, perhaps the best JFK ever gave, was a classic of economic understanding put forth with characteristic Kennedy grace and wit.

[41] *Twentieth Anniversary of the Employment Act—An Economic Symposium* (Joint Economic Committee, 89th Congress, 2d Session, February 23, 1966, Washington, D.C.), p. 81.

[42] *Economic Report of the President*, 1962, pp. 49–53.

[43] *Economic Report of the President*, 1963, pp. ix and xiii.

[44] One source says that under Heller CEA acquired a constituency, namely, the press and the intellectual community. This is true, but it may have acted to exaggerate its real incidence.

[45] Heller, op. cit., pp. 63–64.

Chapter 7

Johnson: The New Economics in Trouble

I believe 1964 will go down in history as the year of the tax cut.
—Lyndon B. Johnson

Lyndon B. Johnson was born in west Texas in 1908, and, in many ways, his economic views bear the stamp of the rural Texas "Populist" sentiment, sharpened and altered by his experience as a young Congressman during the Roosevelt era.

The Texas of Lyndon Johnson's boyhood was not the oil-rich, "Neiman-Marcus" Texas of modern Dallas, Houston, or Fort Worth, but the rugged, poor hill country west of Austin. Though far from rich, the Johnson family was comfortable by virtue of the senior Johnson's numerous business and farming ventures, which had made him a man of local substance and property. The family was also active in local politics. Lyndon's grandfather had been elected to the legislature on the Populist ticket and his father had also served in the legislature. Though by the early 1920s Sam Johnson's financial situation had deteriorated and Lyndon was forced to work his way through college, the Johnsons were still Blanco County gentry.

Johnson's formal academic training was in elementary education at Southwest State Teachers College (now San Marcos State University) at San Marcos. It is unlikely that he contemplated a career in education; rather, as was common in the period and place, he viewed teaching as a

193

vehicle into other fields such as law or business. At any rate, he soon abandoned the teaching profession after a few years as a high school teacher and went to Washington to begin his political career as a congressional secretary serving on the staff of congressman Richard Kleberg. Many young men of the era who became congressional employees attended law school on a part-time basis to further their political ambitions. Johnson chose instead to enter the field directly and apparently, though he venerated education, decided that no more was necessary in his case.

In *The Tragedy of Lyndon Johnson,* Professor Eric F. Goldman, who served in the White House (as a house intellectual) during the administration (and left with bitter feeling on both sides), makes much of the President's low-grade formal education and attributes his lack of interest in reading and his poor sense of history to this source. Certainly, the President was not a scholar, but Goldman also notes that LBJ had a very great mental capacity and feels that it was not exploited by the limited resources of the Southwest State Teachers College of the 1920s.[1]

Like many young men contemplating a political career, LBJ left Washington and returned to Texas in 1935 and became state director of the National Youth Administration (NYA).[2] From that time, with the exception of a short period in the wartime Navy, he was never out of political life until he left the Presidency in 1968.

Professor Goldman and others have noted that LBJ in his early years in Washington had been much impressed by the humanitarian instincts and political skills of Senator Huey P. Long (many years later, in the campaign of 1964, he alluded to Long's philosophy in a New Orleans speech). As a youth, Johnson had also been favorably impressed by the philosophy of Jim Ferguson and his successor, "Ma" Ferguson, Populist-minded governors of Texas in the mid-1920s. There can be little doubt that the Johnsonian economic philosophy was formed in basic outline by the Populist–New Deal ideas, and it is possible, indeed likely, that the impact of the affluent economy of the 1960s (especially on the young) escaped him. His inability to communicate with young persons in the 1960s is symptomatic of this problem. Johnson had observed the severe problems of youth in the 1930s and had taken part in their solution through the NYA. He was unable to appreciate that the affluent young of the postwar years (who had a different set of problems) were not much impressed by similar proposals.

In 1934 Johnson won a special election to the House from the Tenth District, and he now returned to Washington with a better seat from which to observe the workings of the New Deal, his view influenced by men like his fellow Texans Wright Patman, Sam Rayburn, and Vice-President John N. Garner, who successfully blended agrarian economics with New Deal sophistication.

The twenty-four-year-old Congressman arrived in Washington at the peak of New Deal experimentation; Roosevelt, Huey Long, Rex Tugwell, and Hugh Johnson were in the headlines. Can one be surprised that this capable young man, whose formal education and background were limited largely to the rural Texas of the 1920s, was immensely impressed by the scene and convinced that economic salvation lay in the ways of Washington and the New Deal? Of this era, Theodore White writes:

> To understand Johnson, one must recall Washington as it was then, as it lurched from Hoover's Depression to Franklin D. Roosevelt's New Deal. All things were fluid—old ideas were being thrown out, new government structures built, torn down, renamed. Men were heroes one day, nobodies the next, lobbyists thereafter. In the high and creative years of the New Deal, all government seemed plastic and the mission of government itself changed. This above all, was the formative period of Lyndon Johnson's thinking. Young, befriended by a group of youngsters like himself finding their first experience of manhood in this upheaval of order, Johnson acquired a vision of government that has never left him. . . .
> To men like Johnson who lived through the New Deal—as to the Russian Bolshevik generation that made the November revolution—government is a system of movable and replaceable parts.[3]

In the House he quickly became a Roosevelt man, marked by his obvious ambition to move into higher office; and, in 1948 (after a brief Navy stint), he reached the Senate in the famous "landslide" victory.[4]

During his House service, Johnson had moved gradually but steadily to the right in his socioeconomic views. Not only did he need to strengthen his Texas base, he was himself becoming a man of property. Though the family eventually became quite wealthy, all sources agree that Mrs. Johnson was the entrepreneur of the family.[5] Like Roosevelt, Johnson had no real interest in business nor was he marked by depth of thought in economic matters. His formal training was meager. Teachers' colleges fifty years ago were not apt to stress broad training in arts and sciences; and by inclination LBJ had little interest in history, philosophy, and other scholarly subjects requiring wide reading. He was clearly a man who learned by observation, talking, and doing, not by reading and theorizing. He, like Truman, was a highly pragmatic man, quick to

195

see the advantages and disadvantages of a given situation and able to relate any issue to the realities of Texas political life. Also like Truman, he had a computerlike memory for facts.

In the 80th Congress, LBJ voted for the Taft-Hartley Act and, later, to override Truman's veto, thus incurring the wrath of organized labor. He had no difficulty in accommodating himself to the oil interests of his state. As an agrarian Texan, he had been schooled to oppose "eastern bankers," who were the traditional enemy of the western farm and ranch interests. However, as his personal wealth increased and his political goals became more clearly defined, he moved to the right without any apparent damage to his personal convictions and, as a rising Senator, with great advantage to his political ambitions.

The Majority Leader

Johnson's entry into the Senate in 1948 was a major turning point in his career. Though he had been a decade in the Congress and in his House days was an intimate of Franklin Roosevelt, his new base was less secure. The embarrassing eighty-seven-vote margin by which he won was difficult to forget (to his dismay, he became "Landslide Lyndon"). Nonetheless, his political talents were obvious, and he soon found himself admitted to the "Club" of the Senate, becoming especially friendly with two of his fellow freshman Democrats and southwestern millionaires, Clinton Anderson of New Mexico and Robert S. Kerr of Oklahoma.[6]

The new Senator began an almost immediate acceleration of his move toward conservatism, brought about by several factors. The hairline primary victory demonstrated his narrow base in Texas. Postwar urban Texas was moving rapidly toward economic conservatism, a far cry from his west Texas district of the 1930s. Johnson saw the need to make himself more acceptable to the oil industry and other conservative interests who were suspicious of his New Deal ties.

The Senate was in ascendancy. In FDR's time an alliance with the White House was an advantage. Now, in contrast—despite Truman's upset victory in 1948—the Fair Deal agenda was unpopular in the Senate and had little national appeal. The road to Senate power led away from the Truman program.

Though LBJ and his close associates were in general liberals, they were of a different stripe than Paul Douglas of Illinois and Hubert Humphrey of Minnesota who entered with them in the "class of 1948." The Johnson group were Southwestern "wheeler dealers" ("rich

Populists," so to speak), whose liberalism was more flexible and pragmatic. They were ambitious to be in the Senate inner circle, a group then dominated by conservatives such as Richard Russell and Robert Taft.

Always the master politician, LBJ no doubt felt that the New Deal era was gone and saw the national mood drifting to the right, as indeed it was. Johnson himself, though he never forgot his New Deal "salad days," was not so sentimental as to think that the exciting days of 1932–35 would return. Truman was not FDR; and his 1948 victory, though a personal triumph, was not indicative of the national political mood. Can one imagine that Johnson by his move into the Senate considered it possible that he might himself sit in the White House? Before such a move might be made, however, his Senate base must be strengthened; loss of his tenuously gained Senate seat would probably end his political career. A more secure position had to be established without delay.

As a freshman Senator, Johnson remained for two years in relative obscurity and devoted his efforts to ingratiating himself with the Senate leaders and to solidifying his base at home.[7] However, by 1950 he began to move rapidly, and his rise in the Senate was spectacular. To some degree, in fact, his reputation as an "operator" after he became Majority Leader was such as to endanger his reputation with the voting public, who viewed him as a master politician given to "slick deals."

To satisfy Senate liberals, Johnson as leader was forced to favor their views on certain economic issues—those that he could afford to accept without eroding his base of power in the Senate or in Texas. Generally, he backed minimum wage legislation, housing, Social Security, farm legislation, rural electrification, reciprocal trade, and, often, foreign aid. He remained conservative on the budget, oil and gas legislation (e.g., the tideland oil issue), and public power.

The Vice-President

Johnson's economic views became considerably more liberal, at least on the surface, as he began to consider the possibility of seeking the presidential nomination in 1960. His first task was to reshape his image as a southern and a Texas Senator. Although he had been obliged to cultivate oil interests, he now attempted to shift these into the background. The sensational disclosures of undue influence on the part of oil lobbyists in attempting to pass the natural gas bills in the mid-1950s had not helped him in the attempt to soft-pedal the issue, but this was in the past and, with skill and luck, might be overcome.

Likewise, his image with labor was tarnished by the fact that he had to accommodate Texas views at the expense of his national aspirations, but this, too, might be overcome by careful management. Johnson was passing through the familiar process by which a candidate must broaden his views as he seeks higher office. A Congressman can adjust his views to his district; a Senator must give lip service to the economic interests of his state as a whole. A hopeful presidential candidate must appear to be nationally oriented.

In Johnson's case, the move was from left to right and back to left as the Presidency loomed as a realistic goal. Johnson had problems other than his conservative image. He was a performer without peer in Texas politics but was regarded as somewhat "cornball" in the North and East. During the campaign, his movement suffered from the fact that he was trapped in the job of Majority Leader, while Kennedy, Humphrey, and Stuart Symington were free to campaign.

Johnson also had a great philosophical handicap; as White notes:

A third and even greater burden lay on Lyndon B. Johnson. This was the quality of his experience and the difficulty of demonstrating the quality in Presidential politics. If Symington's mind is as fine an executive instrument as Washington possesses, Johnson's is as fine a legislative mind—and as difficult to make known to the commonalty. For Johnson the United States Senate is more than the Senate: it is faith, calling, club, habit, relaxation, devotion, hobby and love. For him the Senate, with its hallowed tradition, is the most glorious instrument of government known to man, and each facet of its life—its majestic decisions, its sordid little deals, it prickly personalities, its open clashes and backroom intrigue—fascinates him. Over twelve years the Senate has become almost a monomania with him, his private domain, and he confuses the United States Senate with life itself.[8]

Johnson's efforts to capture the presidential nomination in 1960 came to naught, and he became instead the vice-presidential candidate. However, the famous Johnson style rose to full flower again in 1964 with his victory over Senator Barry Goldwater.[9] As President in his own right, Johnson was able, and, of course, forced, to take a more liberal and national economic view. When his term ended in 1969, Johnson had completed almost thirty-eight years in public life. Almost a year earlier, he had renounced a second full term of office, but he had left his stamp on the Presidency and its economic policies.

Johnson and the Council

When Kennedy was succeeded by Lyndon Johnson in November 1963, there was immediate speculation as to the future of the Council and its stabilizing role. Liberal Kennedy supporters had not been pleased when Johnson was selected for second place on the ticket in 1960.

Kennedy supporters viewed Johnson as much too conservative in his economic views and were distrustful of his image as an "operator." This ambivalence marked his selection and service as Vice-President. Many of those who viewed LBJ with the greatest suspicion were among the young liberals who looked with the greatest favor upon the performance of the Council and the emergence of the "new economics." Although his relationship with Kennedy and his "vice-presidential attitude" were beyond any criticism, Johnson (with good reason) was not fond of the "Harvard crowd" who had found influential places in the administration. (One observer noted that LBJ referred to anyone who had not graduated from the University of Texas as one of the "Harvard crowd.") In many ways, the Council was the symbol of the ascendancy of the intellectual. Would LBJ, the hard-headed Texan, view CEA as a refuge for "ivory tower" scholars? It seemed altogether possible that the Council's days of glory might be ending.

Contrary to many expectations, the Council increased its participation in affairs. Upon Heller's resignation in 1964, Gardner Ackley became chairman. Ackley, a professor from the University of Michigan, had served several years in OPA, OSS, and other wartime agencies. He had joined the Council as a member in 1967.

Ackley left the Council in early 1968 and was succeeded by Arthur M. Okun, who served until the administration ended. Others who served were John P. Lewis (May 1963–August 1964), Otto Eckstein (September 1964–February 1966), James Duesenberry (February 1966–June 1968), Merton J. Peck (February 1968–January 1969), and the late Warren L. Smith (July 1968–January 1969). Okun, a Columbia Ph.D., had enjoyed a distinguished career at Yale and had served on the CEA staff before becoming a member in November 1964. Eckstein was unique in that he had been on the staff of the Joint Economic Committee and had directed the study on growth that underlay much of Kennedy's campaign. The Johnson Council and staff were much like the Kennedy group—young, well trained, and generally activist. Under Johnson, the Council took a more active part than it had previously in the conduct of national economic affairs, especially those relating to price-wage relationships, such as the guideposts.

199

The expanding participation of the Johnson-Ackley-Okun Council was not without its price. The Council found itself increasingly on the firing line on a day-to-day basis as it was often forced to defend policies based on estimates of a highly fluid situation. Certain similarities appear between the Ackley Council in 1966–67 and the Keyserling Council after the impact of the Korean War began to be felt. The highly fluid Vietnamese War made any rational budgetary policy very difficult to pursue. The Council shared with the Treasury and the Bureau of the Budget congressional displeasure over the rather obvious "budgeteering" techniques the administration used in attempting to secure a "paper" balance.

Johnson's Administration was not marked by severe economic crisis in the usual sense, nor was it notable for innovation. The President grasped the rationale of the Kennedy tax cut, pushed it through the Congress, and extracted a great deal of political mileage from it.

Concerned with social legislation but forced to pursue the Vietnamese War, the administration was from the beginning in an ambivalent position, although many problems did not arise at once. CEA reports were largely devoted to analysis of the continuing upward movement of the economy, and they looked hopefully toward the end of the war.

The 1965 report (under the heading, *The Unfinished Tasks*) spoke of the need for faster economic growth, concluding:

Ceaseless change is the hallmark of a progressive and dynamic economy. No planned economy can have the flexibility and adaptability that flow from the voluntary response of workers, consumers, managements to the shifting financial incentives provided by free markets.

In those activities entrusted to governments—as in those where private profit provides the spur—the search for efficiency and economy must never cease.

The American economy is the most efficient and flexible in the world. But the task of improving its efficiency and flexibility is never done.

American prosperity is widely shared. But too many are still precluded from its benefits by discrimination; by handicaps of illness, disability, old-age, or family circumstances; by unemployment or low productivity; by lack of mobility or bargaining power; by failure to receive the education and training from which they could benefit.

The Council, citing the tax cut as a "watershed of economic policy,"

200

held that the fiscal lessons of 1964 would not soon be lost and that a new era of economic policy was at hand.

After a detailed review of the sustained economy of 1964, the report called for more growth and devoted substantial space to international stability:

> With the help of appropriate policies, we must move decisively toward international balance, thereby reinforcing the position of the dollar as the world's major reserve currency. As we succeed in this endeavor, we can expect to encounter some demand by both private and official foreign holders for additional short-term dollar assets needed to help to meet their growing liquidity requirements. Under such circumstances, the United States can reasonably supply a limited volume of additional dollars in keeping with the ultimate objective of equilibrium in its payments position. . . .

Under the heading, "Economic Tasks of the Great Society," the Council discussed such issues as urban blight, traffic congestion, rural and urban poverty, education, health, and equality of opportunity:

> The steps we take during the next few years will help to determine the quality of life in the year 2000.
> The patterns of building and transportation that we create will determine the character of our cities. The parks and open spaces that we provide will affect the way people spend their increased leisure time.
> With growing population and further urbanization, problems of congestion and pollution—often considered as mere nuisances today—could become obstacles to effective and tolerable city life even before 2000. But imaginative solutions could make the cities of tomorrow not only far more efficient but far more livable than the cities of today.
> The vitality of our rural areas in 2000 will also be affected by the success of our efforts to stem their decline and solve their problems in the coming years.[10]

Thus, in the first full year of his own administration, the President launched a broad offensive on domestic matters that reminded many of the New Deal years.

In the 1967 report, the President again traced the growth of the economy and emphasized such problems as unequal economic progress, price increases, and international payments. He struck a note for more efficient use of the capability of the economy and tried to look beyond Vietnam, anticipating the opportunity

— to consider possibilities and priorities for tax reduction;

— to prepare, with the Federal Reserve Board, plans for quick adjustments of monetary and financial policies;

— to determine which high priority programs can be quickly expanded;

— to determine priorities for the longer range expansion of programs to meet the needs of the American people, both through new and existing programs;

— to study and evaluate the future direction of Federal financial support to our States and local governments;

— to examine ways in which the transition to peace can be smoothed for the workers, companies, and communities now engaged in supplying our defense needs, and the men released from our armed forces. . . .

Under the title, "Strains and Restraints in a Surging Economy," the Council gave much space to the issue of price stability, traced the sequence of recent events, and made the best of what was clearly becoming a bad situation:

The surge in demand for goods and labor created pressures on prices in many areas. From October 1965 to July 1966 the annual rate of advance for industrial wholesale prices stepped up to 3 percent. Prices of industrial crude materials moved sharply upward—at an annual rate of 8 percent from October to April. At the consumer level, demand pressures raised prices of services and non-food commodities and combined with special supply factors in agriculture to push up food prices. . . . All in all, the economy exceeded reasonable speed limits in the period from mid-1965 through the first quarter of 1966.

After years of providing stimulus to the economy, policy changed direction at the turn of the year. Monetary policy accounted for a major share of the restraint during most of 1966. . . .

Fiscal policy also responded effectively. Although the special defense costs necessarily swelled Federal outlays and were highly stimulative, restrictive actions were taken in other areas. Increases in nondefense purchases were held to $300 million from 1964 to 1966. Several restrictive tax measures were proposed in January 1966 and were enacted in mid-March. These included a reinstatement of some of the earlier excise tax reduction restoring about $1 billion to the annual rate of Federal revenues; and a system of graduated withholding for individual income taxes drew off $1½ billion in payroll taxes that took ef-

202

fect at the start of 1966. In addition, revenues were increased in the spring by unusually large payments on 1965 income tax liabilities. . . .

These monetary and fiscal actions helped to bring the rate of over-all economic expansion in line with the growth of capacity. After the first quarter of 1966, gains in GNP slowed to an average of $12½ billion a quarter, no longer outstripping the growth of the potential GNP. The unemployment rate leveled off as employment gains essentially matched the growth of the labor force. Manufacturing output actually rose less than the growth of manufacturing capacity and average operating rates at year-end were below the 91 percent that had been reached in the first quarter. . . .

The change of pace was first clearly noticeable in the spring. Fiscal restraint appreciably slowed the growth of disposable income in the second quarter and contributed to a marked slowdown in consumer spending. During the summer, consumer demand perked up again. But homebuilding, which had declined moderately in the second quarter, was hit hard by the shortage of mortgage financing and took a sharp plunge, holding down the increase in economic activity.[11]

The increasingly serious matter of balance of payments was viewed with enlarged concern:

A country's foreign trade and payments are its main points of economic contact with the rest of the world. The balance of payments of any nation is intimately dependent on policies and developments in the outside world. U.S. exports depend heavily on European, Canadian, and Japanese growth and the foreign exchange receipts of the less developed countries as well as on U.S. growth and price stability. The flow of capital from the United States depends on profit opportunities and monetary conditions abroad as well as those in the United States.

For most of the decade following World War II, U.S. balance of payments deficits provided needed international currency to support the rapid expansion of world trade and economic growth. Other countries were eager to hold more dollars; indeed, it was commonly known as a period of "dollar shortage." Recently, however, as foreign reserves have increased, U.S. deficits have been less welcome.[12]

Despite the early warning notes, the Johnson-CEA efforts at stabilization were largely ineffective for several reasons, most notably Johnson's reluctance to abandon his "Great Society" program, despite the rapid escalation in military expenditures. In its efforts to enhance the prospects of stabilization, the administration made a renewed effort to make the wage-price guideposts viable.

The Guidepost Caper

The famous wage-price guideposts, intended to serve as informal guides to wage-price decisions, were first given formal expression in the *President's Economic Report* in January 1962; thus they were to become a major policy effort and deserve attention.[13] Few economic pronouncements in recent years have given rise to more controversy than the wage-price guideposts or put CEA in a less enviable position. Though, of course, it was not then known, they were also portents of events to occur during the Nixon Administration. The guideposts policy was intended to be something of a halfway house between full-scale wage-price controls, such as those prevailing under wartime or emergency conditions, and the complete wage-price freedom that marks the traditional normal or peacetime economy.

Though the guideposts were effective for a while, companies and unions engaged in wage negotiations soon began to play a "numbers game." In early and mid-1966, as labor became more restive, the strain on the guidepost limits increased. The President and the Council began to be more and more involved with labor-management disputes and industrial price policies. Inexorably, this put the Council more and more often on the firing line and exposed it to increasingly critical comment from those segments of the economy that wished to, or succeeded in, breaking through the guideposts limits. It was impossible under these circumstances to avoid the political implications of the problem. The allowable limits for increases were based loosely on assumed historical gains in productivity (3.2 percent). Unfortunately there are many wage-price decisions where productivity is meaningless, and even in those cases in which the guide is reasonably accurate, there are often strong union efforts to exceed the limits. Business argued that the administration was more apt to be looking the other way when labor stepped over the line than it was when industrial prices were an issue (which may have been true). By mid-1966, with the inflationary settlement of the airline mechanics strike, the guideposts reached the end of their operational usefulness and were, to a degree at least, formally ended in CEA's report for January 1967.

In effect, the administration was attempting to operate a system of control over wages, salaries, and prices, wholly on a voluntary basis. In this time of generally rising prices, during which most of the burden of control rested on monetary policy, wage-price increases beyond the limits of productivity were inevitable.

It seems likely that the guideposts served their purpose, but that their usefulness was short-lived and that there was generally agreement that the time had come to abandon them. Though the Council recognized that the figure of 3.2 percent was no longer viable, it was reluctant to admit that the guideposts were dead. Speaking before the Society of Business Writers in May 1967, Chairman Ackley refused to concede that they had become useless:

> Is there any hope? Are the guideposts really dead? For my part, I can answer questions very easily.
>
> I believe that voluntary restraint in the exercise of private discretion will continue because the national leaders of labor, business, and Government know that it must. They recognize the problem, and know that the answer does not lie in operating the economy with a wastefully, costly, and inhumane margin of slack; in burdensome, inefficient, and ultimately unsuccessful direct controls; in attempts to atomize private concentrations of market power.
>
> And I believe that this continuing system of voluntary restraint must be based on the productivity principle because no other makes economic sense.[14]

Vietnam and Stabilization

LBJ began his administration with a degree of acuity and visibility that reminded historians of the first hundred days of the Roosevelt years. The Kennedy tax cut was pushed to completion and a wide range of socioeconomic programs relating to his domestic proposals (mainly the "war on poverty") were quickly executed. Johnson's relation with the business community appeared to be almost as good as Eisenhower's, and his relationship with the Congress was at first superb. Where Kennedy had been unable to establish an easy rapport with business, Johnson immediately received its full support. He used his standing on Capitol Hill to the best advantage of anyone since FDR.

Despite this vigorous activity and his decisive victory in 1964, Johnson became increasingly ineffective in the economic role. The toll in time and energy of the Vietnam War was inescapable. Further, though the administration had hoped that a productive economy would be able to support both Vietnam and domestic programs, this proved to be only partially the case. Inflation became increasingly a problem as the war continued. But, as late as mid-1966, LBJ was still convinced that the nation could have both "guns and butter," and resisted both a tax increase or attempts to scale down the domestic program.

The last *Economic Report* (under the heading, *Gains in Five Years*) spoke of

— a decline in unemployment to 3.3 percent;
— fewer persons in the poverty class;
— gains in average income;
— rise in corporate profits;
— increase in farm income.

On the deficit side, however, it conceded that "the immediate task [in 1969] was to make a decisive step toward price stability."

Johnson's early training, in the Roosevelt era, seems to have convinced him that there were no socioeconomic problems beyond the reach of government, and he viewed the goals of the Great Society as being essential. The Great Society and the war in Vietnam increasingly entangled economic policy with matters of social justice and international policy. In many ways, the Johnson effort seemed more appropriate to the New Deal era in which he learned his trade. Though a superb political and legislative tactician, the President was curiously ineffective as an economic policy maker, and he lost force rapidly after 1967.

Though the policy of the late 1960s bears the stamp of the Council, it was an odd mixture of the Johnsonian and Rooseveltian, with a patina of modern economics applied by Ackley and Okun.

Minority members of the Joint Economic Committee were, of course, openly critical of the administration, taking it to task for its spending policies and looking with a jaundiced eye on the "new economics."

The budget deficits that were incurred during the Johnson Administration were nothing less than a parody of promises made by Administration economists in the name of the "New Economics." The New Economics maintained that what was important to economic growth and stability was not Federal budget surpluses every year, but a budget balanced over the long-term business cycle, with deficits in periods of slack in the economy, and surpluses in periods of maximum utilization of the economy's potential. We discovered, however, that while the previous Administration found it easy enough to run deficits in a slack economy, it could not, or would not, take the steps necessary to produce surpluses at high employment.

In view of such fiscal irresponsibility, it is not surprising that inflation has grown to disrupting proportions. The Consumer Price Index has increased 12.3 percent since mid-1965 and 4.7 percent over the 12 months of 1968 alone. Although virtually stable from 1958 through 1964, the Wholesale Price Index has risen 6.8 percent since mid-1965, and increased 2.8 percent last year. Early figures for 1969 indicate that this rapid rate of inflation is continuing.

The cost of this inflation to the American people over the last 5 years totals almost $115 billion in higher living costs and $106 billion in erosion of the real value of bank deposits, savings accounts, life insurance and pension fund reserves, and Government bonds. . . .

The primary task for economic policy this year is to reduce inflation, while maintaining high levels of employment. This is a herculean challenge, for the statistical record of industrial countries shows an inverse correlation between the rate of price inflation and the level of unemployment. In other words, there tends to be a trade-off between the two objectives of price stability and low unemployment, where a country has to settle for a little less of one in order to obtain a little more of the other.

The record of the 1960's in this country is clear on this point. As we have managed to reduce the level of unemployment, we have experienced increasing degrees of inflation. This record predicts we would have to accept a less-than-1-percent reduction in the rate of inflation to prevent unemployment from rising above 4 percent.[15]

The Joint Committee members noted the need for advance planning in terms of post-Vietnam economics, foreign trade policy, antitrust policies, and other matters of overall policy formulation. One emerges from a reading of the hearings with a strong impression that the Joint Committee members as well as the staff were deeply involved and had done their homework thoroughly. This increasingly critical comment was hard to answer. Of course, some of it was political, but by no means all of it. Even comment from the minority members of the Joint Committee, though partisan in nature, was often justified. What had happened? What had begun in 1962 as a stellar performance in economic policy making, and had been carried to completion by Johnson, had fallen on evil days. Let us glance back.

In 1965, in the wake of the successful tax cut, hearings on the President's report had begun on an optimistic and congratulatory note. The President seemed to have mastered the art of economic policy making as

207

effectively as he had the art of dealing with the Congress. Professional economists were noting the performance of the President and the Council with approval; a new era had apparently arrived.

The ubiquitous Seymour Harris, as a witness before the Joint Economic Committee, had warm praise for CEA's performance and the fact that Keynesian policies had come to fruition at last:

> It is hard to see how Professors Heller, Tobin, Ackley, Eckstein, and Okun could be improved upon.
>
> In the Treasury, we have a Secretary as able as any since Hamilton. The 1964 Economic Report is a superb document with which I am very largely in agreement.
>
> For the first time, the President of the United States (both Kennedy and Johnson) and the Congress have accepted the implications of modern fiscal policy. Moreover, a large section of the business community now supports the new economics, with the head of the country's largest bank reassuring his financial colleagues that deficit financing is not a danger, and the debt is at a safe level.[16]

Harris was a leading American Keynesian and had been a close Kennedy adviser. Johnson had generally impressed, not only the lay public, but economists of Harris' caliber and experience. Yet, by mid-1968, domestic economic policy had come under severe critical attack; prices were rising; gold was flowing out; the credit "crunch" of 1966–67 had upset housing and other industries. Administration economic policies appeared to be drifting dangerously.

Although the factors that forced the President not to seek reelection were for the most part noneconomic, economic policy problems were formidable. The combination of the demands of the war and the pressures to continue the domestic programs at home put the economy under an intolerable strain. The administration was unable and unwilling (clearly some of both) to resolve these pressures.

What of the much heralded "fine tuning" of the economy? The much advertised "new economics"? The Johnson Council found itself fully occupied with administering and defending the guideposts.

Public attention was focused on the dramatic opposition to the war. Civil rights, poverty, student uprisings, and other symptoms of domestic discord to a degree were rooted in this issue. The administration had badly underestimated the costs of the war and the rate at which they would accelerate with military escalation. In 1966–67 fiscal year the actual cost was some $5 to $7 billion over estimate. Not until the Great Society measures had passed did LBJ admit the true budgetary costs.

The President was understandably reluctant to reduce spending on his domestic programs. Not only did these programs constitute the heart of his Great Society, their elimination or substantial reduction would have further escalated the already considerable unrest among various groups on the domestic scene. In his report, the President did not overlook these issues, and he was careful to note that domestic and international matters were interlocked:

> The American economy is still the ultimate example—the showcase—of free enterprise in action. A sluggish American economy will raise doubts everywhere, and especially in the newly developing nations, about the ability of a free enterprise economy to perform efficiently and to grow continuously. Full utilization and economic growth in the United States are of critical importance to the less developed countries in one further respect. These countries cannot develop without an increasing demand from abroad for their products. They cannot diversify their economies without expert markets for their new products—especially light manufactures. Full utilization and full employment in the United States will not only raise U.S. demand for these imports, but also will—by permitting labor, capital, and enterprise to adjust more readily to changing patterns of supply and demand—make it easier to accept imports of light manufactures even when they compete with domestic production.[17]

Yet these words became increasingly difficult to translate into real operational policy. Domestic price stability began to be a more and more difficult goal as budgetary demands increased far beyond expectations. In the three years 1966, 1967, and 1968, the federal budget rose by some $46 billion, of which about half was attributable to the Vietnam War. The deficit for the three years was $38 billion. *Fortune* magazine noted that the "new economics had failed to mesh with political necessity."[18] "Management of the economy," seemingly within reach in 1964, now appeared much more difficult than many "new economists" had assumed.

In the 1966 *Economic Report*, the President appeared to be trying to forestall trouble by asking and answering three questions:

> Can we avoid bottlenecks in major industries or key skills that would hamper our expansion?
> Can we keep a destructive price-wage spiral from getting under way?
> Can we move ahead with the Great Society programs and at

209

the same time meet our needs for defense?

My confident answer to each of these questions is "YES."

The positive answer seemed, on the surface, to be justified.

The budget receipts (consolidated cash basis) were forecast at $145.5 billion and expenditures at $145 billion. However, to provide a margin against rising expenditures, the President asked in the budget message for an acceleration in the collection of corporate income taxes, withholding of personal income taxes on a graduated scale, and continued postponement of repeal of the "wartime" excise taxes. Nor would he hesitate to ask for increases in other taxes. The Council had warned LBJ in December 1965 that the Great Society, Vietnam and no inflation was impossible without a tax increase. The President was afraid that this would spell the end of his Great Society program and decided to wait. Economists from outside the government gave the same advice—Otto Eckstein, Robert M. Solow, Carl Kaysen, and John T. Dunlop, for example. Had the situation remained as forecast, wise management might have won the day, but at this point the administration became evasive and sensitive about the costs of the war. No new estimate of war costs was presented to the Congress, even though the underestimate was apparent by July 1966. Meanwhile the Federal Reserve had begun (in the absence of fiscal policy moves) to tighten up monetary policy without much coordination with the administration.[19] Although the President (and the CEA) had said he would not hesitate to ask for new taxes, he did, in fact, hesitate. Though it is difficult to know who knew what-when, it appears beyond doubt that the Council was kept as much in the dark about war costs and intentions as the public.

When the President held back, the Fed took action. In December, the Board increased interest rates, and the action made the President and his associates most unhappy. Growing coolness between the Fed and the administration made matters more difficult:

That tempers rose over the discount action is understandable. Within the administration, private discussions among the senior troika members and their staffs had indicated growing concern that inflation would develop before full employment was achieved. But President Johnson, reflecting his strong populist leanings, had long opposed high interest rates and apparently believed that the Federal Reserve authorities and private bankers could indeed hold interest rates down if only they wanted to. Thus, according to one White House aide, the President saw the increase in interest rates as almost a personal vindictive act on the part of Chairman Martin.

In retrospect, the December discount action appears to have been a minor episode. But President Johnson's and Secretary Fowler's resentment produced a new coolness in administration-Federal Reserve relations. Clearly, Federal Reserve action reflected both honest differences of judgment on the economic situation and misunderstanding as to the degree of Federal Reserve commitment. Inadequate information from the Department of Defense on its spending plans underlay the entire situation.[20]

Professor Reuben Slesinger has noted the dangers that the President faced and the logic of the stabilization program:

Furthermore, rising defense requirements clearly complicate the task of economic policy. The stimulative fiscal policies of recent years have achieved their mission. Consumer spending and investment demand have both been invigorated. The same logic that called for fiscal stimuli when demand was weak now argues for a degree of restraint to assure that the pace of the economy remains within safe speed limits. Measures to moderate the growth of private purchasing power are needed to offset, in part, the expansionary influence of rising defense outlays if intensified price and wage pressures are to be avoided. A combination of such measures—affecting excise tax rates and the timing of individual and corporate tax payments—is thus a key proposal in the President's fiscal program.[21]

Administration pleas for observance of the wage-price guideposts in wage negotiations, or for restraint in consumer spending, had a hollow ring as federal expenditures rose rapidly in both defense and nondefense sectors. Thus, the Johnsonian economic policy, which had begun with such promise, became more and more difficult to defend as the 1968 election approached.

By a touch of irony, the highly publicized success of the tax cut of 1964 made the similar success of future administration policies all the more important and highlighted the administration's shortcomings. Herbert Stein and others have noted the 1964 success increased the probability that future decisions would be largely influenced by compensatory finance.[22]

The turnaround in the economy from 1964 to 1968 was, in retrospect, both dramatic and cruelly shattering to the President's expectations. Professor Otto Eckstein has described the move from a high point of economic policy to the dismal days of 1968:

By July 1965, before defense contracts began to rise, un-

211

employment was down 4.5 percent and falling rapidly, the economy was growing at over 5 percent a year, and wholesale prices were still stable and no higher than five years earlier. The economy had shown, at least for 18 happy months, that it could prosper without war with sensible, modern economic management; doubts about fiscal policy were wiped out, and for a year or two economists rode high indeed.

Then came the Vietnam War and the end, for a period at least, of modern fiscal policy. The budget underestimated defense spending by $10 billion for fiscal 1967 and $5 billion for fiscal 1968. The impact on the economy was underestimated by larger amounts because of the greater jumps in defense contracts. If the economic impact of the war had been known, the excise taxes would not have been cut in the summer of 1965. In early 1966 there should have been a broad across-the-board tax increase. But taxes were not increased because the President could not get the American people to pay for the war. In the end, the war paralyzed the political process, producing the surrealistic debate over the tax surcharge from mid 1967 to mid 1968. International financial crises followed one on another. Demand became excessive. The tax surcharge of mid 1968, which Congress voted, finally restored some fiscal order.[23]

The Kennedy-Johnson tax cuts, along with the increase in spending, had brought a tremendous swing in the federal budget. The 1967 full-employment budget showed a *deficit* of $12 billion—welcome, indeed, during the slowdown, but a potential disaster under the rapidly changing circumstances—and by mid-1968 it had increased again to $25.3 billion. The tax surcharge, finally passed in 1968, coupled with a degree of fiscal restraint, reversed the situation dramatically, and by 1969, the second-quarter full employment *surplus* had reached almost $10 billion! Small wonder that matters were difficult to control. As Eckstein sums up the period:

> In the 1960's, expenditures by government rose at a substantially higher rate than the gross national product. The total outlays (on national income account) of all levels of government were 27.1 percent on the GNP in 1960; by 1969, the figure rose to 31.4 percent. The outlays of states and localities rose from 9.9 percent to 13.1 percent of GNP; federal outlays rose from 18.5 to 20.5 percent.
>
> This increase in part represents the Vietnam War, which absorbed about 3 percent of GNP, some of it at the expense of other defense outlays.[24]

212

Thus Johnson in the course of his administration saw the reaction to his economic performance change from warm applause to bitter criticism and positive action shift into stagnant frustration. The Council, though as capable as those that preceded it, found itself with an impossible task. Though Nixon in his campaign made the most of the economic situation, little blame was seriously put on the shoulders of CEA. No doubt economists had to a large degree oversold such items as "fine tuning" in the flush of their 1963–64 success, and clearly "steering" was one thing and "fine tuning" another, but what effect, given the lack of information at their disposal, any degree of professional skill might have had is very questionable.

Second perhaps only to Kennedy, Johnson accepted the Council as an integral part of his administration and in the early years used it with great success. By the end of his Presidency, however, the economic situation was in rapid deterioration, and, while less a factor in the decline of presidential popularity than the war, it was an item of considerable importance.

Basic to the problem was the rapidly rising level of war expenditures superimposed on an already high level of domestic spending. Johnson and his advisers had hoped to be able to control the situation through rising output and by judicious use of the wage-price guideposts. The task proved to be beyond the capacity of the administration to perform. Vietnam also took an increasing toll of the President's time, mental energy, and goodwill.[25]

As prices rose, the pressure on the wage-price guideposts mounted to intolerable levels, and the Council became more and more involved in day-to-day administration of the efforts to keep wages and prices in line. These efforts had the effect of weakening the general moral authority of the Council. More frequent attacks were directed toward it by both management and labor. The Council shared in the general frustration that marked the executive branch of the government, and culminated in LBJ's decision to step aside. The Council was never designed to be an administrative body, but it found itself using more and more time and energy performing tasks for which it was poorly equipped and devoting less and less time to the tasks for which it would have been most useful.

There was, however, no repetition of the episode of 1952, when an incoming Republican administration made the future of the Council so uncertain. By 1968 CEA had become a firmly established institution in both Democratic and Republican circles. As the Okun Council operated in the closing days of the administration, attention shifted to the Nixon appointees.

213

Notes

Chapter 7

[1] Eric F. Goldman, *The Tragedy of Lyndon Johnson* (New York: Knopf, 1969).

[2] NYA was designed as the urban counterpart to the CCC. Urban youths were employed in school libraries, playgrounds, as teaching aides, etc., and were encouraged to stay in school.

[3] Theodore H. White, *Making of the President, 1964* (New York: Signet Books, 1965), p. 55. Copyright© 1965 by Theodore White. Reprinted by permission of the author and Atheneum Publishers.

[4] After complicated legal maneuvering and challenges of votes, Johnson was declared the winner of the Democratic Primary by 87 votes.

[5] Before 1948 when the political future was uncertain, LBJ was more active in the family enterprises, principally Austin radio and television stations acquired at low prices and much improved by the Johnsons; however, after his election to the Senate, Mrs. Johnson became head in fact as well as name. Politics was meat and drink to Johnson, and while money was helpful, making it was clearly of secondary interest. See Rowland Evans and Robert Novak, *Lyndon Johnson: The Exercise of Power* (New York: Signet Books, 1966), pp. 33ff.

[6] Though Anderson and Kerr were far richer than Johnson, the radio and television stations, land, bank stock, and cattle were rapidly increasing the Johnson estate at this time, and he was able to approach them on more or less even terms.

[7] Though Kerr espoused oil-gas interests openly (wearing a Kerr-McGee Company lapel button), Johnson rendered his aid behind the scenes, thus endearing himself to the oil interests but not openly alienating liberal supporters. See for example, Paul Douglas, op. cit.

[8] White, op. cit., p. 159.

[9] Though an economic conservative, Goldwater was not, in all probability, defeated so much on economic grounds as on the basis of his somewhat undeserved image as a "hawk" on Vietnam. Goldwater held that he was offering a choice, not an echo, but in economic terms no major difference was visible between the candidates.

[10] *Economic Report of the President, 1965*, p. 78.

[11] Ibid., p. 99.

[12] Ibid., pp. 197–98.

[13] These matters were discussed in a book published by the University of Chicago Press in 1966. The book embodies the results of a conference of well-known economists and is edited by George P. Shultz and Robert Z. Aliber. See *Guidelines, Informal Controls and the Marketplace* (Chicago, 1966). See also James L. Cochrane, "The Johnson Administration: Moral Suasion Goes to War," in *Exhortation and Controls, the Search for a Wage-Price Policy, 1945–1971*. Cranford D. Goodwin, ed. (Washington: Brookings, 1975).

[14] *Report of the Joint Economic Committee of the Congress of the United States on the January, 1969, Economic Report of the President*, together with minority, supplementary and dissenting views, April 1969.

[15] Ibid., p. 94, 98.

[16] Ibid., p. 37.

[17] *Economic Report of the President*, 1969.

[18] *Fortune*, May 1970.

[19] In June, Chairman Martin of the Fed had made his famous speech in which he drew a parallel between current events and those of 1929, in which he professed to see "disquieting similarities." A round of rebuttal followed from the administration, and LBJ was furious.

[20] Bach, op. cit., p. 125.

[21] Reuben Slesinger, *National Economic Policy: The Presidential Reports* (Princeton:

Van Nostrand, 1968), p. 77.

[22] Stein, op. cit., pp. 456–57.

[23] Otto Eckstein, "The Economics of the 1960's: A Backward Look," *Public Interest* (Spring, 1970), pp. 86–97.

[24] Ibid., p. 38.

[25] The emotional drain of the war was tremendous. The President found himself more and more imprisoned by the issue, less and less able to concentrate and act on other issues. What the administration might have been able to do on the domestic front without the burden of Vietnam is an unanswerable question, but the 3 percent of GNP directly absorbed by the war was far less significant than its emotional toll on the administration, and the resultant reluctance to adjust economic policy to the realities of the situation.

Chapter 8

Nixon and
the New
Federalism

I'm now a Keynesian.
—Richard M. Nixon, 1972

In a recent book Arthur M. Okun (chairman of the Council of Economic Advisers at the close of the Johnson Administration) noted that the high watermark of the "new economics" and of the prestige of the economist in Washington was reached in late 1965.[1] No doubt many economists would agree. This certainly appeared to be a high point for the Council. The success of the tax cut under the Kennedy-Johnson Administration enabled Walter Heller to return to academic life, leaving the Council with a highly polished image. His associates, both on CEA and in the profession, basked in reflected glory.

In the eventful years that have passed since that time, the Johnson Administration passed into history, Richard M. Nixon was elected and reelected; upon his resignation he was replaced by Gerald R. Ford. What are the fortunes of the Council after thirty years?

Even by mid-1973 it was clear that a substantial amount of professional expertise and a great deal of good fortune would be necessary if the plateau of influence and prestige of the mid-1960s was to be held. The last years of the Johnson Administration and the early years of the Nixon Administration put the skills of the federal economist to a severe test.

The new administration took over in troubled times. A long-drawn-

216

out and indecisive foreign war dogged it on the international front. The domestic scene was in ferment with continuing demands for social legislation. The Johnson Administration had found these matters increasingly difficult to contend with. Inflation had become more serious, and the new administration promised to take effective action against it while preserving a high level of employment. Generally, Republicans were expected to be somewhat more apt to stress price stability as opposed to full employment. Yet effective measures to counter inflation were likely to drive unemployment above generally acceptable levels and to bring unpredictable results, further increasing domestic tensions. Indeed, this proved to be the case; as job markets tightened, young people faced the frustrations of unemployment, and their elders grappled with rising prices.

Most economists, while applauding the performance of the Heller Council, agreed that the "new economics" had yet to demonstrate its ability to simultaneously maintain both a stable price level and an acceptable level of unemployment. This goal would be difficult enough under more normal conditions; under the circumstances of the Vietnam War in 1970, it appeared to be almost impossible.

From Whittier to the White House

Nixon came into the Presidency in 1969, having defeated Hubert Humphrey, the Democratic candidate. Nixon's background was entirely in law and politics. Shortly after World War II he was elected as a Representative from California and subsequently served briefly in the Senate. Having become a national figure in the Hiss case, in 1952 he was elected to the Vice Presidency on the Eisenhower ticket.[2]

The Nixon-Humphrey campaign in the fall of 1968 was relatively free from economic debate, although, as the campaign progressed, economic issues became more important. The rapid increase in prices, the tax surcharge, and spending on nondefense projects were all discussed; but emotional issues were the Vietnam War and domestic matters centering on civil rights and law and order; and the apparent widespread dissatisfaction with the manner in which the Johnson Administration had managed them.

In contrast to the 1964 presidential candidate Barry Goldwater, Nixon seemingly represented the younger and more moderate, progressive wing of his party. However, he appeared to be less liberal in his economics than Nelson Rockefeller, George Romney, or other leading conten-

217

ders for the Republican nomination. Few really expected the Nixon Administration to depart in a radical fashion from the economic policies of the preceding administration, since the relevant problems facing the Eisenhower, Kennedy, and Johnson administrations changed only moderately, in degree rather than in direction. Nixon's victory, though decisive, was hardly a mandate for drastic economic change.

Nixon's economic background was much like Johnson's. A youth of modest means, Nixon graduated from Whittier College (a Quaker institution in California) and Duke University Law School. From his graduation in 1939, he practiced law in California, served in the Navy in World War II, and returned to the law upon his resumption of civil life. As a twenty-nine-year-old lawyer, Nixon in 1942 had spent ten months in the wartime OPA. This experience as a low-level bureaucrat left a deep and unpleasant impression on him. He was uninterested in economic matters and appalled by the vast, "nit-picking" tasks of the price-fixing agency. His aversion to the problems stemming from comprehensive price controls remained a strong factor in his economic thinking thirty years later.

Entering politics almost by accident, he served as Congressman, Senator, and Vice-President until his defeat by Kennedy in the 1960 presidential campaign. Nixon was not a man of wealth, and until his years in New York he had never made a large income in private life. Like Johnson, he was a full-time politician. His early role in the Hiss case, his frequent service as political spokesman (often hatchet man) for the Eisenhower Administration, coupled with a degree of immaturity, had branded him as a hopeless conservative. Nixon had been a tough political partisan, while Eisenhower remained "above the battle." This activity did much to incur the wrath of liberals in both parties, to whom Nixon was always the "gutter politician."[3]

In 1962, Nixon was declared politically dead by the news media when he lost the governorship of California to Edmund G. "Pat" Brown, and, indeed, it did appear that his public career was over. He left California for New York to enter the legal circles of the "Eastern establishment" and, to all outward appearances, became another Thomas E. Dewey, a party regular of stature, but finished as a national candidate.

Nixon, however, began a slow comeback. The perceptive observer of presidential elections, Theodore White, has noted that Nixon gained much perspective from his years in private law practice.[4] Changes in his outlook can be summarized as follows:

Nixon became wealthy and for the first time began to shed the "poor-boy-on-the-way-up" image, replacing it with that of one who had "arrived" in the economic sense. His income as senior partner in Nixon, Mudge, Rose, Guthrie, Alexander and Mitchell was $200,000 per year. Now that his income was adequate, he was able to associate on an independent financial basis with men of means. His rise from a modest young suburban lawyer to Vice-President had, in contrast, been so rapid (six years) that his financial status had often. been precarious and his reactions unpredictable. The first "crisis"—the "Nixon fund incident" in 1952—stemmed from his lack of financial resources and had almost cost him his career.

In private life, Nixon had time to read, write, travel, and study problems in depth. His fund of knowledge on national and international issues, like his financial resources, had often been low in his earlier years. A nonpartisan comment about Nixon often heard in the years before 1968 was that he was "superficial" and that he had no really deep understanding of issues or meaningful executive experience. During the Eisenhower years, Nixon as a youthful Vice-President had been considered by many (perhaps by himself) to be a young man who, though having obvious ability, owed his status largely to the fact that he happened to be in the right place at the right time. He could point to no solid business or professional record in private life.[5]

His self-respect by 1968 was much enhanced. Nixon as a capable lawyer and, as a successful member of a respected New York law firm, had achieved success, not on the basis of election coattails or a lucky incident, but on his ability to make it in a "big-time" Eastern law firm of the type that supplies talent to the upper level of the federal establishment.

As senior partner, Nixon took an active part in both the practice and the management of the firm. Yet he also had a good deal of time for national political affairs and, on behalf of his major client, Pepsi-Cola, made numerous foreign trips and began to build a reputation as a foreign expert. These trips, always well publicized, were the tipoff that he was contemplating reentry into presidential politics.[6]

Despite his 1960 loss to Kennedy and his 1962 loss to Brown, 1968 found Nixon in a position of strength for the nomination; and, though some observers noted that Humphrey began to gain as November approached, Nixon won decisively in the election.

Nixon Economics

When he took office, Mr. Nixon proceeded slowly and cautiously in shaping economic policy. The "first hundred days"—

since FDR's time considered a bellwether of future policy—were undramatic. Nixon chose Professor Paul McCracken as CEA chairman. McCracken, then fifty-two, had served as a Council member under Saulnier from December 1956 to January 1969. On the faculty of the University of Michigan, he was a specialist in business policy. McCracken was thought to be something of a "monatrist," or "Friedmanite" economist, "inclined to stress the importance of the money supply. McCracken called himself "Friedmanesque." Herbert Stein, also fifty-two, with a Ph.D. from the University of Chicago, had substantial government experience and was often regarded as the "ambassador" to the academic and business communities.[7] Many observers felt by 1972 that Stein had overshadowed McCracken, who was quiet and reserved by nature. McCracken in many ways was the prototype of the college professor, while Stein was more of an "operator," wise in the ways of Washington. The third member of the Nixon Council, Hendrik S. Houthakker, forty-five, was a Harvard faculty member with a strong background in econometrics and much interest in agricultural economics.

The first two years of Nixon's economic policy can be characterized as generally unimaginative. Much time was used to install the new administration and to position it vis-à-vis Johnson's policies.[8] In general, those who had been strong Nixon supporters before the election were disappointed, while liberals were pleasantly surprised. On the "Hill," still under Democratic control, the Joint Economic Committee continued, with Senator Proxmire in the chair.

A factor that somewhat overshadowed the appointment of CEA members and had portents for the future was the return to Washington of Arthur F. Burns. Burns, who had served with distinction as CEA chairman from 1953 to 1956, was appointed to a new position as counselor to the President, a task which apparently encompassed responsibility for a wide range of socioeconomic matters. Speculation immediately arose whether and to what extent Burns' authority might overlap that of CEA.

Burns' role in his counselor's job was never very clear. Confusion existed as to his jurisdiction with that of Daniel P. Moynihan, who had a similar status, both were concerned with domestic issues as opposed to Henry Kissinger in the area of foreign affairs, where he stood alone. Also the fact that Burns was an economist of reputation naturally caused speculation as to his economic role if any. Evans and Novak report that Nixon had decided early that Burns would replace Martin as chairman of the Board of Governors of the Federal Reserve System and thought of the White House position as being merely temporary.[9] Confusion and speculation ended when Burns was named to the Federal Reserve post in 1970.

The first annual report of the Nixon Council struck a note of cautious optimism and devoted a rather substantial amount of space to the long-range issues of economic policy. The President in his section of the report rejected the idea that a trade-off between employment and price stability was unavoidable.

After 5 years of sustained unemployment followed by 5 years of sustained inflation, some have concluded that the price of finding work for the unemployed must be the hardship of inflation for all.

I do not agree.

It is true that we have just passed through a decade when the economy spent most of the time far off the course of reasonably full employment and price stability. But if we apply the hard lessons learned from the sixties to the decade ahead, and add a new realism to the management of our economic policies, I believe we can attain the goal of plentiful jobs earning dollars of stable purchasing power.

He emphasized the need for the choice of goals, based on information; accordingly, this *Economic Report* "opens up the books" as never before.

We are making available the facts and figures that will enable the people to make more intelligent judgements about the future. If we are to improve the quality of life in this Nation, we must first improve the quality of debate about our national priorities. In this Report, and in the Budget Message, long-range projections are made that will enable the people to discuss their choices more effectively in the light of what is possible. In the real world of economics, there is a place for dreams that are realizable if we make the hard choices necessary to make them come true.[10]

Despite these hopeful words, the Council's report did not shrink from the fact that 1970 would be a year of difficult decision making and that steering a course between inflation and deflation would be a complex exercise in economic statesmanship.

The year 1970 opens with total demand slowed down substantially and real output approximately stable, but with prices still rising rapidly. The objectives of policy for 1970 are to reduce the rise of prices and to revive the growth of output. These objec-

221

tives are difficult to reconcile. Measures that would assure the most rapid stabilization of the price level would almost certainly force a sharp contraction of production and employment. But there is a path of moderate expansion of demand which will yield both a decline of the rate of inflation and a resumption of growth of output. The task of economic policy in 1970 is to achieve this path.[11]

An estimate of future output and claims again it was prepared and the performance of the economy charted up to 1975. In general, the theme of this prognosis was that, despite hopes for the "peace dividend" (much discussed by the Johnson Council), no substantial excess would be available for some time. Claims on GNP, either present or in sight, would for some time balance or exceed increased growth:

The capability of the economy to grow may be different from what has been assumed. Nevertheless, for all of their necessarily hypothetical character, these estimates do highlight three important points that have major implications for fiscal policy. First, existing claims upon the growing available national output already exhaust the probable output and real national income that the economy can generate for several years to come. The satisfaction of a new claim, therefore, necessarily will require the rejection of another claim which now exists. Second, the Federal Government's Fiscal Policies will directly affect which claims on our national income are satisfied—not only the direct Federal claims but also State, Local and Private claims. Federal actions that increase State, Local or Private expenditures—even if those actions are not reflected in the Federal Budget— generate claims against the national output. . . . The budget and the budget surplus should not be regarded merely as conventional symbols of sound finance; they have a profoundly important functional role in achieving national goals.

No one ignored the problem of inflation, and in testimony before the Joint Economic Committee (which was, not surprisingly, less sanguine) McCracken outlined administration strategy:

The change of policy was expected to act upon the rate of inflation in two stages, each of which would take time. First, fiscal and monetary restraint would reduce the rate of growth of total spending. This reduction would not come fully and immediately when policy changed. For example, consumers would at first respond to an increase in their taxes by reducing their saving rates, and most of the effect on consumption spending would come later. Also, businesses and households would at first respond to monetary tightness by reducing liquidity and finding substitutes for money—adjusting their spending more slowly to these changes.

In the second stage of this adjustment process the decline in rate of growth of spending would begin to reduce the rate of price increases. This also would take time, especially after a long period of inflation. Cost increases built in by previous wage contracts and other commitments would continue for a time. Price and wage decisions would for a time reflect the presumption that the long inflation would continue. During this period, when prices continued to rise strongly even though the rate of growth of demand had diminished, the rate of growth of real output would decline. However, in time the slower growth of demand and of production would result in a slower rate of inflation.

Neither wage-price controls nor "guidepost" policy were necessary or useful, starting from the circumstances of early 1969, to achieve the objective of the transition to a more stable price level.[12]

The Joint Committee was not convinced that prices were at a downward turning point and expressed concern about the effect of monetary restraint on the employment picture, which appeared to be increasingly serious. The administration, however, held fast to its view that neither guideposts nor administrative "jawboning" were appropriate. The early Nixon policy was apparently designed to put more emphasis on demand-pull inflation as opposed to cost-push inflation, and to suggest monetary remedies. This line became increasingly hard to hold as 1971 began. In May, an editorial in *Fortune* magazine expressed the view widely held by big business:

Warily and reluctantly, *Fortune* has come to the conclusion that the Federal Government should set up voluntary wage price guideposts, something like those of the early 1960's. We don't like the idea of guideposts, even noncompulsory ones, and we would make only modest claims for their efficacy. Moreover, the advocacy of Government intervention in the workings of the market is philosophically at odds with the principles of economic freedom to which we subscribe. But in the present situation, with psychology getting in the way of economics, with inflation proving more persistent than economists had expected, it could be temporarily useful to establish Governmental standards designed to guide wage settlements and price decisions in the direction of price stability.[13]

Federal Reserve Chairman Burns by late May had reached much the same conclusion. Few economists fully endorse guideposts or income policies with enthusiasm and accept the Nixon view that they are unworkable because the vested interests of corporate and labor leaders use them (whatever their private views may be) to press for unilateral price and wage increases.

The President stuck to his "game plan." He was opposed to direct controls, both on ideological grounds and because he felt strongly that they were impossible to enforce with any reasonable commitment of resources. There was much talk of "inflation alerts" and other measures short of direct controls, but it began to be more and more evident that these largely voluntary measures were not effective. The JEC publication, *The Inflation Process in the United States*, issued in February 1972, found this "hands-off" policy to be a major contributing factor to inflation.

The New Economic Policy

Throughout 1970 and into early 1971, prices continued to rise and unemployment increased. The Administration was understandably increasingly on the defensive as to when prices would begin to recede and substantial wage increases in key industries (e.g., trucking) brought to life new demands for return to the wage-price guideposts. These demands were echoed by second-level Administration officials, but at this time the line from the top level was still opposed to an incomes policy. There were, however, growing signs that some positive action needed to be taken. Several excerpts from the 1972 *Report* indicate the tone of administration thinking at the time:

> The combination of problems created a dilemma for economic policy. A rate of expansion and a level of unemployment less favorable than policy had projected could have been remedied by more expansive fiscal and monetary measures. But this remedy would have made the other problems worse. It would have stimulated the still lively expectations of continuing or even accelerating inflation and it would have speeded up the flight from the dollar. The problems had to be dealt with simultaneously.[14]

There was also a willingness to admit that perhaps the scope and difficulty of the task had been underestimated:

> The problems of managing fiscal policy or monetary policy or both have apparently been underestimated. It can well be that

224

more has been promised than can be delivered with existing knowledge and instruments. Certainly there is need for much additional research. But if the question is not one of keeping the economy on a narrowly-defined path but one of avoiding violent aberrations like the one that began in 1965, our tools are probably adequate, and the problem is more the national will than the techniques of economics and economic policy.[15]

Although the President continued to resist the call for prescribed wage-price policies, he began, in mid-1970, a restructuring of the domestic economic machinery. Secretary of Labor, George P. Shultz, a former dean of the Graduate School of Business at the University of Chicago and a noted labor economist, was appointed to the post of Director of the Office of Budget and Management, a task combining the powerful budget directorship and the management of administration economic affairs in general. Shultz was to have general oversight over federal budgetary and expenditure matters. Robert P. Mayo, Director of the Budget, had never been close to Nixon and worked generally under Treasury Secretary Kennedy, whose protégé he had been. His view of the status and function of the Budget Director was much more limited than that of those who had previously occupied this key position. He left to join the Federal Reserve Bank of Chicago. Shultz was at once tagged as the "Assistant President," "administration strongman," and "house intellectual." Columnist Victor Riesel noted Shultz's task was to make the "New Federalism" work. It is likely that Shultz as a labor economist and successful Secretary of Labor was expected to form a bridge to the labor unions, a group whose support the administration needed most to preserve its domestic policies and whose support was increasingly withheld.

The major economic event of the year seemed to be the alleged conversion of the President to Keynesian economics. The President proposed a budget deficit in order to stimulate economic activity, saying, "I am now a Keynesian." Nixon who had been thought to be a devotee of Professor Friedman's monetary views had apparently embraced a new philosophy. The administration did not try to hide the fact that the planned deficit was designed to put the President in a stronger position for the 1972 election. The President referred to the procedure as a "self-fulfilling prophecy."

Some Washington "insiders" were of the opinion that the shift to Keynesianism was principally the handiwork of Shultz rather than the Council. In any event, by mid-1971 Shultz, not the Council, seemed to be the key to administration economic policies.

McCracken clearly seemed to be far from being another "Burns type chief of staff," nor had he formed the close day-by-day relationship structured by Walter Heller. John Kenneth Galbraith called McCracken the "most compromised economist in the United States." Others pointed to McCracken's quiet personal manner and argued that he was more effective behind the scenes than appeared to be the case. A reading of CEA documents lends strength to this supposition.

In mid-August 1971 the President made a startling reversal in his policy stance and (with characteristic drama) announced a ninety-day wage-price freeze, to be followed by some form of incomes policy with controls akin to the wage-price guideposts. Important international financial controls were also instituted. Thus began a long and confusing series of controls and decontrol of wages and prices lasting until Nixon left office. Needless to say, the move made a tremendous impact, but action was centered, not in the Council, but in the office of the Secretary of the Treasury and in the emergency organizations established to oversee controls.

Reportedly, Herbert Stein had been given much responsibility for planning and implementing Phase II (the post-freeze plans), but CEA seemed again to be only on the fringes of decision making. As the post-freeze structure came gradually into view, CEA remained in the background. A "voluntary" program administered by a group of committees was established. The two key segments of this structure were the Price Commission and the Pay Board, designed to judge the fairness of wage-price increases. The Council as such seemed to play a minor role.

The administration noted that not since 1932 had such dramatic changes been made in the economy, and, indeed, economic commentary in the mass media reached new heights. Despite this, the Council remained strangely in the background, although the chairman was designated vice-chairman of the Cost of Living Council. The 1972 *Economic Report* traced the background and purpose of the "New Economic Policy":

> The decision to embark on the New Economic Policy (NEP) came from an increasing awareness in the Administration that the ambitious goals it had set at the beginning of the year were not being met. Progress in the fight against inflation was proceeding too slowly, and its future success was uncertain. At the same time, the recovery was also progressing, but not fast enough to cut the rate of unemployment. More crucial than either of these for the timing of the decisions was the serious weakening of the dollar in international markets.[16]

It was, of course, pointed out that these controls would be removed as soon as possible, but no one in the administration was willing to speculate about specific dates. For a time these controls were fairly effective but they lost force quickly. It has been suggested that a major reason was Nixon's philosophic dedication to laissez-faire economics. Some economists (though not in the administration) were of the opinion that incomes policies were apt to be a more or less permanent feature of the U.S. economy. This view stems from the belief that a modern industrial economy, with many inflexible elements in the price-wage structure, cannot make sufficiently rapid adjustments in wage rates and prices to maintain continuously an acceptable balance between unemployment and prices. Thus, in order to keep price increases within reason and to preserve an acceptable level of unemployment, controls are mandatory.[17] Nixon of course looked forward to the time when the controls could be ended, viewing them as a symbol of New Deal-Fair Deal interference in business.

At long last (January 1973) the U.S. withdrew from formal participation in Vietnam, but of course the economic consequences were long lived. All talk of a "peace dividend" had long since been abandoned and while a measure of sociopolitical stability resulted from the end of actual fighting, the impact on the inflationary spiral was less detectable. The long delay in facing up to the economic impact of the war took its toll. The economic lessons of Vietnam, like its social costs, had been formidable and the impact was not to be reversed by formal withdrawal.

Shultz, Burns, and Connally

By mid-1971—with the election of 1972 already a major factor in its calculations—the administration found itself in a unique situation. Shultz, whose expertise and experience as an economist had been in labor relations, found himself playing an increasing role as policy adviser in the area of aggregative economics. He made his most dramatic impact with the appearance of his young University of Chicago protégé, Arthur Laffer, who in testimony before the Joint Committee, predicted a gross national product for 1971 of $1,065 billion, a prediction Paul Samuelson greeted with a statement that it would receive the same "Christian charity" we extend to Fidel Castro when he predicts that Cuba will produce ten million tons of sugar! (The 1972 *Economic Report* estimated 1971 GNP at $1,046 billion.) From the Federal Reserve, Burns, who had become a skilled practical politician, was increasingly critical of administration policy.[18] Both federal and independent economists were generally skeptical of the Shultz-Laffer growth estimates. Though Shultz had the President's confidence, it was clear that the Laffer estimates were not shared by the other economists of the administration.

The 1972 *Report* was a bit restrained in its forecast (predicting an increase of about $100 billion) and stressed the difficulties of prediction: "GNP forecasts made by the Council have been qualified in the past by the caveat that they should be viewed as the midpoint of a range of plus or minus $5 billion around the forecast. When GNP was $500 billion, this was the equivalent of a band of uncertainty of ± $10 billion."[19]

In mid-1971, the administration announced that henceforth Treasury Secretary John Connally (a Johnsonian Democrat who succeeded David Kennedy and later became a Republican) would be the administration spokesman on economic matters. Chairman McCracken announced that the administration was admitting defeat in its drive to control inflation in the immediate future.

In late 1971, McCracken resigned and Stein became chairman. The opening on the Council was filled by the appointment of Professor Marina von N. Whitman, a faculty member at the University of Pittsburgh.[20] Houthakker had resigned in July 1971 and had been replaced by Professor Ezra Solomon of Stanford University. Professor Houthakker, although he was highly capable as an economist, had been almost invisible on the Council, and his resignation was little noticed. Connally was replaced as the Secretary of the Treasury by Shultz, who appeared to be the "resident expert" in economic matters. Near the end of the administration, Shultz was replaced by William E. Simon, a former bond trader who carried over under Ford.

What could one say about the Council near the end of the Nixon era? Clearly, it appeared under the Nixon mode of operation to have suffered considerable eclipse, perhaps only temporary but eclipse nonetheless. Let us consider the events that took place from 1969–74. First, CEA was overshadowed by Burns in the role of counselor to the President. Second, it seemingly played a secondary role to Shultz as policy maker. Third, Secretary Connally assumed the dominant role until his resignation in May 1972 when he was replaced by Shultz. In early 1974 Kenneth Rush (a lawyer-business executive) was named economic coordinator. Not since the days of 1950 was the Council so much in the background in the face of the fast-moving events of the Korean War.

It is possible to see a close parallel between Nixon and Truman insofar as their relationship to CEA is concerned. No doubt both Truman and Nixon would object to being bracketed, but the parallel is apt. Truman let the Council mind its business so long as it suited his purpose, showing no interest in day-to-day affairs. Some aspects of the Nixon performance give a similar impression. Every account of the administration makes it clear that like Truman Nixon considered economics a distasteful chore, though he recognized the importance of bread-and-butter political issues. The Nixon White House staff was tightly knit and its procedures were generally formal. No professional economist played the "bridge" role of Gabriel Hauge in the Eisenhower years. Nixon, like Truman, was not really interested in economic affairs except as they related to politics or, in Nixon's case, international relations and diplomacy. Evans and Novak report that he was bored by McCracken's presentations. The Council apparently often had a difficult time penetrating the "Berlin Wall" of H. R. Haldeman and John Ehrlichman in the internal administration of the Nixon White House.[21]

But even after these two left the staff, CEA under Stein fared little better. Rush did not play a strong role as coordinator of policy in 1974, but neither did the Council. Shultz and Roy Ashe (a business executive), the Director of the Office of Management and Budget until early 1975, were reportedly in contention for the strong-man role during the year 1973–74, which has come to be known as the "Watergate Era." Waves of crises shook the administration, culminating in the resignation of the President in 1974 and his succession by Vice-President Gerald R. Ford.

Transition and Survival

One hesitates to judge the Nixon Council harshly in 1973–74 since many other domestic issues seemed to be in a state of limbo. The Council was likely no worse off than many other parts of the federal establishment. Loss of prestige by the administration and the rapid pace of inflation/recession spelled dark days for the federal economist. Herbert Stein, who had been controversial since 1972 when he campaigned for Nixon's reelection, left in the fall of 1974 to become Robertson Professor of Economics at the University of Virginia. Keyserling had been quite active in his era, but he refrained from outright campaigning as did others; Stein departed from this tradition. Only days before his resignation, Nixon appointed Alan Greenspan, a New York consulting economist, to head the Council. Greenspan, then forty-eight, held a master's degree in economics from New York University. (Although the press reported him to be writing a dissertation for the Ph.D., the fact that he received his M.A. degree in 1950 made that unlikely.)

Gary L. Seevers, appointed in July 1973, and William Fellner, appointed in October of the same year, had replaced Professors Solomon and Whitman, who had left in March and August respectively. Except for Stein, who stayed on to ease the transition, none of the original Nixon appointees were left when the President resigned. Fellner left in April 1975, replaced by Burton Malkiel from Princeton University. Seevers also resigned in April and was succeeded by Paul W. MacAvoy of Massachusetts Institute of Technology, a specialist in energy economics.

Thus in 1974, the Council began its tenure under a sixth President. Gerald Ford, a lawyer with more than a quarter century of congressional service, was viewed as generally conservative but not reactionary. Clearly, domestic affairs were destined to play a large part in his administration. Indeed, Ford had hardly assumed office before serious economic difficulties beset him. In late summer, when he took the helm, it appeared that controlling inflation would be the thrust of the administration's economic policy. By late 1974, however, rising unemployment (surpassing any in the postwar era) forced the administration to fight on two fronts. Inflation of some 12 percent in 1974 and unemployment of some 8 percent in early 1975 brought the worse of both economic worlds. To complicate his problems further, the 94th Congress was overwhelmingly Democratic. Watergate was replaced on the front pages by an "Economic Roundup"; not since the 1930s had there been so much national discourse on economic matters. The Council continued to maintain a low profile, throughout 1975 and 1976.

However in mid-1974, there was considerable press speculation that Chairman Greenspan was increasingly influential with the President.[22] There is evidence that matters have improved under Greenspan. By early 1976, he seemed to White House observers to have frequent access to the President and, more important, to have the confidence of the President who has reportedly been impressed by Greenspan's accuracy in prediction, fostered by improving conditions in 1976.

Another favorable point must be noted. Greenspan has reversed the Stein policy of active partisanship, and restored some of the prestige of the Council. Greenspan has seemingly benefited from the paucity of competing economic talent close to the President. William Seidman, the Presidential Assistant for Economic Affairs, is an accountant, and the Director of the Office of Management and Budget, James T. Lynn, is a lawyer. Thus Greenspan enjoys something of a monopoly in the White House. One hopes that the fortunes of the Council have indeed turned upward.

In mid-1976, attention was shifting to the 1976 presidential election. The national mood appeared to be increasingly skeptical of governmental solutions to major problems. Federal economic policy is not exempt from this view, and the future of the Council in this new atmosphere remains to be seen. Let us turn our attention to the Joint Economic Committee.

Notes

Chapter 8

[1] Arthur M. Okun, *The Political Economy of Prosperity* (Washington: Brookings, 1970), p. 59. See also, Robert Lekachman, "The Quarrelsome Economists," *New Leader,* October 13, 1969.

[2] Younger readers may not recall that Alger Hiss, a former State Department official, was convicted of perjury in a celebrated case (after many complex legal actions), lasting throughout the late 1940s and early 1950s. Nixon, as a Congressman, was instrumental in the case. Hiss had been accused of passing certain documents to Communist agents before World War II—acts which Hiss denied. The statute of limitations had ruled out any trial on those charges, and Hiss was tried only on the perjury charge. Nixon, as a member of the House Committee which investigated the matter, won national recognition. He moved rapidly to the Senate and to the Vice Presidency and was in consequence accused of being an opportunist.

[3] *Washington Post* cartoonist, "Herblock," always portrayed the Vice-President as being unshaven, emerging from back alleys or sewers, and in every way, taking the lowest possible road. Nixon did not help his own image by his unfortunate castigation of the press after his defeat in California.

[4] Theodore White, *The Making of the President, 1968* (New York: Atheneum House, 1969).

[5] In May 1969, The Weekly Digest of Presidential Documents carried a financial statement of Nixon listing his net worth as $595,900. This was previous to the purchase of property in San Clemente, California. It is a paradox of politics that Kennedy, who had considerably less of a record of private career accomplishment to point to, was seldom taxed with this fact. At the time of their entry into the House, JFK and Nixon were about equal in their lack of record. Neither made much of a record in the Congress. Both were young men in a hurry; yet Nixon, the prototype of the "bootstrap career boy," was (in a nation where upward mobility is highly regarded) less acceptable than Kennedy, the rich man's son. New York erased this image, and Nixon became a man of substance and self-assurance; Whittier was long in the past.

[6] See Jules Witcover, *The Resurrection of Richard Nixon* (New York: Putnam's 1970), pp. 46ff.

[7] It will be recalled that Leon Keyserling of the Truman CEA was second prize winner of the Pabst Essay Contest on postwar planning. It is interesting that Stein, then 28 (1944) and a young Federal economist, was first prize winner ($25,000) with an essay entitled "A Plan for Postwar Employment."

[8] Rowland Evans, Jr., and Robert D. Novak, *Nixon in the White House, The Frustration of Power* (New York: Random House, 1972), p. 74ff.

[9] *Economic Report of the President, 1970,* p. 3.

[10] Ibid., p. 4.

[11] Ibid., p. 57.

[12] Ibid., p. 83.

[13] *Fortune*, May, 1971. Copyright© Time, Inc.

[14] *Economic Report of the President*, 1972, p. 22.

[15] Ibid., p. 112.

[16] Ibid., p. 29.

[17] See for example, E. Ray Canterbery, "Myths vs. Realities: The Fifties Against the Sixties," Chapter 4, *Economics on a New Frontier* (Belmont: Wadsworth, 1968).

[18] See "A Practical Politician at the FED," *Fortune*, May 1971.

[19] *Economic Report of the President*, 1972, p. 107.

[20] Mrs. Whitman, who holds a Columbia Ph.D., became the first woman CEA member and also the highest ranking female appointee to any post in the Nixon Administration. She had formerly been a CEA staff member. McCracken returned to his Chair at the University of Michigan.

[21] See the discussion, "Economists Consider Economic Reporters and Vice Versa," *Proceedings*, American Economic Association, May 1972, Vol. 62, No. 2.

Part III

CONGRESSIONAL ECONOMICS AND THE COUNCIL

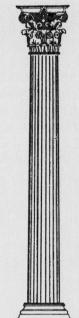

Chapter 9

The View from
Capitol Hill

*I have come to you as the head of the
government, and the responsible leader
of the party in power, to urge action
now, while there is time to serve the
country deliberately in the clear air of
common counsel.*
—Woodrow Wilson

Let us return briefly to 1945, when the legislative
action leading to the Employment Act began, and look at it from the
congressional point of view. The Congress had for some time been aware
of the need to take a firm line in controlling postwar reconversion policy,
and steps had been taken to make sure that the executive branch did not
dominate the situation.[1]

Galvanized into action by various efforts in the executive branch (by
the National Resources Planning Board and others) to stake out this
area, the Congress by March 1945 had established two committees—one
in the Senate (the Special Postwar Economic Policy and Planning Committee under Senator Walter F. George); and another in the House, an
even earlier group under the chairmanship of Representative Charles
Colmer.

These efforts to restore policy making to the Congress were in the
mind of Senator O'Mahoney when, later in the Senate debate on S-380,
he told his colleagues: "Mr. President, this is a bill to vest in Congress
the power and the responsibility of meeting the issue instead of continu-
ally delegating the power to the executive branch of government. This,
Mr. President, is a bill to *restore the functions of Congress.*"[2] [Emphasis
added.]

235

The Senator knew to whom he spoke. New Deal policies, aggressively pursued, had tended to put the legislative branch in a subordinate position. Although the Congress had become much more independent after 1936, recurrent crises had caused many elements in the nation to look to the executive branch for leadership. Wartime conditions had intensified this situation. Thus, the Congress had seen what appeared to be a steady drift of power and public attention down Pennsylvania Avenue. Professor Lester G. Seligman has noted, for example, the desire of the Congress to regain a measure of control by structuring the machinery of the act.[3]

Now the Roosevelt era was drawing to a close and the critical post-war period loomed ahead. Here was an opportunity for the Congress to assert itself. The idea of institutionalizing presidential advice had wide appeal. During the debate, Congressman John J. Cochran of Missouri, a staunch supporter of the proposed legislation, observed that advice from professionals might have been valuable in the past:

> Naturally the Cabinet is not going to be able to take on additional duties. The purpose in setting up the Council of Economic Advisers is to meet the situation that the Secretary of Commerce, Mr. Wallace, and other members of the Cabinet explained to the committee, and that was one of the reasons President Hoover failed to meet the crisis confronting him was that he did not have the proper advice and it was also stated that had President Roosevelt been properly advised in reference to the situation he might have done a better job in meeting the deplorable conditions that existed at the time. Therefore, we are setting up this Council of Economic Advisers because we feel that the men who are to canvass the situation should have nothing else to do. Naturally when the Council makes its report to the President, he will discuss the report and the condition with his Cabinet before sending the message to Congress.[4]

The discourse between Senators Alben Barkley (the Majority Leader) and Taft is also enlightening.

> *Barkley:* We left the President's hands free in looking over the country and in selecting men of experience and vision when making such appointments. The idea of the conferees was that in making these appointments without designating the appointees as representatives of groups, the President would choose men who would be able to speak in a broad way for all the people and at the same time have adequate knowledge with reference to any particular segment of the population.

236

Taft: And while they might tend to represent one or another of the groups I should hope that they would be of such broad experience and knowledge that they would not be merely representatives of any particular groups.

Barkley: The Senator is correct, and what he has stated was the feeling of the conferees. It was hoped that the appointees would be men of such outstanding ability and experience that they would be representing the whole country and at the same time bring to the service of the Council whatever experience they may have had in their respective callings.[5]

All of this was fine, but did all this proposed machinery not focus on the President and give him more adequate tools for policy making than those possessed by Congress? None of this helped the Congress in its power struggle with the White House. Congress' possession of a strong voice in postwar policies was vital. Clearly, the creation of the Council (or a similar body) proposed by the legislation would have merely formalized current practice, that is, would have continued to entrust work to the White House advisers or a group similar to the National Resources Planning Board. The Congress has always had grave doubts about White House aides and advisers, since neither Congress nor the electorate has control over them and they are accountable solely to the President. Legislation to enlarge this force always arouses congressional hostility.

There must, in the eyes of Congress, be a device incorporated into the act that would restore the congressional policy-making power, or the legislation was pointless. The logical move was to incorporate a body that, *as a part of the Congress,* would have at its command adequate professional resources to monitor and comment intelligently on the recommendations and proposals coming from the White House.

The Joint Committee, envisioned as a special review body by both S-380 and HR-2202, seemed to be the answer. Even those who were dubious about the legislation per se or about its details were not apt to question the need for legislative oversight.

Senator George Radcliffe of Maryland (who was not favorable toward the act in general) made a typical comment (noting that the whole matter was perhaps debatable): "But it is desirable that there should be fact-finding facilities in operation. It is desirable that estimates should be made and that suggestions be presented as to what can be done in regard to relieving unemployment *and it is most assuredly desirable that in this matter the Senate and the House should cooperate closely in some suitable way.*"[6] [Emphasis added.]

Some, such as Representative Clare Hoffman, a very conservative Michigan Republican, felt strongly that the Committee would be just another appendage and would serve little function, but this was a minority view.[7] Senator Murray, who had been close to the situation from the beginning, gave what was probably the clearest forecast of the Committee's role:

> From the day this legislation was first introduced, the provision for a joint congressional committee to analyze the President's over-all program has been hailed as a distinct contribution to the improvement of congressional operations.
>
> There is general agreement that such a committee could be extremely helpful in coordinating the separate and diverse activities of the many committees in the Senate and the House of Representatives. For example, let me quote from the Senate Banking Committee's minority report on the full employment bill:
>
> "We believe there should be such a joint committee studying the effect of proposed legislation on economic stability. We question somewhat whether the standing committees will pay much attention to the report of the joint committee, but it should be helpful by revealing to these committees and the individual members of the Senate the relationship of this measure to an over-all economic program."
>
> The Joint Committee on the Economic Report should be a tremendous contribution to the improved organization and operation of the Congress.[8]

Thus, the idea of the Joint Committee arose in part at least from the understandable desire on the part of Congress to regain and expand its authority over and to improve its procedure in dealing with economic policy to prevent a recurrence of its recent unhappiness with the National Resources Planning Board.

There is little doubt that one of the major weaknesses of the NRPB was its unilateral position vis-à-vis the Congress, for the NRPB was entirely a creature of the executive branch. When the Employment Act came under consideration, the Congress was anxious not to surrender its powers again. No doubt, also, many in the executive branch would have agreed that NRPB's detachment from the Congress had been an error that led to its demise. Clearly, despite the mutual desire to retain power, joint efforts were required for success.

After much compromise, the act was finally passed, but almost immediately the Republican victory in the 1946 election threw matters into confusion, and the Committee found itself drifting and for some time unable to organize itself.

As a consequence, the Joint Economic Committee did not begin its life under very favorable circumstances. Indeed, as perhaps befits its bipartisan nature, its first report was issued in an atmosphere of acrimony and partisan dispute. The shift in political power in the 80th Congress from Democratic to Republican hands had upset the flow of work and caused the Joint Committee (then the Joint Committee on the Economic Report) to begin its operations only after some delay. The first *operative* committee consisted of the following:[9]

Senators	*Representatives*
Robert A. Taft (R) *Chairman*	Jesse P. Wolcott (R)
Joseph H. Ball (R)	George H. Bender (R)
Ralph E. Flanders (R)	Robert F. Rich (R)
Arthur V. Watkins (R)	Walter P. Judd (R)/
Joseph C. O'Mahoney (D)	Christian Herter (R)
Francis J. Myers (D)	Edward J. Hart (D)
John Sparkman (D)	Wright Patman (D)
	Walter B. Huber (D)

Several of the Committee members deserve a word of comment. Senator Robert A. Taft, who was to be the new chairman, was an outstanding figure on Capitol Hill. Taft was the Republican leader and candidate for nomination for the Presidency in both 1948 and 1952. He had long been interested in economic legislation and served as chairman of the Committee on Education and Labor. Though conservative, Taft was not a member of the hard-core Republicans who looked with jaundiced eye on all liberal proposals.

Taft's opposite Democratic number, Senator Joseph O'Mahoney of Wyoming, had built a Senate reputation for economic erudition. He had been the guiding light in the Temporary National Economic Committee (TNEC) hearings in the late 1930s and served as TNEC chairman. The TNEC had done pioneering work in industry structure, pricing policy, and other facets of the economy—its work was a landmark for years. A lawyer and a former newspaperman of liberal views, O'Mahoney had been a supporter of the Employment Act from the beginning.

Ralph E. Flanders, a Republican from Vermont, was a self-made industrialist (machine tools) and former president of the Federal Reserve Bank of Boston. He had also been closely identified with the Committee for Economic Development, a liberal business group. All of these Senators had been favorable to the Employment Act.

On the House side, the stalwarts were, of course, Patman and Jesse P. Wolcott. Patman (often called the last of the Populists) was a Texas Democrat, later chairman of the House Committee on Banking and Currency, and always an archfoe of the Reserve System.[10] Wolcott, ranking Republican, was more conservative, but he also had been a supporter of the act.

The original Committee thus consisted on the surface of eight nominal Republicans, who might be expected to take a hostile attitude toward the concept of economic planning, and six liberal Democrats, who might be expected to take a more benevolent view. However, Taft, Flanders, Wolcott, and Bender—all Republicans—had been involved in the original legislation and were generally favorable toward it. This group turned its efforts toward carrying out the mandate of the act, namely:

(1) to make a continuing study of matters relating to the Economic Report;

(2) to study means of coordinating programs in order to further the policy of this Act; and

(3) as a guide to the several committees of the Congress dealing with legislation relating to the Economic Report, not later than March 1 of each year (beginning with the year 1947) to file a report with the Senate and the House of Representatives containing its findings and recommendations made by the President in the Economic Report, and from time to time to make such other reports and recommendations to the Senate and the House of Representatives as it deems advisable.

Charles O. Hardy, formerly of the Brookings Institution and at the time vice president and economist for the Federal Reserve Bank of Kansas City, was appointed the first staff director. The first *Economic Report of the President* caught the JEC largely unprepared for business. In lieu of a formal report, a two-page statement was issued, saying:

These matters are already under consideration by standing committees of Congress which will make a detailed study of each one of them and submit recommendations to the Congress. Most of them are highly controversial. A recommendation from this committee at this time, which could only be casual before our studies are made, would not be helpful to the solution of the problems. The committee will proceed to consider these problems with reference to their effect on the maintenance of a stable economy and continuous employment.

The basic problem which this committee has to consider is the method of preventing depressions so that substantially full employment may be continuously maintained. No problem before the American people is more vital to our welfare, to the very existence of our way of life, and to the peace of the world. It is the most complex and difficult of all the long-range domestic problems we have to face. It involves a study of price levels and wage levels and their relation to each other, a study of methods of preventing monopoly control in industry and labor from distorting prices and wages, a study of individual and corporate savings and a study of many other economic forces bearing on a stable economy.

Until we have further studied and analyzed the basic considerations which underlie this problem, we do not feel we should become involved in controversy on current issues which have many aspects beside their effect on the prosperity of the country.[11]

This seemed unsatisfactory to many. Senator Glen Taylor of Idaho (later to run for Vice-President on Henry A. Wallace's Progressive ticket), an active supporter of the act, issued a blistering statement, criticizing the Committee for not rendering a report, saying Taft had offered instead "a series of excuses."[12]

The Council's midyear *Economic Report* (July 1947) was also given only passing attention, but, in late July, the JEC undertook an extensive study of food prices and followed this with a special study on the cost of living.[13] An elaborate procedure was used, including public hearings held under subcommittees in various parts of the United States. Late in 1948, the Committee also began a series of hearings on the President's message on inflation.[14] The mid-year report was soon abandoned as unnecessary, the last being in June 1947.

Search for Direction

The Committee had a choice of moving in two major directions. It might restrict itself to comments on the President's *Economic Report*, i.e., let the President take the lead and merely respond to his evaluation and suggestions. This would be an easy way to handle the task, but would undoubtedly result in a partisan split along party lines and continue to let the White House dominate the scene. On the other hand, the Committee might take a strong lead, pursuing independent studies, gathering materials, and operating so as to explore issues before they came to executive attention, something that had seldom been done in the past and that would represent an innovation in legislative procedure. This might involve the Committee in a series of jurisdictional disputes with other congressional committees, although this never became a serious problem.

Several characteristics of the Committee and its structure were relevant to the ultimate choice. The outstanding members of the Committee all chaired or sat on other committees. While they had a strong interest in JEC, their time and energies were limited. JEC was the latecomer, and members were burdened with prior and often more rewarding or demanding commitments. Since members have many duties to perform, congressional committees, by tradition, tended to lean heavily on professional staffs. That is, the day-to-day operation of a committee fell largely to its staff. Staff members often constitute the "permanent undersecretariat," whose job was to operate the committee despite changes in chairmanship or membership due to the vicissitudes of elections or death. Nevertheless, committee staffs tended to be small. In the era preceding World War II, the typical committee staff seldom numbered more than six and often less. Much work was routine. A committee counsel and assistant (who often change jobs in the event of a change in political control) and a clerical-secretarial staff of several people were a typical complement. From time to time, when the need arose, experts were borrowed from the executive agencies. Professionals, aside from lawyers, were rare. Staffs tended to be clerical in nature, with much experience and empirical knowledge.[15] These conditions were hardly suitable to the JEC.

At CEA, much attention, even at an early date had been paid to the quality of the staff aides, and their professional standing was high. Even minor jobs were filled with careful attention to professional training. If JEC were to balance its sister organization and speak with equal authority, it would need a high caliber staff.

The key man at JEC, of course, was the staff director (now executive director). This appointee would be, along with the chairman, in a position to direct the work and set its tone and general orientation. Hardy, who served until his death in November 1948 had received a Ph.D. from the University of Chicago in 1916. Like Nourse at CEA, he had spent some years at the Brookings Institution. Though perhaps less known in academia than his CEA counterpart, he was of high professional caliber. He was succeeded in December 1948 by Fred E. Berquist, who served as acting director until August 1949. From that time, until March 1951, the post was held by Theodore J. Kreps of Stanford University. Kreps held a Ph.D. from Harvard and had a long academic career interlaced by federal service, including a tour on the TNEC staff. He was succeeded by Grover W. Ensley, who served until July 1957. In fact, Ensley was in day-to-day charge, since Kreps carried on at Stanford while he served on the staff. Ensley was "chief of staff," and the staff was responsible to him. Ensley held a New York University Ph.D. and had served as economic adviser to Senator Flanders.[16]

Kreps was aware of the need for more professional and nonpolitical staff than was customary, and he insisted (backed by both Taft and O'Mahoney) that tenure practices be followed, in contrast to the patronage system then in vogue.

Kreps told the author, "I told the committee outright that they needed men of mature ability, Ph.D.'s, whom I would not ask to come unless something like a nonpolitical career was possible. They agreed! My first appointment was Grover Ensley as Associate Director. When told that he was to aid Senator Flanders (and would thus presumably espouse a Republican view), I simply said, so what?"[17] Kreps probably found the committee more receptive due to the confusion which had followed the changeover in 1946–47. Kreps credits both Ensley and James Knowles with outstanding performances: "They were the two vital appointments which were made by the committee."[18]

The election of the first Republican Congress since the end of the Hoover Administration put Taft—like Eisenhower some years later—in a strong but ambivalent position. Republicans in Congress, long out of power, had become prone to offering sharp criticism of administration policies without providing positive alternatives. Blunt and strong-minded, Taft was a man who generally put principle ahead of expediency.[19] The Committee, under his chairmanship, became more active and better organized. In early spring, the Committee undertook the preparation and distribution of a questionnaire on business thinking, utilizing the offices of Dunn and Bradstreet. The results of this effort were never released by the Committee, although the firm released them under the title, *Survey of Business Expectations and Government Policies*.

In May the Committee prepared a staff questionnaire, dealing with the principles of long-run stability and short-run stabilization policy, that was sent to many nongovernment economists. A second questionnaire was distributed to businessmen, contractors, financiers, and representatives of labor and agriculture. These data were used in the preparation of hearings on "Current Price Developments and the Problem of Economic Stability," which began in midsummer of 1947.

These activities brought up the question of CEA-JEC cooperation.

243

Hardy sent Nourse a copy of the questionnaire and indicated that he (Hardy) would like to sit in on CEA deliberations. Nourse felt this was impossible but at the same time indicated that two-way cooperation was welcome *on the staff level,* and Nourse encouraged his staff to consult with their JEC counterparts. Nourse wisely saw that the bipartisan nature of the JEC would spell trouble if it were privy to CEA information at all levels. This issue was to increase in complexity and intensity as time passed.

By the time the second *Economic Report* appeared, the Joint Committee was much better organized; however, the central question remained unsolved, namely, how to deal with the divergent opinions that were bound to arise. When the Committee requested an extension of time to file the 1948 report, rumors began to circulate regarding a possible "majority" report and a "minority" report. On May 12 Senator O'Mahoney indeed released a "minority" report that, among other things, criticized the majority for slowness and inaction.

The Committee's report was divided into Part I, "Committee Findings"; Part II, "Staff Report"; Part III, "Summary of Recommendations Offered in the Economic Report of the President"; and Part IV, "Minority Views on the President's Report." All eight Republicans signed Part I, and all six Democrats signed Part IV.

The Joint Economic report noted that the Committee had not been able to give sufficient time to the President's report of 1947 but now:

> We have carefully examined and studied the *Economic Report of the President* of January, 1947, and the *Economic Report of the President* of 1948. We have further examined the reports made by the Council of Economic Advisers to the President of the United States. *The Economic Reports of the President* give extremely valuable assistance to all those who are interested in solving the problems of continuous full employment. Necessarily, the President has to enter into more controversial fields than his advisers and deal with policies which frequently have political implications. We feel, however, that the operations under the act have fully justified its passage and have given us a good start on the national economic policy guided by more information and study than we have ever had before. To the extent that we present any criticism of the reports, we do not intend to reflect in any way on the manner in which this work has been done.

The "Staff Report" (Part II), written by Dr. Hardy, was a highly technical piece of work. Nourse speculates that the Committee found Part II difficult to understand, but was impressed, and hesitated to incorporate the findings in its own report, although it was reluctant to reject them.

By late 1948 the Committee was still seeking direction and orientation. At the December meeting of the American Economic Association, Grover Ensley (then still adviser to Senator Flanders) made a brief presentation, surveying gaps in economic knowledge that the Committee hoped to fill by its own or by outside efforts.[20]

The Republicans before they relinquished control undertook a significant piece of work—significant not so much in content as in methodology. Considerable discussion had centered around the issue of corporate profits, and the *President's Report* had made numerous references to them, causing Senator Taft to establish a subcommittee under Senator Flanders to consider this matter. A series of open hearings were held with testimony from outside experts—from academia, business, labor groups and others.[21] This procedure, i.e., an open hearing with expert testimony and opportunity for cross-questions and general seminar type discussion, was a portent of the future.

During the year, the committee concerned itself with a number of matters, of which the most important was the initiation of publication of the monthly statement, *Economic Indicators*. This document, prepared by CEA, had been supplied in multigraph form to various high-level officials. The Committee undertook responsibility for publishing and distributing this document more widely, as explained by Chairman Taft:

> In carrying out its mandate under the Employment Act of 1946, the Council has found it desirable to bring together in concise and graphic form the most important facts showing current trends in the Nation's economy. Thus, the Executive Office is in a better position to point up the key problems of national economic policy and to promote the improvement and coordination of the Federal Government's widespread statistical services."

The close of 1948 was marked by Hardy's death, as well as a change in congressional control. Thus, substantial changes were afoot.

The Joint Economic Committee at Work

The Republicans, who had captured the 80th Congress in 1947, lost it again in 1949, upon which occasion Senator O'Mahoney resumed the chairmanship of JEC. O'Mahoney chaired the Committee through the 81st (1949–50) and 82nd (1951–52) Congresses. In 1953, the Republicans again organized the Congress, and Representative Wolcott served as chairman. Senator O'Mahoney was defeated for the 84th Congress, and, when the Democrats took over again in January, Senator Paul H. Douglas of Illinois became chairman. Senator Sparkman was senior to Douglas, but he stepped aside to chair the Senate Committee on Banking and Currency, though he remained on JEC. Douglas alternated with Patman as chairman until Douglas was defeated in 1966. Douglas thus served as chairman in the 84th, 86th, and 88th Congresses, while Patman headed the Committee in the 85th, 87th, and 89th. (In the 85th Congress, Senator Sparkman served as vice-chairman.) For many years, Douglas had been a professor of economics at the University of Chicago and was president of the American Economic Association in 1947.

The issues in dispute between the Committee and the administration reflected the larger differences between the parties in control of the White House and the Congress. Within the Committee, of course, these differences generally, though not always, manifest themselves along party lines. In the usual case, the members in opposition tend to oppose the President's proposals, and those of his own party tend to support them. These "Pavlovian" or "knee-jerk" reactions can be anticipated, but upon occasion more fundamental issues of economic or political philosophy complicate the situation. Many of these instances have been recounted in the chapters dealing with CEA, but some major instances of JEC-CEA controversy might be mentioned.

For example, the major point of difference between the Eisenhower Council and the JEC was the issue of inflation versus economic growth. The administration generally was fearful of inflation, while the Democratic elements of the Joint Committee were apt to be advocates of expansion and economic growth. Douglas and the other liberal members were critical of the administration for being too cautious and too much concerned with budget balancing.

Douglas was far from convinced on the administration's general view that inflation was a major threat. In March 1958 the JEC issued a report noting that, in the majority (i.e., Democrat) view, achieving a higher rate of growth deserved the "major emphasis in public policy." The argument was fueled by rising cost of money as interest rates increased.

The "growth" debate was illustrated by several specific issues. The Cabinet Committee on Price Stability for Economic Growth issued four "informational reports," backstopping the administration view as to the high priority of price stability. The reports rejected wage-price controls as being more harmful than helpful. Senator Douglas opposed this view and characterized the committee proposals as a "collection of bromides."

In 1959, JEC launched an extensive "study of employment growth and price levels" (to be completed in 1960). These studies were instigated by Lyndon Johnson in preparation for the 1960 campaign.

No action was taken on Eisenhower's request to amend the Employment Act to make "reasonable price stability" a goal of national economic policy. This matter had been often considered, and—while most economists and businessmen were favorable—organized labor generally opposed it, holding it to be in conflict with full employment and fearing that it would open the door to undesirable changes in the act.

The Committee study, *Employment, Growth, and Price Levels,* gave rise to considerable controversy, since it was generally critical of the Eisenhower Administration policies. Some observers assigned the report a large share of credit for Kennedy's election in 1960, and there is no doubt that many of JFK's speeches on the theme of "getting America moving again" were drafted with this material in mind. The Committee thus found itself in the middle of presidential politics (Republican Congressman Thomas B. Curtis, a long-time and influential JEC member, was highly critical of the "Eckstein Report"). One notes that a decade later there was general agreement that the economy had been too tightly held in check for far too long a period, and the report is accepted as a valid comment.

For the most part, the Douglas-Patman team (which served the whole Kennedy period) treated Kennedy's economic policies with kindness, since they generally reflected JEC's positions. Kennedy came in for a share of critical comment from the minority, but, largely, his (or Heller's) policies were applauded by both Douglas and Patman.

As we have noted, Heller used the JEC hearings as a "launching pad" for new concepts. Both Nourse and Burns had been wary of the Committee (though, of course, Burns was willing to testify), but Heller often turned the task of testifying to his own and the President's advantage.

The relative economic tranquillity of the Eisenhower-Kennedy years began to wane as prices increased in late 1967. The "credit crunch" of the previous year had symbolized increasing economic difficulties. The much-vaunted "new economics" hailed by Lyndon Johnson after the 1964 tax cut began to lose some of its charm. The Joint Committee became increasingly restive and was especially distrustful of the wage-price guideposts. Referring to long-run trends, the Committee noted that "The record of the 1960's in this country is clear on this point. As we have managed to reduce the level of unemployment, we have experienced increasing degrees of inflation. This record predicts we would

247

have to accept a less-than-one-percent reduction in the rate of inflation to prevent unemployment from rising above 4 percent."[22]

The Joint Committee members noted the need for advance planning in terms of post-Vietnam economics, foreign trade policy, antitrust policies, and other issues. One emerges from a reading of JEC hearings with a strong impression that the Joint Committee members as well as the staff were deeply involved and had done their homework thoroughly.

The Committee has fulfilled its role as a body intended to comment on administration policies, but in some ways this has been the least meaningful of its various roles. In reading the hearings, it is difficult to escape the partisan flavor. All too often the members who adhere to the President's party "point with pride" while the opposition predictably "views with alarm" without regard to economic merit. The hearings on the report make interesting reading and they clearly demonstrate the economic erudition of many members of the Congress, but their impact on policy is not easy to measure. The most meaningful contribution of the Joint Committee has been its independent studies and publications.

Proxmire and New Directions

When Senator William Proxmire became chairman of the Committee in 1966, with the beginning of the 90th Congress, the Committee considerably enlarged its role.[23] Studies undertaken by earlier chairmen or members, dealing with broad issues of military costs, consumer credit, urban problems, and other areas, have been enlarged.[24] Patman continued as vice-chairman. Richard Bolling had served in the 88th Congress as vice chairman.

Proxmire thus took over the Committee in the second half of the Johnson Administration, when the "new economics" had begun to fall from its recent rise to grace. Two trends were to mark the decade 1966–76. The Committee was to become increasingly active in issues not formerly considered to be in its realm and, second, the Committee was to become increasingly critical of the administration policy of Johnson, Nixon, and Ford. This criticism became more intense as the administration passed into Republican hands in 1968.

From 1946 until 1967, the Committee for the most part had restricted its operations to matters directly concerned with economic policy in the narrow sense. That is, it commented on the *President's Report* and made studies of such matters as interest rates, cost of living, productivity, and related issues. Senator Proxmire, a liberal Democrat from Wisconsin, took a broader view. The new direction of the Committee can best be described as "activist." For example, the Committee injected itself into the supersonic transport (SST) controversy in 1971; it has recommended the abolition of the Highway Trust Fund, castigated Pentagon officials for cost overruns, entered the dispute on the Lockheed matter (Lockheed had been aided with public funds), and, in general, has become a prime critic of the so-called military-industrial complex. It has made forays (initiated by Bolling) into urban economics and has continued in the forefront of productivity studies (begun by Douglas). Perhaps the most controversial matter in which the Committee, and especially Senator Proxmire, were involved was the SST program. The controversy over the supersonic transport was deeply intermixed with semieconomic issues such as ecology, health, national transportation policy, and "national prestige." The whole Congress, of course, became more concerned with economic matters in 1974–75 as inflation/recession hit home and "fuel crises" continued.

The "investigative" approach, such as that used in the cost overrun studies, has put the Committee much in the news, but there is some feeling that the prestige of the JEC has been somewhat diminished by its move out of the mainstream of traditional economic matters and that its talents have been spread thin in many directions. Whatever the merit of these active moves (and to what degree they might continue in the event of a more conservative chairman is impossible to say), they have clearly put the Committee on the firing line as never before.[25]

Like CEA's involvement in the guidepost policies, one cannot view the matter with complete satisfaction. Many of the issues, such as that of the SST, go far beyond the jurisdiction of JEC (or any other single committee). Further, there is some danger that in going so far afield JEC will outrun its expertise and credibility. True, the SST has economic impact, but matters of ecology are not clearly within the capability of the Committee. Another, more important matter must be considered: JEC does not have unlimited resources. As it expands its interests, it must face the danger of giving only passing attention to some of its other duties. It would be most unfortunate if it were to neglect its traditional duties in order to ride off on various hobbyhorses, depending on the whim of its chairman.

Clearly, the JEC is a much different creature than the CEA, and its effectiveness must be judged by different criteria. By its nature, the Committee is in a position to "second guess" the Council. That is, it can examine the President's *Report*; call witnesses, either friendly or hostile, and it has to some degree the benefit of hindsight, since time will have elapsed since the data upon which the President's *Report* was based were collected. Clearly, one of the major functions of the Joint Committee is to force the Council and the administration to coordinate economic matters with the Congress and to provide a channel of communication, and in this area it has generally been successful.

The 94th Congress arrived in Washington in an ambivalent mood. Democrats had been elected in large numbers, but it soon became clear that the electorate was in a grim mood. Inflation and unemployment plagued the economy, and no one was willing to wait long for, if not a solution, at least action to ease the situation. Euphoria of election faded quickly into grim reality.

Further, the Congress was in a rebellious mood in its own house. Senior chairmen came under attack, and several were unseated by the "reform minded," much strengthened by the election of numerous young newcomers. The grand old man of the Joint Committee, Patman, fell to a challenge from his younger colleague, Henry S. Reuss, of Wisconsin, who aspired to become chairman of Banking and Currency, a post Patman had held for a generation. Patman remained unimpaired on the JEC, however, as vice chairman, until his death early in 1976. Hubert Humphrey, for a quarter of a century, a public figure as a former Vice-President and presidential candidate, replaced Proxmire as JEC chairman, though Proxmire remained on the Committee. Humphrey's approach was aggressive, and it appeared that the "activist" tradition would continue. Humphrey was anxious to enlarge the concept of full employment by making provision for public jobs if necessary. Congressional action appeared unlikely. Perhaps the declining image of the CEA in the Nixon-Ford era would be a factor in strengthening the position of the Joint Committee. The organization of the 94th Congress resulted in a number of changes in Committee membership. No Democratic Senators left except for J. W. Fulbright, who was defeated, his place being taken by Edward M. Kennedy of Massachusetts. James B. Pearson of Kansas and Schweiker of Pennsylvania, both Republicans and not very active, left the Committee. They were replaced by Robert Taft, Jr., of Ohio and Paul J. Fannin of Arizona. On the House side, two Democrats left— Martha Griffiths of Michigan, who had been very active, and Hugh Carey of New York. They were replaced by Lee H. Hamilton of Indiana and Gillis Long of Louisiana. The three junior Republicans—William B. Widnall (New Jersey), Barber B. Conable, Jr. (New York), and Ben B. Blackburn (Georgia)—all departed. These vacancies were filled by Garry Brown (Michigan), Margaret Heckler (Massachusetts), and John H. Rousselot (California). It is, of course, much too early to see what impact these new members will have on the Committee philosophy.

The Committee as an Institution

Congressional committee assignments are considered desirable insofar as they offer prestige or power, or relate to a personal or political interest of the member. Membership on the Senate Foreign Relations Committee or the Appropriations Committee would thus be almost universally desirable, while a Senator might seek appointment to another committee because of personal or regional interests. For example, in 1975 Sparkman moved up to chair Foreign Relations, vacated by Fulbright. Proxmire vacated the chair at JEC (though he stayed on the Committee) to move up to chair Banking and Currency, of which Sparkman had been chairman. Humphrey then took the chair on the Joint Committee.

Although on the surface the Joint Committee is much like other committees, it is to a degree unique, since, unlike most committees, it has investigative or research jurisdiction over the whole economy. Most economically oriented committees are concerned with some specific phase of the economy: agriculture, transportation, monopoly, etc. The province of the Joint Committee, on the other hand, is the aggregate economy. Consequently, the member is concerned with the national interest in the broadest sense. He cannot point with pride to what he has done for potatoes, peanuts, or beef; on the contrary, he has ample opportunity to step on the toes of powerful economic interests. Successful service involves hard work in difficult areas.

The task of the Joint Economic Committee is as difficult as it is novel in our frame of government. If taken seriously, it entails long and painstaking work and does not carry emoluments of power or prestige (like Appropriations, Defense, or Foreign Affairs Committees.) Its requirements are not met by the technical competence of the lawyer or the flair and experience of the politician. It calls for training and practice in the fields of economics, business, finance and social psychology. The Senator or Representative who gives the needed measure of time and thought to the work of this committee must not merely curtail to that extent the effort given to legislative work and to rendering personal (and sometimes menial) service to the claims of his constituents or to mending his political fences. Beyond this, he is sure sooner or later, in larger or smaller measure, to find himself, in seeking to advance the national economic interest more soundly, to be refusing support to or actively opposing a pet project of his state or district or of a special interest group that is strongly represented among his constituents.[26]

251

Service on the Joint Committee presents many problems, but, as we shall note later, it also offers some tangible benefits. One writer has characterized the Committee:

In many ways the Joint Economic Committee is the most exciting contemporary invention of Congress. Established originally to react to the annual Economic Report of the President, it roves at will over the economic spectrum, studying broadly or intensively any problem which attracts the interest of Committee or Congressional leadership. The Joint Economic Committee is a Congressional anomaly. It is a planning and theory group in a culture fiercely devoted to the short run and the practical. It is committed to the panoramic view in a system which stresses jurisdictional lines. It signifies recognition that economic problems are related, by a body which deals with them piecemeal.[27]

Fortunately, the Committee, particularly in its early years, had members and chairmen who were deeply interested in its success. In *Making Monetary and Fiscal Policy,* G. L. Bach notes that JEC chairmen have often been among the "intellectuals" of the Senate. Most senior members also serve on other committees that deal with economic issues, providing opportunity for considerable cross-fertilization of ideas (also for some jurisdictional disputes, which, fortunately, have been kept to a minimum; in the early period, it was feared there would be problems regarding the relationship of the Joint Economic Committee to those committees having specific jurisdictions, but these fears proved largely groundless).

Though the Committee staff has more leeway than the CEA, and the staff director or other senior staff members have more influence over direction, this advantage is somewhat balanced by the fact that, while CEA gets its orders from and serves only the President, JEC must please many bosses. Another major difference is apparent: The Council staff works for the Council, a body speaking (in public) with one voice; but in the Congress the majority and the minority articulate their views.

While it has unique features, the Joint Committee must fit into the framework of the legislative process. Above all, the Committee is an arm of the Congress and must reflect the divergent views and interests of that body, a matter very much in the minds of those who drafted the original legislation. When the situation under discussion is fluid and controversial and Committee members are knowledgeable, cross-examination can become penetrating.[28] The Council presents to the Congress a program or a series of economic programs that the Joint Committee may examine at its leisure and subject to searching examination. This is, at least in a formal sense, a one-way street, since the Council, no matter what its reservations about JEC, is not in a position to hold hearings or subject JEC reports to formal examination. Further, while the Council must stick closely to its task of preparing the annual report, JEC can pick and choose issues largely as the membership and staff decide. As we have seen, Senator Proxmire has broadened the mandate of the Committee in recent years. The Council would not be able to extend its activities in such a manner on its own initiative, although, to be sure, it has expanded its activities somewhat over the years since 1946. A second basic structural difference is found in the bipartisan nature of the Joint Committee. Committee members who represent the opposite party, although they need not and do not take issue with CEA proposals at every turn, will naturally be inclined to seek out weak spots or methodological differences and exploit them for political purposes.

Perhaps in large part because of JEC's efforts, there seem to be fewer instances of fundamental disagreement in economic views among Congressmen than was the case a few decades ago. It would be difficult to imagine views such as those expressed by Congressmen Hoffman and Manasco during the debates on the Employment Act being put forth seriously today.[29] Nonetheless, there will be differences, real or otherwise, and they cannot be ignored. Thus, JEC and CEA will be apt to deal with each other at arm's length; that is, they recognize the virtues of cooperation, but its perils are equally obvious.

Differences between minority and majority members are minimal insofar as popular goals are concerned, but there is much debate about means. Republicans and Democrats alike are opposed to inflation and in favor of economic growth, economic freedom, and the American version of the capitalistic system. Such differences as occur are in the method of achieving these goals. The opposition party will take issue with the President's analysis of events or with his forecast of the future. Since, presumably, both Council and Committee have access to the same basic data, differences in interpretation are all that can occur. But even if there are no basic differences, the fact that the economic report is to be subject to vigorous analysis is salutary.

To what degree should the JEC reports be separated or reconciled as to majority or minority views? Until Senator Douglas became chairman, the general practice was to issue a reconciled report, insofar as possible. Grover Ensley, then staff director, is quoted in the *National Journal* as saying, "I'm very proud that during my time most of the JEC material was either unanimous or at least not a clear split."[30] In the same publication, however, Senator Douglas and former Research Director James

Knowles defend the divided report—Knowles noting that calm, quiet consideration of issues is not the style of the day.[31]

There are, of course, two aspects of this matter. From the viewpoint of the professional economist, basic agreement is indicative of scientific maturity and, therefore, is generally desirable; on the political side, however, differences are bound to be exploited to the utmost. Douglas rightfully opposes "artificial and strained agreement" for its own sake. Yet in the final analysis, general agreement seems a worthwhile goal, if, of course, it reflects full knowledge and concern for public welfare.

The tendency for JEC to broaden its area of operations has, to be sure, increased its interrelationships considerably. Senator Proxmire's interest in "overruns" and in defense procurement has taken JEC into matters of defense policy, while interests in consumer economics have brought it into possible conflict or overlap with the regulatory agencies. Further expansion of JEC under an aggressive chairman understandably might move it into many areas of "economics" not now considered to be in its domain.

During his chairmanship, Senator Proxmire indicated his philosophy by the character of his staff. In those years, several young, activist staff members were added, whose interests were clearly broad in scope and far from being confined to traditional economics. Presumably "undue" expansion would be noted and brought to a halt by chairmen of other committees if they saw their interests endangered. This is not, however, a simple matter in practice. Where does one draw the line between JEC and the committees on Armed Services or Appropriations insofar as procurement costs are concerned, or between JEC and the Senate Committee on Finance with regard to tax policies?

The relationship with executive or regulatory agencies is still another matter. JEC is an arm of the Congress and, as such, it is free to examine such matters as agricultural policies or stock market practices as it sees fit. The Department of Agriculture or the Securities and Exchange Commission might be upset by what they regard as JEC invasions, but they are hardly in a position to dictate to the Congress. Thus, as far as JEC retains the confidence of the Congress, it can roam more or less at will.

Performance and Personnel

Expanding involvement has also brought JEC into multifaceted relationships with numerous outside groups. In some cases, these relationships are scholarly and helpful, designed to ex-

254

change information or enhance mutual interests. Committee and staff members maintain relationships with such groups as the American Economic Association, American Statistical Association, National Association of Business Economists, and others. In recent years, for example, a JEC report listed the following meetings, conferences, etc., in which JEC staff took part, wrote papers, or otherwise had outside contact:

American Bankers Association—Symposium on public policy and economic understanding

American Economic Association—Annual meeting

American Enterprise Institute—Seminar on federal income-tax laws

American Statistical Association—Annual meeting

American Statistical Association—New York chapter outlook conference

Brookings Institution—Forum for business leaders

Business Council—Technical consultants

Business Week—Conference on the economic outlook (New York City)

Federal Statistics Users' Conference—Conference on quarterly estimates of GNP by Office of Business Economics

Government Economists on Regulatory Problems—Seminar

Harvard University, John F. Kennedy School of Government, and Massachusetts Institute of Technology—Seminar on systematic analysis and planning, programming, and budgeting in government decision making

Industrial College of the Armed Forces—Annual meeting of the Mobilization Readiness Division of the American Ordnance Association

Joint Council on Economic Education—Twentieth anniversary of the council

McGraw-Hill—Annual meeting of the Informal Conference of Business Economists

Makah Indian Reservation—Meetings on economic development program

National Association of Business Economists—Annual meeting

National Association of Tax Administrators—Conference on revenue estimating

National Council for Indian Opportunities—Meeting

National Economists Club—Weekly meetings

National Industrial Conference Board—Economic forum

National Institute of Public Affairs—Regular meetings

National Manpower Policy Task Force—Meeting

President's Task Force on Aging

255

Resources for the Future—Fellowship Advisory Council
Washington Statistical Society—Meeting

Papers were written or address made to:

Air Force Academy
American Bankers Association—Annual conference of university professors
Economists Club, Washington, D.C.
Federal Executive Seminar, Kings Point, New York—Current economic policy issues
Federal Natural Resources Development
George Washington University Law School—Graduate seminar on corporation law
Massachusetts Institute of Technology
Michigan State University
Monthly Labor Review
National Congress of American Indians
New York University Graduate School of Public Administration—Centennial address
Saturday Review
U.S. Civil Service Commission—Round table for executives
United Steel Workers of America—Executive board conference on the military-industrial complex
University of Minnesota—Seminar on government contracts
University of Wisconsin—The Center for the Advanced Studies in Organization Science
Water Resources Research

In addition, various members of the staff conducted seminars, lectured graduate courses at local universities, and consulted with representatives of various foreign nations seeking information about JEC activities.

Other outside contacts are apt to be more mundane in nature. Needless to say, the numerous trade associations resident in Washington are interested in JEC activities. The lobby groups concerned with defense procurement responded with alacrity to Senator Proxmire's probings of defense costs. Such groups as the Chamber of Commerce of the United States, the National Association of Manufacturers, the AFL-CIO, and others have always been vitally interested in JEC activities. Partisan lobby groups, of course, have a selfish interest and their views are narrow. Other organizations—such as the National Planning Association and the Committee for Economic Development—are more apt to take a broad-gauge view. One notes with interest that some trade associations (e.g., NAM) that opposed (or ignored) the Employment Act at the time of its passage now recognize the usefulness of both Committee and Council.[32]

These external contacts are most useful. The Committee staff has multiple sources of information and opinion. It is likely that these activities are unique among congressional committees. To be sure, all committees work closely with the industries or groups with which they are concerned, but the mandate of the JEC is so broad that it comes into contact with many heterogeneous groups.

Internally, the Committee has been subject to the stresses and strains that affect the typical congressional committee. Such mundane matters as pay, office space, and status must be considered. Organization of the Committee is largely at the discretion of the chairman. Reorganization, promotion, or demotion rest in his hands, although, of course, other members may, if they care to make an issue, force his hand. Presumably, the chairman, desiring to make the Committee effective, will pay attention to professional qualifications and morale of staff, but little tenure exists insofar as assignments are concerned. Turnover has been high. One former staff director told the author, "No one stays long enough to know where the bodies are buried." A great deal of work must be duplicated and outside contacts needlessly renewed because of staff changes. JEC has never had adequate physical arrangements. In the 1970s, it was split between the New Senate Office Building and the Rayburn (House Office) Building. Quarters were crowded, with senior staff separated only by bookcases from the general working quarters. The contrast with CEA, still housed in the old (but spacious and dignified) Executive Office Building ("Old State"), is striking.[33]

Senior staff members, with some exceptions, have not had the public exposure and reflected White House glory (and heat) accruing to CEA members. CEA members appear more often in the mass media and, no doubt, have a much higher "recognition factor" than their JEC counterparts. Can one doubt that a poll among college students would find much greater recognition of Alan Greenspan than John R. Stark (not that recognition would be very high in any event!)? On the Hill things work differently. Staff members generally are faceless—committee members take the bows. Consequently, the JEC staff is not apt to be well known to the public generally or even to fellow economists. The majority of professional economists are academicians; and, from their viewpoint, professional stature is measured differently from the standards applied by professionals in government or industry.

Nourse, Burns, and Heller have probably been the three outstanding CEA chairmen. No JEC staff director has approached them in scholarly output or in prestige among their fellow academic economists. Hardy, Ensley, Knowles, and Stark have all been sound economists and capable staff directors, but their professional reputations in academia do not equal those of their counterparts on CEA. Kreps was the most academic of the group and never really left the campus. In sum, JEC personnel have tended to be more the hard-working empirical economists, while CEA has had a number of "superstar" economists among its ranks.[34]

One has the impression that the staff director is thought of perhaps more as an executive function than a research function. Until Greenspan was appointed, all CEA chairmen, with the exception of Keyserling, had been, at least some time in their careers, academic economists. The JEC staff directors have been a more varied group.

Hardy, Kreps, and, to a degree, Ensley were more or less "standard" academic economists, although Ensley's academic career has been of much less importance than his research career. Lehman, Knowles, and Stark have been essentially nonacademic. Lehman spent a long period in the Bureau of Labor Statistics in various positions and was in TVA and NRPB. He has a master's degree in economics from the University of Wisconsin. Knowles, with an M.A. from Columbia, had a long career in economic and statistical analysis and served for some time on the faculty of the College of the City of New York (1938–44). Stark has a law degree, an M.A. in economics, and served in the Bureau of Labor Statistics and in the Bureau of the Budget. Riley, Johnson, and Berquist, who served for short periods, were civil servants drawn from various departments, e.g., the Department of Commerce. To say that these men fit less into the academic economist mold (Ph.D., long academic career) than their CEA counterparts in no way questions their professional ability. They were "know-how" pragmatic types who ran a complex organization with obvious skill.

CEA staff and members have tended to be "academic," and a good deal of crossing back and forth from the Council to academic life has taken place. Burns, Heller, Nourse, Ackley, and others have (through publications, etc.) been well-known academics, although Nourse had not been active in academic circles for many years at the time of his appointment. JEC staff directors, on the other hand, have been more inclined toward being pragmatic economists, and few have had an academic reputation. Much the same is true of professional staff members. JEC staff members are apt to have more diverse backgrounds than those at the Council. No doubt this is, to a degree, due to the different atmosphere "on the Hill" from that prevailing "downtown." Conventional "experts" are more revered in the agencies than in the Congress, where a more pragmatic view prevails.[35]

One JEC staff member pointed out to the author that qualities much admired in academic economists would be likely to be of little value in congressional service. Many outstanding academic economists may be too theoretical, or too much enamored of the limelight, to operate successfully on Capitol Hill. Also, they may embrace fads or untried ideas, since they have no real responsibility for policy results.

> The staff [JEC] did not make the mistake of originating any of a number of ideas that the profession has been guilty of and which led to serious mistakes of public and private economic policy. Certainly most of us were not guilty of such nonsense as the Philips curve trade-off, the so-called balanced budget multiplier, the monetary-fiscal policy debate, or the "inflation is not nearly as dangerous as unemployment" illusion. All of these must seem illogical in the extreme to anyone well versed in the structure and functioning of economic and political institutions, yet they all have received widespread blessing from the professional academics. They are all ideas commonplace in leading economic texts written by the "superstars." I wonder what the profession can be proud of in this.

Committee staff members are more akin to business economists, and as the nonacademic segment of the profession grows in size (as it is doing) relative to the academic group, these economists will become more influential in the profession. One might note that in 1946, when the Employment Act was passed, only a handful of well-trained nonacademic types were on hand. Nowadays, the situation is different and will change more as time passes.[36]

Considerable assistance to the JEC staff and committee members has come from the legislative reference section of the Library of Congress. This remarkable group, with many experts available to it, makes its services available to members of Congress in general in the preparation of reports and studies of many kinds. It also lends out staff to congressional committees. Like a small academic economics department, the JEC tries to keep a staff of generalists on hand, who are able to deal with most of the issues that arise. For example, in mid-1970, specialities represented on the staff were fiscal policy, urban economics, economic statistics, money and banking, international economics, regulatory policies, and investment policies. Notably absent were such specialities as Soviet economics, human resources, transportation economics, and other areas with which the Committee is often concerned. When specialized economists—as, for example, Soviet experts—are needed, they can, of course, be borrowed from educational institutions or the federal executive agencies.

The Committee has had some problems in the impermanence of the staff director, clearly the key man in the organization, but the situation has become more stable in recent years. (See Table 8.)

Table 8. **JEC STAFF DIRECTORS AND CEA CHAIRMEN, 1946–76**

JEC Staff Director		CEA Chairman	
Hardy	Mar. 1947 Nov. 1948	Nourse	Aug. 1946 Nov. 1949
Berquist*	Dec. 1948 Aug. 1949	Keyserling	Nov. 1949 Jan. 1953
Kreps	Aug. 1949 Mar. 1951	Burns	Mar. 1952 Dec. 1956
Ensley	Apr. 1951 July 1957	Saulnier	Dec. 1956 Jan. 1961
Lehman*	Aug. 1957 Mar. 1958 Jan. 1960 Feb. 1961	Heller	Jan. 1961 Nov. 1964
Riley	Mar. 1958 Dec. 1959	Ackley	Nov. 1964 Feb. 1968
Johnson	Feb. 1961 Feb. 1963	Okun	Feb. 1968 Jan. 1969
Knowles	Feb. 1963 Jan. 1967	McCracken	Jan. 1969 Jan. 1972
Stark	Jan. 1967	Stein	Jan. 1972 Aug. 1974
		Greenspan	Aug. 1974

*Acting

From 1946 to 1976 the Joint Committee had a total of nine directors with Ensley serving more than six years. Others served briefly, except for Knowles, who served almost four years, and Stark, who by 1976 had served for nine years. In the same period, the CEA had ten chairmen, but, except for Okun, their tenure has been generally uniform and balanced, most serving roughly three years. Clearly, the turnover in the early period of the Joint Committee was detrimental to smooth organization.

The key here, of course, is the mechanism of appointment. CEA chairmen are chosen by the President, with considerable publicity and congressional approval. JEC staff directors, on the other hand, are selected by the committee chairman on criteria largely of his own making; the chairmanship is the key to the directorship. The new chairman, of course, wants to be successful, and he desires an able man to direct his committee. He also wants someone with whom he can work and in whom he can repose trust. Further, the chairman wants to avoid intra-committee friction, which might arise from arbitrary action. Thus, he may seek the views of his fellow members and perhaps staff as well, but the choice will be his. This may be a difficult task. From the standpoint of a working relationship, the Senator might prefer someone from his personal staff, but such a person might lack strong professional background. A generation ago, staff apppointments were made most often on a purely patronage basis, but the complexity of the modern Congress has made this a hazardous procedure.

No President (so far as is known) has yet removed a CEA chairman. Neither has a chairman carried over from one administration to another when the party changed.

It is likely that a greater degree of stability would be helpful, but, on the other hand, it is difficult to point to serious shortcomings arising from the situation. One interesting fact is that, whereas most former CEA chairmen left to return to academic life (Burns, Saulnier, Heller, Ackley, McCracken, and Stein), only Kreps returned to academia (Stanford) upon leaving the Committee. Knowles retired in 1972 to become a consultant, and Ensley went into the business world as president of the National Association of Mutual Savings Banks.

It was noted that committee service is usually appealing as a source of power or prestige or as a matter of personal interest and background. Since JEC has little power or prestige, the apparent willingness to serve must be because of interest in its activities.[37]

In fact, service on the Committee has become much sought after. While it lacks the great prestige of Foreign Relations or the power of Appropriations, it has attracted numerous aspirants, and many who have served have found the experience valuable. The increasing role of the Committee on the national scene has enabled a number of its members to find a platform they otherwise might never have found. Two members, Patman and Sparkman, were charter members, still serving on the Committee in the 94th Congress. Douglas served through eight Congresses until his defeat in the election for the 90th Congress.[38] Taft served from the formation of the original Committee until his death in

1952. Martha Griffiths of Michigan served since the 87th Congress, leaving in 1974. Senator Jacob Javits also began his service in the 87th Congress and was still serving in the 94th. Other well-known figures served only briefly, passing on to other, more attractive assignments.

Among JEC alumni who served only a term or so are John F. Kennedy (86th Congress, 1959–60) and Barry Goldwater (83rd Congress, 1953–54).[39] Like most committees, JEC has had both active and inactive members. Among the more active members over the years have been Taft, Flanders, O'Mahoney, and Wolcott in the early period; Douglas, Bolling, Reuss, Curtis, and Mrs. Griffiths in the middle period; and Reuss, Javits, Proxmire, Stuart Symington, Abraham Ribicoff, Hale Boggs, W. E. Brock, and Mrs. Griffiths in recent years. Sparkman is difficult to place. Though a charter member, his role on the Committee has not been very active and he has never served as chairman, although he has been the ranking Democrat since the 82d Congress.[40] Patman spanned the whole period! (Patman died March 7, 1976; he had earlier announced his intention to retire at the end of the current session.) Taft, O'Mahoney, Wolcott, Patman, Bolling, Reuss, Curtis, and Mrs. Griffiths were trained as lawyers. Patman and O'Mahoney, however, were deeply interested in economic issues as well. Symington, Flanders, and Brock had business backgrounds. Proxmire has had both academic and business experience. Thus, the active members of the Committee have various backgrounds, and no clear pattern can be determined.[41]

To some degree, Committee organization, like its physical quarters, may appear to be transitory and haphazard. Yet, clearly, flexibility is essential. The Committee has more or less worked out its own format as it has gone along. It was evident at an early date that the traditional procedure of congressional committees was inadequate for JEC's needs. The seminar-style, academic atmosphere of the Committee has not been entirely accidental, but it was not contemplated by the original legislation—which did not specify any procedure—and it is clear that no fixed ideas existed as to exactly how the Committee would function. The evidence is strong that the original thinking relative to JEC was only that it must serve to stake out economic policy formulation as an area of congressional interest and thus demonstrate that the Congress was not willing to leave it entirely to the executive branch. JEC, of course, has encompassed much more than that over the years. Not surprisingly, its organizational form has changed and it will doubtless change further as time passes.

Most congressional committees depend heavily on the subcommittees, and JEC is no exception. To some degree, Committee organization allows the members, and especially the chairman, to "ride his hobbyhorse" (when Mr. Patman was chairman, anti-Federal Reserve Policy dominated), and the subcommittees carry this even further. The subcommittees enable the Committee to spread the workload and make maximum use of both member interest and staff talent.

The Committee has made much use of outside talent and deserves substantial credit for bringing into its ranks outstanding economists for special studies. In this respect, it is more flexible than the Council, and a number of outstanding men have been used in this capacity.[42] JEC, as a legislative arm, has more leeway than CEA for bringing in temporary staff and borrowing from executive agencies, although both have a good record in this regard.

Much, of course, depends upon the personalities of the members. As we have seen, the original membership of the Committee was somewhat mixed, by good fortune, with a cadre of interested members. Over the years, this general pattern has been followed.

There is little need to comment at length on the multiple duties of the active legislator, many of which have little to do with legislation as such. Aside from these practical problems, there are philosophic issues that make it difficult for him to function with complete effectiveness as a JEC member. His economic outlook will be dominated by the pragmatic as well as the philosophic. He must pay heed to the economic interests of his state or district. Only when these matters have been secured can he turn his interest to more national or global matters.[43] His national posture may be widely different from his home state stance.

This microeconomic outlook does not mesh with the Joint Committee task, since it transcends regional interest and focuses upon national interests. It would be naive to believe that when a member enters the JEC committee room he sheds his state or district interests or forgets his inherent, parochial, and perhaps incorrect economic beliefs. However, service on the Joint Economic Committee has been a form of higher economic education, and the Committee and its staff have rendered a valuable service to the Congress and to the nation.

The Committee has been a unique experiment in legislative operation. Indeed, in some ways the impact of the Employment Act has been more marked in the legislative area than in the executive. Much of the function prescribed by the act had already been a part of the executive branch although done informally. The act added little to the *power* of the executive branch but a great deal to its *responsibilities*. In contrast, it enlarged the power of the legislative branch as well as its responsibilities.

James Knowles, who was associated with the Joint Committee more than twenty years and served as staff director, has told the author: "The failures under the Employment Act since 1946 are legislative failures, and the successes are likewise legislative in character. I seriously doubt that a case can be made for a single important policy success under the Act that was beyond question the consequence of executive leadership. I say this despite my own deep admiration for many who have served on the CEA and other executive agencies over this period."[44] This view may be a bit extreme, and perhaps Knowles' outlook is to some extent limited by his long service to the Committee, but it cannot be disregarded.

The Educational Role

No one can read the JEC hearings without becoming fully aware of the two-way educational process that takes place. Nor can one escape the fact that the members involved have most often spent considerable time on their "homework." Not only does the Committee have the benefit of the views of the Council, but also of a large number of distinguished outside economists who are invited to testify. In addition, high-level officials appear as witnesses. It cannot be expected that every member of the Committee has the time or inclination to absorb and digest this vast amount of complex information (the hearings on the CEA report alone run five to six hundred pages), but, overall, the value of the procedure is beyond calculation. For a legislator to keep up with all the hearings, legislative studies, etc., would mean reading thousands of pages each week, in addition to his many other duties. Some of these duties are superficial, but duties nonetheless.

Having seen committees at work on complex economic matters, a cynical observer might be excused if he had little faith in the JEC. To be sure, the Committee has not been beyond reproach. However, its performance has been most rewarding over the years. As John W. Lehman says,

Not only have the committee's studies affected a broad range of legislation, but their direct influence, both current and long range, on the actions of executive agencies has been impressive. Today's concerns over restoring excise tax cuts and increasing tax rates remind us of the Joint Economic Committee's unanimous resolution in July, 1950, calling for an immediate increase in taxes to finance the Korean War on a pay-as-you-go basis and how it changed current policy of that time. There was the

264

Treasury-Federal Reserve "accord" which came out of the Subcommittee on Monetary Policy's studies and hearings—and the new or improved statistics initiated as a result of the studies of the subcommittee working so intensively in that area. Studies of balance of payments and foreign economics bore fruit in the Trade Expansion Act and some of the corrective measures involving the balance of payments. The Agriculture Subcommittee's presentation of alternative agricultural programs also shows how hearings and reports lay the ground for executive as well as legislative action.

We could go on through study after study to illustrate in depth this role of the Joint Economic Committee in the early identification of public economic problems and in the long, oft-times repetitive process of public education so essential to the acceptance of an idea. As Walter Heller noted, we could document the development of the "New Economics" of last year's tax cut in the studies of the Fiscal Policy Subcommittees, in the "Study of Employment, Growth, and Price Levels," and that 1954 best seller, "Potential Economic Growth in the United States in the Next Decade." [45]

Probably the most worthwhile result of the JEC has been its role as "educator." Lehman's comments are again pertinent:

[Who would have foreseen] that the committee would bring the kind of reciprocity between academia and the Congress that would prompt a reference shelf writer 18 years later to say that—

"The Joint Economic Committee is the nom de plume of the world's largest class in economics, in which astute and overworked Congressmen and Senators take turns being pupils and instructors to most of the Nation's economists.

"The Committee surely was not set up to be the voice urging and defending adequate and proper economic statistics, but it has been and it continues to be, in the clearest of tones."

Nor did anyone, I suspect, even anticipate that the Joint Committee would virtually have to invent a hearing format and method in order that the wide-ranging views of many kinds of witnesses could be fairly and effectively presented. The use by the Joint Committee and other congressional groups of the round-table, seminar-type hearing, and the compendium of witness papers prepared and distributed in advance is so common now as to make us forget their origin.

Or would one have thought in 1946 that an experimental hearing, bringing together physical and social scientists in 1955 for a discussion of "Automation and Technological Change," would have highlighted the need for improved educational standards at all levels, three years before the traumatic impact of Sputnik I? And it was the Joint Economic Committee which about the same time began the series of pioneering studies that have led us through the maze of economic statistics we must tread if we are to understand comparative rates of growth between the United States and the Soviet Union.[46]

The educational role, though somewhat accidental, is no less useful to both the public and the business community. To be sure, the educational role is not unique. Many organizations (other than those engaged in higher education) play a part in economic education or indoctrination. Such activity is carried on at three levels. On the first and most common level, various industry lobby groups promote partisan views favorable to their economic interests. Trade associations publish, their representatives testify at hearings, and in various ways they promote their viewpoint. On the second and broader level, associations of various kinds attempt to convert citizens to their overall economic viewpoints. The U.S. Chamber of Commerce and the National Association of Manufacturers, for example, espouse the virtues of laissez-faire economics. On the third level, organizations of a nonpartisan nature attempt to acquaint literate citizens with economic issues on an unbiased basis. The Twentieth Century Fund, the Committee for Economic Development, and the National Planning Association are typical. These groups attempt to remain unbiased and to present factual material on complex issues, allowing the interested individual to arrive at informed rational conclusions. The Joint Committee performs somewhat the same function, but it has several unique advantages.

First, JEC has resources far beyond those of even the most affluent private group. Given sufficient interest, JEC can tap almost unlimited resources in comparison to those commanded by such groups as CED or NPA.

Second, the Joint Committee has a forum unmatched by its competitors. Even relatively dull congressional hearings have some news value. Senator Proxmire or Senator Humphrey can command some attention from the media, and, while reports by the CED are carefully noted by the professional journals, JEC studies are reviewed by the *New York Times*, the *Washington Post*, and the *Wall Street Journal*.

The tutorial role has been enhanced by several hundred JEC publications on a wide variety of topics. The Committee has indeed become a major educational force.

Withal, the impact of the Committee is not easy to evaluate. Its

266

educational force has been tremendous, and its role as sounding board has been invaluable. Nonetheless, it must be kept in mind that what counts in the Congress is the vote, and the operational "line" committees are important here. The Joint Committee is, in the final analysis, a staff group, although it has had a large degree of success on a number of issues. No matter how sound its analysis or how valuable its comment, it is dealing with political creatures, and it is part of a partisan body. Despite these problems, it has played a valuable role, but its role is limited and shaped by the structure of the Congress. Although its origin was very much based in the congressional desire for a stronger voice in economic policy making, the evolution of the Committee has been more encompassing.

Notes

Chapter 9

[1] A brief history of the legislation appears in *Twentieth Anniversary of the Employment Act*, Economic Symposium, Joint Economic Committee, U.S. Congress, February 23, 1966, appendix. See, for example, the volumes, *History of Manpower Policy in the United States*, U.S. Senate, Subcommittee on Employment Manpower of the Committee on Labor and Public Welfare, U.S. Senate (Washington, 1965).

[2] *Congressional Record*, September 27, 1945, p. 9204.

[3] Lester G. Seligman, "Presidential Leadership: The Inner Circle and Institutionalization," *Journal of Politics*, 13 (August 1956), pp. 410ff.

[4] *Congressional Record* (70th Congress, 2nd Session, Vol. 29, Part I, February 6, 1946), p. 980.

[5] *Congressional Record* (79th Congress, 2nd Session, Vol. 92, Part I), p. 1138.

[6] *Congressional Record* (79th Congress, 1st Session, Vol. 91, Part 7), p. 9026.

[7] In a colorful statement, Hoffman characterized the Act as "chasing the devil of unemployment round the stump, and never quite catching him."

[8] *Congressional Record* (79th Congress, 1st Session, Vol. 91, Part 7), p. 9026.

[9] The original committee was organized in the 79th Congress with Senator O'Mahoney as Chairman. He had been an original backer of the Act. Before the committee could become operative, however, the new Congress was elected and control shifted to the Republicans. Only Taft, O'Mahoney, Patman, and Huber, Judd, and Rich carried over to the new committee in the 80th Congress. Judd resigned April 17, 1947, and was replaced by Herter (see Appendix C).

[10] By 1974, Patman and Sparkman were still the only two in office. Patman remained an unreconstructed foe of the Fed. Patman announced his retirement in 1976.

[11] Originally mimeographed but later printed as S. Doc. No. 11 (80th Congress, 1st Session).

[12] Nourse, op. cit., p. 187.

[13] Senate Report 1565, June 9, 1948 (80th Congress, 1st Session).

[14] U.S. Congress, "The President's Program to Deal with the Problems of Inflation," 80th Congress, 1st Session, *Senate Report 809*.

[15] The prewar pace on the Hill was not demanding. Sessions were shorter, and the congressional staff was accustomed to taking things easy. Since that time, the situation has changed greatly. The war had, of course, a profound influence. Several committee staffs

dealing with war issues such as contracts, etc., built up to 50 or 75 staff members, mostly borrowed from other federal agencies. These carefree days were shaken not only by the war but by the "crisis of 1947," when the 80th Congress was elected. Democratic staff members on the Hill on "patronage" were thrown out wholesale by gleeful Republicans who had been "out" since 1932. Much to everyone's dismay, it was discovered that many tasks required some expertise and in a number of embarrassing cases those who had been separated were brought back to run the shop. This and other incidents caused the key personnel to be placed on a more formal basis than that which had prevailed since colonial times. In the years since, long sessions, complex legislation, and other demands have increased workload and staff beyond what anyone imagined in the quiet pre-war era.

[16] Like his CEA associate, Keyserling, Ensley had been a winner of the Pabst Brewing Company Essay Contest on Postwar Economic Planning.

[17] Personal Correspondence, August 30, 1970. Ensley notes that no one raised the question of his party ties. He voted in his home state of Washington where registration by party is unnecessary. Personal correspondence, December 19, 1974.

[18] Ibid.

[19] Taft appears in John F. Kennedy's *Profiles in Courage* on the basis of his unpopular stand in opposition to the Nuremberg Trials.

[20] Grover W. Ensley, "Suggested Lines of Economic Research Needed to Carry Out Objectives of the Employment Act," *American Economic Review*, Papers and Proceedings, May 1949, pp. 453ff.

[21] *Profits* (80th Congress, 2nd Session). Report of a Subcommittee of the Joint Committee on The Economic Report on Profit, Hearings (Joint Committee Print).

[22] *Statement of Committee Agreement, Minority and Other Views*, Joint Economic Committee, 90th Congress, 1st Session: March 17, 1967, p. 18.

[23] Proxmire, who went on the Committee in the 87th Congress, jumped over Sparkman and Fulbright who were senior to him but preferred to chair other committees.

[24] Typical of the new titles appearing recently are *Federal Reserve Discount Mechanism* (1969), *Standard for Guiding Monetary Action* (1968), *Economic Analysis of Public Investment Decisions: Interest Rate Policy and Discounting Analysis* (1968), and *Economic Effect of Vietnam Spending* (1967); urban problems have also occupied the Committee and a two-volume study, *Urban American: Goals and Problems*, emerged in 1967.

[25] If the Republicans should organize the Congress soon, the chair would pass to Javits or Representative Clarence Brown.

[26] Nourse, op. cit., pp. 429–30.

[27] Ralph K. Huitt, "Congressional Organizations in the Field of Money and Credit," *Fiscal and Debt Management Policies* (Englewood Cliffs: Prentice-Hall, 1963), p. 477.

[28] See, for example, the questioning of Chairman Ackley by Representative Thomas B. Curtis, *Hearings of January, 1965, Economic Report of the President*, 89th Congress, 1st Session, Part I, 1965.

[29] Both Hoffman and Manasco, though very different in outlook, bitterly opposed the Employment Act and expressed economic views more appropriate to the late nineteenth century.

[30] *National Journal*, May 20, 1970, p. 1293.

[31] Ibid. However, in a letter to the author, Knowles emphasized that he and Ensley were talking about different periods and situations. He and Ensley had been in general agreement at the time Ensley was staff director. (Personal correspondence, April 24, 1973).

[32] Some still oppose it, but none ignore it.

[33] Despite vast expenditures, space on the Hill always seems to be a problem. "Temporary" quarters are used for decades. (The Temporary Monopoly Subcommittee is also poorly housed.) Most congressional offices are crowded with desks set in hallways and alcoves. In this regard, the JEC is little worse off than others, but it contrasts badly with CEA. One always has the feeling that congressional committees are just moving in or out even though some have occupied the same space for years. The "new" Senate Office

Building did not seem to help much, and in 1974–75 a move was afoot for an additional building.

[34] See Hugh S. Norton, *The World of the Economist* (Columbia: University of South Carolina Press, 1973).

[35] One might say that probably the emphasis placed on educational attainment as measured by formal degrees is excessive in academia and that many federal economists who lack the terminal degree or a long record of publications would likely do very well in academic life.

[36] See Norton, *World of the Economist*, op. cit., especially Chapter 3.

[37] As the prestige of the JEC grows, it may be able to attract people much like Foreign Relations does.

[38] Douglas was the only professional economist in the Congress who served on the committee, and, of course, only a handful has served in the Congress at all.

[39] JFK had been anxious to serve on the Committee, but by 1959 he had other concerns and his interest was minimal.

[40] Sparkman served as Chairman of Banking and Currency until 1975 and waived his seniority on JEC, a common congressional practice.

[41] It must be noted that in several cases (e.g., Patman, who had served in Congress since 1928) professional training is more or less moot. Patman could hardly be described as a practicing lawyer. Likewise, Proxmire holds a degree in English Literature from Yale and an MBA from Harvard, but has no specific professional field. He worked briefly for J.P. Morgan & Company.

[42] This was especially the case in the study of *Growth and Price Levels*. This study was studded with "name-brand" economists.

[43] One recalls that only after LBJ became secure in his Texas base did he allow himself to be "liberal" on national economic issues. Proxmire, in contrast, from a liberal state can take a more liberal line, but even he must keep fences mended at home.

[44] Letter to the author, April 24, 1973.

[45] John W. Lehman, "Administration of The Employment Act," *Twentieth Anniversary Symposium*, p. 89.

[46] Ibid., p. 88.

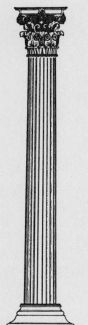

Chapter 10

Impact of the Employment Act

Societies, like individuals, have their moral crises and their spiritual revolutions. The student can observe the results which these cataclysms produce, but he can hardly without presumption attempt to appraise them, for it is at the fire which they have kindled that his own small taper has been lit.
—R. H. Tawney

Can one doubt that making economic policy on the federal level is a process that lacks a systematic approach and is not adaptable to precise measurements? Timing, the interface of personalities, the press of events, and other tenuous forces play parts that are not easily traced.

The View from 1600 Pennsylvania Avenue

Presidents are responsive to events in the light of their training, experience, and the constraints within which they must operate. Neither Harding nor Coolidge was an aggressive President; but the times did not call for such qualities, and their contemporaries generally were satisfied with their performance. Harding was an embarrassment to the Republican party after his death, but the embarrassment stemmed, not from his lackluster performance as a policy maker, but from the unfortunate laxity of his administration in a moral and petty fiduciary sense. In contrast, Hoover was the soul of personal honesty and moral uprightness, and in a sense his administration was efficiently operated; yet his failure as a policy maker drove his party from office and

270

kept it out of the White House for twenty years. Roosevelt's virtues and defects as a policy maker will long be debated by historians, but the impact of his administration on economic policy making is beyond dispute.

Perhaps the first point to emerge from our observation is that the Presidency is surprisingly open-ended in the realm of economic policy making. Roosevelt did much and Coolidge did little, yet their formal powers were much the same. Of course, open-endedness applies to other domestic issues and foreign policy as well. Truman in Korea, Eisenhower in Little Rock, and Kennedy and Johnson in Vietnam illustrate the point clearly. The President must, by the nature of his office, take the initiative. In 1933, the nation was in a severe economic crisis; the President took the lead and, generally, the Congress followed. By 1936, the crisis appeared to be less threatening, and the Congress pursued a more independent line.

Economic issues, of course, had always been important in the Presidency, but they became all encompassing by the early years of the decade 1930–40. The impact of World War I, followed quickly by economic crisis, brought economic matters to the forefront of national policy and public awareness. Harding, Coolidge, and, to a degree, Hoover—operating under a philosophy that can be characterized generally as one of laissez-faire—saw no distinction between economic problems as such and those of business in general. Working with small and informal White House organizations, their mode of operation was more akin to that of the nineteenth century than that of the twentieth.

Harding and Coolidge escaped the cataclysm, but Hoover faced the almost total collapse of old economic relationships. Calling on such advice and using such machinery as was available, Hoover grappled with these problems but was reluctant to abandon his old values and continued to view governmental economic policy narrowly.

Roosevelt, entering the White House amid chaos, created an economic three-ring circus. Though he clung tenaciously to the basic concept of capitalism, FDR was more than willing to experiment with economic ideas. He was not adverse to economic planning and had a strong faith in public regulation. Without economic training and by nature an unsystematic administrator, he never did (and never cared to) weld together a cohesive economic philosophy. Thus began the age of the amateur. Though a few professional economists had begun to appear in governmental circles, those close to Roosevelt, especially in the first New Deal, had a wide range of backgrounds. Macroeconomics was in the formative stages, and few had a clear concept of the aggregate

271

economy. However, changes were afoot. Though most professional economists still regarded themselves as academicians, others heeded the call to Washington, as did many who had no claim whatsoever to economic expertise.

As a group, the economists who served on the White House level as advisers were much castigated. Tugwell was the most extreme example, but in general others were also not well regarded by press and public. Why was this the case? Not a single businessman, lawyer, or economist came forward with a viable solution to the problem of the Great Depression; yet the businessman (though he fell from his pedestal in 1929) was not subjected to the type of abuse that was Tugwell's lot.

Several reasons seem likely. The "economist," as we have noted, was often anything but an economist in the modern sense, and the title was used by the press to refer to a wide variety of people. In general, the "economists" who were in the headlines in the Roosevelt years were "nonprofessional" by modern standards. No less a person than former Secretary of State Dean Acheson (at that time Assistant Secretary of the Treasury), for example, has referred to Raymond Moley as "Professor of Economics at Columbia."[1] Moley, a lawyer, was, in fact, a professor of government and public administration with a Ph.D. in political science and made no pretense of being an economist. Few people would have been interested in the distinction. Even many of those who had been formally trained in economics would hardly have been comparable to their modern counterparts, so vastly have standards risen.

Second, many of those who became well known in the Roosevelt years were, to be honest, prime targets for their critics. Tugwell *was* arrogant and a political ignoramous. His book *The Brains Trust,* written thirty years later, leaves no doubt on both counts! Many of his associates in the Agricultural Adjustment Administration *were* prototypes of the absent-minded and impractical college professor. It is notable that it was largely the tough, practical minded, and well-qualified men who survived. Robert Nathan, Leon Henderson, Isador Lubin, and Mordecai Ezekiel, for example, were pragmatic men who survived the New Deal program.[2] The professional shortcomings of the New Dealers become obvious when compared to their successful modern-day counterparts: Walter Heller, Gardner Ackley, Paul McCracken, and Paul Samuelson.

Third, unlike their successors, the New Deal economists had no framework within which to operate. FDR put them into various slots where they operated "catch as catch can." Informal advisers have certain advantages, but there are many shortcomings as well and, overall, the latter seem to outweigh the former.

272

The upshot of this was, of course, that, while by 1940 businessmen had fallen from grace, the economist had by no means risen in public esteem to the point where his training might be useful in policy making. FDR neither understood nor liked economics. Conservative businessmen viewed with contempt those "who never met a payroll" or, at best, looked on them with considerable distrust. To the general public, their works were incomprehensible. One notes with interest that during World War II the Congress had decreed that no one who had not had experience in business or industry should hold a policy level job in OPA. Some, but by no means all, of this distrust had disappeared by 1946 when the Employment Act was passed.

It has been pointed out that planning during wars strongly supported by the public is always more successful for those who do the planning, since fluid conditions can always be pointed to, if necessary, as a good reason for the failure of the plan. Also, World War II provided clear-cut and popular goals that have not generally existed in peacetime or during unpopular wars. Planning and planners became more acceptable in the years 1940–45. Nonetheless, the Truman-Nourse and, especially, the Truman-Keyserling Councils suffered from a residue of suspicion.

By 1950 much had happened within the economics profession. The "Keynesian Revolution" in economic thinking had been gaining adherents since the late 1930s and early 1940s. Keynes' *General Theory* had come into the world in 1936 and by 1940 had become an important part of economic training. Wartime service in the early 1940s had matured economists; many of them demonstrated their skills and began to establish a reputation for expertise. Problems of materials shortages, price control, allocation of goods, and other matters were more concrete than had been true of their Depression counterparts and thus lent themselves to analysis, especially by the neoclassical economists, whose tool kit was appropriate for these tasks. Keynes foresaw the influence of wartime planning on the profession. In 1941 he wrote to the American economist, Walter S. Salant:

There is too wide a gap between the intellectual outlook of the older people and that of the younger. I have been greatly struck during my visit by the quality of the younger economists and civil servants in the Administration. I am sure that the best hope for good government of America is to be found there. The war will be a great sifter and will bring the right people to the top. We have a few good people in London, but nothing like the *numbers* you can produce here.[3]

273

Numerous economists served capably in such agencies as the Office of Strategic Services, the War Production Board, the Board of Economic Warfare, the Office of Price Administration, and, after the war, in the Agency for International Development, the Central Intelligence Agency, and in the Korean War agencies. The role of the academic economists was especially important in the war agencies, since a fair number of them remained in the federal service or returned at frequent intervals. Harvard professor Edward S. Mason, who served as chief economist in the Office of Strategic Services, brought to Washington several young economists who later served in key positions.

Even businessmen who had been loud in their condemnation of "the professors" became more aware of some practical value of the economist's skills. Growing complexities of the government-business relationship made it necessary for the businessman to pay some attention to the atmosphere in which a firm operated. This situation became a factor at first in the traditionally regulated industries, such as transportation and public utilities. As the 1930s progressed, the area of federal influence was greatly expanded into the whole range of industry. The war, in particular, with the necessity for assignment of priorities and other matters, made it necessary to have a good picture of industry as a whole and greatly stimulated the gathering and analysis of economic data. For this purpose the economist was well suited.

More progressive firms began to recognize the value of staff specialists of all types as business problems became more complex and, also, as the businessman became accustomed to and grew less hostile toward those entering the firm through formal education.

Economic data, the raw material for the economist, began to be accumulated, and he was able to perform his functions more efficiently. These changes were brought to a head by World War II, and the "new economist" began to emerge.

Why, then, did the "Age of the Professional Adviser" not dawn? Why was Truman more of the informal FDR period? Truman, like Roosevelt, was an economic conservative and, likewise, generally an economic illiterate. Can one doubt that when the time came to appoint a chairman for the newly created Council, someone suggested that Nourse be appointed? Nourse was well thought of—a conservative who had been for years in the highly respected Brookings Institution. It is not unlikely that Mr. Truman, pausing in the midst of other duties, said: "Fine, fine, go ahead." Nourse was by age and background well suited to pioneer an agency whose future was uncertain. He stood well among his peers, he was mature and conservative, and he had spent long years in

274

Washington. He was noncontroversial. Had Keyserling been selected as the first chairman, the heavens would have fallen. Truman (like everybody else) was in favor of full employment. No doubt Nourse would fill the post of "manager-of-full-employment" with as little wave making as one might reasonably expect.

Truman was not one to shrink from making waves, but he wanted to choose the issue. He knew little of economics and cared less. If it appeared that Nourse was a good man for the job, he was willing to appoint him. One can think of a half dozen academic or Washington-based economists who, had they been suggested, might have been appointed. Nourse and other sources make it clear that while the President had nothing against him and regarded him as a capable professional, to Truman he was always "Dr. Nourse" or "the Doctor." The President really expected little of substance from the Council, and no news was good news.

Personality cannot be ignored. Truman was warm and friendly with a liking for "courthouse" politics. Both Nourse and Truman were, by any measure, gentlemen and men of character, but their surface qualities were very different. Nourse was a scholar—cool, precise, and, on occasion no doubt, pedantic. He was a careful researcher and the complete opposite of the courthouse type.[4] The two were never on the same wave length. On one occasion, the President misquoted percentage increases in GNP in a radio address. When Nourse called this to his attention, the President took it lightly, pointing out that no one would know the difference. Truman was probably right, but Nourse, the scholar, was shocked. The President said in a jocular mood that he was glad Nourse told him, since he learned that Nourse had actually heard the program. Nourse was not amused.

Yet, the President, Nourse, and Keyserling, with the other members of the Council and staff, laid the firm foundation that supports the present Council. Without a Nourse and a Keyserling there would have been no Burns, Heller, or Ackley. Without the confused days of 1946–47, the confident days of 1960 would never have come to pass.

Despite frustrations and cross purposes, the process of formal advice became established and has survived for a third of a century. Though it was now on a formal basis, policy making remained fragmented. Fragmentation is not necessarily bad if there are, for example, resident economists in the White House who can interpret and coordinate matters, using the resources of the Council. Unfortunately, this was not the case. Truman took little interest in, and had no one to guide him through, the shoals of methodological difference between Nourse and Keyserling, or Keyserling and those who felt that the Council was becoming too partisan. No complex institution begins to be viable on the day it opens its doors for business.

Some years were to pass before the Council would be a viable and accepted institution, and, when the long Democratic era ended in 1952, the Council faced the most crucial test yet. Nonetheless, the crisis-filled years since 1920 had at long last resulted in the formalization and professionalization of Presidential economic advice. The President would become increasingly dependent upon the men who occupied the third-floor suite of "Old State."

Institutional Development of the Council

It is apparent that each chairman has organized the Council in a highly personal way, which is appropriate to an advisory group and to a group that has remained small and flexible. Throughout its life, the Council has followed the original idea of using the services of other federal agencies and concentrating its own efforts on synthesis and analysis. In recent years the professional staff has numbered only twelve to fifteen persons, a remarkably small number for an agency in operation for so long a period. In addition, the Council makes use of part-time consultants (twenty-five to thirty in recent years), mostly from outside the government.

Though it must work systematically, the Council must face the frustrations of adjusting its workload to fit the daily or weekly crisis facing the Presidency. Although the *Economic Reports* and other documents emerge on schedule, unforeseen strikes, price incidents, and other emergencies requiring the services of "the fire brigade" constantly arise. The Council could, of course, assume a minor role in these affairs, but access to the President is only potential and not guaranteed. If the Council wants to be a real part of the operations, the members must undertake a wide range of activities not contemplated by or spelled out in its original mandate.

Presidential Staff Duties   In its early years there was some sentiment expressed that the Council should assume an olympian, apolitical stance, rendering detached advice upon call. Paul McCracken has commented on this viewpoint:

> For obvious reasons this was unrealistic. The President's time and energy are two of Washington's most scarce commodities, and a group obviously not a member of the team could hardly

276

expect to get much of the President's time or have much influence on Administration policy. On such a basis, said Roy Blough of Columbia (and a former Council member) "the influence of the Council might be somewhat above that of a group of university professors with research and publishing facilities, but probably not much above it." On the other hand it was necessary to learn from painful experience that the Council can become too political. In 1952 relations between the Council and the Congress became so strained that appropriations were voted only for operation through the remainder of President Truman's term (January 1953). Arthur Burns, therefore, actually began his career as an Economic Adviser to the President, and the new Administration then had to take steps to revive the Council. If the Council starts to become too political in the narrow sense of the term, it no longer serves well the Administration or the nation. In a conference with him before I became a member, President Eisenhower said that he wanted from the Council the straight economic advice because others in the Administration might start out thinking themselves. This puts very well the danger of the Council's becoming too actively political. Experience has demonstrated that the Council must be on the Administration's team, but it and the Members must preserve their professional status. This is not a wide path, but the Council has successfully kept on it through the Administrations of the last three Presidents.[5]

It is the nature of any organization, governmental or otherwise, to be anxious to extend the scope of its activities. In the White House, where interest in affairs is intense, this tendency is endemic. Consequently, activities that in the Roosevelt days were carried on by anonymous presidential assistants have fallen into the hands of the Council. Further, the Council, having formulated certain working policies such as the wage-price guideposts, finds itself forced to comment on or defend these policies and thus is more and more frequently embroiled in day-to-day affairs.

The Council is relatively small and by itself constitutes a modest empire compared to the vast establishments involved in policy creation in the executive branch of the government. On almost every matter of policy there is generally a Cabinet officer who is immediately responsible for policy formulation and implementation. Professor McCracken notes that, despite this competition, the Council is in a strong position:

The Council is sufficiently well-positioned to have become through the years a major influence on national economic policy.

277

What accounts for this? There are about three major reasons. First, the Council is in the Executive Office of the President, and it reports directly to the President. So long as the President has confidence in the advice he receives, thus having direct access to the occupant of the oval office assures the Council of Economic Advisers an important participation in policy discussions and decisions. Much here depends, of course, on the personal relationship between the President and the Chairman of the Council. Clearly these relationships between Presidents Kennedy and Johnson and Messrs. Heller and Ackley have reflected cordiality and confidence. It was also true for President Eisenhower and Messrs. Burns and Saulnier. Second, the Members of the Council can meet formally and socially on even terms with other senior Administration officials. This is important. While economists have long been in Government, it was with the Employment Act of 1946 that economists became the Principles of an agency. Thus the wisdom of economics is assured of an opportunity to do its leavening influence in numerous ways. The Chairman regularly attends Cabinet meetings and periodically makes presentations. Members serve on Administration committees, including Cabinet committees. The Chairman and Members of the Council often represent this Government at international meetings. The last Economic Report, in the section reporting on the Council's activities, enumerated at least 47 of these ventures in which Members and staff had been engaged during the year. Third, the Council has a major impact on policy through its responsibility for the preparation of the Economic Report. This is the Administration's major annual articulation of the case for its programs and policies. And articulation shapes, even makes, policy. Naturally other officials and agencies influence the result, and the Reports inevitably must reasonably reflect the policy posture of the whole Establishment, but there is still a major advantage in holding the pen that is put to paper.[6]

The Council is much involved, but involvement in current affairs is not without an element of danger. Although the Council must be in the mainstream of events, when it becomes embroiled in labor relations or commodity price increases, for example, it is open to serious trouble because it is always easier to attack the President's staff than the President himself. In the Roosevelt days, Hopkins, Rosenman, and Tugwell were the target of those who did not choose to attack Roosevelt personally. Dr Steelman absorbed criticism directed at Truman, and Walter Heller was Kennedy's economic lightning rod. As part of the

278

official family, and involved in policy making as it is, CEA can be expected to receive a share of abuse. Interestingly enough, by the 1960s and 1970s, either the political climate had changed or the personalities were different in that Nixon and Ford as well as Johnson were more often attacked directly.

Unfortunately also, the Council, like any governmental official or agency, can become quickly overexposed. The currency of speech making and television appearances is subject to rapid depreciation, and the Council must take care to see that it does not fall into this trap. An additional danger of overinvolvement is that the Council builds up a vested interest and is apt to react subjectively when opposition arises. All highly placed officials must guard against this, and the Council member is no exception.

External Relations   The pronouncements of the Council and its formal reports have become widely read documents, subject to widespread comment in the business press. The Council is also in the limelight when it is called upon for public testimony. It will be recalled that Nourse was reluctant to appear before the Congress, but since that day CEA members have appeared routinely. As their policy-making role has grown, so too has the necessity of defending those policies before Congress and its committees and in the business community.

The Council has also increased its activities in relation to other federal agencies. In recent years, it has participated in many interagency activities as a routine matter, although, in the 1950s, Keyserling was much criticized for the practice.

The Council has a broad public exposure in other ways—members of the Council appear on television, are the subject of frequent comment in the press, and often address professional and business groups. There is no objection to such activity; it is, indeed, desirable. Yet, again, there is potential danger, and the Council members must always be aware of the fact that they wear the Council brand. No matter how much the members emphasize the fact that they speak as individuals, it is evident that others consider this impossible. This is especially true of young staff members who have not built a reputation independent of their service on the Council. Nourse was a man of established reputation within the profession (though not known to the general public) before he was appointed to the Council. Young staff members and some Council members of recent years, although they have high professional qualifications, have no identity outside CEA. Even though an economist may have a professional reputation prior to Council service, his *public* reputation rests on his Council activities. Arthur Burns, Walter Heller, and James Tobin, for example, were well known to and highly respected by their fellow economists before their Council service. However, most segments of the public and the business community are aware of these men solely in their role as members or former members of the Council. This, of course, is true of all advisers. Paul Samuelson (a Nobel Prize winner) is one of the best-known economists in the world, but his *public image* stems largely from his role as a Kennedy adviser, Nixon critic, and commentator on economic affairs.

A by-product of the Council's high degree of visibility is the fact that much has been written about it, and this material has been widely read. In 1956 and again in 1966, on the tenth and twentieth anniversaries of the act, the professional journals and, to a lesser extent, the lay press devoted much space to evaluations and critical analyses of the CEA, the Joint Committee, and the advisory process in general. In 1966 the Joint Economic Committee sponsored a one-day symposium in Washington that featured brief addresses by those who had served on the Council or Joint Committee, or who had been instrumental in the passage of the act. These remarks were printed and circulated. In early fall a second volume consisting of invited comments was released. In some cases, these were merely comments on what was said in the symposium; however, the title of the volume was *Directions for the Future* and new ground was broken.

Many commentators at the twenty-year point suggested minor alterations or additions to the structure of the Council or the Joint Committee, designed to improve forecasting or promulgation of policy. For ease of presentation, these comments will be divided into two categories: those relating to the administration of the act as it now exists, and those relating to proposed changes of a more philosophical nature that relate to the structure of the act and suggest future changes.

In the first category, recommendations were in regard to several facets of Council procedure. John W. Kendrick, for example, wondered if the CEA should not enlarge its staff and extend its intra-agency contacts.[7] Very little was said about the administration of the act and almost nothing about the organization of the Joint Committee. Either these matters were proceeding satisfactorily or they were not considered of sufficient importance to merit consideration in light of other, more pressing problems.

In the relationship of the Council to other agencies, two major problems were cited. The first of these is the seeming lack of coordination

280

between the Council and the monetary authority; and, second, the fact that the act makes no direct reference to international financial relations. These two problems have assumed major importance in recent years. Both were noted by several commentators: Professors William R. Allen, James W. Angel, Leo Fishman, and Seymour Harris.[8] Especially troublesome was the lack of coordination between the Board of Governors and the policy of any given administration as promulgated by the Council. These problems were, by all odds, the most serious mentioned.

Keyserling was concerned about what he viewed as an overly passive attitude on the part of the Council. In his view, economics should "move beyond forecasting toward purposeful policy, and increasingly from defensive to affirmative action." In general, he advocated a return to the procedures he himself advocated as chairman. Keyserling was also concerned with the guideposts, noting characteristically that they were apt to slow down the pace of economic progress. Most were less critical. Former Chairman Walter Heller had no "burning desire" for change in the formal organization of economic advice in government, although he saw the situation as fluid and was not committed to the status quo.[9]

Surprisingly little criticism was registered concerning the structure of the Council and the Joint Committee. In general, the various Councils have reacted in surprisingly uniform fashion to the problems with which they, and their Presidents, were confronted.

Most segments of the public, no longer fearing a catastrophic depression, now demand that the Council provide for stable growth, control of inflation, and reasonable employment. Along with this added responsibility, the Council has acquired more effective tools and techniques to cope with its problems. The performance of a given Council cannot be evaluated in relation to the changing conditions that it faces over time; nor can the effectiveness of the various Councils be compared, except in relation to the problems each has faced. Each Council has built upon the experience of its predecessors. Nourse fought battles that Keyserling did not have to repeat, just as Heller enjoyed a heritage from Burns and passed benefits on to Ackley; Ackley, in turn, provided experience for Okun and McCracken to draw upon. Though in the early 1970s Stein drew critical comment for political activity, the passage of time may vindicate his position.

Nourse, as befitted the first chairman, attempted to maintain an objective and scientific approach. Keyserling, on the other hand, as an unreconstructed New Dealer embarked on a much more activist course. Burns, as part of an administration dedicated to reducing the area of governmental influence, acted more as a consultant to the President.

281

Saulnier faced new problems of controlling inflation. Heller, the prototype of the modern economist, was a man of confidence and extended the influence of the Council into new areas.

Although the basic approach to major economic problems has changed little, the Council, both by design and by good fortune, has remained a highly personal and noninstitutional organization. The personal nature of the Council-President relationship has been much more significant than one would have expected. To what degree the Council has been forced to remain small because of budget limitations or because of design is difficult to say, but the important point is that it has remained small and informal in its organization.

The generally academic tone of the group and, under Heller's chairmanship especially, the frequent use of part-time personnel and consultants has helped to assure that isolation and bureaucratic tendencies would be minimized. The "this-is-the-way-we-always-did-it" syndrome of the typical government agency has largely been avoided. Nonetheless, each chairman had to make clear to the permanent staff that a new era had begun.

As a consequence of these efforts, the tie between the academic and business communities and the Council has remained viable. Many former members of the Council and personnel of its staff have accepted positions with academic institutions, research groups, or businesses. They have retained their Council interests and often have returned for short stints. Thus, the Council benefits from a constantly expanding cadre of alumni who have knowledge of its operations and who provide it with useful contacts on many levels of both academic and business life.

The Council over the years has been in competition with individuals and institutions for the position of being the primary, if not the sole, source of presidential economic advice. The Council must compete for the President's limited time and energy with Cabinet officers, Senators, delegates from home, visiting heads of state, war heroes, and countless others. In arriving at a major decision, the President must weigh many noneconomic factors. The formal power structure (Treasury, Defense, and other agencies with their many serious problems, all calling for immediate solution) is a formidable competitor. No Council has interposed itself between the President and these old-line agencies. Heller, with all of his influence, could not have displaced Dillon, nor did he try to do so.[10]

In competing for the President's ear, the Council must remain largely passive. It can pass him memoranda, but it cannot force him to read them. The Council must wait until the President takes the lead in asking for its services. It may "assist and advise," "analyze and interpret," "develop and recommend."

The Council has no executive power, no field staff, no clientele like the Department of Agriculture; no power comparable to that possessed by the Office of Management and Budget to involve itself in programs; and no congressional champions like those who safeguard the interests of the Air Force or the Navy. It does, however, have a few congressional "fans" such as Reuss of Wisconsin. The Council must rely on what reflected glory it can attract from its position close to the President and on the use of its wits to call attention to the needs that it can fill by virtue of its professional expertise. With the passage of time, however, the Council has acquired a number of partisans both in the Congress and throughout the nation. It is unlikely that the events of 1952 (when congressional action almost phased CEA out) could be repeated without substantial opposition.

Despite its lack of formal power and its host of competitors, the Council is more than a mere facade. First and foremost, the Council is the visible symbol of the presidential responsibility for economic welfare, but it is more than a symbol. The Council has performed tangible, important, and unique services for the Presidency. The Council, as *the* expert group on economic matters serving the President on a highly personal basis, has provided him with a vehicle by which he can take the initiative in the continuous power struggle with the Congress and, indeed, with the independent agencies and with his own executive departments. The Council has been able to coordinate and synthesize the views of the various specialized and expert groups within the executive branch.

The Council not only gives the President expert economic advice in private, but also backs up his authority with professional weight in public. It has been useful in this way, thanks largely to the battle for professional objectivity fought by Nourse and his successors. Overall, the Council has acquired a reputation for being objective. Thus, it is useful to the President as it never could be if it were thought of as a totally partisan, "rubber-stamp" organization. How much weight the Council carried in backstopping President Kennedy in his dispute with the steel industry, for example, cannot be determined, but no doubt its moral force and expertise was useful to him as he injected himself into a complex argument involving such matters as price increases, productivity, and other esoteric economic issues.

The Council, via either its reports or in oral testimony, is a useful channel for putting before the public or the Congress matters that the

President wishes to ventilate but does not care to embrace wholly in a policy sense. The Council, like any good staff arm, can take the blame if such matters prove to be embarrassing. In fact, the Council may serve the President as well in defeat as it does in victory. Rejection, or apparent rejection, of the Council viewpoint may not mean that its economic advice has been found defective, but that more serious problems have intervened or that different values have been forced upon the President for consideration. Flexibility is provided by the ability of the President to accept or reject the Council's advice at his discretion. The Council's strength lies in the fact that the President is not required by law to accept its advice or, indeed, even to listen to it. Its success has come when it was needed and its advice asked for. Its failures (under Nixon, for example) have come for the most part when it was ignored.

Perhaps the most powerful of CEA's competitors—though, of course, not formally an advisory group to the President—is the Board of Governors of the Federal Reserve System. Although the Federal Reserve has worked closely with the Council in recent years, it is by no means prepared to subordinate its views to those of CEA. Designed to be independent of both Congress and President, the Federal Reserve since its inception has guarded its independence closely. The Federal Reserve–Treasury dispute during the Truman Administration was the only open controversy between the administration and the Federal Reserve in recent years, but the independence of the Board in policy making has frequently caused friction under the surface.

Without direct political accountability, the Federal Reserve nevertheless has great influence on the course of the economy and the political fortunes of the President and the Congress. Former Chairman Patman of the House Banking and Currency Committee had long argued that the Fed should be brought to heel, and in the 1970s, despite his removal from the chairmanship, he appeared to be gaining converts.[11]

Numerous students have charged the Federal Reserve Board with excessive errors in policy formulation.[12] Regardless of the record of being "right" or "wrong," the fact remains that the Board is probably the single most important economic policy-making body outside the direct control of the executive.

Suggestions for less Fed autonomy have been made but, given the prestige of the organization in the Congress and in the business community, the chance of such proposals succeeding in the near future seems extremely remote. (Former Chairman Martin, in particular, had prestige almost equal to that of J. Edgar Hoover, and his forced removal from the chairmanship would have required enormous political courage.)

Cooperative arrangements between the Fed and CEA have been informal, though nonetheless effective. Burns, Saulnier, Heller, Ackley, and others were successful in maintaining contact.

The Treasury, of course, has primary responsibility for conducting the government's business and overseeing its financial affairs. In any case, it is a strong competitor of the Council as a policy-making body, and under a strong secretary it is almost overwhelming.

Other Cabinet agencies may press for programs not compatible to CEA. The Labor Department, for example, may be more anxious to avoid unemployment than the Council, and thus may be apt to press for more liberal policies than the Council. The Council must be aware of these agencies and their problems but, in general, it must deal with them at arm's length.

Impact on Other Agencies   Not surprisingly, the Council has had substantial influence upon the agencies with which it has been associated. The relationship of greatest significance, of course, has been with the Joint Committee. Although this might have been a delicate relationship, it has been largely amicable and beneficial for both. Similarly, the existence of the Council has been conducive to interest in economic research in other agencies. We have seen that CEA has depended upon the various federal agencies for information, rather than building up a large research staff of its own.

Located within the White House family, the Council enjoys substantial prestige and public exposure not available to other organizations. In part, it has passed this standing on to other research groups with which it has worked. The Council gives all these organizations a sense of participation at the White House level that was seldom experienced before 1946. Also, the Council has concentrated attention on statistical gaps and on lack of uniformity in reporting information, thus increasing the effectiveness of the whole process of data collection and analysis on the federal level. The movement of staff from the Council to and from other agencies has also been important in unifying economic advice. Despite its successes, however, several minor shortcomings or potential problems can be delineated.

The most serious problem, which has so far resisted solution, is that of maintaining independence from full commitment to the administration program while, at the same time, enjoying the confidence of the President and participating in the administration's general policy. It seems likely that no wholly satisfactory solution will ever be found. Perhaps this is at least partially a matter of appearance rather than substance. Keyserling, for example, was fully committed to the Truman program and made no secret of the fact, a position which made him controversial. Obviously, no one expects the Council members to be *against* the administration, but perhaps they must be careful to keep a low profile and seem to support the administration solely because its views are always economically sound, as Arthur Burns did. Though each chairman has built on the past, each will face unique problems and personalities, and the relationship between each Council, President, and administration must be established anew on an *ad hoc* basis. Again we must remind ourselves that three decades is a brief time in the life of an agency. With the passage of time, the Council will acquire a patina of tradition that will be more difficult to break through. One of the major advantages of the Council has been its flexibility; it would be unfortunate if, in gaining maturity and stature, it also acquired rigidity.

The Council and Its Future

No doubt the passage of time will bring about changes in the organization of the Council as was done in the case of Reorganization Plan No. 9, which gave the chairman more authority. New conditions and new personalities will always make changes necessary.

In the years of its existence, the Council has faced many problems, both philosophical and organizational. While its solutions have seldom met with universal acclaim, the experiment of providing formal economic advice on the highest level of government has been, on the whole, highly successful. CEA has been forced to develop its philosophy and its goals as it went along, and it has had to do this, not in the calm of academia, but in the political arena during perhaps the most momentous years in American history.

In considering the impact of the Act of 1946, one must first recall the lukewarm reception which the act received. Not much was expected from the battered piece of legislation that emerged from Congress, weakened by compromise and diluted so as to offend a minimum number of vested interests.

Galbraith wrote twenty years after the Act was passed:

One wonders whether, on preliminary form, there was ever a more unpromising piece of legislation than the Employment Act of 1946. The title itself was a hedge; reference to full employment was too controversial. Any mention of methods by which employment would be sustained was avoided. To have hinted at deficit financing would have been fatal. Three economic advisers

286

were provided which, it would be foreseen, was a certain formula for endless disagreement. They had no visible executive authority. A Congressional Committee was authorized but with no legislative powers, a point emphasized in its name. As a substitute for solid function, an improved system of reports was provided for. One remembers discussing the legislation in 1946 with Gordon Gilbert who was one of its architects. We agreed that it was principally a gesture though probably a useful one. He thought it more useful than I did. Yet in retrospect the Employment Act appears as the most important single piece of economic legislation of the postwar years. The Council of Economic Advisers which it created has, a few early months apart, functioned harmoniously as a powerful general staff on economic policy. It has far outstripped the Secretary of Commerce and the Federal Reserve Board in influence. Probably it is now more powerful than the Treasury. The Joint Economic Committee, as it has been retitled, if a less spectacular success, is the most respected forum of economic discussion in the Congress. How did it come about?[13]

By almost any measure, the Council has performed more effectively than most observers would have forecast in 1946. Several circumstances seem to account for this success. First, the Council has not had to cope with a major economic downturn of a magnitude comparable to that of 1929. Hopefully, the Council's actions have, indeed, helped to prevent such a major breakdown. The dimensions of the decline of 1975 were certainly severe, but far different from 1929–32. To what degree the CEA would have been effective in 1929, given the philosophy of the Hoover Administration, is a matter of speculation. The Council faced and passed a severe test in 1953–54 and again in 1960–61. However, an economic breakdown of the magnitude of 1929 has not occurred, and, to that degree, the Council (along with other such devices) remains untested. Second, the Council has both benefited from and contributed to the increasing acceptance of economic analysis in government and business. The performance of economists during World War II and in the difficult years since has been creditable, and the usefulness of economic analysis at high levels of business and government has been demonstrated. Finally, and of most importance, was the acceptance of the Council's function by the President, who, of course, is the key to the process. Without such acceptance, the Council would have had, at least in the early years, no real purpose. Perhaps, now that it has become firmly established, it would be very difficult for the President to ignore it. Truman, while supporting the Council idea, was apparently unwilling to use it to its full potential. The record indicates that he looked upon it essentially as a political device. This judgment may be harsh, but it seems to be supported by the historical facts. Eisenhower, after a somewhat tenuous beginning, became an enthusiastic supporter, though it would probably have perished in 1952 had not bipartisan congressional support saved the day. Burns' great contribution was that he established the Council's reputation for usefulness in an administration not generally thought to be sympathetic to economic planning and research. Kennedy was known to be a warm supporter of the Council, with some personal interest in research methodology. Johnson, although more in the Truman mold, continued the Kennedy activist tradition insofar as the Council was concerned. Nixon seemingly was inclined to keep the Council in a somewhat subordinate position vis-à-vis other agencies, such as the Treasury; and Ford, at least at this time (early 1976), seems bent on the same course. A third factor in the success of the Council has been good fortune in choice of chairmen. All have performed in admirable fashion, although, to be sure, their modes of operation have been widely different.

No chairman has served a full presidential term, with the exception of Heller, whose term overlapped the Kennedy-Johnson years; but all have remained for more than three years. The change from Nourse to Keyserling was a shift in mode of operation, in economic philosophy, and personality. The Burns-Saulnier shift was only mildly noticeable in the form of operating technique, as was that from Heller to Ackley to Okun. It is notable also that in every case, until Nixon named Greenspan in 1974, when a chairman has resigned during an administration his replacement has come from within the Council. However, the move toward continuity was enhanced when Nixon in 1969 reached into the ranks of former Council members to appoint McCracken. When Johnson succeeded Kennedy, he made no change until Heller resigned in November 1964. The Council members have been orthodox professional economists; although they have represented varying views, none has been an adherent to "far-out" schools of thought, such as those that flourished in the 1930s.

While thirty years is a short time in the life of a federal agency, the Council seems firmly established and has indeed become a strong competitor with the older agencies for influence on economic policy. Even if the Council should itself be eliminated, the function of formal advice seems well-enough established to survive in another framework.

There can be no question that the Employment Act of 1946 in its thirty years has been a success. From the uncertain years of 1946 to the end of the Truman Administration, through the years of confidence in the Kennedy and Johnson administrations, and a seeming decline under the Nixon and Ford administrations, the Council has had its troubles and triumphs, but the general course has been upward. There seems to be no serious opposition to the Council as an institution. The Council and its counterpart, the Joint Committee, have reached a high level of influence in national affairs. The paucity of suggestions for improvement of the act in the 1966 symposium is symptomatic of the general esteem in which these agencies are held. We must remember, however, that the years since 1946 have presented economic problems mainly of an inflationary nature. Thus, the major objectives of the Employment Act, although somewhat altered to be sure, have been relatively within reach. Less success has been achieved with the objectives of price stability and growth, which also come within the purview of the act as now interpreted.

Ironically, the educational successes of the Council and the Joint Committee have made the public more demanding and more aware of economic phenomena. In an article based on his presidential address to the American Economic Association, "Progress Toward Economic Stability," Burns noted that the success of the Council had made the public more sensitive to economic policy.[14] Much credit is due to other federal agencies and to the business community, which have, like the Council, become more sophisticated in their formulation of economic policies. Obviously, CEA and the Joint Committee, essentially coordinating agencies, would not have been able to carry out their programs unaided.

The question of success or failure must in the end be answered in relation to the objective of the organization in question. It is obvious that the goals of the Employment Act have shifted since 1946. The original objective of the act was to prevent a major postwar depression or a sliding back into the slough of 1937–39. For many reasons, this has not occurred and over the years that have elapsed the original goal has been supplemented by the dual objectives of economic stability and economic growth. What began as defense against deflation has turned largely into a battle against both inflation and deflation, with the purpose of achieving a reasonable stability.

One must also note that what was a suitable objective for the Council three decades ago is hardly adequate today. In 1946, Truman gave the Council its "sailing orders," namely, to get the national income up to $200 billion.[15] It was then $180.9 billion and first exceeded $200 billion in 1948; by this measure, it had achieved its objective within two years.

Likewise, it has done its job in preventing a major depression. The recessions of 1948–49, 1953–54, and 1960–61 were mild. In no case did unemployment exceed 8 percent nor GNP fall by more than 3.7 percent; in every case, the reversal in trend took place within thirteen months. The 1974–75 downturn, though pronounced, and durable, was far from the crisis of the 1930s. In a sense, the Council has been the victim of its success. Not satisfied with the prevention of catastrophic depression, the increasingly demanding public has expected the Council to prevent unwelcome price increases and to promote growth. Within a decade, the goal of a national income of $200 billion jumped to $350 billion (1956), and by 1966 anything less than $600 billion would have been considered pedestrian. In the 1970s, $900 billion to $1,200 billion or more was a realistic goal! Economic growth, not even mentioned in the original act, has become an objective of major interest, though less emphasized now than a decade ago. It is likewise a measure of public awareness that the demands on President Ford and the Congress to take action against inflation/deflation were immediate and vocal. Congressional and executive inaction were clearly not to be tolerated by any significant segment of the population, liberal or conservative.

Though the Council has had a great measure of success, it has so far failed to demonstrate its ability to cope effectively with inflationary pressures. Here, of course, it encounters the greatest political difficulties. Everyone enjoys expansionary policies, but restrictive policies are popular with few.

The core of this matter is, of course, the fact that CEA is an advisory group. Whatever need it may see for restrictive action, it can do no more than call the matter to the President's attention. It seems quite obvious in the 1970s that President Johnson in the mid-1960s was quite unwilling to pursue such policies as were doubtless suggested by the Council. The "new economics" and "fine tuning" of the system are, in this regard, more apparent than real.

Although the basic approach to major economic problems has been consistent, the Council, as we have seen, has remained a small, highly personal, noninstitutional organization. One can speak in meaningful terms about the "Burns Council" or the "Heller Council," whereas one would not speak of a "Benson Department of Agriculture" or a "Dillon Treasury." The personal nature of the Council-President relationship has been much more significant than one would have expected it to be.

The educational role, of course, has strengthened the public interest in, and intensified the President's responsibility for, economic activity, thus providing feedback to the Council itself. As Edward S. Flash says,

"The Council has supplied information and analysis, but even more it has articulated the concepts needed for determination and defense of policy. The value of such an organization has been gradually recognized and accorded legitimacy by politician and bureaucrat, by economist and layman."[16]

On Capitol Hill, the Joint Economic Committee has performed a unique function, equally essential to the success of the act. Harvey C. Mansfield notes:

> If the JEC has helped change the climate of thinking, it would be something else again to argue that it has been specifically responsible for any identifiable policy change. A study group is not an action group, let alone a policy-making group. Before 1955 its annual reports were unanimous, or nearly so; since then, majority and minority reports, strictly along partisan lines, have been the rule. Some critics have deplored this; Senator Douglas welcomes it, on the ground that unanimity necessarily requires covering over real differences with innocuous generalities. A middle course might seek to state matters of agreement and isolate differences, in order to define issues more sharply; but this would not be easy where differences are ideological and not merely technical, as economic arguments are apt to be. Other critics have urged changes in procedure and format to dramatize the committee's output; experiments in this direction will probably have to wait on changes in leadership that would make them congenial.
>
> It is perhaps significant that the committee's work, like Senator Jackson's studies in the field of national security organization, attracted the greatest attention in a period when Democrats controlled the Congress and Republicans the White House. When the same party controls both, there is less room—and less incentive—for developing, from a congressional committee base, major alternatives in policy to those espoused by the administration in office.[17]

It will be recalled that an objective of the Joint Economic Committee was to regain, or at least to preserve, a measure of congressional influence vis-à-vis the President. It might seem that this would have created a highly competitive situation perhaps detrimental to the objective of the act. After a third of a century of experience, however, this is not the case. Indeed, one might argue that the JEC-CEA relationship has been a link between the legislative and the executive functions, instead of a wedge. This linkage is on several levels. First, the professional staffs of the two groups have a fairly close relationship and speak the same professional language. Although there are party differences separating a portion of the committee membership from the President, many, if not most, of these differences disappear at the staff level. Second, the JEC format has provided a useful platform for the views of the administration, but it has been equally effective for the Congress.

The Joint Committee has enlarged the congressional role and improved the quality of legislative processes in the realm of economic policy making. It is true, as Mansfield notes, that a study group is not an action group. Yet the Joint Economic Committee role has been invaluable. Its extended activities under Senator Proxmire have brought it into areas not envisioned by the Employment Act, and the results of this move remain to be seen.

Though the Council and the Joint Committee have discharged their functions with considerable success in the past three decades, it may be that the present arrangement will cease to exist. Some years ago, Professor Blough suggested that the Council, like its members, might be expendable. No governmental agency is immortal. Yet it seems unlikely that the functions of the Council and the Committee will be entirely dispensed with. The advantages of a group advising the President and a comparable group acting as a sounding board in the Congress have become obvious over the years. Likewise, the degree of federal involvement in the economy has become more pronounced and seems to be destined for further expansion.

It is clear, however, that the functions performed by the CEA cannot be effectively performed under any and all circumstances. Form and organization are important. Several requisites for effectiveness seem to emerge.

1. The agency must be independent of other established executive departments in order to remain objective in its views.
2. The agency must remain relatively small and informal in organization.
3. Though it must have a degree of organizational stability to function effectively, it must also remain flexible with a maximum interchange of ideas and personnel between itself and other organizations, both in and out of government.
4. It must retain its standards of professional competence.
5. It must remain close to the President both in terms of organization and physical location.
6. It must be subject to comment by a comparable body (now the Joint Economic Committee) in order for executive and

292

congressional views to mesh with the maximum effect. The relations between these bodies must be close and friendly but at arms length.

7. The agency should involve itself in the President's program, but avoid commitment to the point of losing objectivity.

8. It seems desirable to have a resident economist in the White House to field the wide variety of economic issues that arise and to bridge the gap between the President and the advisory group. Care must be taken, however, to see that he acts as a bridge and not a barrier.

If it adheres to these principles, the name of the agency or, in fact, its organizational status will be of minor import. The Act of 1946, after a third of a century, has established a successful pattern, and these principles seem to contain the formula for future success.

The impact of the Act of 1946 has been immense. It has created not only a new mechanism for dealing with or for viewing economic problems, but also a continuing awareness of what must and can be done to influence the course of economic events. Begun almost solely as a device to prevent depression, the act has become much more—an economic gyroscope acting to stabilize the economy. It has created a viable force for economic education and a meaningful framework for economic discourse within and without the government.

By most measures the Council has been successful as an institution, but what has been its policy-making responsibility and its impact on the Presidency? Can it be said that policy making in the sphere of economics has been more systematic or more intelligent than it was in pre-Council days? Would policy have remained much the same without it? Would other organizations have served the same purpose? Was the Council a routine response to a presidential need or a genuine and far-reaching innovation in the art of modern government? Clearly, it has been some of both, but the innovation aspect seems to have emerged more strongly. With its origins in the desperate need to prevent mass unemployment, the Act of 1946 has apparently created a fourth branch of government, essential to modern economic policy.

Notes

Chapter 10

[1] Dean Acheson, *Present at the Creation* (New York: Norton, 1969).

[2] In 1976 they were all alive, and Nathan and Lubin were both active economists.

[3] Roy Harrod, *Life of John Maynard Keynes* (New York: Harcourt, Brace & World, 1951), p. 509.

[4] In personal interviews Nourse's colleagues referred to him as "Ed," but one suspects that few people did so in the office. He was never "Ed" to the President.

[5] Paul McCracken, "The Political Position of the Council on Economic Advisers," Address, Western Michigan University, January 19, 1966 (mimeographed). These comments were made after his service on the Eisenhower Council but before his service as Chairman under President Nixon.

[6] Ibid.

[7] Invited Comments, *Directions For the Future*, Supplement to Hearing, Joint Economic Committee, 89th Congress, 2nd Session, Washington, D.C., 1966, p. 76.

[8] Ibid.

[9] Heller, *New Dimensions in Political Economy*, op. cit., p. 56.

[10] No matter how well established, it is most unlikely that CEA would be able to obtain an absolute monopoly on economic advice and it is, no doubt, just as well. Presidents will have and should have access to multiple sources of information and advice on all aspects of the national interest.

[11] Professor Canterbery suggests that if Fed policy had been more effective and correctly aimed Herbert Hoover would have been reelected in 1932; a plausible thought if, as Friedman argues, proper monetary policy would have prevented or ended the Depression.

[12] See for example, E. Ray Canterbery, "A New Look at Federal Open Market Committee Voting," *The Western Economic Journal*, 6 (December 1967), pp. 25–38; Franco Modigliani, "Some Empirical Tests of Monetary Management and of Rules Versus Direction," *The Journal of Political Economy*, 72 (June 1964), pp. 211– 45; Thomas Havrilesky, "A Test of Monetary Policy Actions," *The Journal of Political Economy*, 75 (June 1967), p. 203.

[13] Review by John Kenneth Galbraith of Edward S. Flash's "Economic Advice and Presidential Leadership," *American Economic Review* (December 1966), p. 1249.

[14] *American Economic Review* (March 1960), Vol. I, No. 1, p. 1. See also, Otto Eckstein, "The Economics of the 1960's, A Backward Look," *Public Interest* (Spring, 1970), pp. 86–87.

[15] Nourse, op. cit., p. 109.

[16] Flash, op cit., p. 325.

[17] Harvey C. Mansfield, "The Congress and Economic Policy," *The Congress and America's Future*, David B. Truman, ed., *The American Assembly* (Englewood Cliffs, N.J.: Prentice Hall, 1965), p. 147.

APPENDIX A

Members of the Council, 1946–76

Name	Position	Oath of Office Date	Separation Date
Edwin G. Nourse	Chairman	August 9, 1946	November 1, 1949
Leon H. Keyserling	Vice Chairman	August 9, 1946	
	Acting Chairman	November 2, 1949	
	Chairman	May 10, 1950	January 20, 1953
John D. Clark	Member	August 9, 1946	
	Vice Chairman	May 10, 1950	February 11, 1953
Roy Blough	Member	June 29, 1950	August 20, 1952
Robert C. Turner	Member	September 8, 1952	January 20, 1953
Arthur F. Burns	Chairman	March 19, 1953	December 1, 1956
Neil H. Jacoby	Member	September 15, 1953	February 9, 1955
Walter W. Stewart	Member	December 2, 1953	April 29, 1955
Raymond J. Saulnier	Member	April 4, 1955	
	Chairman	December 3, 1956	January 20, 1961
Joseph S. Davis	Member	May 2, 1955	October 31, 1958
Paul W. McCracken	Member	December 3, 1956	January 31, 1959
Karl Brandt	Member	November 1, 1958	January 20, 1961
Henry C. Wallich	Member	May 7, 1959	January 20, 1961
James Tobin	Member	January 29, 1961	July 31, 1962
Kermit Gordon	Member	January 29, 1961	December 27, 1962
Walter W. Heller	Chairman	January 29, 1961	November 15, 1964
Gardner Ackley	Member	August 3, 1962	
	Chairman	November 16, 1964	February 15, 1968
John P. Lewis	Member	May 17, 1963	August 31, 1964
Otto Eckstein	Member	September 2, 1964	February 1, 1966
Arthur M. Okun	Member	November 16, 1964	
	Chairman	February 15, 1968	January 20, 1969
James S. Duesenberry	Member	February 2, 1966	June 30, 1968
Merton J. Peck	Member	February 15, 1968	January 20, 1969
Warren L. Smith	Member	July 1, 1968	January 20, 1969
Hendrik S. Houthakker	Member	February 4, 1969	July 15, 1971
Paul W. McCracken	Chairman	February 4, 1969	January 1, 1972
Herbert Stein	Member	February 4, 1969	January 1, 1972
	Chairman	January 1, 1972	September 5, 1974
Ezra Solomon	Member	June 17, 1971	March 25, 1973

Marina von			
N. Whitman	Member	March 16, 1972	August 15, 1973
Gary L. Seevers	Member	July 18, 1973	April 15, 1975
William J.			
Fellner	Member	October 31, 1973	February 25, 1975
Alan Greenspan	Chairman	September 5, 1974	January 20, 1977
Paul W.			
MacAvoy	Member	June 13, 1975	January 20, 1977
Burton Malkiel	Member	July 22, 1975	January 20, 1977

APPENDIX B

Biographical Sketches of CEA Members, 1946–76

EDWIN G. NOURSE (1883–1974). CEA Chairman, 1946–50.

Nourse received a Ph.D. from The University of Chicago in 1915. For many years, he followed a typical academic career, teaching in the field of agricultural economics at Arkansas, Iowa State, and at the University of Pennsylvania. In 1929 he joined the Brookings Institution and became its vice-president in 1942. He served as president of the American Economic Association during 1942.

LEON H. KEYSERLING (1908–   ). CEA Member, 1946; Chairman, 1950–53.

Keyserling received an A.B. from Columbia in 1928 and an LL.B. from Harvard in 1931. He did additional graduate work in economics at Columbia in the early 1930s. Moving to Washington at the peak of the New Deal, he served in AAA, as assistant to Senator Robert F. Wagner, and rose to be general counsel of the Housing Agencies. After leaving CEA, he has had an active career as founder-president of the Conference on Economic Progress. He is consulting economist-lawyer and an active commentator on CEA affairs.

JOHN D. CLARK (1884–1959). CEA Member, 1946–53.

Clark was born in Nebraska in 1884 and graduated from the University of Nebraska in 1905. He obtained an LL.B. from Columbia in 1907 and had a successful business career, rising to a vice-presidency of Standard Oil of New Jersey. In 1931 he received a Ph.D. from Johns Hopkins and began a second career. When he was appointed to the Council, he was Dean of the School of Business at the University of Nebraska.

ROY BLOUGH (1901–   ). CEA Member, 1950–52.

Blough received the Ph.D. from the University of Wisconsin in 1929.

Like most of his age group, Blough held many academic and federal appointments, serving in the Treasury and other agencies. He also served in the United Nations and was advisor to various foreign governments. In the late 1950s he was on the faculty of Columbia University and was associated with the Ford Foundation.

ROBERT C. TURNER (1908–   ). CEA Member, 1952–53.

Like Blough, Turner had a long career intermixing federal service and academic appointments. He received the Ph.D. from Ohio State in 1937. On the faculty of Indiana University after the Second World War, he served in many federal agencies.

ARTHUR F. BURNS (1904–   ). CEA Chairman, 1953–56.

Burns is a native of Austria but was brought to the United States as a child. He obtained his Ph.D. from Columbia in 1934, taught at Rutgers and Columbia, and was closely associated with the National Bureau of Economic Research, rising to Director of Research. After serving as CEA Chairman, Burns returned to the National Bureau in 1956, but appeared in Washington again in 1969 as counselor to President Nixon. In 1971 he became chairman of the Board of Governors of the Federal Reserve System. Burns served as president of the American Economic Association in 1959.

NEIL H. JACOBY (1909–   ). CEA Member, 1953–55.

A Canadian, Jacoby obtained his Ph.D. in 1938 from the University of Chicago. He became dean of the graduate school of business at UCLA after a long career in both teaching and research. In 1972 Jacoby was a member of the Nixon Pay Board and served on the UCLA faculty.

WALTER W. STEWART (1885–1958). CEA Member, 1953–55.

Stewart had a long career as adviser and federal economist. Born in Kansas, he received a degree in economics from the University of Missouri in 1909. He was academician, investment banker, and first Director of Research for the Fed. At the time of his appointment, he was at the Institute for Advanced Study, at Princeton University.

RAYMOND J. SAULNIER (1908–   ). CEA Member, 1955–56; Chairman, 1956–61.

Saulnier was born in Massachusetts. In 1938 he received the Ph.D. from Columbia and, a long-time Columbia faculty member, spent his entire career there interlaced with frequent Washington service. Saulnier served on the staff of the Fed, U.S. Treasury, and other agencies. He was made a CEA staff member and rose to membership. Saulnier returned to Columbia in 1961, following his CEA term.

JOSEPH S. DAVIS (1885–   ). CEA Member, 1955–58.

Davis was born in Pennsylvania and obtained a Harvard Ph.D. degree in 1912. For many years he was at Stanford as director of the Food Research Institute and returned there after his CEA term.

PAUL W. McCRACKEN (1915–   ). CEA Member, 1956–59; Chairman, 1969–72.

McCracken served as a member in 1956–59 and returned as chairman in 1969, serving until 1972. An Iowa native, he holds a Ph.D. from Harvard granted in 1948. McCracken's career has been almost equally balanced between academic and federal service. In 1972 he returned to Ann Arbor to his chair as professor of business policy. He remained a frequent commentator on CEA affairs writing on a regular basis for the *Wall Street Journal*.

KARL BRANDT (1899–   ). CEA Member, 1958–61.

Brandt, like Davis, was a food expert and agricultural economist. A native of Germany and educated at the University of Berlin (Dr. Ag.), he immigrated to the United States in 1933. He served on the faculty of the New School for Social Research and at Stanford.

HENRY C. WALLICH (1914–   ). CEA Member, 1959–61.

Also a native of Germany, Wallich was born in Berlin, but received his higher education in the United States, receiving a Ph.D. from Harvard in 1944. Wallich, unlike most CEA members, has extensive background in finance and banking. He returned to Yale after his CEA term ended, but later was appointed to the Board of Governors of the Federal Reserve System.

JAMES TOBIN (1918–   ). CEA Member, 1961–62.

James Tobin was born in Champaign, Illinois, but emigrated eastward to obtain a Ph.D. from Harvard in 1947. During the Second World War, Tobin, like many of his generation, had extensive federal service in WPB, OPA, etc. He served on the Yale University faculty both before and after his CEA service. Tobin, a very distinguished academic economist, was winner of the Clark Medal and president of the American Economic Association in 1971.

KERMIT GORDON (1916–1976). CEA Member, 1961–62.

A rare bird among contemporary professional economists, Gordon has only the A.B. Degree (Swarthmore, 1938). However, he had done extensive graduate work, was a Rhodes Scholar, and held high-level academic posts. Gordon had extensive federal wartime service and was

Director of the Budget, 1962–65. In 1967 he became president of the Brookings Institution.

WALTER W. HELLER (1915–   ). CEA Chairman, 1961–64.

Heller was born in Buffalo, New York. His career has embraced both federal and academic service. After obtaining the Ph.D. from Wisconsin in 1941, he served in the Treasury and other agencies. He has been on the faculty of the University of Minnesota since 1946 and returned there after his CEA service. He continues active in CEA affairs and his views appear frequently in the press.

H. GARDNER ACKLEY (1915–   ). CEA Member, 1962–64; Chairman, 1964–68.

Ackley, like his associate Heller, was in the early stage of his career when the war agencies called. Serving in OPA, OSS, etc., he returned to the academic world and received his Ph.D. in 1947 from the University of Michigan. Ackley succeeded Heller in 1964 and served until 1968. After his CEA years, he returned to Michigan, after a short period as ambassador to Italy (1968–69).

JOHN P. LEWIS (1921–   ). CEA Member, 1963–64.

Lewis was born in Albany, New York, and received the Ph.D. from Harvard in 1950. Having served as CEA staff member, on the United Nations, and in various federal agencies, Lewis went to Indiana University in 1953. His post-Council service has included a United States AID mission and a senior fellowship at Brookings.

OTTO ECKSTEIN (1927–   ). CEA Member, 1964–66.

Another German-born economist, Eckstein served on both the JEC and CEA staffs. He received a Harvard Ph.D. in 1955. He organized and became president of a consulting firm in Cambridge—Data Resources, Inc.

ARTHUR M. OKUN (1928–   ). CEA Member, 1964–68; Chairman, 1968–69.

Okun was born in Jersey City, New Jersey. After being granted the Ph.D. from Columbia in 1956, he served on the Yale faculty and as a Cowles Commission staff member. In 1969 he joined the Brookings Institution as senior fellow.

JAMES S. DUESENBERRY (1918–   ). CEA Member, 1966–68.

Duesenberry received the Ph.D. from Michigan in 1948. A long-time Harvard faculty member, Duesenberry served on the Council from 1966 to 1968 and returned to Cambridge following his CEA term.

MERTON J. PECK (1925–   ). CEA Member, 1968–69.

Born in Cleveland, Ohio, Peck received a Harvard Ph.D. in 1954. A veteran of several academic appointments and federal study groups, he returned to academic life at Yale in 1969.

WARREN L. SMITH (1914–72). CEA Member, 1968–69.

Smith, a Michigan faculty member, served only a brief period on CEA. A native of Watertown, New York, Smith spent much of his career in Ann Arbor after obtaining his Michigan Ph.D. in 1949.

HERBERT STEIN (1916–   ). Member CEA, 1969–72; Chairman, 1972–74.

Stein, winner of the *Pabst Essay Contest on Postwar Planning* in 1944, was born in Detroit and obtained his Ph.D. from Chicago in 1958. Long a staff member of the Committee for Economic Development, where he rose to be Director of Research, Stein also served as a Brookings fellow. Later, he became Willis J. Robertson Professor of Economics at the University of Virginia.

HENRIK S. HOUTHAKKER (1924–   ). CEA Member, 1969–71.

Houthakker was born in Amsterdam in 1924 and educated at the University of Amsterdam, where he obtained the degree of doctor in economics in 1951. Houthakker came to the United States in the same year, where he became associated with the Cowles Commission and joined the Harvard faculty in 1960. He won the Clark Medal in 1963.

EZRA SOLOMON (1920 –   ). CEA Member, 1971–73.

A University of Chicago Ph.D., Solomon has served on the faculties of both Chicago and Stanford. At Stanford, Solomon served as Dean Whitter Professor of Finance.

MARINA von N. WHITMAN (1935–   ). CEA Member, 1972–73.

So far the only female member to be appointed and the daughter of the well-known economist John von Neuman, Mrs. Whitman was born in New York. She holds a Columbia Ph.D. (1961) and has been a member of the University of Pittsburgh faculty since 1963.

GARY L. SEEVERS (1937–   ). CEA Member, 1973–75.

One of the younger members of the Council, Seevers was promoted from staff to membership. A Michigan Ph.D., Seevers was on leave from Oregon State University.

WILLIAM J. FELLNER (1905–   ). CEA Member, 1973–75.

Unlike many CEA members, Fellner is essentially a theoretical economist. A Hungarian by birth, Fellner holds a Ph.D. from the University of Berlin. He came to CEA from Yale, where he has been Sterling Professor since 1959.

ALAN GREENSPAN (1926–). CEA Chairman, 1974–77.

Greenspan is the first CEA member to come from the ranks of business economists. Greenspan holds an M.A. from New York University and was president of Townsend-Greenspan & Co., a consulting firm located in New York.

PAUL W. MAC AVOY (1934–). CEA Member, 1975–77.

Mac Avoy was born in Haverhill, Mass., and holds a Ph.D. from the University of Chicago. He is on leave from Massachusetts Institute of Technology where he is Henry R. Luce Professor of Public Policy. Mac Avoy is a specialist in the economics of energy and public utility regulation.

BURTON MALKIEL (1932–). CEA Member, 1975–77.

Born in Boston, Malkiel holds a Princeton Ph.D. and is on leave from that institution where he is Gordon S. Rentschler Professor of Economics. Malkiel is a specialist in industrial structure and in finance.

APPENDIX C
JOINT ECONOMIC COMMITTEE
MEMBERSHIP, 1946–76
(79th through 94th Congress)

SEVENTY-NINTH CONGRESS (1946)

SENATE	HOUSE OF REPRESENTATIVES
Joseph C. O'Mahoney of Wyoming	Edward J. Hart of New Jersey
	Wright Patman of Texas
James M. Tunnell of Delaware	George E. Outland of California
Abe Murdock of Utah	Walter B. Huber of Ohio
Francis J. Myers of Pennsylvania	George H. Bender of Ohio
Robert A. Taft of Ohio	Walter H. Judd of Minnesota
Styles Bridges of New Hampshire	Robert F. Rich of Pennsylvania
Robert M. La Follette, Jr. of Wisconsin	

House Members were appointed on March 11, 1946, and Senate Members on July 2, 1946. No business was transacted in the 79th Congress. From the 79th through the 85th Congresses the majority party was represented by four Senators and four Representatives and the minority party by three Senators and three Representatives.

EIGHTIETH CONGRESS (1947– 48)

SENATE	HOUSE OF REPRESENTATIVES
Robert A. Taft of Ohio, *Chairman*	Jesse P. Wolcott of Michigan, *Vice Chairman*
Joseph H. Ball of Minnesota	
Ralph E. Flanders of Vermont	George H. Bender of Ohio
Arthur V. Watkins of Utah	Robert F. Rich of Pennsylvania
Joseph C. O'Mahoney of Wyoming	Christian A. Herter of Massachusetts
Francis J. Myers of Pennsylvania	Edward J. Hart of New Jersey
John Sparkman of Alabama	Wright Patman of Texas
	Walter B. Huber of Ohio

Representative Herter was appointed on April 17, 1947, to fill the vacancy created by the resignation of Walter H. Judd from the Joint Committee on the same date.

Note.—The following were appointed as temporary members of the Joint Economic Committee to assist in the hearings on high prices of consumer goods pursuant to Senate Concurrent Resolution 19, agreed to July 26, 1947:

Eastern Subcommittee:
  Senator Raymond E. Baldwin of Connecticut
  Representative Clarence E. Kilburn of New York
Mid-Continent Subcommittee:
  Senator James P. Kem of Missouri
  Representative Henry O. Talle of Iowa
Western Subcommittee:
  Senator Zales N. Ecton of Montana
  Representative Walt Horan of Washington
  Representative Norris Poulson of California

EIGHTY-FIRST CONGRESS (1949–50)

SENATE	HOUSE OF REPRESENTATIVES
Joseph C. O'Mahoney of Wyoming, *Chairman*	Edward J. Hart of New Jersey, *Vice Chairman*
Francis J. Myers of Pennsylvania	Wright Patman of Texas
	Walter B. Huber of Ohio
John Sparkman of Alabama	Frank Buchanan of Pennsylvania
Paul H. Douglas of Illinois	
Robert A. Taft of Ohio	Jesse P. Wolcott of Michigan
Ralph E. Flanders of Vermont	Christian A. Herter of Massachusetts

Arthur V. Watkins of Utah

Robert F. Rich of
Pennsylvania

EIGHTY-SECOND CONGRESS (1951–52)

SENATE	HOUSE OF REPRESENTATIVES
Joseph C. O'Mahoney of Wyoming, *Chairman*	Edward J. Hart of New Jersey, *Vice Chairman*
John Sparkman of Alabama	Wright Patman of Texas
Paul H. Douglas of Illinois	Richard Bolling of Missouri
William Benton of Connecticut	Clinton D. McKinnon of California
Robert A. Taft of Ohio	Jesse P. Wolcott of Michigan
Ralph E. Flanders of Vermont	Christian A. Herter of Massachusetts
Arthur V. Watkins of Utah	J. Caleb Boggs of Delaware

Representative McKinnon was appointed on June 3, 1951, to fill the vacancy created by the death of Frank Buchanan, April 27, 1951.

EIGHTY-THIRD CONGRESS (1953–54)

HOUSE OF REPRESENTATIVES	SENATE
Jesse P. Wolcott of Michigan, *Chairman*	Ralph E. Flanders of Vermont, *Vice Chairman*
Richard M. Simpson of Pennsylvania	Arthur V. Watkins of Utah
Henry O. Talle of Iowa	Barry R. Goldwater of Arizona
George H. Bender of Ohio	Frank Carlson of Kansas
Edward J. Hart of New Jersey	John Sparkman of Alabama
Wright Patman of Texas	Paul H. Douglas of Illinois
Richard Bolling of Missouri	J. W. Fulbright of Arkansas

Senator Carlson was appointed September 29, 1953, to the existing vacancy due to the death of Senator Taft, July 31, 1953.

EIGHTY-FOURTH CONGRESS (1955–56)

SENATE	HOUSE OF REPRESENTATIVES
Paul H. Douglas of Illinois, *Chairman*	Wright Patman of Texas, *Vice Chairman*
John Sparkman of Alabama	Richard Bolling of Missouri
J. W. Fulbright of Arkansas	Wilbur D. Mills of Arkansas
Joseph C. O'Mahoney of Wyoming	Augustine B. Kelley of Pennsylvania
Ralph E. Flanders of Vermont	Jesse P. Wolcott of Michigan
Arthur V. Watkins of Utah	Henry O. Talle of Iowa
Barry Goldwater of Arizona	Thomas B. Curtis of Missouri

EIGHTY-FIFTH CONGRESS (1957–58)

HOUSE OF REPRESENTATIVES	SENATE
Wright Patman of Texas, *Chairman*	John Sparkman of Alabama, *Vice Chairman*
Richard Bolling of Missouri	Paul H. Douglas of Illinois
Hale Boggs of Louisiana	J. W. Fulbright of Arkansas
Henry S. Reuss of Wisconsin	Joseph C. O'Mahoney
Henry O. Talle of Iowa	of Wyoming
Thomas B. Curtis of Missouri	Ralph E. Flanders of Vermont
Clarence E. Kilburn of New York	Arthur V. Watkins of Utah
	John D. Hoblitzell, Jr. of West Virginia

Representative Boggs was appointed on January 27, 1958, to fill the vacancy created by the death of Augustine B. Kelley, November 29, 1957.

Representative Reuss was appointed on February 17, 1958, to fill the vacancy created by the resignation of Wilbur D. Mills from the joint committee on January 27, 1958.

Senator Hoblitzell was appointed on March 20, 1958, to fill the vacancy created by the resignation of Barry Goldwater from the joint committee on the same date.

EIGHTY-SIXTH CONGRESS (1959–60)

SENATE	HOUSE OF REPRESENTATIVES
Paul H. Douglas of Illinois, *Chairman*	Wright Patman of Texas, *Vice Chairman*
John Sparkman of Alabama	Richard Bolling of Missouri
J. W. Fulbright of Arkansas	Hale Boggs of Louisiana
Joseph C. O'Mahoney of Wyoming	Henry S. Reuss of Wisconsin
John F. Kennedy of Massachusetts	Frank M. Coffin of Maine
	Thomas B. Curtis of Missouri
Prescott Bush of Connecticut	Clarence E. Kilburn of New York
John Marshall Butler of Maryland	William B. Widnall of New Jersey
Jacob K. Javits of New York	

Representative Coffin was appointed on February 18, 1959, and Senator Kennedy on March 19, 1959, under the provisions of Public Law 86–1, approved February 17, 1959, which increased the membership of the joint committee from 14 to 16.

Appendix C

EIGHTY-SEVENTH CONGRESS (1961–62)

HOUSE OF REPRESENTATIVES

Wright Patman of Texas,
Chairman
Richard Bolling of Missouri
Hale Boggs of Louisiana
Henry S. Reuss of Wisconsin
Martha W. Griffiths of Michigan
Thomas B. Curtis of Missouri
Clarence E. Kilburn of
New York
William B. Widnall of
New Jersey

SENATE

Paul H. Douglas of Illinois,
Vice Chairman
John Sparkman of Alabama
J. W. Fulbright of Arkansas
William Proxmire of
Wisconsin
Claiborne Pell of
Rhode Island
Prescott Bush of Connecticut
John Marshall Butler of
Maryland
Jacob K. Javits of New York

EIGHTY-EIGHTH CONGRESS (1963–64)

SENATE

Paul H. Douglas of Illinois,
Chairman
John Sparkman of Alabama
J. W. Fulbright of Arkansas
William Proxmire of
Wisconsin
Claiborne Pell of
Rhode Island
Jacob K. Javits of New York
Jack Miller of Iowa
Len B. Jordan of Idaho

HOUSE OF REPRESENTATIVES

Richard Bolling of Missouri,
Vice Chairman
Wright Patman of Texas
Hale Boggs of Louisiana
Henry S. Reuss of Wisconsin
Martha W. Griffiths of
Michigan
Thomas B. Curtis of Missouri
Clarence E. Kilburn of
New York
William B. Widnall of
New Jersey

EIGHTY-NINTH CONGRESS (1965–66)

WRIGHT PATMAN, Texas, *Chairman*

PAUL H. DOUGLAS, Illinois, *Vice Chairman*

HOUSE OF REPRESENTATIVES

Richard Bolling, Missouri
Hale Boggs, Louisiana
Henry S. Reuss, Wisconsin
Martha W. Griffiths,
Michigan
Thomas B. Curtis, Missouri
William B. Widnall,
New Jersey
Robert F. Ellsworth, Kansas

SENATE

John Sparkman, Alabama
J. W. Fulbright, Arkansas
William Proxmire, Wisconsin
Herman E. Talmadge,
Georgia
Jacob K. Javits, New York
Jack Miller, Iowa
Len B. Jordan, Idaho

APPENDIX C

NINETIETH CONGRESS
JOINT ECONOMIC COMMITTEE (1967–68)
WILLIAM PROXMIRE, Wisconsin, *Chairman*
WRIGHT PATMAN, Texas, *Vice Chairman*

SENATE	HOUSE OF REPRESENTATIVES
John Sparkman, Alabama	Richard Bolling, Missouri
J. W. Fulbright, Arkansas	Hale Boggs, Louisiana
Herman E. Talmadge, Georgia	Henry S. Reuss, Wisconsin
Stuart Symington, Missouri	Martha W. Griffiths, Michigan
Abraham Ribicoff, Connecticut	William S. Moorhead,
Jacob K. Javits, New York	Pennsylvania
Jack Miller, Iowa	Thomas B. Curtis, Missouri
Len B. Jordan, Idaho	William B. Widnall, New Jersey
Charles H. Percy, Illinois	Donald Rumsfeld, Illinois
	W. E. Brock 3d, Tennessee

NINETY-FIRST CONGRESS
JOINT ECONOMIC COMMITTEE (1969–70)
[Created pursuant to sec. 5(a) of Public Law 304, 79th Cong.]

WRIGHT PATMAN, Texas, *Chairman*
WILLIAM PROXMIRE, Wisconsin, *Vice Chairman*

HOUSE OF REPRESENTATIVES	SENATE
Richard Bolling, Missouri	John Sparkman, Alabama
Hale Boggs, Louisiana	J. W. Fulbright, Arkansas
Henry S. Reuss, Wisconsin	Herman E. Talmadge, Georgia
Martha W. Griffiths, Michigan	Stuart Symington, Missouri
William S. Moorhead,	Abraham Ribicoff, Connecticut
Pennsylvania	Jacob K. Javits, New York
William B. Widnall, New Jersey	Jack Miller, Iowa
W. E. Brock III, Tennessee	Len B. Jordan, Idaho
Barber B. Conable, Jr., New York	Charles H. Percy, Illinois
Clarence J. Brown, Ohio

NINETY-SECOND CONGRESS (1971–72)
JOINT ECONOMIC COMMITTEE
WILLIAM PROXMIRE, Wisconsin, *Chairman*
WRIGHT PATMAN, Texas, *Vice Chairman*

SENATE	HOUSE OF REPRESENTATIVES
John Sparkman, Alabama	Richard Bolling, Missouri
J. W. Fulbright, Arkansas	Hale Boggs, Louisiana
Abraham Ribicoff, Connecticut	Henry S. Reuss, Wisconsin
Hubert H. Humphrey, Minnesota	Martha W. Griffiths, Michigan
Lloyd M. Bentsen, Jr., Texas	William S. Moorhead,
Jacob K. Javits, New York	Pennsylvania

Jack Miller, Iowa
Charles H. Percy, Illinois
James B. Pearson, Kansas

William B. Widnall, New Jersey
Barber B. Conable, Jr., New York
Clarence J. Brown, Ohio
Ben B. Blackburn, Georgia

NINETY-THIRD CONGRESS (1973–74)
JOINT ECONOMIC COMMITTEE
WRIGHT PATMAN, Texas, *Chairman*

WILLIAM PROXMIRE, Wisconsin, *Vice Chairman*

SENATE	HOUSE OF REPRESENTATIVES
John Sparkman, Alabama	Richard Bolling, Missouri
J. W. Fulbright, Arkansas	Henry S. Reuss, Wisconsin
Abraham Ribicoff, Connecticut	Martha W. Griffiths, Michigan
Hubert H. Humphrey, Minnesota	William S. Moorhead,
Lloyd M. Bentsen, Jr., Texas	Pennsylvania
Jacob K. Javits, New York	Hugh L. Cary, New York
Charles H. Percy, Illinois	William B. Widnall, New Jersey
James B. Pearson, Kansas	Barber B. Conable, Jr., New York
Richard S. Schweiker,	Clarence J. Brown, Ohio
Pennsylvania	Ben B. Blackburn, Georgia

NINETY-FOURTH CONGRESS (1975–76)
JOINT ECONOMIC COMMITTEE
HUBERT H. HUMPHREY, Minnesota, *Chairman*

WRIGHT PATMAN, Texas, *Vice Chairman*

SENATE	HOUSE OF REPRESENTATIVES
John Sparkman, Alabama	Richard Bolling, Missouri
William Proxmire, Wisconsin	Henry S. Reuss, Wisconsin
Abraham Ribicoff, Connecticut	William S. Moorhead,
Lloyd Bentsen, Texas	Pennsylvania
Edward Kennedy, Massachusetts	Lee H. Hamilton, Indiana
Jacob Javits, New York	Gillis W. Long, Louisiana
Charles H. Percy, Illinois	Clarence J. Brown, Jr., Ohio
Robert Taft, Jr., Ohio	Garry Brown, Michigan
Paul J. Fannin, Arizona	Margaret M. Heckler,
	Massachusetts
	John H. Rousselot, California

307

EMPLOYMENT ACT OF 1946, AS AMENDED, WITH RELATED LAWS
(60 Stat. 23)

[PUBLIC LAW 304—79TH CONGRESS]

AN ACT To declare a national policy on employment, production, and purchasing power, and for other purposes.

Be it enacted by the Senate and House of Representatives of the United States of America in Congress assembled,

SHORT TITLE

SECTION 1. This Act may be cited as the "Employment Act of 1946".

DECLARATION OF POLICY

SEC. 2. The Congress hereby declares that it is the continuing policy and responsibility of the Federal Government to use all practicable means consistent with its needs and obligations and other essential considerations of national policy, with the assistance and cooperation of industry, agriculture, labor, and State and local governments, to coordinate and utilize all its plans, functions, and resources for the purpose of creating and maintaining, in a manner calculated to foster and promote free competitive enterprise and the general welfare, conditions under which there will be afforded useful employment opportunities, including self-employment, for those able, willing, and seeking to work, and to promote maximum employment, production, and purchasing power. (15 U.S.C. 1021.)

ECONOMIC REPORT OF THE PRESIDENT

SEC. 3. (a) The President shall transmit to the Congress not later than January 20[1] of each year an economic report (hereinafter called the "Economic Report") setting forth (1) the levels of employment, production, and purchasing power obtaining in the United States and such levels needed to carry out the policy declared in section 2; (2) current and foreseeable trends in the levels of employment, production, and purchasing power; (3) a review of the economic program of the Federal Government and a review of economic conditions affecting employment in the United States or any considerable portion thereof during the preceding year and of their effect upon employment, production, and purchasing power; and (4) a program for carrying out the policy declared in section 2, together with such recommendations for legislation as he may deem necessary or desirable.

(b) The President may transmit from time to time to the Congress reports supplementary to the Economic Report, each of which shall include such supplementary or revised recommendations as he may deem necessary or desirable to achieve the policy declared in section 2.

(c) The Economic Report, and all supplementary reports transmitted under subsection (b) of this section, shall, when transmitted to Congress, be referred to the joint committee created by section 5. (15 U.S.C. 1022.)

HISTORICAL NOTE

1956 Amendment.—Subsection (a) amended by Public Law 591, 84th Congress, 2d session, cited to text, by striking out "at the beginning of each regular session (commencing with the year 1947)."

COUNCIL OF ECONOMIC ADVISERS TO THE PRESIDENT

SEC. 4. (a) There is hereby created in the Executive Office of the President a Council of Economic Advisers (hereinafter called the "Council"). The Council shall be composed of three members who shall be appointed by the President, by and with the advice and consent of the Senate, and each of whom shall be a person who, as a result of his training, experience, and attainments is exceptionally qualified to analyze and interpret economic developments, to appraise programs and activities of the Government in the light of the policy declared in section 2, and to formulate and recommend national economic policy to promote employment, production, and purchasing power under free competitive enterprise. The President shall designate one of the members of the Council as Chairman.[2]

(b) The Council is authorized to employ, and fix the compensation of, such specialists and other experts as may be necessary for the carrying out of its functions under this Act, without regard to the civil service laws and the Classification Act of 1949,[3] as amended, and is authorized, subject to the civil service laws, to employ such other officers and employees as may be necessary for carrying out its functions under this

---

[1] In the original Act, before amendments, this read: "within sixty days after the beginning of each regular session (commencing with the year 1947)". This was changed to "at the beginning of each regular session" in the Legislative Reorganization Act of 1946, Public Law 601, 79th Congress, 1st session.

[2] The original Act, before amendments, read: "The President shall designate one of the members of the Council as chairman and one as vice chairman, who shall act as chairman in the absence of the chairman."

[3] Originally Classification Act of 1923. This act was completely rewritten in 1949.

Act, and fix their compensation in accordance with the Classification Act of 1949, as amended.

(c) It shall be the duty and function of the Council—

(1) to assist and advise the President in the preparation of the Economic Report;

(2) to gather timely and authoritative information concerning economic developments and economic trends, both current and prospective, to analyze and interpret such information in the light of the policy declared in section 2 for the purpose of determining whether such developments and trends are interfering, or are likely to interfere, with the achievement of such policy, and to compile and submit to the President studies relating to such developments and trends;

(3) to appraise the various programs and activities of the Federal Government in the light of the policy declared in section 2 for the purpose of determining the extent to which such programs and activities are contributing, and the extent to which they are not contributing, to the achievement of such policy and to make recommendations to the President with respect thereto;

(4) to develop and recommend to the President national economic policies to foster and promote free competitive enterprise, to avoid economic fluctuations or to diminish the effects thereof, and to maintain employment, production, and purchasing power;

(5) to make and furnish such studies, reports thereon, and recommendations with respect to matters of Federal economic policy and legislation as the President may request.

(d) The Council shall make an annual report to the President in December of each year.

(e) In exercising its powers, functions, and duties under this Act—

(1) the Council may constitute such advisory committees and may consult with such representatives of industry, agriculture, labor, consumers, State and local governments, and other groups as it deems advisable;

(2) the Council shall, to the fullest extent possible, utilize the services, facilities, and information (including statistical information) of other Government agencies as well as of private research agencies, in order that duplication of effort and expense may be avoided.

(f) To enable the Council to exercise its powers, functions, and duties under this Act, there are authorized to be appropriated such sums as may be necessary. (15 U.S.C. 1023.)

310

Appendix D

HISTORICAL NOTE

1961 Amendment.—Subsection (f) amended by Public Law 87– 49 cited to text, by striking out "To enable the Council to exercise its powers, functions, and duties under this Act, there are authorized to be appropriated (except for the salaries of the members and the salaries of officers and employees of the Council) such sums as may be necessary. For the salaries of the members and the salaries of officers and employees of the Council, there is authorized to be appropriated not exceeding $345,000 in the aggregate for each fiscal year."

JOINT ECONOMIC COMMITTEE

SEC 5. (a) There is hereby established a Joint Economic Committee, to be composed of eight Members of the Senate, to be appointed by the President of the Senate, and eight Members of the House of Representatives, to be appointed by the Speaker of the House of Representatives. In each case, the majority party shall be represented by five members and the minority party shall be represented by three members.

(b) It shall be the function of the joint committee—

(1) to make a continuing study of matters relating to the Economic Report;

(2) to study means of coordinating programs in order to further the policy of this Act; and

(3) as a guide to the several committees of the Congress dealing with legislation relating to the Economic Report, not later than March 1,[4] of each year (beginning with the year 1947) to file a report with the Senate and the House of Representatives containing its findings and recommendations with respect to each of the main recommendations made by the President in the Economic Report, and from time to time to make such other reports and recommendations to the Senate and House of Representatives as it deems advisable.

(c) Vacancies in the membership of the joint committee shall not affect the power of the remaining members to execute the functions of the joint committee, and shall be filled in the same manner as in the case of the original selection. The joint committee shall select a chairman and a vice chairman from among its members.

(d) The joint committee, or any duly authorized subcommittee thereof, is authorized to hold such hearings as it deems advisable, and, within the limitations of its appropriations, the joint committee is empowered to appoint and fix the compensation of such experts, consul-

---

[4] In the original act, before amendments, this read: "May 1." This was changed to "February 1" in the Legislative Reorganization Act of 1946, and subsequently to "March 1" in Public Law 405, 80th Cong., 2d sess.

tants, technicians, and clerical and stenographic assistants, to procure such printing and binding, and to make such expenditures, as it deems necessary and advisable. [The cost of stenographic services to report hearings of the joint committee, or any subcommittee thereof, shall not exceed 25 cents per hundred words.][5] The joint committee is authorized to utilize the services, information, and facilities of the departments and establishments of the Government, and also of private research agencies.

(e) To enable the joint committee to exercise its powers, functions, and duties under this Act, there are authorized to be appropriated for each fiscal year such sums as may be necessary, to be disbursed by the Secretary of the Senate on vouchers signed by the chairman or vice chairman.

(f)[6] Service of one individual, until the completion of the investigation authorized by Senate Concurrent Resolution 26, 81st Congress, as an attorney or expert for the joint committee, in any business or professional field, on a part-time basis, with or without compensation, shall not be considered as service or employment bringing such individual within the provisions of sections 281, 283, or 284 of title 18 of the United States Code, or of any other Federal Law imposing restrictions, requirements, or penalties in relation to the employment of persons, the performance of services, or the payment or receipt of compensation in connection with any claim, proceeding, or matter involving the United States. (15 U.S.C. 1024.)

HISTORICAL NOTE

1956 Amendment.—Section 5 (a) of such Act and the heading thereof are each amended by striking out "Joint Committee on the Economic Report" and inserting in lieu thereof "Joint Economic Committee"; and any other statute in which the name "Joint Committee on the Economic Report" appears is amended to conform to the foregoing change in the name of the Joint Committee. (60 Stat. 25; 15 U.S.C. 1024) Public Law 591, 84th Congress, 2d session.

1959 Amendment.—Section 5 (a) amended by Public Law 86–1, February 17, 1959, cited to text. The original Act provided that "The party representation on the joint committee shall as nearly as may be feasible reflect the relative membership of the majority and

---

[5] Amended by Public Law 624 (84th Cong., 2d sess.) as follows: "Compensation for stenographic assistance of committees paid out of the foregoing items under 'Contingent expenses of the Senate' hereafter shall be computed at such rates and in accordance with such regulations as may be prescribed by the Committee on Rules and Administration, notwithstanding, and without regard to any other provision of law." (70 Stat. 360.)

[6] This subsection no longer in effect.

minority parties in the Senate and House of Representatives", and be composed of seven Members of the Senate and seven Members of the House of Representatives.

1964 Amendment.—Section 5 (e) amended by Public Law 88–661, October 13, 1964, cited to text. In the original Act, before amendments, the appropriation authorization was $50,000. This was changed to $125,000 in Public Law 330, 81st Congress, 1st session, October 6, 1949.

JOINT RESOLUTION OF JUNE 23, 1949

The Joint Economic Committee is authorized to issue a monthly publication entitled "Economic Indicators," and a sufficient quantity shall be printed to furnish one copy to each Member of Congress; the Secretary and the Sergeant at Arms of the Senate; the Clerk, Sergeant at Arms, and Doorkeeper of the House of Representatives; two copies to the libraries of the Senate and House, and the Congressional Library; seven hundred copies to the Joint Economic Committee; and the required number of copies to the Superintendent of Documents for distribution to depository libraries; and the Superintendent of Documents is authorized to have copies printed for sale to the public. (15 U.S.C. 1025.)

REORGANIZATION PLAN NO. 9 OF 1953

(Prepared by the President and transmitted to the Senate and the House of Representatives in Congress assembled, June 1, 1953, pursuant to the provisions of the Reorganization Act of 1949, as amended)

COUNCIL OF ECONOMIC ADVISERS

The functions vested in the Council of Economic Advisers by section 4(b) of the Employment Act of 1946 (60 Stat. 24), and so much of the functions vested in the Council by section 4(c) of that Act as consists of reporting to the President with respect to any function of the Council under the said section 4(c), are hereby transferred to the Chairman of the Council of Economic Advisers. The position of Vice Chairman of the Council of Economic Advisers, provided for in the last sentence of section 4(a) of the said Act, is hereby abolished.

The basic strategy of those favoring the passage of S-380 (and its identical companion in the House, HR-2202) was to secure widespread bipartisan backing. The increasingly conservative attitude in the Congress as the postwar era began made this especially important, and the real battle proved to be in the House, much less liberal than the Senate.

SENATE

Although there were several cosponsors of S-380, four Senators, all Democrats, were instrumental, due either to their interest in the legislation or their overall influence and prestige in the Senate: James E. Murray, Montana; Robert F. Wagner, New York; Elbert Thomas, Utah; and Joseph C. O'Mahoney, Wyoming.

Though less involved, the leading Republican, the late Robert A. Taft, Sr., of Ohio, lent his general support, a factor of considerable influence in view of the desire for bipartisan involvement. Other Republican cosponsors were Wayne Morse, Oregon; William Langer, North Dakota; George Aiken, Vermont; and Charles W. Tobey, New Hampshire. Morse and Langer were special cases. Morse later switched to the status of "independent," and later still became a Democrat. Langer, though a Republican, was unorthodox and unpredictable, usually voting with liberals.

The final vote was 71 to 10 for approval. Those voting nay were: C. Douglas Buck (R), Delaware; Harry F. Byrd, Sr. (D), Virginia; Peter G. Gerry (D), Rhode Island; Chan Gurney (R), South Dakota; John McClellan (D), Arkansas; Eugene D. Millikan (R), Colorado; E. .H. Moore (R), Oklahoma; Lee O'Daniel (D), Texas; Edward V. Robertson (R), Wyoming; Kenneth Wherry (R), Nebraska.

HOUSE

Despite the large number of cosponsors, the prospects for easy passage in the House were not nearly so bright. There were 116 cosponsors of HR-2202 of which the most important were Wright Patman (D), Texas; George Outland (D), California; John J. Cochran (D), Missouri; Mike Mansfield (D), Montana; and Henry M. Jackson (D), Washington.

House Cosponsors of HR-2202*

STATE Congressman	Party	District
ALABAMA		
Luther Patrick	D	9

Appendix E

ARIZONA
| Richard Harless | D | A.L. |
| John R. Murdock | D | A.L. |

CALIFORNIA
Helen G. Douglas	D	14
Clyde Doyle	D	18
Frank R. Havenner	D	4
Ned R. Healy	D	13
Chet Holifield	D	19
Ed V. Izac	D	23
Clair Engle	D	2
Cecil R. King	D	17
Gordon McDonough	R	15
George P. Miller	D	6
George E. Outland	D	11
E. E. Patterson	D	16
H. R. Sheppard	D	21
J. H. Tolan	D	7
Jerry Voorhis	D	12
Richard J. Welch	R	5

CONNECTICUT
James P. Geelan	D	3
H. P. Kopplemann	D	1
Clare Booth Luce	R	4
Joseph F. Ryter	D	A.L.
Chase Going Woodhouse	D	2

DELAWARE
| Philip A. Traynor | D | A.L. |

ILLINOIS
Emily Taft Douglas	D	A.L.
William L. Dawson	D	1
Thomas S. Gordan	D	8
Martin Gorski	D	4
Edward A. Kelly	D	3
William A. Link	D	7
Thomas J. O'Brien	D	6
Melvin Price	D	22
Alexander J. Resa	D	9
William A. Rowan	D	2
Adolph J. Sabath	D	5

INDIANA
| Ray J. Madden | D | 1 |

315

KENTUCKY
Joe B. Bates	D	8
Earle C. Clements	D	2

MASSACHUSETTS
Thomas J. Lane	D	7

MICHIGAN
John Lesinski	D	16
John D. Dingell	D	15
Frank E. Hook	D	12
George D. O'Brien	D	13
Louis C. Rabaut	D	14
George G. Sadowski	D	1

MINNESOTA
William J. Gallagher	D	3
Frank T. Starkey	D	4

MISSOURI
A. S. J. Carnahan	D	8
John J. Cochran	D	13
John B. Sullivan	D	11

MONTANA
Mike Mansfield	D	1

NEVADA
Berkeley L. Bunker	D	A.L.

NEW JERSEY
Edward J. Hart	D	14
Mary T. Norton	D	13
Charles A. Wolverton	R	1

NEW YORK
Joseph Clark Baldwin	R	17
William B. Barry	D	4
Charles A. Buckley	D	25
William T. Byrne	D	32
Emanuel Cellar	D	15
James J. Delaney	D	6
Samuel Dickstein	D	19
Walter A. Lynch	D	23
Vito Marcantonio	American Labor Party	18
Joseph L. Pfeffer	D	8
Adam C. Powell	D	22
Peter A. Quinn	D	26
Leo F. Rayfiel	D	14
George F. Rogers	D	40
John J. Roomey	D	12

James H. Torrens	D	21
OHIO		
George H. Bender	R	A.L.
Walter E. Brehm	R	11
Edward J. Gardner	D	3
Walter B. Huber	D	14
Michael Kirwan	D	19
Homer A. Ramey	R	9
William R. Thom	D	16
Michael A. Feighan	D	20
OKLAHOMA		
William G. Stigler	D	2
Victor Wickersham	D	7
OREGON		
Homer D. Angell	R	3
PENNSYLVANIA		
William A. Barrett	D	1
Michael J. Bradley	D	3
Herman P. Eberharter	D	32
Daniel J. Flood	D	11
William T. Granahan	D	2
William J. Green, Jr.	D	5
Daniel K. Hoch	D	13
Augustine B. Kelley	D	27
Herbert J. McGlinchey	D	6
Thomas E. Morgan	D	24
John W. Murphy	D	10
Samuel A. Weiss	D	14
RHODE ISLAND		
John E. Fogarty	D	2
Aime J. Forand	D	1
TENNESSEE		
Albert Gore	D	4
Estes Kefauver	D	3
J. Percy Priest	D	6
TEXAS		
J. M. Combs	D	2
Wright Patman	D	1
UTAH		
Walter K. Granger	D	1
J. W. Robinson	D	2
VIRGINIA		
John W. Flannagan	D	3

317

WASHINGTON		
John M. Coffee	D	6
Hugh De Lacy	D	1
Henry M. Jackson	D	2
Charles R. Savage	D	3
WEST VIRGINIA		
Cleveland M. Bailey	D	3
E. H. Hedrick	D	6
John West Key	D	5
Matthew M. Neeley	D	1
Jennings Randolph	R	2
WISCONSIN		
Andrew J. Biemiller	D	5
Alvin E. O'Konski	R	10

* Source: *Congressional Record* 79th Congress., 1st Session, February 15, 1945.

The vote in the House was 126 for and 225 opposed; however, it was agreed that this was not a true reflection of opinion since there was considerable confusion. The bill had been amended on the floor to the point that some who were in favor of the concept voted against the bill believing it to be worthless as it stood, others voted for it merely as a symbol. Certainly, the number who were opposed to the basic bill were in the minority. As a result of its failure to pass, the bill went to a conference committee consisting of the following:

SENATORS

C. Douglas Buck (R) Delaware
George Radcliffe (D) Maryland
Robert A. Taft (R) Ohio
Glenn H. Taylor (D) Idaho
Alben Barkley (D) Kentucky
Abe Murdock (D) Utah
Charles W. Tobey (R) New Hampshire

REPRESENTATIVES

Clare Hoffman (R) Michigan
Carter Manasco (D) Alabama
William Whittington (D) Alabama
John J. Cochran (D) Missouri
George H. Bender (R) Ohio

The conference committee was a badly split group. Buck, Radcliffe, Hoffman, and Manasco were outspoken opponents of the legislation,

318

while Taylor, Tobey, and Cochran were strongly in favor. The resulting product was skillfully redrafted by Bertram Gross, who had drafted the original bills, and passed by the House on February 8, 1946, by a wide margin (230 to 84). Two days later, the conference bill passed the Senate (71 to 10) and was signed by the President on February 20. Three decades later only McClellan, and Jackson were still in Congress. Senator Buck of Delaware was defeated at the next election, and many observers attributed his fall to his vote on S-380. Radcliffe was defeated in the 1946 primaries, Manasco and Murdock were defeated in the 1948 primaries. Their defeat was not clearly linked to the legislation. Cochran resigned in 1946 due to failing health.

Nay votes on the Conference Bill (S-380) in the House, February 6, 1946*

STATE Congressman	Party	District
ARKANSAS		
E. C. Gathings	D	1
W. F. Norrell	D	6
CALIFORNIA		
John Phillips	R	22
GEORGIA		
John S. Gibson	D	8
John S. Wood	D	9
ILLINOIS		
Leo E. Allen	R	13
Leslie C. Arends	R	17
C. W. Bishop	R	25
Ralph E. Church	R	10
Noah M. Mason	R	12
Jessie Sumner	R	18
INDIANA		
Charles A. Halleck	R	2
IOWA		
James I. Dolliver	R	6
John W. Gwynne	R	3
Charles B. Hoeven	R	8
Ben F. Jensen	R	7
Karl M. LeCompte	R	4
Thomas E. Martin	R	1
Henry O. Talle	R	2

KANSAS

Frank Carlson	R	6
Clifford R. Hope	R	5
Errett P. Scrivner	R	2
Thomas W. Winter	R	3

KENTUCKY

Andrew J. May	D	7

LOUISIANA

Paul H. Maloney	D	2

MAINE

Frank Fellows	R	3
Robert Hale	R	1

MARYLAND

Dudley G. Roe	D	1

MASSACHUSETTS

Angier L. Goodwin	R	8
Pere C. Holmes	R	4

MICHIGAN

Fred L. Crawford	R	8
George A. Dondero	R	17
Clare E. Hoffman	R	4
Bartel J. Jonkman	R	5
Paul W. Shafer	R	3
Roy O. Woodruff	R	10

MINNESOTA

H. Carl Andresen	R	7
Harold Knutsen	R	6

MISSISSIPPI

Thomas G. Abernethy	D	4
Dan R. McGehee	D	7
John E. Rankin	D	1
Jamie L. Whitten	D	2
Arthur Winstead	D	5

MISSOURI

Walter C. Ploeser	R	12
Max Schwabe	R	2
Dewey Short	R	7

NEBRASKA

Howard H. Buffett	R	2
Carl T. Curtis	R	1
A. L. Miller	R	4
Karl Stefan	R	3

NEW YORK
Ralph W. Gwinn	R	27
Clarence E. Hancock	R	36
Jay LeFevre	R	30
John Taber	R	38

OHIO
Clarence J. Brown	R	7
Cliff Clevenger	R	5
Charles H. Elston	R	1
Thomas A. Jenkins	R	10
Robert F. Jones	R	4
Frederick C. Smith	R	8

OKLAHOMA
Ross Rizley	R	8
George B. Schwabe	R	1

OREGON
Harris Ellsworth	R	4
Lowell Stockman	R	2

PENNSYLVANIA
Leon H. Gavin	R	19
William D. Gillette	R	14
Louis E. Graham	R	25
Chester H. Gross	R	21
J. Roland Kinzer	R	9
John C. Kunkel	R	18
Samuel K. McConnell Jr.	R	16
Robert F. Rich	R	15
Robert L. Rodgers	R	28
Richard M. Simpson	R	17

TENNESSEE
Clifford Davis	D	10
John Jennings Jr.	R	2
B. Carroll Reece	R	1

TEXAS
Paul J. Kilday	D	20
Fritz G. Lanham	D	12
Tom Pickett	D	7
Milton H. West	D	15

WEST VIRGINIA
Hubert S. Ellis	R	4

WISCONSIN
John W. Byrnes	R	8
Lawrence H. Smith	R	1

* Source: *Congressional Record*, 79th Congress, Second Session, February 6, 1946.

Proposals for Changing the Employment Act

For an act in force for thirty years, the Employment Act has been surprisingly durable. Few suggestions for change have been made and fewer still have been enacted.

In 1949, the Hoover Commission recommendations for administrative change were made (lodging more authority in the Chairman), but not changing the act in any basic way.

From time to time, suggestions have been made for incorporating the goal of "reasonable price stability" into the act. So far this proposal has been successfully opposed by organized labor.

In 1966 amid the wage-price guidepost difficulties, Representative Henry S. Reuss proposed that the guideposts be codified and that the CEA would be required to transmit them each January 20th to the Joint Economic Committee for approval. The CEA figures would remain in effect unless Congress changed them. There was also at this time some consideration of some permanent type of wage-price agency. Neither idea survived.

In the early part of Nixon's second term, his domestic counsel, John Erlichman, suggested an executive branch reorganization which would create several "super cabinet" posts, including one devoted to economics. This proposal was lost in "Watergate," but apparently it would have interposed a layer of authority between CEA and the President.

In the 94th Congress, Senator Hubert H. Humphrey and Congressman Augustus Hawkins introduced legislation to define unemployment at 3 percent of the labor force and to provide public jobs for those unable to obtain private employment. This proposal had made no progress by mid-1976.

Bibliographic Note

The amount and quality of material concerning economic policy in the various administrations differs widely. The Roosevelt years are by far the most extensively covered. Due no doubt in part to its length and the number of people involved, almost every facet of the administration and all aspects of FDR's personality have been intensively examined.

While many of these works are superficial, they often contain fragments of historical information otherwise overlooked. Schlesinger's monumental *Age of Roosevelt* is the most readable and comprehensive source of information on the period just prior to and during the New Deal. Rosenman's *Working with Roosevelt* and Tugwell's *The Brains Trust* and *The Democratic Roosevelt* are especially valuable to the economist.

The crisis atmosphere of the early months of the administration is well portrayed in Acheson's two books, *Morning and Noon* and *Present at the Creation*, and in Feis' *Characters in Crisis*. FDR's economic views and training are well covered in Daniel Fusfeld's *The Economic Thought of Franklin Roosevelt and the Origins of the New Deal*. The pre-Roosevelt years are well treated in H. G. Warren's *Herbert Hoover and the Great Depression* and in Schlesinger's *Age of Roosevelt*, Volume I, *Crisis of the Old Order*.

The volume of material on the other administrations is neither so extensive, nor so varied in its scope. However, given the brief span of the Kennedy Administration, the volume of material is immense, although much of it is superficial. Notable exceptions are Sorensen's *Kennedy* and Schlesinger's *A Thousand Days*.

The onset of depression stimulated the output of material on employment and planning. A very comprehensive bibliography of these efforts appears in *History of Employment and Manpower Policies in the United States*, Parts III and IV, Committee on Labor and Public Welfare, U.S. Senate, 88th Congress, 2d Session.

With the organization of the Council in 1946, the output of specific economic information became more systematic, and, in addition to official documents, extensive accounts have been written including the following: Nourse, *Economics in the Public Service;* Burns, *The Management of Prosperity;* Jacoby, *Can Prosperity Be Sustained?;* and Heller, *New Dimensions of Political Economy.* Devoting a great deal of space to the pre-Employment Act period and early efforts at stabilization, Nourse is by far the most comprehensive.

Of the Presidents considered, by 1976 only four—Coolidge, Hoover, Truman, and Johnson—have published their own memoirs; however, none of these are very helpful from the standpoint of the economist. Except for Hoover, economic discussion is almost ignored or treated superficially. They tend to emphasize foreign affairs; for example, Johnson's *The Vantage Point* is mainly concerned with the Vietnam War and mentions the Council only in passing. Truman gives CEA brief treatment.

The events leading up to the passage of the Employment Act are thoroughly discussed in Bailey's *Congress Makes a Law,* and the outlook at the ten-year point is well portrayed by the late Gerhard Colm in his National Planning Association symposium, *The Employment Act, Past and Future.* The book by Edward Flash, Jr., *Economic Advice and Presidential Leadership,* also covers the early period (through Kennedy). Herbert Stein's *The Fiscal Revolution in America* is also excellent as a source of information in the New Deal and Postwar years. While little has been written about the Joint Economic Committee as such, its own output has been extensive and is a valuable information source. Several former Council members have made valuable contributions to the periodical literature, such as articles by Blough in the *American Economic Review* and the Jacoby article in *History of Political Economy.* The work of economists in the interwar period, leading up to the concept of full employment (a much-neglected area), is well recounted in the round-table discussion headed by Paul Sweezey in the *American Economic Review* (cited under his name). An equally good source on this period is the recent book by J. Ronnie Davis, *The New Economics and the Old Economists.*

A good general source of information dealing with presidential advice in recent years in found in Milton S. Eisenhower's *The President Is Calling.*

The presidential libraries contain a massive amount of information in the form of memoranda and letters concerning the Council, and future scholars may be able to mine this information and correlate it into logical sequence; however, much is yet unavailable. Several scholars have commented on the fact that the immense volume of raw material in the recently established presidential libraries, coupled with the "sensitive" nature of much of it, has made its use cumbersome. For example in 1975, twelve years after his death, very little of the Kennedy material is usable. It is likely that some years will have to elapse before materials relating to the CEA are available in readily usable form.

SELECTED BIBLIOGRAPHY

GENERAL WORKS

Acheson, Dean G. *Morning and Noon.* Boston: Houghton Mifflin Co., 1965.

———. *Present at the Creation.* New York: W. W. Norton & Co., Inc., 1969.

Ackley, Gardner, "Vandeveer Memorial Lecture." Southern Illinois University, October 26, 1966 (mimeographed).

Adams, Samuel H. *Incredible Era, The Life and Times of Warren G. Harding.* Boston: Houghton Mifflin Co., 1930.

Adams, Sherman. *Firsthand Report: The Story of the Eisenhower Administration.* New York: Harper & Bros., 1961.

Allen, Frederick Lewis. *Only Yesterday: An Informal History of the Nineteen Twenties.* New York: Harper & Bros. Publishers, 1931.

Allen, Robert S., and Shannon, William V. *The Truman Merry-Go-Round.* New York: Vanguard Press, 1950.

Anderson. Patrick. *The President's Men.* Garden City: Doubleday & Company, Inc., 1968.

Bach, G. L. *Making Monetary and Fiscal Policy.* Washington, D.C.: The Brookings Institution, 1971.

Bailey, Stephen Kemp. *Congress Makes a Law.* New York: Columbia University Press, 1950.

Baus, Herbert M., and Ross, William B. *Politics Battle Plan.* New York: The Macmillan Co., 1968.

Beard, Charles A. *The Idea of National Interest: An Analytical Study of American Foreign Policy.* New York: The Macmillan Co., 1934.

———. *The Myth of Rugged American Individualism.* New York: Harper & Bros. Publishers, 1932.

Benedict, Murray R. *Farm Policies of the United States, 1790–1950: A Study of Their Origins and Development.* New York: Twentieth Century Fund, 1953.

Bennett, David H. *Demagogues in the Depression, American Radicals and the Union Party, 1932–1936.* New Brunswick: Rutgers University Press, 1969.

Biddle, Francis B. *In Brief Authority*. Garden City: Doubleday & Company, Inc., 1962.

Blum, John M., ed. *From the Morganthau Diaries*. Vol. I, *Years of Crisis, 1928–1938*. Boston: Houghton Mifflin Co., 1958.

Boulding, Kenneth. *The Skills of the Economist*. Cleveland: H. Allen, 1958.

———. *Economics and Public Policy*. Washington, D.C.: The Brookings Institution, 1955.

Brogan, D. W. *The Era of Franklin D. Roosevelt*. New Haven: Yale University Press, 1950.

Burns, Arthur F. *The Management of Prosperity*. Pittsburgh: The Carnegie Institution of Technology, 1955. New York: Columbia University Press, 1966.

Burns, James McG. *John Kennedy: A Political Profile*. New York: Harcourt, Brace and World, 1960.

———. *Roosevelt, The Lion and The Fox*. New York: Harcourt Brace and Company, 1956.

———. *Roosevelt, Soldier of Freedom*. New York: Harcourt Brace Jovanovich, 1971.

Byrnes, James F. *Speaking Frankly*. New York: Harper & Bros. Publishers, 1947.

Canterbery, E. Ray. *Economics on a New Frontier*. Belmont: Wadsworth Publishing Co., Inc. 1968.

———. *The President's Council of Economic Advisers*. New York: Exposition Press, 1961.

Chapple, Joe Mitchel. *Life and Times of Warren G. Harding*. Boston: Houghton Mifflin Co., 1924.

Childs, Marquis. *Eisenhower, Captive Hero*. New York: Harcourt, Brace and Company, 1958.

Clark, Joseph S., and other Senators. *The Senate Establishment*. New York: Hill and Wang, 1963.

Clinch, Nancy Gager. *The Kennedy Neurosis*. New York: Grossett and Dunlap, 1973.

Cochran, Thomas C., and Miller, William. *The Age of Enterprise: A Social History of Industrial America*. New York: The Macmillan Co., 1942.

Coit, Margaret. *Mr. Baruch*. Boston: Houghton Mifflin Co., 1957.

Colm, Gerhard. *The Employment Act, Past and Future: A Tenth Anniversary Symposium*. Washington, D.C.: National Planning Association, 1956.

Commons, John R., et al. *History of Labour in the United States, 1896–1932*. New York: The Macmillan Co., 1935.

Corwin, Edward S. *The President: Office and Powers*. New York: New York University Press, 1957.

Cotter, C. P. *Government and Private Enterprise.* New York: Holt, Rinehart & Winston, 1960.

Dahl, Robert A., and Lindbloom, Charles E. *Politics, Economics and Welfare.* New York: Harper & Bros. Publishers, 1953.

Daniels, Jonathan. *Man of Independence.* Philadelphia: J. P. Lippincott and Co., 1950.

————. *The Time Between the Wars: Armistice to Pearl Harbor.* Garden City: Doubleday & Company, Inc., 1966.

Davis, J. Ronnie. *The New Economics and the Old Economists.* Ames: Iowa State University Press, 1971.

Dillard, Dudley. *Economic Development of the North Atlantic Community.* Englewood Cliffs, N.J.: Prentice-Hall, Inc., 1967.

Donovan, Robert J. *Eisenhower, The Inside Story.* New York: Harper & Bros. Publishers, 1956.

Dorfman, Joseph. *The Economic Mind in American Civilization, 1918–1933*, Vol. III. New York: The Viking Press, 1959.

Douglas, Paul H. *In The Fullness of Time.* New York: Harcourt Brace Jovanovich, 1972.

Eccles, Marriner. *Beckoning Frontiers.* New York: Alfred A. Knopf, 1951.

Einaudi, Mario. *The Roosevelt Revolution.* New York: Harcourt, Brace and Company, 1959.

Eisenhower, Dwight D. *Mandate for Change: 1953–1956, the White House Years.* Garden City: Doubleday, & Company, Inc. 1963.

————. *Waging Peace: 1956–1961.* Garden City: Doubleday & Company, Inc., 1965.

Eisenhower, Milton S. *The President Is Calling.* Garden City: Doubleday & Company, Inc. 1974.

Ekirch, Arthur A., Jr. *Ideologies and Utopias, The Impact of the New Deal on American Thought.* Chicago: Quadrangle Books, 1969.

Ellis, Edward R. Nation in Torment. New York: Coward-McCann, 1970.

Evans, Rowland, and Novak, Robert. *Lyndon Johnson, the Exercise of Power.* New York: Signet Books, 1966.

Ezekiel, Mordecai. *Jobs for All Through Industrial Expansion.* New York: Alfred A. Knopf, 1939.

————. *$2500 A Year.* New York: Harcourt, Brace and Company, 1936.

Federal Economic Policy. Washington, D.C.: *Congressional Quarterly Service*, 3rd Ed., 1968.

Feis, Herbert. *1933: Characters in Crisis.* Boston: Little, Brown & Company, 1966.

Finer, Herman. *The Presidency: Crisis and Regeneration.* Chicago: University of Chicago Press, 1960.

327

Flash, Edward S., Jr. *Economic Advice and Presidential Leadership: The Council of Economic Advisers.* New York: Columbia University Press, 1965.

Freidel Frank. *Franklin D. Roosevelt,* Vol. I, *The Apprenticeship.* Boston: Little, Brown & Company, 1952.

Fusfeld, Daniel. *The Age of the Economist.* Glenview, Ill.: Scott, Foresman & Co., 1966.

————. *The Economic Thought of Franklin Roosevelt and the Origins of the New Deal.* New York: Columbia University Press, 1956.

Galbraith, John Kenneth. *Ambassador's Journal.* Boston: Houghton Mifflin Co., 1969.

————. *The Great Crash, 1929.* Boston: Houghton Mifflin Co., 1961.

————. *The Liberal Hour.* Boston: Houghton Mifflin Co., 1960.

————. *Economics, Peace and Laughter.* Boston: Houghton Mifflin Co., 1971.

Ginzberg, Eli. *The Illusion of Economic Stability.* New York and London: Harper & Bros. Publishers, 1939.

Goldman, Eric F. *Rendezvous with Destiny.* New York: Alfred A. Knopf, 1952.

————. *The Tragedy of Lyndon Johnson.* New York: Alfred A. Knopf, 1969.

Gruchy, Allan. *Modern Economic Thought: The American Contribution.* New York: Prentice-Hall, 1947.

Hacker, Louis M. *American Problems of Today.* New York: F. S. Crofts & Co., 1938.

————. *A Short History of the New Deal.* New York: F. S. Crofts & Co., 1934.

Hansen, Alvin. *The American Economy.* New York: McGraw-Hill Book Co., 1957.

Harris, Seymour E. *Economics of the Kennedy Years.* New York: Harper & Row Publishers, 1964.

————., ed. *The New Economics.* New York: A. Knopf, 1947.

Harrod, Roy. *Life of John Maynard Keynes.* New York: Harcourt, Brace and Company, 1951.

Heller, Dean, and Heller, David. *The Kennedy Cabinet.* Derby, Conn.: Monarch Books, 1961.

Heller, Walter W. *New Dimensions of Political Economy.* Cambridge: Harvard University Press, 1966.

Kearns, Doris. *Lyndon Johnson and the American Dream.* New York: Harper & Row Publishers, 1976.

Kennedy, John F. *Kennedy and the Press; the News Conferences.* Edited by Harold W. Chase and Allen H. Lerman. New York: Thomas Y. Crowell Co., 1965.

––––––. *To Turn the Tide*. Edited by John W. Gardner. Selection of President Kennedy's Public Statements. New York: Harper & Row, Publishers, 1962.

Koenig, Lewis W. *The Invisible Presidency*. New York: Rinehart & Co., 1961.

Krock, Arthur. *Memoirs, Sixty Years on the Firing Line*. New York: Funk and Wagnalls, 1968.

Larson, Arthur. *Eisenhower, The President Nobody Knew*. New York: Scribners, 1968.

Lash, Joseph. *Eleanor and Franklin*. New York: W. W. Norton & Co., Inc., 1971.

Lawrence, Joseph Stagg. *Wall Street and Washington*. Princeton: Princeton University Press, 1929.

Leuchtenburg, William E. *The Perils of Prosperity, 1914–1932*. Chicago: The University of Chicago Press, 1958.

––––––, ed. *The New Deal, A Documentary History*. Columbia: University of South Carolina Press, 1968.

Lindley, Ernest K. *The Roosevelt Revolution*. New York: Viking Press, 1933.

––––––. *Halfway with Roosevelt*. New York: Viking Press, 1936.

Link, Arthur S. *Woodrow Wilson and the Progressive Era, 1910–1917*. New York: Harper & Row, Publishers, 1954.

Lyons, Eugene. *Herbert Hoover, A Biography*. Garden City: Doubleday & Company, 1964.

Mansfield, Harvey C. "The Congress and Economic Policy." *Congress and America's Future*. Edited by David B. Truman. The American Assembly. Englewood Cliffs, N.J.: Prentice-Hall, Inc., 1965.

Mason, Alpheus T. *Brandeis: A Free Man's Life*. New York: Viking Press, 1946.

Mazo, Earl, and Hess, Stephen. *Nixon: A Political Portrait*. New York: Harper & Row, Publishers, 1969.

McCloskey, Robert G. *American Conservatism in the Age of Enterprise*. Cambridge: Harvard University Press, 1951.

McConnell, Grant. *Steel and the Presidency, 1962*. New York: W. W. Norton & Co., Inc., 1963.

McCoy, Donald R. *Calvin Coolidge, The Quiet President*. New York: The Macmillan Co., 1967.

McCracken, Paul W. *The Political Position of the Council of Economic Advisers* (mimeographed). Western Michigan University, January 19, 1966.

Mellon, Andrew. *The Peoples' Money*. New York: The Macmillan Co., 1924.

Mitchell, Broadus. *Depression Decade*. New York: Holt, Rinehart & Winston, 1947.

Moley, Raymond. *After Seven Years*. New York and London: Harper & Bros. Publishers, 1939.

————. *The First New Deal*. New York: Harcourt, Brace & World, 1966.

Moulton, H. G., and Pasvolsky, Leo. *War Debts and World Prosperity*. Washington, D.C.: The Brookings Institution, 1932.

Mowry, George E. *The Era of Theodore Roosevelt, 1900–1912*. New York: Harper & Bros., Publishers, 1958.

Myers, William S., and Newton, Walter H. *The Hoover Administration: A Documented Narrative*. New York: Charles Scribner's Sons, 1936.

Neustadt, Richard E. *Presidential Power, The Politics of Leadership*. New York: Wiley, 1960.

Nevins, Allan. *The New Deal and World Affairs*. New Haven: Yale University Press, 1950.

Nixon, Richard M. *Six Crises*. Garden City: Doubleday & Company, Inc., 1962.

No Author. The Unofficial Observer. *The New Dealers*. New York: Literary Guild, 1934.

Norton, Hugh S. *National Transportation Policy: Formation and Implementation*. Berkeley: McCutchan Publishing Co., 1967.

————. *The Role of the Economist in Government Policy Making*. Berkeley: McCutchan Publishing Co., 1969.

————. *The World of the Economist*. Columbia: University of South Carolina Press, 1973.

Nourse, Edwin G. *Economics in the Public Service*. New York: Harcourt Brace and Company, 1953.

————. *Professional Background of the First Chairman of the Council of Economic Advisers*. Harry S. Truman Memorial Library.

Okun, Arthur. *The Political Economy of Prosperity*. Washington, D.C.: The Brookings Institution.

Patterson, James K. *Mr. Republican, A Biography of Robert A. Taft*. Boston: Houghton–Mifflin Co., 1972.

Perkins, Dexter. *The New Age of Franklin Roosevelt, 1932–1945*. Chicago: University of Chicago Press, 1957.

Perkins, Frances. *The Roosevelt I Knew*. New York: The Viking Press, 1946.

Phillips, Cabel. *The Truman Presidency*. New York: The Macmillan Co., 1966.

Pusey, Merlo J. *Eisenhower, The President*. New York: The Macmillan Co., 1956.

Reedy, George E. *The Presidency in Flux*. New York: Columbia University Press, 1972.

Richberg, Donald. *The Rainbow*. Garden City: Doubleday, Doran & Co., 1936.

Robbins, Lionel (Baron Charles). *Autobiography of an Economist.* London: The Macmillan Co., 1971.

Roberts, Chalmers W. *LBJ's Inner Circle.* New York: Delacorte Press, 1965.

Robey, Ralph. *Roosevelt vs. Recovery.* New York and London: Harper & Bros., Publishers, 1934.

Romasco, Albert U. *The Poverty of Abundance.* New York: The Oxford University Press, 1965.

Roosevelt, Elliot, and Brough, James. *An Untold Story: The Roosevelts of Hyde Park.* New York: G. P. Putnam's Sons, 1973.

Roosevelt, James (with Sidney Shallett). *Affectionately, FDR.* New York: Harcourt, Brace and Company, 1959.

Roseman, Samuel I. *Working with Roosevelt.* New York: Harper & Bros., Publishers, 1952.

Rossiter, Clinton. *The American Presidency.* New York: Harcourt, Brace and Company, 1956.

Rourke, Francis. *Bureaucratic Power in National Politics.* Boston: Little, Brown & Company, 1965.

Rovere, Richard H. *The Eisenhower Years.* New York: Farrar, Straus & Cudahay, 1956.

Rowen, Hobart. *The Free Enterprisers, Kennedy, Johnson and the Business Establishment.* New York: G. P. Putnam's Sons, 1964.

Russell, Francis. *The Shadow of Blooming Grove.* New York: McGraw-Hill Book Co., 1968.

————. *The President Makers.* Boston: Little, Brown and Company, 1976.

Safire, William. *Before the Fall—An Inside View of the Pre-Watergate White House.* Garden City: Doubleday & Co., Inc., 1975.

Saloutos, Theodore, and Hicks, John D. *Agricultural Discontent in the United States, 1900–1939.* Madison: University of Wisconsin Press, 1951.

Samuelson, Paul A., et al. *New Frontiers of the Kennedy Administration: The Texts of the Task Force Reports Prepared for the President.* Washington, D. C.: Public Affairs Press, 1963.

Saulnier, Raymond J. *The Strategy of Economic Policy.* New York: Fordham University Press, 1963.

Schlesinger, Arthur M., Jr. *A Thousand Days.* Boston: Houghton Mifflin Co., 1964.

————. *Crisis of the Old Order,* Vol. I, and *The Politics of Upheaval,* Vol. III, of *The Age of Roosevelt.* Boston: Houghton Mifflin Co., 1955 and 1957.

Schriftgiesser, Karl. *Business and Public Policy.* Englewood Cliffs, N.J.: Prentice-Hall, 1967.

331

Seligman, Ben B. *Main Currents in Modern Economics*. Glencoe: Free Press of Glencoe, 1962.

Seven Harvard and Tufts Economists. *An Economic Program for American Democracy*. New York: Vanguard Press, 1933.

Shannon, David A. *Twentieth Century America*. Chicago: Rand, McNally & Co., 1963.

Shultz, George P., and Aliber, Robert Z., eds. *Guidelines, Informal Controls, and the Market Place*. Chicago: University of Chicago, Graduate School of Business, 1966.

Sidey, Hugh. *John F. Kennedy, President*. Greenwich, Conn.: Fawcett Publications, 1963.

Slesinger, Reuben. *National Economic Policy: The Presidential Reports*. Princeton: D. Van Nostrand Co., 1968.

Sorensen, Theodore C. *Decision Making in the White House, the Olive Branch or the Arrows*. New York: Columbia University Press, 1963.

————. *Kennedy*. New York: Harper & Row Publishers, 1965.

Soule, George. *Prosperity Decade*. New York: Rinehart & Co., 1947.

Spaulding, Henry D. *The Nixon Nobody Knows*. Middle Village, N.Y.: Jothanan David, 1972.

Stein, Herbert. *The Fiscal Revolution in America*. Chicago: University of Chicago Press, 1969.

Stolberg, B., and Vinton, W. J. *The Economic Consequences of the New Deal*. New York: Harcourt, Brace and Company, 1935.

Tanzer, Lester, ed. *The Kennedy Circle*. Washington, D. C.: Robert B. Luce, Inc., 1961.

Theobald, Robert. *Free Men and Free Markets*. New York: C. N. Potter, 1963.

Tobin, James. *The Intellectual Revolution in the U.S. Economic Policy Making*. Noel Buxton Lecture. University of Essex, England, January 18, 1966 (mimeographed).

————. *National Economic Policy*. New Haven: Yale University Press, 1966.

————. *The New Economics, One Decade Older*. Princeton: Princeton University Press, 1974.

Truman, Harry S. *Years of Decisions*, Vol. I, *Memoirs*. Mentor Edition. Garden City: Doubleday and Company, Inc., 1955.

Tugwell, Rexford G. *The Brains Trust*. New York: Viking Press, 1968.

————. *The Democratic Roosevelt*. Garden City: Doubleday and Company, Inc., 1957.

————. *FDR, Architect of an Era*. New York: The Macmillan Co., 1967.

Tully, Grace. *FDR, My Boss*. New York: Charles Scribner's Sons, 1949.

Ulmer, Melvin. *The Welfare State: U.S.A.* Boston: Houghton Mifflin Co., 1969.

Vinyard, Dale. *The Presidency.* New York: Charles Scribner's Sons, 1971.

Warren, H. G. *Herbert Hoover and the Great Depression.* New York: Oxford University Press, 1959.

Weinberg, Arthur, and Weinberg, Lila, editors. *The Muckrakers, 1902–1912.* New York: Simon & Schuster, 1961.

Whalen, Richard J. *The Founding Father: The Story of Joseph P. Kennedy and the Family He Raised to Power.* New York: New American Library Publishers, 1964.

White, Theodore H. *The Making of the President, 1960.* New York: Atheneum Publishers, 1961.

———. *The Making of the President, 1964.* New York: Atheneum Publishers, 1965.

———. *The Making of the President, 1968.* New York: Atheneum Publishers, 1969.

———. *The Making of the President, 1972.* New York: Atheneum Publishers, 1973.

White, William Allen. *Puritan in Babylon: The Story of Calvin Coolidge,* New York: The Macmillan Co., 1938.

Wilhite, Virgle. *Founders of American Economic Thought and Policy.* New York: Bookman Associates, 1958.

Wilkins, B. H., and Friday, C. B., editors. *The Economists of the New Frontier.* New York: Random House, 1963.

Williams, T. Harry. *Huey Long.* New York: Alfred A. Knopf, 1969.

Wills, Garry. *Nixon Agonistes.* Boston: Houghton Mifflin Co., 1970.

Winning Plans in the *Pabst Postwar Employment Awards.* Pabst Brewing Company (undated).

Witcover, Jules. *The Resurrection of Richard Nixon.* New York: G. P. Putnam's Sons, 1970.

Zinn, Howard, ed. *New Deal Thought.* Indianapolis: Bobbs-Merrill Co., 1966.

FEDERAL DOCUMENTS

Congressional Record, 79th Congress, 2d Session, September 27, 1945, 9204.

Congressional Record, 80th Congress, 2d Session, 29, February 6, 1946, 980.

Congressional Record, 79th Congress, 1st Session, 1945, 12267; 79th Congress, 2d Session, 92, Part 1, 1138.

Congressional Record, 79th Congress, 1st Session, 91, Part 7, 9026.

Economic Report of the President, 1947, 1948, 1949, 1950, 1951, 1952,

1953, 1954, 1955, 1956, 1957, 1958, 1959, 1960, 1961, 1962, 1963, 1964, 1965, 1966, 1967, 1968, 1969, 1970, 1971, 1972, 1973, 1974, 1975.

General Management of the Executive Branch. Commission on Organization of the Executive Branch (Hoover Commission). Washington: U.S. Government Printing Office, 1949.

Hearings on the Independent Offices, Appropriations Bill, Fiscal Year, 1952, 82d Congress, 1st Session, U.S. Congress Senate Committee on Appropriations, 90, 91.

History of Employment and Manpower Policies in the United States. Committee on Labor and Public Welfare, U.S. Senate, 88th Congress, 2d Session, U.S. Government Printing Office, 1965.

Hoover, Herbert C. *State Papers*, I, 34.

Hoover, Herbert C. *State Papers*, II, 572.

Hoover, Herbert C. *State Papers*, II, 257.

Hoover, Herbert C. *State Papers*, II, 262.

Joint Economic Committee. *Federal Reserve Discount Mechanism*. Washington: U.S. Government Printing Office, 1969.

Joint Economic Committee. *The Inflation Process in the United States*. Washington: U.S. Government Printing Office, February, 1972.

Joint Economic Committee. *Interest Rate Policy and Discounting Analysis*. Washington: U.S. Government Printing Office, 1968.

Joint Economic Committee. *Recent Inflation in the United States*. Washington: U.S. Government Printing Office, 1970.

Joint Economic Committee. *Standards For Guiding Monetary Action*. Washington: U.S. Government Printing Office, 1968.

Joint Economic Committee. *Study of Employment, Growth and Price Levels*. Washington: U.S. Government Printing Office, 1959.

Joint Economic Committee. *Twentieth Anniversary of the Employment Act—An Economic Symposium*. Washington: U.S. Government Printing Office, 1966.

Joint Economic Committee. *Urban America, Goals and Problems*. Washington: U.S. Government Printing Office, 1967.

Joint Economic Committee. *Vietnam Spending*. Washington: U.S. Government Printing Office, 1967.

Keyserling, Leon H. *How Well Is the Employment Act of 1946 Achieving Its Goal?* Washington: U.S. Department of Labor, 1966.

Lehman, John W. "Administration of the Employment Act." *Twentieth Anniversary of the Employment Act, An Economic Symposium*. Washington: Joint Economic Committee, 1966, pp. 67–99.

"Monetary Policy and the Management of the Public Debt." *Hearings* Before the Subcommittee on General Credit Control and Debt Management, 82d Congress, 2d Session, March, 1952.

National Resources Planning Board. *The Economic Effects of Federal Public Works Expenditures, 1933–1938*, J. Kenneth Galbraith, editor, 1940.

334

Profits, Eightieth Congress, 2d Session. Report of a Subcommittee of the Joint Committee on the Economic Report, 1947.

Report of the Joint Economic Committee of the Congress of the United States on the January, 1969, *Economic Report of the President*.

Roosevelt, Franklin D. *State Papers*, I, 860.

Roosevelt, Franklin D. *State Papers*, IV, 97.

Statement of Committee, Agreement, Minority and Other Views. Joint Economic Committee, 90th Congress, 1st Session, March, 1967.

U.S. Congress, Joint Economic Committee. *Study of Employment Growth and Price Levels*, 1965.

U.S. Congress. "The President's Program to Deal With the Problem of Inflation." Eightieth Congress, 1st Session, *SR 809*.

U.S. Senate, Committee on Labor and Public Welfare. *History of Employment and Manpower Problems in the United States.* Eighty-eighth Congress, 2d Session, 1964.

U.S. Senate, *Report 1565*, June 9, 1940. Eightieth Congress, 1st Session.

Weekly Digest of Presidential Documents, May 10, 1969.

PERIODICALS

Ackley, Gardner. "Contributions of Economists to Policy Formation," *Journal of Finance*, 21, No. 2 (May, 1966), 170ff.

"A Practical Politician at the Fed." *Fortune*, May, 1971.

Bailey, Stephen Kemp. "Political Elements in Full Employment Policy," Papers and Proceedings, *American Economic Review* (May, 1955), 341–51.

Blough, Roy. "Political and Administrative Requisites for Achieving Economic Stability," *The American Economic Review*, 40, No. 2 (May, 1950), 176ff.

Blough, Roy. "The Role of the Economist in Federal Policy Making," *Bulletin No. 28.* Urbana, Ill.: Institute of Government and Public Affairs, University of Illinois, 1953.

Burns, Arthur F. "Progress Toward Economic Stability," *American Economic Review*, 50, No. 1 (March, 1960), 1ff.

Canterbery, E. Ray. "A New Look at Federal Open Market Committee Voting," *Western Economic Journal*, 6 (December, 1967), 25–38.

Carson, Robert B. "Changes in Federal Fiscal Policy and Attitudes Since the Employment Act of 1946," *The Social Studies*, 58, No. 7 (December, 1967), 308–14.

Eckstein, Otto. "The Economics of the 1960's; A Backward Look," *Public Interest* (Spring, 1970), 86–97.

Editorial. *Fortune*, May, 1970.

Ensley, Grover. "A Budget for the Nation," *Social Research*, 1, No. 2 (September, 1943), 280ff.

Foster, W. T., and Catchings, Waddill. "Mr. Hoover's Road to Prosperity," *Review of Reviews* (January, 1930).

Forum, July, 1931.

Galbraith, John Kenneth. Review, "Economic Advice and Presidential Leadership," *American Economic Review* (December, 1966), 1249.

Goldenweiser, E. A. "Research and Policy," *Federal Reserve Bulletin*, 30, No. 4 (April, 1944), 312–17.

Hamilton, Walton H. "The Place of Value Theory in Economics," *Journal of Political Science*, 26 (March, 1918), 345–407.

Hansen, Alvin. "Keynes After Thirty Years," *Welt Wirtschaftliches Archiv Band*, XCVII, Heft 2, 1966.

Hansen, Alvin. "Economic Progress and Declining Population Growth," *American Economic Review*, 29, No. 2 (March, 1939), 1–15.

Harris, Seymour. "The Gap Between Economists and Politicians." *New York Times Magazine*, April 14, 1965.

Harris, Seymour E. "Economic Policies under Kennedy in 1962 and Fiscal Year 1963: Introduction and Summary," *The Review of Economics and Statistics*, 45 (February, 1963), 137–46.

"How Political Must the Council of Economic Advisers Be?" Panel Discussion, *Challenge* (March–April, 1974), 28–42.

Havrilesky, Thomas. "A Test of Monetary Policy Actions," *The Journal of Political Economy*, 75 (June, 1967), 703ff.

Heller, Walter W., et al. "Economists Consider Economic Reporters and Vice Versa," *American Economic Review* (May, 1972), 373–90.

"How Political Must the Council of Economic Advisers Be?" Panel Discussion, *Challenge* (March–April, 1974), 28–42.

Jacoby, Neil H. "The President, the Constitution and the Economist in Economic Stabilization," *History of Political Economy*, 3, No. 2 (Fall, 1971), 389–414.

"Joint Economic Committee," *National Journal* (June 20, 1970), 1291–303.

Keyserling, Leon. Letter to Editor, *Journal of Commerce* (December 31, 1968).

Keyserling, Leon H. "The Wagner Act: Its Origin and Current Significance," *George Washington Law Review*, 19, No. 2 (December, 1950).

Lekachman, Robert. "The Quarrelsome Economists," *The New Leader* (October 13, 1969).

Lewis, John P., and Gross, Bertram. "The President's Council of Economic Advisers During the Truman Administration," *American Political Science Review*, 48 (March, 1954), 114ff.

Mencken, H. L. "Three Years of Dr. Roosevelt," *The American Mercury*. 37, 1936.

Modigliani, Franco. "Some Empirical Tests of Monetary Management and of Roles Versus Discretion," *Journal of Political Economy*, 72 (June, 1944), 211–95.

Salant, Walter S. "Some Contributions of the Truman Council of Economic Advisers to the Intellectual Revolution in American Economic Policy-Making," *History of Political Economy*, 4, No. 2 (Fall, 1972).

Seligman, Lester. "Presidential Leadership: The Inner Circle and Institutionalization," *Journal of Politics*, 13 (August, 1956), 410ff.

Slichter, Sumner. "Postwar Economic Prospects," *Harvard Business Review* (Autumn, 1942).

Slichter, Sumner. "Structural Changes in the U.S. Economy," *Graphic* (April 1, 1924), 1ff.

Shanahan, Eileen. "The Economists Dilemma." Washington Report, *The New York Times*, October 14, 1973, 8-F.

Soule, George. "Full Employment After the War," *The New Republic* (August, 1942).

Stein, Herbert. "The Principles Behind the Policies," *Challenge*, 16, No. 1 (March/April, 1973), 32–38.

Sweezy, Alan, and Others. "The Keynesian Revolution and Its Pioneers," Proceedings, *American Economic Review*, 62, No. 2 (May, 1972), 116–41.

Tobin, James C. "Growth Through Taxation," *New Republic* (July 25, 1960).

Tullock, Gordon. "A Modest Proposal," *Journal of Money Credit and Banking* (May, 1971), 263ff.

Wallich, Henry C. "The American Council of Economic Advisers and the German Sachverstalentigerat; A Study of the Economics of Advice," *Quarterly Journal of Economics*, 83, 349–79.

White, Theodore H. "The Action Intellectuals." *Life*, June 9, 1967.

CORRESPONDENCE AND INTERVIEWS

Correspondence

David E. Bell	November 1969
Marriner Eccles	March 1967
Grover Ensley	December 1972
Mordecai Ezekiel	April 1967
Alvin Hansen	November 1966
Seymour E. Harris	February 1967
Walter W. Heller	March 1967
Leon Keyserling	June 1971
James Knowles	April 1973

John W. Lehman	October 1970
Theodore Kreps	June 1967
Theodore Kreps	August 1970
Paul McCracken	April 1973
Edwin G. Nourse	December 1969
Winfield Riefler	March 1967
Hobart Rowen	October 1974
Walter S. Salant	April 1967
Paul Samuelson	June 1966
George Soule	May 1966
John R. Stark	February 1972
Henry C. Wallich	February 1966
Ralph A. Young	November 1966

Interviews

Gerhard Colm	Atlanta	November 1966
	Washington	July 1967
Grover Ensley	New York	July 1967
Mordecai Ezekiel	Washington	July 1967
Gabriel Hauge	New York	July 1967
Leon H. Keyserling	Washington	June 1968
Isadore Lubin	New York	July 1967
James Knowles	Washington	December 1969
Robert Nathan	Washington	June 1968
Edwin G. Nourse	Washington	June 1968
Arthur Okun	Columbia, S.C.	November 1971
Charles B. Warden, Jr.	Washington	June 1968

Index

339

347